The Weight of Their Votes

The Weight of Their Votes

Southern Women and Political Leverage in the 1920s

Lorraine Gates Schuyler

The University of North Carolina Press

Chapel Hill

Designed by April Leidig-Higgins
Set in Minion by Copperline Book Services, Inc.

The paper in this book meets the guidelines for
permanence and durability of the Committee on
Production Guidelines for Book Longevity of the
Council on Library Resources.

Library of Congress Cataloging-in-Publication Data
Schuyler, Lorraine Gates.
The weight of their votes: southern women and political
leverage in the 1920s / Lorraine Gates Schuyler.
p. cm.   Includes bibliographical references and index.
ISBN-13: 978-0-8078-3066-6 (cloth: alk. paper)
ISBN-10: 0-8078-3066-6 (cloth: alk. paper)
ISBN-13: 978-0-8078-5776-2 (pbk.: alk. paper)
ISBN-10: 0-8078-5776-9 (pbk.: alk. paper)
    1. Women in politics — Southern States — History
— 20th century.   2. Women — Suffrage — Southern
States — History — 20th century.   3. Political
participation — Southern States — History — 20th
century.   4. Voting — Southern States — History —
20th century.   5. Southern States — Politics and
government — 20th century.   I. Title.
HQ1236.5.S676S38   2006
324.975'042 — dc22   2006017813

cloth   10 09 08 07 06   5 4 3 2 1
paper   10 09 08 07 06   5 4 3 2 1

for Ridge — at last

Contents

Illustrations

Acknowledgments

After the long process of researching and writing this book, I am honored to have the opportunity to thank the many people who made this project possible. This is the part of the book I have long wanted to write.

First, I would like to thank the history department at the University of Virginia for its generous financial support of my graduate education in general and of this project as both a dissertation and a manuscript. Chuck Mc-Curdy, as chair of the department, provided me with research and travel support at critical moments, for which I am truly grateful. Duke University, the Herbert Hoover Presidential Library Association, and the Virginia Historical Society also provided grants for research in their collections. A fellowship from the Miller Center of Public Affairs allowed me to focus an entire year on finishing my dissertation, with the added luxuries of an office and a wonderful community of scholars in the Fellowship Program.

While conducting the research for this project, I relied on the talent and assistance of countless archivists and librarians. I owe a special debt of gratitude to the archivist at Delta State University and to the helpful staff of the Herbert Hoover Presidential Library. Lew Purifoy and the Inter-Library Loan staff at the University of Virginia's Alderman Library have been spectacularly helpful, persistently tracking down the obscure sources that I requested and, more than once, mailing them to me when I was on the road. Staff in the Geostat Lab showed extreme patience as they taught me how to code old electoral data, use SPSS, and make maps that pulled it all together. Two outstanding undergraduates, Kate Baylor and Anna Krome-Lukens, provided thorough research assistance.

At the University of Virginia, the Southern Seminar, the Twentieth Century Seminar, and the Miller Center of Public Affairs offered forums for me to share draft chapters of this project. The suggestions that were offered by scholars there encouraged me to improve the manuscript in ways that I would not have and saved me from many mistakes that I otherwise would have made. Skeptical audiences and generous co-panelists at meetings of the Southern Historical Association, the Organization of American Historians, the Social Science History Association, the Miller Center of Public Affairs, and the Southern Association for Women Historians all helped to refine my arguments and bolster my evidence. I am especially grateful to Liette Gidlow, Glenda Gilmore, Grant Hayden, Georgina Hickey, Darlene Clark Hine, Lisa Materson, Elisabeth Perry, Patricia Schechter, and Anne Firor Scott, whose helpful comments and hard questions ensured that every conference presentation improved the final book. William Link was probably surprised when I took him up on his offer to read the manuscript, and I appreciate his close attention to it and all of the comments he offered. Members of the C. Vann Woodward Dissertation Prize Committee also gave this project a thoughtful read, and I especially appreciate the comments that Jack Temple Kirby shared with me. Elizabeth Hayes Turner and Pamela Tyler offered generous and thorough readings of the original manuscript. Their suggestions vastly improved the book.

At the University of Virginia, I was fortunate to have the support of several gifted scholars who allowed themselves to be roped into this project. Grace Hale offered detailed criticism and pushed me to make this project better at every turn. Cindy Aron and Sid Milkis provided the sage advice of skeptical readers on my dissertation committee. Paul Freedman patiently explained ecological inference and helped me make the best use of the quantitative data available.

Brian Balogh nurtured this project from a very early stage and encouraged me to say what I really thought. This book had its earliest expression in a seminar paper for Brian, and he saw its potential long before I did. In trying to answer his many good questions, I finally saw it as well. Brian adopted this project almost as his own. He found books I should read, sent me to Iowa, reminded me about the importance of appropriations requests, and tenaciously believed that I was getting it right. No one has read more drafts of this book, not even Ed. Unfortunately, this book could never be an adequate expression of my appreciation for his support over the years.

My adviser, Edward Ayers, has been the best mentor a graduate student could ask for. He helped me conceive this project out of the "anonymous women" I stumbled across in earlier research, and he helped to turn my inchoate thoughts into polished analyses, all the while allowing me to believe that I had done the hard thinking myself. On more than one occasion he found the resources to extend my research trips for "just a few more days," and he read countless drafts of this book, as both a dissertation and a manuscript. His penetrating critiques of numerous drafts and the encouragement with which he offered them have made this book much better than it would otherwise have been. I can't thank him enough.

In addition to these institutional and intellectual debts, I would like to acknowledge a few personal ones. Angie and Michael Tschantz made being on the road much more enjoyable by providing good company and a home away from home while I conducted research in South Carolina. Loch and

Leena Johnson welcomed me into their home and took great care of me while I spent week after week doing research in Georgia. Amy and Jenry Morsman provided advice, encouragement, friendship, and, on occasion, a place to sleep. I miss our evenings at CD. Sarah Gadberry encouraged me to take this path in the first place. Nancy Schuyler, and all of the Neales and Schuylers, helped take great care of my boys so I could go into hiding and finish this book. I know they are as happy to see it completed as I am. My grandmother set an exacting standard for my writing and helped me to keep my audience in mind. My parents and my sister have provided a lifetime of love and encouragement. I appreciate all of the diversions that they provided from this project and that they never asked when I was going to finish it.

Finally, I am profoundly grateful to Ridge. Since I began this project, Ridge has been a gentle but insightful critic, a thorough editor, and an unwavering booster. I am truly blessed to be married to my best friend. The arrival of our first son, Charlie, in the last year of my dissertation, and of Sam a few years later, gave me daily reminders of what is most important in life.

The Weight of Their Votes

Introduction

Does voting really matter? From the time of the Revolution to recurring debates over redistricting, Americans have fought for the right to vote. The Founding Fathers created a government by elected representatives to ensure that propertied white men were ruled by a government they could control. Since then, other Americans have fought to share in that power by securing the franchise for themselves. This book assesses the significance of those struggles by exploring the effects of woman suffrage in the repressive Jim Crow South.

Two long, fierce struggles illustrate the importance Americans have placed on the right to vote. In 1848, the pioneering women who gathered at Seneca Falls insisted that, like white men, they too were deserving of ballots. In the ensuing battle for woman suffrage, activists marched in the streets, picketed outside the White House, endured jail sentences, and staged hunger strikes to secure their full participation in the American polity. Their battle for suffrage rights lasted more than seventy years.

When the Civil War ended, newly freed slaves insisted that Emancipation would be meaningless if they did not have ballots with which to protect themselves. As black men exercised their voting rights for the first time in the wake of the Fourteenth and Fifteenth Amendments, white southerners organized campaigns of violence and intimidation before resorting to "legal" disfranchisement statutes to ensure that the prized right of voting would remain the privilege of white men only. For nearly a century, African Americans continued to fight for full access to the polls. In the face of poll taxes, literacy tests, and violence that eviscerated black voting rights, black southerners staged Freedom Schools and public protests, faced beatings and hostile registrars, risked humiliation and even death to exercise their right to vote.

Voting rights have been vigorously—even violently—contested in the United States because they are so powerful. Since the earliest days of the republic, those Americans with suffrage rights have used their votes not only to elect representatives to office but also, and more importantly, to influence the policies of government. As President Lyndon Johnson affirmed in 1965, there is nothing more effective than voting rights; they provide a power "that all the eloquence in the world won't bring, because," as he told Martin Luther King Jr., legislators "will be coming to you then, instead of you calling" them.[1] That is certainly what American women believed when they fought for their own voting rights. For decades before the ratification of the Nineteenth Amendment, women sought changes in the nation's prohibition laws and social welfare policies. During those fights women became convinced that their policy concerns would never receive adequate attention until they could back their demands with their ballots. In the months and years that followed the ratification of the Nineteenth Amendment, women found that the vote did make a difference.

This book is about the difference that women's votes made, and, by extension, the significance of the vote itself. The American South in the 1920s may seem an unlikely place to look for meaningful democratic participation.[2] Disfranchisers, determined to secure their control over the region's political system, had enacted an incredibly thoroughgoing system of voting restrictions in the decades prior to the ratification of the Nineteenth Amendment. In the South, potential voters faced not only poll taxes and literacy tests but registration and tax deadlines that passed months before any campaigning began. Registrars in many states were required to open the enrollment books only a few days per year. Citizens who did manage to register successfully faced confusing ballot-marking procedures, which made it easy for election officials to disqualify the ballots of dissident voters. Historian Dewey Grantham has described this as the "classic period of southern politics," marked by Democratic Party dominance and white supremacy.[3] No more than one in five southerners voted from 1920 to 1930.[4]

Yet after decades marked by the removal of millions of men from the electorate and the consolidation of political power in the hands of a few white men, the ratification of the Nineteenth Amendment signaled a dramatic break with the past. In the weeks and months that followed the enfranchisement of women, the closed system of southern politics opened up for hundreds of thousands of southern women who for the first time were able to participate directly in the southern body politic. After fighting for decades for the right to vote, those southern women who were able to cast ballots found that their legislators treated them with a new respect. As the election season got under way in the fall of 1920, politicians suddenly added women to their campaign staffs and eagerly sought invitations to campaign before women's organizations. Most importantly, the substance of the political debate changed as well, as prohibition enforcement, age of consent laws, and other issues of concern to women rose to the top of the political agenda.

As suffragists had long expected, voting rights gave organized women new political leverage. After 1920, these politically savvy activists added ballots to their already formidable political arsenal.

DESPITE THE DETERMINATION with which women fought for suffrage, and the tenacity of antisuffragists who sought to deny votes to women, scholars and even contemporary observers have questioned the significance of the Nineteenth Amendment. By the late 1920s, articles in popular magazines and newspapers frequently examined the question of whether (or why) woman suffrage had been a failure. National organizations of women, like the League of Women Voters, were on the defensive as observers pointed to low voter turnout and the small number of female officeholders as evidence of the "failure" of the Nineteenth Amendment. Since then, scholars have examined women's political participation and legislative reform efforts in the 1920s and concluded that the enfranchisement of women made little difference in the lives of women or to the American political system.[5] Women were active politically long before they obtained the right to vote, and they continued their reform efforts after they won the right to vote, but, the story goes, the Nineteenth Amendment did not mark a "Great Divide."[6]

In recent years, historians have explored the role of women and gender in southern political life and the regional peculiarities of the fight for woman suffrage.[7] Scholars have highlighted the continuities of women's reform activities in the pre- and postsuffrage eras, expanding our definition of the political and transforming our understanding of American political history.[8] Important works in southern history have revealed the remarkable ways in which white women and African Americans exercised power within a political system that denied them the vote.[9] These studies have shown that even people who were systematically kept from the levers of power could influence politics and exercise some control within their society. Through all of these revisions and reconceptualizations of political history, however, a consensus has prevailed that the enfranchisement of women had relatively little effect on the political activities and political power of southern women in the 1920s.[10] "This initial enthusiasm for political participation dwindled rapidly," Elna Green concluded in her study of woman suffrage in the South, "the promise of change by enfranchisement went unfulfilled. . . . It appeared that women's voluntary associations, and not politics, would continue to be the source of change in the postratification South."[11]

Certainly, the clubwomen who voted for the first time in 1920 were not political neophytes. Women, particularly middle- and upper-class white women, began in the late nineteenth century to pursue expanded public roles by insisting that fulfillment of women's private duties required women's public action. Often referred to as "municipal housekeepers," these Progressive Era activists articulated a new kind of public authority for women based on their traditional duties as mothers and homemakers. Excluded from the ballot box and denied the levers of power available to men, these women devised ingenious political strategies to achieve their goals, and by some accounts pioneered the interest group politics of the twentieth century.[12]

Prior to the enfranchisement of women, female temperance workers spearheaded successful efforts to enact local, state, and, ultimately, federal legislation that prohibited the sale of alcohol. Organized women pressed for state support of reformatories for delinquent boys and girls. States increasingly established women's prisons, as female activists pressured lawmakers to eliminate conditions that led to sexual harassment and abuse. Working with organized labor, women's groups helped push the enactment of protective labor legislation for women in thirty-nine states between 1909 and 1917.[13] In one of their greatest victories, women reformers working through the Congress of Mothers, the General Federation of Women's Clubs, and other female organizations secured the passage of mothers' pension laws in dozens of states before 1920. The creation of the Children's Bureau in 1912 signaled the power of organized women. This federal agency was led and staffed by female reformers who used it "as a base of operations from which . . . to establish a monopoly over child welfare policy."[14] As one scholar put it, women's groups in the early twentieth century were "at the height of their own organizational prowess" and they could "credibly claim to be the broadest force of the day working for the public interest."[15]

To achieve these remarkable policy victories, unenfranchised women staged sophisticated publicity campaigns, built extensive reform coalitions, and took advantage of the ideology of separate spheres to speak with public authority on issues relating to children and the home.[16] They signed petitions, wrote letters to political leaders, and testified at legislative hearings. They used file systems to categorize political leaders as friend or foe of their cause, and they used personal connections to gain access to influential men. They helped set the public agenda by engaging in what one scholar has called "a politics of public education."[17] Once they had identified the problem they wished to solve, organized women created handbills and brochures that outlined the issues. They made public presentations, spoke before church circles, and lobbied their husbands. Perhaps most effectively, they worked with newspapers and magazines to dramatize the problems and pressure political leaders for solutions. National organizations served as clearinghouses for information, and women from all parts of the country worked to build coalitions with other like-minded men and women to press for reform.

Through their victories and voluntarist associations, women created a public "dominion" for themselves, asserting (and being accorded) tremendous authority over public questions having to do with women and children, despite the fact that they remained voteless.[18]

Yet, even as they achieved these victories, women reformers became increasingly convinced that women needed the right to vote in order to see all of their policy goals enacted. When male legislators refused women's demands to increase the age of consent or to protect a widowed mother's right to the custody of her children, women reformers grew "increasingly impatient."[19] Thus, the battle for woman suffrage became the most active fight for many of these women reformers. The movement for woman suffrage came late to the South, and it divided women reformers as it did the nation. Suffragists and antisuffragists disagreed over the proper role of women in public life and the necessity of the vote to influence public policy. Even those women who were committed to securing the ballot often disagreed about who was fit to vote and how their goals could best be achieved. In the South, these questions were exacerbated by the region's peculiar politics, by a civic culture that put white women on a pedestal far removed from public life, and by fiery debates about race and states' rights. Deeply invested in the system of white supremacy that buttressed their privileged position, white southern suffragists publicly supported disfranchisement and denounced claims that the enfranchisement of women might provide votes for black women, too. Yet, throughout this long fight, female activists remained convinced that the vote would mean the difference between policy-makers politely ignoring women's petitions and legislators seriously weighing the demands of their constituents. No longer supplicants, these suffragists believed, women would be able to leverage their votes for reform.[20]

In the end, however, scholars have concluded that in the 1920s, after their suffrage fight was won, organized women pursued their goals in the ways they always had, relying on "educational politics," petitions, networks of influence, and their gendered position as agents of moral suasion. Through these kinds of efforts, women obtained some notable policy victories, including federal and state appropriations for maternal and infant health programs under the Sheppard-Towner Infancy and Maternity Protection Act of 1921. Nevertheless, scholars have determined that, divided over the Equal Rights Amendment and protective labor legislation, unable to form a woman's bloc to leverage their votes, and distanced from the political process by men who tenaciously protected their political turf, suffragists' faith in the power of the vote turned out to be "naïve."[21]

As historians of women have focused increasingly on the role of women and gender in state policy-making and political historians have paid increasing attention to female agency and activism, both groups have articulated an important and public role for organized women in the state at the same time that they have discounted the importance of voting. To be sure, the political strategies refined by organized women in the years before 1920 continued to be important to their successful lobbying efforts in the postsuffrage era, and women voters divided along lines of race, class, region, party, and ideology, just as did men voters. Yet it seems hard to reconcile the portraits of these organized women at once so politically savvy that they are able to accomplish remarkable things even though they are disfranchised and at the same time so politically naive that they fail to realize that the vote will not give them "the power they dreamed of."[22] How could these women have so effectively worked the political system without the vote, and at the same time be unable to distinguish the real levers of power from those that yield nothing?

THIS BOOK IS AN EFFORT to answer those questions, to reexamine the meaning of the Nineteenth Amendment and explore the connections between electoral mobilization and political power. This story looks at female agency and activism through one of the most prized tools of American democracy — the vote. Even as recent scholarship has demonstrated the political potency of extrapolitical forms of activism, such as marches, labor strikes, petition campaigns, associational activity, and even more quotidian forms of resistance like stealing and dancing, the power of electoral mobilization has been neglected.[23] As a result, not only is our historiography incomplete, but our understanding of the means by which ordinary Americans gain access to political power has been profoundly distorted.

By analyzing a variety of sources, including the papers of politically active women and their reform organizations, the correspondence of male politicians, political party records, legislative journals, newspapers, and broadsides, this study poses a direct challenge to the standard interpretation of the meaning of the Nineteenth Amendment. It argues that southern women, who were so adept at wringing power from powerless situations before 1920, were no less adept at using the ballot to achieve their political goals after 1920. If early-twentieth-century politics was shaped by notions of a proper gender order and influenced indirectly by groups and individuals formally excluded from the political process, it was also guided by concerns about patronage, campaigns, constituents, and reelection. Once they were enfranchised, southern women gained the political currency to participate directly in the male-dominated formal politics from which they had so long been excluded. The Nineteenth Amendment offered a rare redistribution of political power in the New South, and a close examination of its effects suggests that woman suffrage was important not only symbolically but also structurally and substantively.

Symbolically, the enfranchisement of women indicated that women no longer deferred to men. The presence of women voting, politicking, and lobbying in spaces formerly reserved for men marked a profound change on the southern political landscape and disrupted what had heretofore been a male preserve. Immediately following the ratification of the Nineteenth Amendment, southern white women began serving as campaign stump speakers, voter registrars, election judges, city council members, party delegates, and state legislators — roles in which women had never before served. In private, as well as in public, woman suffrage challenged the authority of white men. No longer the sole voices of their households on public matters, southern white men were forced to acknowledge that women had political opinions potentially different and equally valuable at the polls. Empowered by their ballots, white female activists worked to clean up polling places and demanded that political leaders participate in new political rituals devised and controlled by white women. At the same time, white men were forced to defer to the wishes of white women in order to court their votes.

In an even more dramatic spectacle, the ratification of the Nineteenth Amendment encouraged black southerners to reassert their place at the polls. African American women staged citizenship schools and organized registration drives, suggesting that the feminization of the polls would threaten not only male privilege but white supremacy itself. In southern states, thousands of black women cast ballots and thousands more flooded courthouses and registrars' offices attempting to enroll. In some parts of the region, African American women ran for public office, organized voters' leagues, and even served as national committeewomen. As a result of the determination of African Americans to exercise their right to vote, white men not only were forced to recognize the equality of white women at the ballot box but found that African American women, too, were casting ballots that carried the same weight as their own.

As they eagerly embraced the political authority that came with the ballot, newly enfranchised women challenged not only the southern gender order but also the structure of southern politics that put white men on top. After two decades of declining voter turnout following the passage of the disfranchising statutes, the ratification of the Nineteenth Amendment brought more than a million new people into the political system in the South. With the threat of Populism a fresh memory, Democratic Party elites in 1920 faced an unpredictable bloc of new voters whose party loyalties could not be discerned. At the same time, southern Republicans saw an opportunity to build a viable opposition party with the support of white women voters.

While Republicans courted these newly enfranchised voters, southern white women denounced party regularity and worked to bring new voters to the polls. From the moment they were enfranchised, southern women, white and black, worked to expand the electorate. And to the dismay of southern Democratic Party leaders, white women staged their get-out-the-vote efforts with apparent disregard for who might show up at the polls. To be sure, white women did not work to mobilize black voters, but they publicized registration and balloting information without obvious concern about who might make use of it. As southern women worked to open up the South's closed political system, they threatened to revive the partisan political competition that Democrats had so effectively stifled.

By working to mobilize new voters and undermining the structure that leading white men had set in place to suppress political dissent, southern white women heightened the anxiety — and the responsiveness — of Democratic Party leaders who feared an electoral revolt. Contrary to what southern Democrats had hoped and many scholars have assumed, southern white women did not simply double the Democratic electorate. By maintaining organizational nonpartisanship, by refusing to ally with any Democratic faction, and by threatening to vote Republican, southern white women convinced male political leaders that their political loyalty was in question. In so doing, they increased the attentiveness of legislators to their policy concerns. For the first time, organized southern white women had ballots with which to back their policy requests, and in the 1920s they very carefully honed that electoral threat and wielded their ballots for legislative reform.

Whatever power enfranchisement initially conferred upon women, scholars argue, those benefits had waned by 1928.[24] Yet in that year Virginia and North Carolina voted for a Republican presidential candidate for the first time since Reconstruction and Republicans made gains in southern state and local offices as well. The Republican insurgency was widely blamed on white women voters, and the election returns reiterated the threat that women voters posed to the established political structure. In the years that followed, southern white women continued to leverage their electoral power for legislative policy, including state appropriations for the Sheppard-Towner program — even after federal funding for the program was eliminated. As Democratic Party elites worked to manage the political instability that attended woman suffrage and granted policy concessions long demanded by white clubwomen, the meaning of the Nineteenth Amendment was clear. Despite disfranchisement and despite politicians' calls for Democratic Party loyalty, the vote dramatically enhanced the power of southern white women.

While the ratification of the Nineteenth Amendment immediately and permanently altered the ways in which male politicians responded to the demands of white clubwomen, disfranchisement ensured that most black women would remain unable to approach their representatives as constituents. Where they could vote in sufficient numbers, African American women, too, capitalized on women's new position as voters to demand policy concessions from southern politicians. For the most part, however, organized African American women had no ballots to leverage. Nevertheless, they did not meekly acquiesce to their disfranchisement. When white southerners refused to enroll black women or turned them away from the polls, African American women turned to the Republican Party, the courts, and the federal government to demand their rights as citizens. They called for congressional reapportionment and federal enforcement of the Nineteenth Amendment, and they worked inside the Republican Party in the hopes that their service would be rewarded with full citizenship rights. Instead, southern black women found themselves in much the same place their men had been since the turn of the century. By the end of the decade, after the Republican Party had repeatedly failed them, growing numbers of black women began to look elsewhere. As African American women in the region considered the first ten years of woman suffrage, the power of the ballot was as clear as it was unattainable.

Even with the ballot, of course, there was a limit to the political power of white women. Although the presence of white women at the polls quickly became commonplace and the Nineteenth Amendment greatly enhanced the power of organized white women as lobbyists, woman suffrage did not translate into widespread female officeholding. In part, this was the result of predictable resistance from southern white men. The spectacle of white women serving in public or party office signaled how profoundly woman suffrage had transformed women's relationship to the state and epitomized the threat of women's new political authority. For some white women, as well, female officeholding seemed to defy southern norms of proper female behavior. More surprising, organized white women specifically chose not to use their new political power to elect women to office. Despite the extensive voter mobilization drives organized by white women and the support that women legislators often gave to white clubwomen's policy priorities, organizations of white women did not focus their energies on electing their own. They wanted their issues represented, not their "identity," and they recognized that their political capital could be more effectively spent shoring up their electoral threat, lobbying their representatives, and getting out the vote.

ALTHOUGH THIS IS a story about formal politics, in a time and place where formal politics was restricted to a small minority of people, this is not a study of political elites. Certainly, the thousands of African American women and men who were able to cast ballots and participate in the South's electoral politics in the 1920s were unusual, but they could hardly be considered political elites. Nor could the hundreds of thousands of white women who flooded the polls on election day. Hundreds of women appear in these pages fairly anonymously, representative of thousands of others. This examination of what southern women did with the vote is an attempt to understand how the majority of southerners, white and black, male and female, reacted to the most dramatic expansion of voting rights between the Civil War and the modern civil rights movement. Clubwomen in every county and town in the region mobilized in new ways after 1920 to take advantage of the opportunities that the Nineteenth Amendment offered. They were joined by rural women who were politicized through farm councils, by home demonstration agents, and at county fairs. Moreover, the Nineteenth Amendment threatened not only the white male political leaders who had for so long controlled the region's politics. As the new political authority wielded by some women challenged their privileged place in southern society, woman suffrage also affected ordinary southern white men, even those who could not vote.

Formal politics affected all southerners, and the southern women newly empowered by their ballots found the greatest opportunities to wield that power at the local level. In a race for city council or state legislature, a few hundred or even a few dozen votes could change the outcome of the election. The presence of new women voters at the polls not only elected candidates who would otherwise have lost, but it *threatened* to do so, which forced all politicians to treat seriously the concerns of organized southern white women. Moreover, southern voters in the 1920s, both male and female, seemed to care more about their state and local politics. Newly enfranchised southern women identified problems in their own communities that they wanted the political system to solve, and by working at the local level they could mobilize substantial political pressure on their representatives to take action.

Ironically, the thoroughgoing system of disfranchisement in the South may have given some politically active white women, the ones who could vote, more opportunity to leverage their ballots for political power than women enjoyed elsewhere in the country. In the context of disfranchisement, with voter turnout rates in many southern states below 20 percent, organized white women could operate as swing voters in a region where it did not take many voters to effect a swing. At the same time, of course, African American women in the South were generally unable to obtain access to the polls. Thus the effects of the Nineteenth Amendment for southern black women differed not only from southern white women but also from black women elsewhere in the country.[25] The experiences of African American women after 1920 provide a powerful counterexample to those of enfranchised white women in the region, and they offer insights into the alternate political strategies that the region's disfranchised members pursued.

Despite the distinctiveness of southern disfranchisement, the ability of southern white women to leverage their ballots for real political power was not a regional anomaly. The legislative victories of southern white women were not simply cheap concessions offered by the leaders of a region whose social policies lagged behind the rest of the nation. These southern white women believed that they were pursuing the same kinds of political activities as other American women, and they saw national organizations of women as clearinghouses for information about the best ways to advance their political goals. By focusing on local and state politics, this study tells a story different from the one that we know, not because southern women were distinctively empowered or because the South was a legislative laggard, but because the story is, in fact, a local one. A political activist in North Carolina once described her work as an effort to "create new interest in local affairs first — then take up the bigger things as we grow up to them."[26] The movement for woman suffrage may have been a national one, but the best measure of what women were able to do with those hard-won ballots is not the enactment of federal legislation or the election of women to office. Instead, we should measure the weight of their votes where they did — in their own communities and state legislatures.

In the short run, hundreds of thousands of white women and a few thousand African American women in the South joined white men in the formal political arena. The entrenched political machinery of the Democratic Party had to account for these new voters and try to control them, and that, by definition, changed the way they operated. Moreover, as they used their ballots to demand legislative changes, activist women insisted that their state and local governments enact legislative remedies that women's groups had sought for years. By exercising their right to vote and by helping other southerners obtain and use their own ballots, these women also began the long, slow process of opening the political system to all comers. In the long run, the ways that southern women, white and black, took advantage of the Nineteenth Amendment not only challenge our understanding of women's history and the role of women in American politics but also provide new insights into the meaning and the power of the vote.

Chapter One

Now You Smell Perfume

The Social Drama of Politics in the 1920s

WHAT WILL YOU BE? A Man or a Jelly Bean?"[1] This is the question that antisuffragists posed to southern men on the eve of ratification. For years, and at an even more fevered pitch in the last months before the Nineteenth Amendment was ratified, antisuffragists made apocalyptic predictions of the doomsday that would arrive in the South if women received the vote. According to these "antis" the entire southern social order would collapse in the wake of woman suffrage, as it threatened to bring "Negro Domination" and the ruin of the white southern family. While the antis' most dramatic claims failed to materialize, the sudden influx of women into public politics transformed the social drama of politics and challenged the supremacy of white males in ways that many antisuffragists had predicted with dread.[2] As white and black women embraced their new status as voters, the Nineteenth Amendment blurred the lines of gender and race that were so central to the order of the Jim Crow South.

IN THE YEARS immediately preceding the ratification of the Nineteenth Amendment, white southern men sat atop a political system exclusively within their control. The threats from Populists, Republicans, African Americans, and even poor whites had been answered with poll taxes, understanding clauses, literacy tests, violence, and other legal and extralegal means of disfranchising disruptive voters. Voter participation rates in the South were appallingly low, even by low national standards, and on election days politically active southern white men gathered at the polls to share in the male political rituals of smoking, spitting, brawling, coarse joke-telling, drinking (despite laws to the contrary), and, not least, casting ballots, which symbolized their superiority to white women and children, all African Americans, and even other white men who lacked the means or education to share in southern political life.

Determined to protect this status quo, southern antisuffragists, both male and female, used theological, "scientific," and sociological arguments to condemn women's demands for the ballot.[3] Ministers, leading male politicians, and female antisuffragists used biblical injunctions to remind southerners of the divine inspiration for woman's separate sphere. Moreover, they argued, women were mentally and physically unfit for the strenuousness of politics and public life. But more often, antis based their attacks on the threat that woman suffrage posed to the southern social order. Woman suffrage, they argued, would foster unhealthy competition between men and women, "discourage marriage," and "lessen women's attractive qualities of modesty, dependence, and delicacy."[4] While antisuffragist men were often content to let the women antis take center stage in public debates over the issue, thereby furthering their contention that southern ladies did not really want the ballot, antisuffragist broadsides reveal surprisingly frank concerns about the effects of woman suffrage on southern manhood.

One broadside put it simply, "Block woman suffrage, that wrecker of the home."[5] Another pamphlet warned that "more voting women than voting men will place the Government under petticoat rule."[6] It was a cartoon published in Nashville, however, that really got to the heart of the matter. Titled "America When Femininized [sic]," it pictured a rooster left to care for a nest full of eggs as the hen departed the barn wearing a "Votes for Women" banner. This scene was supplemented by text that cautioned "Woman suffrage denatures both men and women; it masculinizes women and feminizes men." The broadside warned that the effects of woman suffrage, this "social revolution . . . will be to make 'sissies' of American men — a process already well under way."[7] Another notice printed in Montgomery, Alabama, highlighted the same themes when it asked: "Shall America Collapse from Effeminacy? . . . The American man is losing hold. He is swiftly but surely surrendering to the domination of woman."[8]

As these broadsides suggest, white southern men had a lot to be anxious about in 1920. In addition to the threat of woman suffrage, recurrent agricultural crises, labor unrest, a rising tide of African American activism, the Great Migration, and social changes symbolized by flappers and an increasingly independent youth culture all combined to make white southern men feel very uneasy as they entered the postwar decade.[9] Historian Nancy MacLean has demonstrated that many white southerners believed that the hierarchical relations of power that provided the foundation for southern society were in danger of collapse, and hundreds of thousands turned to

Antisuffrage broadside (courtesy Tennessee State Library and Archives)

the Second Ku Klux Klan as a way to restore order.[10] Nevertheless, many historians looking back on the 1920s have contended that antisuffragists' claims were mere "political hyperbole."[11] To many white men who watched southern women go to the polls for the first time in 1920, however, the dire predictions of antisuffragists must have seemed eerily prescient.

WHAT WILL YOU BE?

A Man or a Jelly Bean?

Shall America Collapse from Effeminacy?

"Its Up to You, Son!"

WOMEN GET "DROP;" MAN LOSING HOLD—DRY LAW TYPICAL OF MODERN PURITAN MANIA, RENOWNED SCIENTIST SAYS.

(Special to New Orleans States.)

CHICAGO, March 11. The American man is losing hold. He is swiftly but surely surrendering to the domination of woman. Degeneracy and effeminacy among the sterner set is increasing at an alarming rate in the larger cities of the country, particularly in New York and Chicago.

Dr. William J. Hickson, head of Chicago's psychopathic laboratory and internationally renowned as a psychopathologist has spent several months investigating these subjects. He says:

"The war brought women to the front. It emancipated them in a way. They stepped into responsible positions. They were practically the backbone of the war hysteria. It was the women who yelled loudest for killing. They served on committees in uniforms. They took up smoking and fell into masculine ways physically.

WOMEN GET "DROP" ON MEN.

"Prohibition is typical of the modern puritan mania. The church movements are also typical. They with prohibition with so called high standard of morality result in a deterioration of masculine physical and mental virility, a falling off of creative ability, of the birth-rate—the latter already noticeable.

"American pep, which was the result of a masculine-dominated country, will soon be a thing of the past. With the collapse of the male ascendency in this country we can look forward to a nation of degenerates.

"The effimination of man is already to be observed and studied scientifically in America. The army had a great deal to do with this. We are receiving in our laboratory more and more degenerates.

TO BE JELLY-BEAN NATION.

"This is always a running mate with puritanism. The suppression of sex in America will ultimately have its harvest in a decadence—a phenomenon already beginning.

"The male today is inferior in most respects to the female. He is aping her in the matter of clothes—wearing tight fitting skirted coats. He boosts her legislation and vaguely whoops it up for her reform.

"He is fast taking second place, and with his fall there is no question that production in the United States, lental and material, will decline.

"In fact, the present decline in production is as much due to the decline in the male as to other economic conditions.

"Our politics is a form of effeminate idealism. An inversion is obviously taking place, and there is no way to stop it. The nation apparently has put its head in the noose of the Puritanism, and the degeneration of individual and national fiber resulting is inevitable."

BROWN PRINTING CO. MONTGOMERY.

Antisuffrage broadside (courtesy Bennehan Cameron Papers, Southern Historical Collection, Wilson Library, the University of North Carolina at Chapel Hill)

DESPITE DETERMINED opposition from the region's leading men, women in nearly every southern state cast their first ballots in November 1920.[12] In August 1920, Tennessee's legislature provided a narrow margin in support of ratification, becoming the essential thirty-sixth state to ratify the Nineteenth Amendment and joining Arkansas, Kentucky, and Texas as the only southern states to vote in support of the federal amendment. By contrast, many other southern states not only refused to ratify the amendment but passed rejection proclamations. Alabama, Georgia, South Carolina, and Virginia sent such resolutions to Washington, announcing to the nation their antipathy for woman suffrage. Even after the Nineteenth Amendment was added to the Constitution, Mississippi and Georgia refused to make the necessary changes in their registration laws to permit women to vote in the 1920 presidential election. Indeed, as one historian has noted, "the all-male electorate of Mississippi rejected woman suffrage in a referendum the same day that women in most of the country voted for the first time."[13] Up until the last moment, it seemed, southern white men fought to maintain the political sphere as their own domain.

Once that moment had passed, the presence of women voting, politicking, and lobbying in spaces formerly reserved for men marked a profound change on the southern political landscape. The appearance of women, both white and black, made the polls look different on election day and signaled that formal politics would no longer be the exclusive privilege of white men. As the *Richmond Times Dispatch* editorialized in 1923, "Somehow we couldn't visualize members of the fair sex in Virginia taking part in 'unfair' politics. The whole thing was incongruous."[14] Figure 1 and table 1, showing the increase in the popular vote in the first presidential election in which women voted, provide visual evidence of how widespread the disruption was for white men who had gone to such lengths to retain control of southern politics.[15]

In Alabama, 79 percent more voters, more than 100,000 additional people, cast their ballots for president in 1920 than had done so in 1916. In North Carolina, nearly a quarter million additional voters crowded the polls on election day in 1920, an increase of 86 percent. In Louisiana, more than 47,000 women registered to vote in the 1920 presidential election.[16] Regionwide, the increase in voting was 56 percent in the states in which women were permitted to vote. The addition of more than one million new voters to the southern polls in November 1920 was not due exclusively to the entrance of women into the system, but in the absence of new women voters, Georgia and Mississippi suffered declines in the popular vote cast for president that year of 7 and 4 percent, respectively. While we cannot know precisely how many southern women voted in 1920, the presence of women at the polls was widespread and numerically strong enough to make southern white men take note.[17]

Newspapers across the South took great notice of the first ballots cast by members of the "fair sex." On election day 1920, Virginia women went to the polls by the tens of thousands, and the state's largest newspaper noted that women "were early at the polls and stayed late" providing instructions to

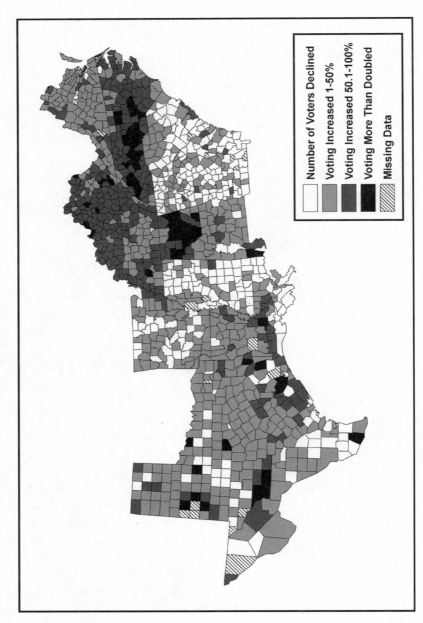

Figure 1. Change in Voter Turnout after Suffrage, 1920 Presidential Election

Table 1. Trends in Voter Turnout before and after Suffrage, 1912–1920

	Change in Turnout 1912–1916	Change in Turnout 1916–1920	Change in No. of Voters 1916–1920
Alabama	11%	79%	103,516
Arkansas	36%	8%	13,517
Georgia	32%	−7%	−11,030
Kentucky	15%	77%	398,264
Louisiana	17%	36%	33,262
Mississippi	34%	−4%	−3,741
North Carolina	19%	86%	248,812
South Carolina	27%	4%	2,858
Tennessee	8%	57%	155,846
Texas	24%	30%	113,139
Virginia	11%	52%	78,975

Source: The data utilized to create this table and table 2 were made available through the online database *U.S. Historical Election Returns* from the University of Virginia Geospatial and Statistical Data Center, ‹http://fisher.lib.virginia.udu/collections/ stats/elections/us.elections›.

first-time voters and working diligently to get out the vote.[18] On the day after the election, the editor of the *Richmond Times Dispatch* hailed the political involvement of the state's women: "Because of the lack of a strong minority party, Virginia campaigns have become rather cut and dried, but this year the women have given the color and zest needed for a complete revivification."[19] A South Carolina newspaper headline declared, "Women at Booths Attract Attention," and articles in newspapers throughout the South described the spectacle of women voters at the polls and provided local tallies of their participation in the day's election.[20]

Once the Nineteenth Amendment was ratified, politically active white women worked to make the polling places their own, and they transformed the polls into respectable spaces. In its election assessment, the *Charlotte Observer* lamented that in elections past, "there were plenty of idle moments in which to pass joke and quip; the air was usually foul with tobacco smoke and the floor spattered with juice and littered with paper, and sometimes the men would become unduly argumentative and a fight or two would enliven the proceedings." But with the arrival of women at the polls, the men "found no time to indulge in the amenities that characterized the elections of former days; instead of it being a day of fun and leisure for them, it was a day of diligent application to work."[21] When the women of Tennessee went to the polls for the first time, the *Chattanooga News* noted that "there was certainly a contrast in the election scenes today and in the city election four years ago." In deference to the women voters, "loud talking and the threats of betting are absent," and "everything was orderly as a Sunday school assemblage."[22] The election in Newberry, South Carolina, was described as "a very quiet and ladylike" one, a characterization antisuffragists might have predicted with fear.[23]

On the morning after the election, one South Carolina newspaper declared, the "Sun Still Shines Though Women Vote." Many men, however, might have disagreed with the reporter's assessment that "nothing untoward happened," as men in the courthouse "took off their hats, failed to chew the usual amount of tobacco, and stood aside for the ladies, while waiting their turns at the ballot box."[24] In yet another southern polling place, the policeman assigned to the precinct facilitated the balloting by holding women's babies as they cast their ballots.[25] Women in Aiken, South Carolina, were credited with casting their ballots "with all sang-froid of old timers," but it was clear from newspaper accounts that times had changed: "Husbands and wives went to the polls together; mothers and daughters drove up and alighted from their automobiles; young matrons left their babies in go-carts and carriages on the pavement or led their little tots along with them."[26] All of these changes that women voters wrought at the polls prompted one Georgia observer to comment, "If I hadn't known it was election day I would have thought the men and women were gathering for an afternoon reception or community sing."[27]

Throughout the decade, women voters worked to "clean up" politics in general and polling places in particular.[28] In Fulton County, Georgia, white women voters protested various "indignities" and "inconveniences" they suffered as they exercised the franchise. While highlighting a particularly "disgraceful episode" involving "two drunks" and "a gambling matter," which had obstructed voters' access at the Peachtree and Sixth Street precinct, these women went on to chastise public officials for forcing voters to "stumble over perfume and candy counters" in local retail establishments that served as polling places on election day.[29] Although these women sincerely believed that such inconveniences interfered with the "dignity" of voting, many of Fulton County's white men must have thought that politics as they knew it had passed once candy counters and perfume played any role at all in election days.

With the advent of woman suffrage, men not only had to acquiesce to the presence of women at the polls, but they also had to contend with the designs of women determined to make polling places more like parlors than saloons. In North Carolina, members of the Franklin League of Women Voters urged the sheriff to clean up the courthouse and construct a ladies restroom in advance of the election, and a Wake County woman voter complained that "much improvement was necessary" in the condition of her polling place.[30] The Charleston, South Carolina, Democratic Executive Committee acted in 1924 to change its rules for the enrollment of primary voters so that "no enrollment books shall be opened or kept in a place conducting an illegal business."[31] Apparently, local male party activists had previously enjoyed practicing their politics in shadier establishments.

One southern man recalled that before woman suffrage, "election day was dreaded. No lady would be seen on the street." With the arrival of women at the polls, however, "a day of fighting, drinking, and foul language" was transformed.[32] In Kentucky, as elsewhere, it was newly enfranchised women who did the transforming. Days after the ratification of the Nineteenth Amendment, one Kentucky woman wrote to the Democratic Party in her state complaining that polling places, "as a rule," were located "in the worst section of the voting precincts . . . some in vacant saloons, blacksmith shops, little 2 by 4 shacks, and other buildings with little or no conveniences." This partisan warned that the Democratic voting strength of newly enfranchised women would be jeopardized by such conditions, and she suggested that voting booths be moved to "school-houses or private houses" and that "a woman officer be appointed for every precinct."[33]

The changes that followed in the wake of woman suffrage did more than render previously male spaces gender-neutral. Masculine political spaces became feminized. Indeed, in calling on Democratic men to move the location of voting and registration in Tennessee, one woman highlighted the contrast, as well as the cultural import of the change: "You know how many women won't go to the polls because only men are there and tobacco smoke or worse," she admonished, "think how you'd feel if obligated to go into a women's pink tea parlor to vote and could only vote for a woman."[34] While most southern polling places were not moved to "pink tea parlors" in the aftermath of the Nineteenth Amendment, they increasingly resembled feminized domestic spaces. As one Georgia man said to the newly elected female legislator from his district, "You used to smell liquor at the polls, but now you smell perfume."[35] The robust masculinity of polling places before 1920 was a reflection of women's distance from political power. The feminization of those same spaces after 1920 was a corollary to women's increasing political authority.

NOT ONLY WERE THESE political rituals becoming feminized, but even the language of politics seemed to require changes once women received

.the vote. One prominent Virginian grappled with this problem quite openly when he wrote to congratulate Mary Munford on her election to the city school board: "I do not know a position in which a citizen of Richmond can be more useful to 'his or her' city. Under woman suffrage that awkward expression 'his or her' will mar our style until one pronoun swallows the other. I am wondering which pronoun will survive in our political vocabulary."[36] In 1922, a South Carolina newspaper asked its readers, "Should one say alderwomen, or women aldermen?" as it reported on the election of a woman to that post.[37] And when the Jefferson County, Alabama, registrar asked potential voters their names, newly enfranchised women routinely responded, "Do you want my name or my husband's?"[38]

The inclusion of women in the body politic did not immediately result in the common acceptance of their presence in political language. In the years after women were enfranchised, the terms "voter," "citizen," "Republican," and "Democrat" often required embellishment to assure that the correct meaning was conveyed. In an essay on the need for "Political House Cleaning," one man addressed his audience "Mr. and Mrs. Good Citizen," as if it would not be clear to whom he was speaking if he failed to use gendered titles.[39] In Newport, Arkansas, Democratic Party leaders specified that "not only the men, but the ladies as well" should "attend the polls and vote."[40] In their correspondence, party organizers often instructed their operatives to get "men and women" Democrats registered, or to see that the poll taxes of "every Republican man and woman in your precinct" had been paid.[41] The Republican county chairman of Russell County, Virginia, advertised a political rally with handbills inviting "all the citizens of the County, men and women, to attend this speaking."[42] To the white men who managed southern politics, these terms had always referred to men. As they reconfigured their political operations to deal with woman suffrage, they felt compelled to use extra words to ensure that their underlings solicited the votes of women. Even in political cartoons, artists felt compelled to clarify that their messages were intended for men and women alike. One election-eve pitch for Congressman Montague was thus addressed to "Mr. and Mrs. Voter."[43] As southerners adjusted to the presence of women in politics, it seemed to some that nothing, not even their language, remained the same.

IT WAS NOT JUST WHITE women who made southern politics look different; newspapers and observers took particular note of the presence of African American women at the polls. Just two decades after Democratic leaders had ended the Republican threat and nearly eliminated the participation of African Americans in the South's political system through disfranchisement,

The Right Man On the Job!

KEEP HIM HERE, MR. AND MRS. VOTER!

A. J. MONTAGUE

MEMBER OF CONGRESS
THIRD DISTRICT
VIRGINIA

FRED O. SEIGEL

Voice of the People

Political cartoon making an election-eve pitch to both male and female voters
(courtesy Library of Virginia)

African American women set about to take advantage of the federal amendment and exercise their rights as citizens. In South Carolina, one report on the number of women registering to vote was headlined, "960 Women Register in Union County, Some Are Negroes."[44] In a front-page story about women voters, the *Chattanooga News* noted, "At several of the voting places some colored women were voting, and from the dispatch with which they marked and handed in their ballots they showed they were adept pupils."[45] An Alabama paper described a "long line of negro women making application for registration" and reassured its white readers that "the negro women qualifying were recommended by some of the most prominent men and women in Birmingham."[46] The tone of a Virginia newspaper was less sanguine, as it proclaimed: "Negro Women Continue to Outnumber White."[47]

If the feminization of the polls threatened white southern manhood on a psychic level, many white men believed that the feminization of the polls threatened white supremacy more concretely. The disfranchisement of African Americans rested on violence, or at least the threat of violence. Yet it was assumed that white women could not be counted on to defend the polls with force, and the feminization of polling spaces made it increasingly unlikely that white men would exercise such violence in white women's presence. Moreover, some African Americans believed that white men would have more difficulty keeping black women from the polls than black men. As one observer put it, "Not even the 'cracker' can treat a woman with quite the same brutality with which he treats a man."[48] Thus, while white men surely did not doff their hats to African American women, the Nineteenth Amendment provided some African American women with an opportunity to exercise their rights as citizens. The feminization of the polls even may have, as one historian argued, "cleared a narrow path for black men to return to electoral politics."[49]

Just as antisuffragists had warned, the ratification of the Nineteenth Amendment fueled the demands of African Americans for full citizenship rights. Precise figures are not available, but accounts from around the region signaled the determination of African Americans to vote. In Louisiana, nearly 2,000 African American women registered to vote in less than two months, joined by more than 300 African American men who had not previously been registered.[50] In Lexington, Kentucky, 3,067 "Negro Republican women" had registered by the end of the first week in October.[51] "Thousands" of African American voters "stormed" the polls in Houston.[52] Even in Edgefield, South Carolina, a white woman reported that nearly 10 percent of the new women registrants were African American.[53] One southern black woman put it plainly, "We are going to exercise our rights under the law. We fear no evil; we will not be bluffed away from the polls. If bodily harm is resorted to, there are two sides to the question, and we may as well begin to prepare for a decision, a peaceful one, we fondly hope. Why should we be denied our votes?"[54]

Despite their best efforts, white political leaders could not prevent the blurring of racial and gender lines that attended woman suffrage. In Richmond, Virginia, for example, the attempts by African American women to qualify as voters "swamp[ed] . . . race segregation" as dozens of black and white women "were milling about giving each other suggestions and instructions" on how to register.[55] The white *News Leader* devoted considerable space to this story, announcing, "One Time This Morning Negro Women Were in Possession, With White Women Standing Outside in Corridor."[56] As white and black women worked to take advantage of the Nineteenth Amendment, they found that their presence in politics undermined the physical separation of the races that segregation demanded. Moreover, in an era when black men and white women could not even share a public sidewalk, the enfranchisement of women placed black men and white women face to face, and even side by side each other at the polls. In Alexandria, Louisiana, for example, a black man sought registration from a white woman registrar.[57] In Newport News, Virginia, woman suffrage resulted in an even more dramatic spectacle on election day as "[white] women were forced to wait for hours in a long line [at the polls], sandwiched in between colored men and colored women."[58]

While the physical closeness of white women and black men at the polls challenged the hierarchies of race and gender that segregation was meant to secure, the advent of woman suffrage also challenged southern power relations away from the polls. In Kentucky, one white woman sought the support of her black maid on behalf of the Democratic ticket. As the domestic servant described it, white southerners in her community were "after all the colored people to vote the Democratic ticket. My madam's been after me for three weeks." In an act of defiance that symbolized the threat that woman suffrage posed to the racial and gender order in the South, however, the black woman forcefully rejected her mistress's request. As she put it, "Miss Charlotte . . . I works for you and dats enouf; I sho' ain't goin' to vote for you."[59] For more than two decades, white southerners had insisted that African Americans not vote at all. The disfranchisement statutes had been an essential component of a broader campaign to legally enforce the submissiveness of black southerners. By opening the door to greater African American political participation in the region, the Nineteenth Amendment threatened that system of white supremacy that ordered the Jim Crow South.

Certainly, the number of African American women who succeeded in voting in southern elections during the 1920s was quite small. Nevertheless, their efforts were widespread, suggesting that the discomfort they caused to white southerners' sense of racial politics far outweighed any real risk they posed to white control of the polls. From Nashville, Tennessee, to Mound Bayou, Mississippi, and from Charlotte, North Carolina, to Birmingham, Alabama, came reports that African American women were organizing voter registration clubs.[60] In rural Kingsville, Texas, Christia Adair led a group of African American women to the polls on the first election day that women were granted primary suffrage. "We dressed up," she recalled, "and went to vote."[61] One image speaks volumes to the changes on the southern political landscape in the 1920s. The photograph, dated 1921, shows the members of the "First Colored Women's Voters Club of Ettrick," Virginia, and puts faces to the fears of the South's leading white men.[62]

Throughout the debates over woman suffrage, antisuffragists warned that a federal amendment would result in votes for both white and African American women. Though suffragists accurately countered with the argument that white women would out-vote black women, and that black women would be kept from the polls by the same methods that disfranchised their husbands, the Nineteenth Amendment did provide a very small number of African American women with an opportunity to participate in southern politics as citizens. With much fanfare, the Nineteenth Amendment brought new people to the polls — people who not only made politics look different but whose presence forced white men to acknowledge the symbolic equality of the ballot and the consequent diminution of their own manhood. As they stood alongside, or behind, women voters to cast their ballots and were forced to abandon the male rituals of election day, some southern white men must have thought that the antisuffragists' dire predictions had come true.

AS WOMAN SUFFRAGE brought profound changes to the social drama of southern politics, white men responded in subtle, and some not-so-subtle, ways to these attacks on male privilege. In Alabama, one newspaper reported on the registration of newly enfranchised women voters, noting that "those men who had inadvertently been caught in this maelstrom of femininity audibly sighed with relief when they reached the street."[63] On the evening following the Democratic primary in 1921, a Virginia newspaper gave front-page attention to problems at the polls and favorably reported on a legislative proposal for the "establishment of convenient places at which women may vote instead of having to stand in line for hours."[64] Certainly hours-long lines at the polls were a problem, but it may have been more than just chivalry that motivated men to support separate polling places for women. As one woman put it, "some men are taking votes for women mighty hard."[65]

Throughout the South, male political elites resisted the entrance of women

African American women organized to take advantage of the Nineteenth Amendment in 1921, Ettrick, Virginia (courtesy Johnston Memorial Library, Virginia State University)

into politics, just as they had rejected woman suffrage. In many places, "registrars of the old anti-suffrage school" resigned their posts rather than register women.[66] Both Democratic and Republican Party leaders preferred the establishment of separate party committees for men and women. To the extent possible, political leaders distanced women from the centers of political power by creating separate party organizations for women or naming women as alternate delegates to real decision-making bodies. Individual men refused to pay their wives' poll taxes, and a woman in Georgia worried that without sufficient publicity, many women would not even know they had been enfranchised.[67] As one woman put it, "women have not been very enthusiastically received by the men in the inner circle of politics."[68]

Despite the chivalry on which white southern men prided themselves, their displeasure with woman suffrage was often poorly hidden. More than a year after the Arkansas General Assembly had granted partial suffrage to women of that state, one man wrote to the state's largest newspaper to announce the humiliation he felt with the arrival of women in politics. As he put it, "When woman knocks at the door of the political arena, it reflects upon my chivalry," and he urged his representatives to "expunge this silly and effeminate law from the statutes of the great state of Arkansas."[69] In Texas, another white man took his concerns to court, challenging the constitutionality of the state's primary suffrage law.[70] While these southern men publicly denounced the new political order, other white men aimed their displeasure at the women voters in their midst. For example, when two Georgia men found their sister's name listed in the newspaper as a would-be voter, "they were very indignant and for a while made things very uncomfortable for her."[71] White men's failure to accept the entrance of women into politics seemed so widespread that a South Carolina newspaper cautioned its male readers not to "ridicule or scorn women's efforts to qualify themselves for voting," and apologetically described the advent of woman suffrage as a "rather puzzling state of things for us men."[72]

Throughout the South, white women organizers reported male opposition, particularly from husbands, as an obstacle to women's full exercise of the franchise.[73] A South Carolina woman "heard a man say that if his wife registered and tried to vote, she could find another home!"[74] After his wife had been asked to join the League of Women Voters, another southern man reportedly responded, "Tell them, 'No.' You are Tom Jones' wife and he does your thinking for you."[75] Unable to prevent the enfranchisement of women in the region, many white men looked to their households as a bulwark of that male privilege. In Georgia a white man, "terribly hurt and surprised" at his wife's efforts to register, berated her: "I never thought the time would come . . . when my wife would take part in politics."[76] A Texas man burned his wife's poll tax receipt to ensure that she would not.[77]

Even before women obtained the right to vote, antisuffragist rhetoric revealed that white southern men believed there was a close link between male control of politics and male control of the household. Despite such public demonstrations of male chivalry as removing hats, refraining from smoking, and escorting female relatives to the polls, white men clearly felt their authority challenged by the sudden of influx of women into public politics and the feminization of formerly male spaces. One female observer put it plainly: "The fear of having their license questioned and eventually taken from them no doubt figures largely in the minds of many men who do not favor the women voter[s]."[78] As white men had feared, women's increased political authority seemed to threaten an attendant decline in the authority of men in their own homes. In Waycross, Georgia, a man prohibited his wife from getting involved in politics, yet in defiance of his wishes, she promised the League of Women Voters that she would work to organize women voters and drive them to the polls.[79] Another woman confided to a friend that she had refused to tell her husband how she would vote.[80]

In Birmingham, the experience of Margaret Burnett epitomized the fears of white men. When the Nineteenth Amendment was ratified, Burnett was engaged to a young veteran. She was a secretary for Alabama Power Company, and neither she nor her mother had ever had much sympathy for the "suffragette women" who were advocating the vote.[81] Burnett's fiancé shared her general aversion to woman suffrage, concluding, "I just don't think it's very lady-like."[82] Nevertheless, in September 1920, Burnett's mother insisted that her daughter accompany her to the courthouse to register as voters. Burnett recalled that white men "lined up on the streets to see these crazy women go down to the courthouse."[83] Once enrolled, Burnett was reluctant to tell her fiancé what she had done. Indeed, when Burnett voted for the first time at the drugstore on the corner of 55th Street and First Avenue, her fiancé did not accompany her. He could not vote. The strict residency requirements in Alabama disfranchised her young fiancé, whose service in the military and business travel prevented him from qualifying.[84] When Burnett's husband finally did enroll as an Alabama voter, it was the result of Burnett's own intervention with the registrar, as she vouched for his membership in the community and convinced the official to permit him the vote. As Burnett recalled years later, "I registered him."[85]

For the first months of their marriage, Burnett was the only qualified voter in the household, a fact that turned paternalistic notions of a "household vote" on their head. For years antisuffragists had argued that women did not need the ballot, because their interests were represented at the polls by the men who headed their households. Antisuffragist ideology rested on assumptions about the centrality of the family and the distinct roles for men and women within it. Women, antisuffragists reasoned, exercised great influence on the men who represented them at the polls, and those men cast their ballots "as an expression of the needs of the family."[86] The threat that woman suffrage posed, then, was to acknowledge that family members — husbands and wives — did not always have the same political interests. Indeed, as one antisuffragist from Memphis warned, "There would inevitably be two sides and these in many instances hotly contested. It is an old saying that a man and his wife should not play chess. Surely, it is a graver question whether they should play at the dangerous game of politics."[87]

Although often overshadowed by the hyperbole of antisuffragists' racial and states' rights arguments, this notion of a household interest was a central pillar of southern white men's power. As historian Stephanie McCurry has demonstrated, all southern white men, regardless of class, shared a common privilege as "masters of their households."[88] Though the scope and nature of this "mastery" had certainly changed in the decades that followed the Civil War, southern white men in the early twentieth century could still point to the public representation of their dependents as evidence of their superior position in southern society. Woman suffrage changed that. After 1920, southern white men were forced to acknowledge and, when they courted women's votes, even embrace the presence of two separate and politically valuable opinions within southern households.

Consequently, the ratification of the Nineteenth Amendment brought all southerners into the debate about the role of women in politics. In particular, rural women who had not typically been engaged in the struggle for the vote had to decide what they would do with it. As one woman reported from Dry Ridge, Kentucky, "most of our women are farmers' wives and they have never given voting a thought."[89] News reports and the work of political activists, however, ensured that the region's rural women would be confronted with their "duty to vote."[90] Prior to 1920, only a small minority of southern women were suffragists, and like their counterparts in towns and cities across the South, many rural white women cast ballots and became active in politics for the first time in the 1920s. These expanded opportunities for women disrupted established patterns of gender relations and male authority in rural communities.

In 1923, a debate over woman suffrage and its implications for politics, marriage, and family relationships raged for three months in the editorial pages of Tennessee's *Putnam County Herald*. As these letters to the editor demonstrate, rural men and women were keenly aware of the connections between women's expanded political authority and challenges to male authority in the home. Representing one extreme in the debate, "Not an Old Maid" wrote that "some of the old-timey women still think the only way to appeal to a man is through his stomach." She chided fellow women that "this idea keeps you over a hot cook stove when you might be holding a good position down town making a nice salary. . . . So, women, don your short skirts, bob your hair, get into your car, go to the polls and vote."[91] At the other extreme, some wives and mothers in this rural county contended that politics was no place for women and expressed their support for the existing patterns of male authority: "I don't believe in women voting. If I did and my husband did not want me to I wouldn't. This is love."[92] Still other women agreed that a woman's place was in the home but felt that the ratification of the Nineteenth Amendment obligated them to cast their ballots wisely.[93]

Despite these wide-ranging opinions, nearly all the letters to the editor reflected a belief that woman suffrage portended changes not just at the polls but in households and marriages as well. Like the antisuffragists' rooster left to care for a nest full of eggs, one Putnam County man predicted that with women "run[ning] the government machine," chaos would reign in the home. Among the election day "misfortunes" he anticipated were babies badly burned in dishwater as husbands took on the duties of voting wives; young boys, he feared, would be enticed into early marriage by aging spinsters while their mothers served in public office. He also warned of an utter reversal of gender roles as women took jobs installing telephone lines and men were praised as "a splendid cook and a nice housekeeper."[94] The author of this letter did not live to see such dire consequences from women's ballots, but even in his rural community woman suffrage transformed the social drama of southern politics. Leaders from both parties urged the women of his region to go to the polls, and before the end of the decade several women from the region were elected to county offices.[95] Moreover, in the *Putnam County Herald* and in local polling places women publicly asserted their right to vote without consultation or interference from men. As one young reader put it, "When I get old enough I'll vote and the men won't hinder me."[96]

Indeed, white men found that they could not always hinder women even from holding office. It would be easy to assume that women's engagement in electoral politics in the 1920s, like southern women's suffrage activism, was mostly an urban phenomenon. Yet the men of rural Winslow, Arkansas, were among the first to be governed exclusively by women. Frustrated by the way that the men had governed the town, a group of white women organized an all-female slate of candidates for the April 1925 elections. In what has been described as "bemused condescension," the men of the town agreed to "let the women take a turn" and offered the women no opposition on the ballot.[97] As the election drew near, however, some men grew wary of this gender bending, and they organized a write-in campaign to challenge the women. Their efforts were unsuccessful, and the women's slate defeated the men by a margin of two to one.[98]

Certainly, not all, nor even a majority of, southern women voted in the 1920s. Many white women resisted entry into "dirty politics" and clung to the belief that politics remained outside a lady's proper sphere. Most African American and poor white women were disfranchised by the same legal and extralegal tactics that prevented their male relatives from voting. And even among women who did vote, such blatant public rejections of male authority were rare. Nevertheless, all white men could feel to some degree that woman suffrage was an affront to their masculinity. Antisuffragists had warned specifically that woman suffrage would "encourage women to disrespect the men of the family" and "take away from his happiness and self respect."[99] As a result of woman suffrage, political elites no longer enjoyed a day of coarse jokes and political brawls at the polls. Ordinary white men found that their wives and daughters were just as important as they were to party organizers on election day. Poor and illiterate white men were forced to watch as some women exercised a right they did not share. Whatever their position in the social hierarchy, southern white men could see that the relationship between white men's dominance in public politics and their supremacy in the privacy of their own homes was not just a convoluted twist of antisuffragist logic.

WHILE THE NOTIONS of gender equality implied by woman suffrage unsettled white men who stood atop the region's social hierarchy, African American men were much less threatened by the efforts of their wives and daughters to cast ballots. Instead, African American men generally viewed the Nineteenth Amendment as an opportunity to enhance their own political power and that of their race. Immediately after ratification, southern black men looked to the women of the race to seize their citizenship rights. The *Atlanta Independent*, for example, called on black women to "pay their taxes and register."[100] As a result of the cumulative poll tax laws, many black and white men in Georgia could not afford to become enfranchised. Many black men consequently called on black women to register, noting that "it is much easier for our women to qualify and vote than the men," because new women voters as yet owed no back taxes at the polls.[101] The *Savannah Tribune* issued a similar call to black women, insisting that registration "will never be easier than now!"[102] "Now that our women are going up in such large numbers to be registered," the *Tribune* continued, "the men should be put upon their mettle to keep pace with them."[103] *The Crisis* put it simply, "Every black man and woman ought to vote."[104]

Privately, as well, African American men seem to have provided little opposition to the women of their households when they desired to vote. In Virginia, one woman reported that her husband had provided her a "type written copy" of the registration application for her to study. When, despite the "perfection" of her application, the registrar denied her application to vote, this woman's husband "appealed the case."[105] An NAACP representative investigating the disfranchisement of African American women in the South reported that the women of Hampton and Phoebus, Virginia, had prepared thoroughly for their attempts to register, adding that "most had been drilled by their men-folk."[106] In Savannah, leading African American women voters publicly thanked the black men of their community "who encouraged us in our efforts and backed us up with their presence and help at all times."[107] In a survey of more than 1,000 black southerners about suffrage restrictions and political conditions, not a single respondent indicated that black men discouraged black women from voting.[108] African American men and women alike had faith that the power of the ballot would mean "the passing of Jim-Crowism, industrial slavery, lynching and all the despicable institutions which depend upon political power, and upon each other."[109]

Thus, African American men welcomed newly enfranchised black women to "the opportunity to aid the men" in "one of the greatest privileges citizens can enjoy."[110]

In contrast to white political women who routinely complained that the antisuffragism of husbands prevented white women from voting, African Americans, both male and female, focused on the hostile white registrars and the legal structure of disfranchisement that posed the greatest obstacles to black women's political participation. Indeed, an African American woman from Louisiana specifically denied that antisuffragist black men in her state "influenced their wives not to vote."[111] Instead, she blamed the small number of African American women voters in her state on "unfair methods used by registrar[s]" and demanded that "national elections be controlled by U.S. Marshalls [sic] in the South."[112] In the face of these "unfair methods," African American men actively demonstrated their support for women voters. In Columbia, South Carolina, the president of the local NAACP branch wrote to the national headquarters to describe the conditions that faced would-be voters in his area and to express his determination to fight their disfranchisement "until hell freezes over."[113] Women in South Carolina were exempt from the poll taxes that men had to pay, and as he lauded black women's efforts to enroll as voters, this local leader made clear his support for woman suffrage as a political strategy for his race. "We mean to stay in the fight," he explained, "until every woman who possesses the qualification is registered or fight the case through the Supreme Court."[114] When black women in Birmingham organized a "women voters' club," the *Birmingham Reporter* applauded their efforts and urged the support "of the sober and thoughtful male members of the race."[115] In contrast to the white southern men who effectively disfranchised their wives by refusing to pay the women's poll taxes, black men in the South were outraged by the "flagrant manner in which our women were discriminated against" and, in most cases, eagerly joined the women of their communities to fight for black women's right to vote.[116]

Nevertheless, some black women did complain that the men failed to adequately support their efforts. A group of women from Pine Bluff, Arkansas, for example, wrote to national leaders in the NAACP to report that male leaders in their city had denounced the women's attempts to press their right to vote in court as "absolutely un[n]ecessary."[117] Similarly, Mrs. William Mann of New Bern, North Carolina, sought assistance from national leaders when her efforts to "enlist the support of colored men in a fight to secure the registration of colored women" ended in disappointment.[118] These African American women were eager to press their cases, and they expressed frustration when local black men refused to stand with them. Yet, unlike many white men, the black men in question did not object to women voting. They simply disagreed about the wisdom of pressing black women's voting rights in court.

The public outcry in response to a letter from James Dudley, president of North Carolina Agricultural and Technical College, further suggests that black men's support for woman suffrage was widespread after 1920. Following the ratification of the Nineteenth Amendment, Dudley published a letter advising African American women not to attempt to vote. In it he warned the women of his race that "your entrance now in the political field will add fresh fuel to the fires of race prejudice and political hate."[119] His admonition to black women to stay away from the polls generated condemnations from around the country. *The Crisis* characterized Dudley's advice as "grave and astonishing" and insisted that his "arguments deserve no particular consideration."[120] In a private letter, Dr. A. M. Rivers of North Carolina reported universal "hostil[ity] to Dudley" among African Americans in his state, and he blamed Dudley's "antebellum utterances" for growing white resistance to African Americans' attempts to register.[121] The editorial rebuke from the *New York Age* was so excoriating that Dudley himself described it as an "attempt to hold me up upon the cross of public ridicule and prejudice."[122] The chairman of the board of the NAACP dismissed Dudley's explanation of his remarks as "fully unconvincing."[123]

This apparent uniformity of support by black men for black women's participation in politics is striking, particularly in contrast to the response of white men. Although the ratification of the Nineteenth Amendment made public converts of many leading Democratic politicians in the South, southern white men commonly issued public and private denunciations of women's entry into the male political arena. These lingering antisuffragist sentiments, however, did little more than aggravate white suffrage supporters. They certainly did not arouse the national condemnation that attended Dudley's discouragement of black women voters. Moreover, while there were certainly white men who accompanied their wives to the polls and even encouraged them to vote, these white men did not, as many southern black men did, send women in their place. Indeed, when faced with the financial burdens of Georgia's cumulative poll tax system, the white men of Clarksville refused to pay their wives' poll taxes.[124] Undoubtedly, some black men continued to hold the antisuffragist sentiments they had harbored before 1920, but there is little evidence that black opponents of woman suffrage felt their manhood threatened by the enfranchisement of women.

On the contrary, southern black manhood was fortified by defending black women voters. In *The Crisis*, Dudley's "familiar remarks about 'women in the home'" were derisively dismissed and his advice was characterized as "but one false note" in the chorus of support for "the woman voter."[125] When African American women in Birmingham were turned away from the registrar's office, the *Birmingham Reporter* fueled calls "that the husbands and sons . . . protect the rights of these women."[126] In private letters and public pronouncements, "real men" were those who resisted disfranchisement for themselves and for the women of their race.[127] Indeed, even Dudley did not object to woman suffrage as an affront to black manhood. Rather, he feared that the assertiveness of black women voters would rekindle racial violence.

Voting was an act of manhood, but for southern black men the presence of women at the polls did not diminish that act or undermine male authority. Only the failure to value the vote was considered a "surrender of our manhood."[128] This relationship between suffrage and male authority in the household was made plain in the aftermath of the 1921 bond election in Savannah, Georgia. That spring, African American women mobilized thousands of black women in support of funding for local schools. These black women monitored the polls, checked registration lists, and followed up to ensure that voters cast their ballots. When the votes were counted, however, the bond issue had failed and unregistered African American men took the blame. In an election postmortem, the *Savannah Journal* wrote that "if our men do not act the MAN and register," then women "will, finally, make you stay at home and wash dishes. . . . If she must act the part of a man in one important act, she will act as such, of course in less important things."[129] In this case, women's participation in politics *did* emasculate black men, but not because women joined them in the electoral fray. Savannah's black men were rhetorically reduced to female drudges because they did not join the fray at all.

To the extent it was possible, African American men supported the attempts by black women to register and vote. But just as for black women, the dictates of white supremacy often made it difficult for southern black men to act. In the presidential election of 1920, five African Americans "lost their lives trying to vote in Louisiana."[130] Whites in Clinton, North Carolina, threatened a black schoolteacher with the "reenactment" of "such scenes as marked the Wilmington riots" if she persisted in her efforts to register.[131] In addition to the threat of violence, some southern officials jailed African Americans for merely attempting to register. And, of course, African Americans also faced economic intimidation. Even in parts of the South where voting was a private affair, registration was not. Lists of qualified voters were routinely printed in newspapers and posted in public locations. In Alabama, such lists were not only made public but were also organized by race, gender, and ward, making it very easy for local whites to target would-be black voters.[132] For obvious reasons, then, connections between voting and male authority in the household were less salient for southern black men than for their white counterparts. African American men had little interest in defending the privilege of voting as a male domain, insisting instead that "no public officer would dare insult a whole people who had the ballot and the unrestricted privilege to use it."[133] In the end, it was the opposition of hostile white registrars, not black men, that kept most black women away from southern polls.

WHILE AFRICAN AMERICAN women and men struggled to obtain basic access to the polls and white men grappled with the challenge that woman suffrage posed to established patterns of private gender relations, some white women staged increasingly determined attacks on men's public authority as well. On the day of the primary election in the summer of 1922, Gertrude Weil went to her polling place near the Wayne County (N.C.) Courthouse. When she arrived she found the election judges and managers, all men, fraudulently marking "all the ballots in sight" for the candidate of their choice. Horrified, she proceeded to tear all the marked ballots into small pieces before the eyes of the "dumfounded" men. When one of the election officials finally recovered his senses, he challenged the woman voter to "bring a man in the court house to do her fighting." But, in an act that only furthered the poor official's humiliation, Weil turned, "paid no attention to him, but continued to look for marked ballots."[134]

The story of Weil's "spunk" was widely reported in the state's newspapers, and reporters and editors lauded her for cleaning up politics, declaring that more such women were needed to protect North Carolina ballot boxes.[135] One woman could barely contain her glee, remarking: "I can't help laughing up my sleeve at the consternation you must have caused."[136] Yet while the press and her friends reveled in Weil's act of defiance, the election officials and other male observers must have greeted the event with considerable ambivalence. One could argue, perhaps, that only the most prickly men would feel threatened by the mere presence of women at the polls; undoubtedly white men found other occasions to participate in rituals of manhood once election days became adorned with feminine decoration. But what of the man marking the ballots? Unable to restore his manhood through an old-fashioned fight, and with the story of his humiliation published in newspapers throughout the state, he must have felt quite like the antisuffragists' "sissy." Perhaps more significantly, this event symbolized just how profoundly women voters jeopardized white men's control over the political system. Not only did women's votes count equally to those of men, but some women flatly rejected the means by which some politicians had heretofore remained in power. As some white women enthusiastically exercised their new power, southern white men were forced not only to adjust to the presence of women in politics but to acquiesce to their new political authority as well.

The presence of female poll watchers, election officials, and registrars was a sudden and ubiquitous example of the new public power of enfranchised white women. Female political leaders across the region demanded that white women be named to these posts, and in order to make their sisters comfortable at the polls, white female political leaders made themselves conspicuous. Moreover, in order to ensure that newly enfranchised women took advantage of their new voting rights, many white women worked as registrars. Though they frequently sought such posts in order to encourage other women to enroll as voters, official duties made these white women responsible for the registration of men as well as women. Some white southern men had resigned their posts in 1920 rather than register women voters.[137] In the decade that followed, many white men found women registrars more than willing to sit in judgment of men's fitness for the franchise. And in those areas where black men dared attempt to register, white women registrars served as the guardians of white supremacy.[138]

Despite the hopes of some men, and the claims of some observers, white women were not merely "docile ballot-droppers."[139] As white women engaged in electoral politics, they mounted a steady critique of men's traditional political methods. Their efforts to clean up the polling places were a criticism of men's ways of voting, and when women organized voter registration drives or get-out-the-vote efforts, they censured men who had prided themselves on keeping the system closed. Moreover, these attacks on male politics were often executed in distinctly female ways. For example, when the Alabama League of Women Voters staged an exhibit designed to increase voter turnout, it arranged elaborately costumed dolls in the window of a Birmingham bank building to illustrate Americans' low voter participation rate in comparison to other democratic countries. While league leaders claimed that crowds were always gathered around the display during the weeks that the dolls were exhibited, surely male politicians must have cringed at the sight of women adorning the heated summer primary battles with girls' toys.[140]

In contrast to the raucous partisan rallies of the nineteenth century, or even the private, backroom, masculine rituals of the more recent past, women's politicking was transparent, "clean," and distinctly feminine. Newly enfranchised women held teas and "Coming Out Part[ies]" complete with cake and decorations to register women voters.[141] They staged voter mobilization drives not just in the streets but in private parlors and church sanctuaries. They carried poll books house to house and decorated ballot boxes. In South Carolina, one white woman carried the voter registration books "all over the county" in order to register newly enfranchised women. Her efforts concluded one afternoon when she stopped at a local store where women had gathered to register. The store was decorated with flowers, and when the business of registering had been completed, refreshments were served and "it was more like a reception than anything else."[142]

While southern white men struggled to adapt to the new political realities of woman suffrage, many white women demanded acceptance as equal partners in politics and access to all of the privileges attendant to citizenship. For some politically active white women, membership on Democratic Party committees ranked chief among those privileges. Like voting, party office-holding symbolized the power and authority of white men. Before the ratification of the Nineteenth Amendment, party leaders exercised their control of politics in groups composed exclusively of men, and they often conducted their business in establishments unsuitable for white women. In South Carolina, local Democratic Club meetings were held in places so inappropriate for white women that party leaders felt compelled to move gatherings of the Democratic Clubs to local schools after 1920, "so that the women voters shall be assured of decent and respectable places of meeting."[143] Despite their reluctance to welcome women into party decision-making bodies, Democratic leaders recognized that "it might prove fatal to their interests to neglect or ignore the women."[144] Consequently, white women from around the region were named to party committees and men were forced to adapt their meetings and manners to the presence of their new partners in politics.

In Alabama, the state's national committeewoman petitioned for greater female representation on the state Democratic Executive Committee. By a very narrow vote, male party leaders agreed to increase the number of voting members temporarily, allowing one woman from each congressional district to be added to the committee.[145] It was clear from the opening moments of the first meeting to which women were invited, however, that the men of the committee were not entirely sure what to make of their presence, as a Mr. Nesbitt moved that "our lady members be invited to seats up in front; and we ask permission that we may smoke."[146] Desiring to extend appropriate courtesies to their new female members yet equally determined that the presence of women would not completely transform the conduct of their political meetings, Alabama's party leaders offered up their seats but continued to smoke.

In North Carolina, male party leaders were described as "speechless" and "too dumbfounded to remember their manners" when white women made their first appearance at Democratic precinct meetings.[147] In what the *News and Observer* described in its front-page story as a "coup," the white women of Raleigh made a surprise appearance at city precinct meetings in 1920 to "demand recognition as Democrats" and their rightful representation at the state convention.[148] When the men of the party recovered from the shock of this "invasion," they acknowledged the political authority of the women of their state and sent several of them as delegates to the state convention.[149]

As the language from North Carolina newspapers makes clear, southern white men did not embrace the feminization of their traditionally male spaces. In South Carolina, male party leaders vigorously resisted feminine inroads into party authority and refused to consider nominations of or by white women at the Aiken County Democratic convention. When a white female activist finally seized the floor to express "how keenly women resented their action," a man suggested that women be named as alternates. The women present at the convention refused this offer, however, and filed out of the convention hall, infuriated at their treatment by party leaders.[150] As one South Carolina woman noted, "If what happened at the Aiken County Democratic convention is a sample of an oncoming reaction, women need not count on laying their armor by."[151]

In the debates over woman suffrage, antisuffragists had warned that voting rights for women would make men a "subject sex."[152] Persistent fears of gender "inversion" marked southern antisuffragism, and nothing so clearly symbolized this disruption of the gender order as female officeholding.[153] One antisuffrage broadside pointed to the states in which women already voted, noting that all were "bedevilled by some form or other of harem government."[154] Another warned, "It is not the right order of affairs to expect men to take orders or directions from women officials, to train men to do so, or encourage women to exert that authority."[155] Yet after 1920, male voters and Democratic Party leaders often had to face white female precinct officials, white female campaign workers, and even white female candidates on election day. The Nineteenth Amendment opened the doors of elective and party offices to women, and white southern men saw women officeholders as the full expression of the threat that the Nineteenth Amendment posed.

The spectacle of women running for office was perhaps the most dramatic change in the social drama of southern politics following the Nineteenth Amendment. As early as the November elections of 1920, southern women ran for and were elected to public office. Throughout the decade, newspapers reported on the elections of white southern women as aldermen, sheriffs, mayors, and state legislators. The widespread coverage of women's political campaigns testified to the spectacle. Under ordinary circumstances, after all, the election of an alderman in Georgia would not be noticed in South Carolina and the election of a southern state legislator would not garner the attention of the *New York Times*. The headlines, too, often framed victory for a woman as a loss for men. When the tiny town of Winslow, Arkansas, elected an all-female city government in 1925, the *Southwest American* announced: "Mere Man Shoved Aside in Winslow," and a *New York Times* headline described Winslow as the town "Where Women Rule."[156] The election of Mary Elliott Flanery as Kentucky's first woman legislator was cast as an invasion when, in the absence of a cloakroom for women legislators, Flanery declared herself "one of the boys" and "took a peg" in the "Gentlemen's Cloak Room."[157] The frequency of these accounts in the 1920s demonstrated that, as the antisuffragists had feared, some southern white men would have to submit to the authority of white women, but their content and novelty also suggested the durability of the gender order.

Quite unsurprisingly, southern white men resisted this most aggressive entry of women into electoral politics. One Georgia white man spoke for many when he was asked to cast his ballot for a woman: "No, I won't vote for her . . . an' if that's her settin' out there in that car I don't keer ef she hears me."[158] Many female candidates encountered similar resistance from men who were simply "against a woman" serving in public office.[159] In 1922, suffragist Belle Kearney ran unsuccessfully for the U.S. Senate; one leading Mississippi politician registered his disgust for women candidates as he remarked to a friend, "When I cast my ballot for a woman, you can rest assured she is going to be a good-looking one and not so d—n old as Miss Belle."[160]

With real power at stake in these races, many campaigns took on the nasty tone of the mudslinging between men in presuffrage days. Some candidates publicly challenged their feminine rivals on gendered grounds, denouncing them as unfit for a "man's job."[161] Others were not above the race-baiting that had so often proved successful in bitter campaigns among men. In Mississippi, an incumbent congressman accused his female opponent of being married to a man with "negro blood in his veins."[162] When the first female city alderman from Macon, Georgia, ran for her seat, Mrs. Charles C. Harrold's opponents accused her of everything from encouraging African American women to vote to having big feet.[163] She was forced to respond to charges that she was Catholic, that she wanted all women workers to wear uniforms, and that she wore cotton stockings.[164] In North Carolina, "the same racist devices used to discourage black women from voting, and to incite white women to vote Democratic, were used to kill the campaign of a southern white Republican woman," Mary Settle Sharpe, who ran unsuccessfully for state superintendent of public instruction.[165] As one Democratic Party stalwart put it, "If women are not thick skinned they had better stay at home."[166]

In the midst of these heated battles, both men and women faced a cultural minefield as they attempted to determine what behavior was appropriate on the campaign trail. As they challenged men for public office, white women placed white men in the unfamiliar position of antagonist rather than protector. Consequently, southern white men struggled to find ways of attacking their female opponents that were at once effective and chivalrous. In Mississippi, one congressional candidate, unused to facing female opponents, suffered the wrath of the state's politically active white clubwomen when he failed to observe the dictates of southern chivalry. In their weekly newspaper, these women publicly gloated as the bewildered male candidate "found himself seriously crippled by his attacks" upon his female primary opponent.[167] Referring to another candidate's loss in the primary, these same activists declared that the candidate "has found with the women voting that it does not pay to turn aside from the great important issues of the day and cast little personal flings at a good woman."[168] In Macon, Georgia, a candidate for city alderman faced an uncertain political future after sending letters to women voters attacking his female opponent for that office. As male candidates faced female opponents, white southerners struggled to contain this new political drama within the boundaries of the established social order. Thus, supporters of "Mrs. Harrold's" candidacy publicly called on "not only every good woman but every good man to resent with their ballot an attack on a good woman."[169]

With direct attacks frequently off-limits, many male candidates found it difficult to express their true opposition to female opponents. As one political operative from South Carolina reported, attacks against female candidates had to be "rather diplomatic" so as not to create a backlash.[170] In Georgia, an editorial gently attacked the candidacy of Viola Ross Napier for state legislature. Obviously disdainful of women in politics, the author fumbled awkwardly to attack Napier's bid for the legislature without attacking Napier herself. While he specifically shied away from rejecting Napier's candidacy, this opponent condemned the idea of women officeholders, explaining that "the trouble with them may be . . . that they lack the required muscle for this job."[171] Careful not to appear unchivalrous, he continued, "Nevertheless, a few women officeholders scattered here and there will give new life and new color and perhaps a much-needed variety to the great and serious business of statesmanship."[172] Having carefully negotiated the boundaries of proper male conduct, this critic, like many male candidates, found that good southern manners made for ineffective political strategy. Napier won more votes than all but one of her male opponents to secure a seat in the legislature.

Other men attacked their female opponents in ways that could hardly be considered chivalrous, but they did so anonymously, in the hope that they could avoid public condemnations for their conduct. When male office-seekers suggested that their female rival had affiliations with the Klan, encouraged African Americans to vote, was unfit for office because of her gender, or was married to someone who had African American ancestry, newspapers often reported such accusations as rumors. Macon's would-be alderman, for example, "invaded" the campaign headquarters of one of her rivals "in search of one of the men who has been 'telling stories on'" her.[173] Despite her suspicions about the origins of these attacks, the newspapers consistently reported them as "stories," "charges," or "reports," without attribution.[174] Although newspapers widely reported his assertion that governing was a "man's job," Sallie Booker's opponent for the Virginia General Assembly would not repeat it when challenged to a public debate.[175] Georgia legislator Viola Ross Napier never did determine who had started the rumor about her affiliation with the Klan.[176] By using rumors rather than direct attacks, male candidates worked to employ their most effective, and offensive, ammunition against their female opponents without alienating southern voters by appearing to attack a white woman.

For white women, the challenge was to compete aggressively against their male opponents without appearing to dismiss the cultural expectations about appropriate femininity. The spectacle of female candidates publicly promoting themselves and stumping for office upended southern gender hierarchies and made a mockery of southern notions of female deference. In a letter to the editor, an anonymous man from middle Georgia wrote in to comment on the "young lady" running for state legislature. While "everybody knows she is a nice girl and very able," he reported, "everybody" agrees the Georgia legislature "is no place for a woman."[177] In Cabon Hill, Alabama, the editor of the local newspaper lambasted a female candidate for state legislature who had the temerity to question the policies of Alabama Power Company while touring the company's steam plant. As the editor described it, "Mrs. Maner in her zeal to further her political ambitions went so far as to completely overlook the fact that she should above all else conduct herself as a lady."[178] For southerners in the 1920s, however, it was not altogether clear how one could successfully run for office and "conduct herself as a lady."

Just as white southern voters insisted that candidates conduct their competition for votes within the boundaries of the established social order, many southern newspapers downplayed the threat of female political authority by focusing attention on officeholders' "ladylike" qualities. A Kentucky newspaper story was headlined "Mrs. Flanery, Politician, Likes Housework." That article went on to describe the "rest" this state legislator found "among flowers and vegetables after [a] strenuous [legislative] session."[179] South Carolina senator Mary Gordon Ellis was a determined politician; she had run for her senate seat as an act of revenge after the incumbent state senator sponsored legislation stripping her of her powers as county superintendent of education.[180] Despite this obvious willingness to assert her authority, or perhaps because of it, a local reporter emphasized Ellis's domestic credentials in his article. "Senator Ellis can go into the kitchen and broil a steak to perfection," the reporter declared, "a meal good enough to put before a king."[181] Miriam "Ma" Ferguson was the first woman to serve as governor in the South, but one newspaper article nevertheless described her as "a kindly, motherly woman . . . a typical middle-class housewife."[182] With great regularity, news reports about female politicians also made note of the woman's appearance. Emma Guy Cromwell, Kentucky's secretary of state, was described as a "slender little woman" with "delicate features" and "delightfully feminine smiles."[183] Less flatteringly, when Minnie Fisher Cunningham opened her campaign for U.S. Senate in 1928, one Texas newspaper described her as "less mannish and political looking" than one would expect a "woman candidate for the Senate to be."[184] To "prove that a woman politician is also a home keeper," southern observers praised women officeholders for their femininity, their cooking, their housekeeping, and their attention to maternal duties.[185] Newspapers' stubborn insistence on the stability of the domestic order did little to reassure white southerners, though. Throughout the decade female officeholding remained rare and noteworthy as white men resisted this most powerful symbol of the increased authority of enfranchised women.

IF FEMALE OFFICEHOLDERS provided white men with the most frightening example of women's new political power, the political activities of antisuffragist women offered perhaps the most discouraging one. Unsurprisingly, former suffragists were quick to embrace their new rights, and they actively engaged in political campaigns, registration efforts, and other public exercises of politics. In an ironic twist, however, white antisuffragist women also seized their ballots and used their new political power in ways that signified the profound changes that attended the Nineteenth Amendment. Many former antisuffragists, echoing the calls of Democratic Party leaders, believed that once enfranchised it was a woman's civic duty to cast her ballot.[186] Some prominent antis, however, did much more than simply go to the polls. In Alabama, Marie Bankhead Owen, a former antisuffragist leader, worked with former suffragists to organize white women voters on behalf of Senator Underwood's 1924 reelection bid.[187] Ivy Hill, of Cleveland, Mississippi, was a virulent antisuffragist before 1920, arguing in public forums that "the evils arising from such a privilege would be a stigma to ideal womanhood."[188] Despite her contention that a woman's place is in the home, Hill was found campaigning for the office of Bolivar County superintendent of education soon after women won the right to vote.[189] Dolly Blount Lamar, a Georgia antisuffragist, began casting ballots as soon as the women of her state won the right and by her own account was "somewhat active in politics. . . . making public my attitude on measures and candidates and speaking and writing for what I believed right."[190] In Tennessee, antisuffragists waged a successful campaign to unseat Governor A. H. Roberts, their bitter foe during the ratification fight in August 1920.[191] When antisuffragist women, the very southern ladies who had claimed for years that they did not want the vote, proudly announced that their ballots had brought down Tennessee's governor, they not only flouted southern gender conventions but also signaled the electoral threat that the region's women voters now posed.

AFTER 1920, white southern men were forced to adapt their campaigns, their public polling places, and their notions of southern ladyhood to accommodate new women voters. Woman suffrage transformed the look and feel of southern politics, and white men could no longer refer to the franchise as evidence of their superiority over white women or even African American women. For the first time in decades, a trickle of new African American voters demanded the right to vote. Moreover, the spectacle of white women representing themselves in public undermined one of the pillars of white southern manhood: white men as protectors of white women.[192] In the words of one Alabama newspaper, women acquired "the status of male voters" when the Nineteenth Amendment was ratified.[193] And just as antisuffragists had warned, the enfranchisement of women undermined the hierarchies of gender and race that ordered the Jim Crow South.

Chapter Two

More People to Vote
Woman Suffrage and the Challenge
to Disfranchisement

In August 1924 an officer in the Atlanta League of Women Voters discovered that in order to vote in the city elections, citizens had to register not only at the courthouse but also at city hall. Georgians already faced significant hurdles to their political participation, including a literacy requirement and, even more daunting, a cumulative poll tax that had to be paid six months before the election. To female political activists, the dual registration requirements were yet another example of the closed political system that had "gagged the people of the city for a generation."[1] Determined to "beat the politicians at their own game," these white women devised a "movable registration booth" that could travel throughout the city, registering voters where they lived and worked. After convincing the city clerk to participate in their plan, the women persuaded the NuGrape drink company to loan them a truck that could be transformed into their portable registration booth. On the Saturday before their registration week efforts, a bugler attracted crowds while the women rode up and down Peachtree and Whitehall streets, tossing voter information from the NuGrape truck, newly adorned with a banner urging citizens to register. When, on the first day of the registration campaign the driver of the truck informed the women that he could not act as their chauffeur, the women created a further spectacle by simply driving the big truck themselves from ward to ward, stopping at designated spots to register voters. During that single week, Atlanta's newly enfranchised women added 1,500 voters to the city's poll books. The effort was so successful that the league made it a central focus of their election year activities for the rest of the decade, as they worked to expand the electorate that southern white men had persistently endeavored to contract in recent years.[2]

AT THE TURN OF the century, Democratic political leaders had enacted a comprehensive set of voting restrictions in the South that had effectively eliminated popular participation in politics. As a consequence, southern women, both black and white, faced substantial structural obstacles when they entered the political system after the ratification of the Nineteenth Amendment. One of the greatest challenges they faced was the infrequency of opportunities to register. In Mississippi, the enrollment books closed four months prior to an election, and registrars were required to spend only one day in each precinct during the registration period. Similarly, registration was held for just one day each year in Virginia election districts. South Carolina had a seemingly generous registration period by contrast; county registration books were open the first Monday to the first Wednesday of every month and from August 1 to August 15 of an election year in counties with populations over 50,000 inhabitants. Nevertheless, traveling to the county seat was a prohibitive burden to many South Carolina voters, who had to wait for the one day each election year when the county registrar was required to visit each town, village, or industrial settlement. While registration, once accomplished, was permanent in most southern states, Tennessee required reregistration every two years, and many cities, like Atlanta, required separate and more frequent reregistration to participate in municipal elections.[3]

Even where registration was permanent, voters had to pay their poll taxes months in advance of the next election in order to cast their ballots.[4] As one Texan put it, "Paying a poll tax in February to vote in November is to most folks like buying a ticket to a show nine months ahead of time."[5] In Arkansas and Texas, voters faced no formal registration system, but the poll tax requirement amounted to an annual reregistration that closed months before the polls opened. In Georgia and Alabama, poll tax liability was cumulative, so voters had to pay back taxes for any year they chose not to vote in order to be readmitted to the polls. Voters in Mississippi, while not subject to such unlimited accruals of back taxes, did have to pay their poll taxes in the off years, as well as during election years, in order to remain eligible, and state law required presentation of poll tax receipts for both years as proof of eligibility.[6] As V. O. Key explained in his famous study of southern politics, "Southern tax authorities make it neither convenient for the tax to be paid nor embarrassing for it not to be paid."[7] Both the cost of voting and the administration of the tax, then, barred hundreds of thousands of southerners from the polls.[8]

Even those who could satisfy the poll tax hurdle, or who lived in a state without the tax, faced literacy provisions and understanding clauses that further complicated registration.[9] Many southern states framed their literacy provisions as an ability to read and write any section of the state or federal constitution. State law and local practice often opened the door to more intense scrutiny, however. Citizens of Georgia and Louisiana were required to understand the "duties and obligations of citizenship," and local registrars were the ultimate arbiters of any would-be voter's "understanding."[10] Applicants for registration in North Carolina and Virginia were legally required to answer any relevant question posed by the registrar. A potential voter in Virginia was also required to make application "in his own handwriting, without aid, suggestion, or memorandum."[11] While many local registrars offered white applicants forms to fill out, would-be black voters were regularly asked to submit all the required information on a blank piece of paper. In practice, few white voters in any state were subject to literacy or understanding provisions by 1920. The absolute discretion granted to registrars provided, as one scholar put it, "legal means of accomplishing illegal discrimination."[12]

Given these obstacles, it is no wonder that voter participation in the region hovered just above 20 percent.[13] Politically active women were nevertheless determined to increase those figures, and as the Atlanta voter registration effort so colorfully demonstrated, newly enfranchised women recognized that election laws and disfranchising statutes were the greatest impediments to their work. After 1920, southern women worked to open up this closed system. Using sophisticated voter mobilization campaigns, black and white women in the region undermined disfranchisement by bringing more than one million new voters to the polls. Moreover, through their legal battles and demands for electoral reform, newly enfranchised women attacked the very structure of disfranchisement itself.

ANTISUFFRAGISTS HAD warned of the threat that woman suffrage posed to disfranchisement. Although southern voting restrictions had robbed millions of men, both white and black, of the franchise, the region's political leaders were particularly determined to keep African Americans from the polls. In the South, debates over woman suffrage had been marked not only by apocalyptic predictions about the emasculation of white men and the demise of the white southern family but also by shrill cries of "the black peril" and states' rights.[14] For many white southerners, Reconstruction, Populism, and the days of vigorous Republican competition in the South were not distant memories but vivid historical lessons that seemed destined to recur should white southern Democrats weaken in their resolve. As one antisuffragist broadside put it bluntly, "Shall History Repeat Itself?"[15] Opponents of woman suffrage warned that the enfranchisement of women, particularly if it came by way of federal amendment, would reopen the polls to African American voters and result in federal oversight of southern elections. Historian Elna Green has found that "across the region, former leaders of the movement to disfranchise blacks now rose up to protect their prior handiwork by preventing the enfranchisement of women."[16] One North Carolinian warned of the dire consequences suffragists' efforts would bring: "So sure as the sun rose this morning, I believe the negro will be put back in politics, then woe to our free south land. All of the old Democrats['] work will be done away and a new issue will take hold and our freedom will be gone. . . . You may think this will never be again, but there is a saying history repeats itself, and what has been will be again."[17]

Given this racially charged atmosphere, many African American women in the South had maintained a low profile during the suffrage debates, concerned that their support for woman suffrage would only hurt the cause. The ratification of the Nineteenth Amendment, however, freed them to begin the difficult work of taking advantage of the political opportunity the federal amendment offered. More than a decade before the better-known voter registration drives that emerged in the wake of the New Deal, African American clubwomen throughout the South used the Nineteenth Amendment to attack disfranchisement. Columbia, South Carolina, was the site of just one of many such campaigns. There, in the weeks that followed the ratification of the Nineteenth Amendment, African American women began preparing other black women for the labyrinth of rules and regulations they would have to navigate in order to enroll successfully as voters.

Like other voters in the region, would-be voters in South Carolina faced a daunting system of disfranchisement, which had successfully kept African Americans and a majority of white men from voting for more than two decades. In addition to strict residency requirements, South Carolinians had to read and write any section of the state constitution submitted to him (or her) by the registrar. This literacy requirement was administered at the full discretion of the registrar, and the only legal exemption was for voters who had paid taxes on property assessed at $300. In addition, male voters (though not female ones) were subject to a $1 poll tax.

Aware of these obstacles and prepared to read and write the constitution, dozens of African American women in Richland County went to register to vote on September 8th, the first day of registration in September 1920.[18] Although southern antisuffragists had long contended that woman suffrage would bring African American voters to the polls, election officials seemed unprepared for the realization of their own warnings. The black women successfully "took the registrars by surprise," one observer described, "as the latter seemed to have no concerted plan for dealing with the colored women except to register them like the white women."[19] Indeed on that first day, registrars did not even subject African American women to the literacy test, in effect registering them just like the white women who applied—white women who were rarely subject to literacy requirements. At the end of the day, one exasperated white man demanded, "Who stirred up all these colored women to come up here and register?"[20]

If election officials had been unprepared for these politically assertive black women during the first day of registration, they "evidently held a council of war at night."[21] The next morning, would-be African American women voters faced a much more hostile registration process. In addition "to being tortured by long standing," as they were forced to wait until every white applicant had been registered, these African American women also "were greeted with scowls, rough voices, and insulting demeanor." In addition, "They were made to read and even to explain long passages from the constitutions and from various civil and criminal codes, although there is no law requiring such an inquisition."[22] The registrars even brought in a lawyer, as one observer described it, "apparently for the special business of quizzing, cross-questioning and harassing the colored women, in the manner of opposing counsel in court. He asked questions about all sorts of things from all sorts of documents."[23] Some sample questions included: "How much revenue does the Baptist Church pay the State?" and "Explain a *mandamus*."[24] Many black women registrants were refused simply because they mispronounced a word, "in the mere opinion of the registrar, with never an appeal to Webster."[25]

These legal and quasi-legal efforts to use existing disfranchisement laws to keep black women from the polls were coupled with threats of violence. Yet despite threats from the white sheriff to "git out an' let de whahte people register—an' stay out! An' if you don' stay out, dey'll be some buckshot to keep yo' out," Columbia's African American women expressed a singular determination as they continued to line up at the polls.[26] One observer noted that "some colored women were even stimulated to go and assert their right to register because they heard that others of their race had been unjustly turned away. . . . No discouragement, no 'test,' no petty insult stopped them."[27] By mid-September, 703 white women and 136 African American women had registered to vote in Richland County, South Carolina, which included Columbia.[28]

With the ratification of the Nineteenth Amendment, African Americans saw the federal government use its power to expand the electorate in the South for the first time since Reconstruction, and they hoped to capitalize on this new use of federal power to reassert their place at the polls. In Kentucky, where black voters and Republicans both enjoyed greater freedom than in other parts of the South, African American women voters filled the Frankfort Baptist Church for a Republican rally that demonstrated their willingness to "work for the success of the Republican ticket this November."[29] But as the efforts of Columbia's black women demonstrated, the mobilization of black women voters was not restricted to the Upper South. In Savannah, Georgia, more than 1,700 African American women registered to vote in the weeks before the November 1920 elections. Even though the strict registration deadlines in Georgia prevented *any women* — white or black — from casting votes in that election, African American women in Savannah and "in every ward in Atlanta" attempted to vote anyway.[30] When black women voters in Houston "demonstrat[ed] their citizenship in such a substantial manner with the ballot" that one was arrested on false charges, "the brave female voters of color redoubled their efforts and urged every qualified voter to go to the polls."[31] Such determined efforts signaled black women's commitment to challenge not only the exclusion of black southerners from the polls but also the letter of disfranchisement laws.

Furthermore, these efforts were more than the individual acts of defiant black women. Throughout the South, African Americans organized systematic campaigns to use the Nineteenth Amendment to reopen the polls and reinvigorate the Fifteenth Amendment. In September 1920, Maggie Lena Walker, Ora Brown Stokes, and a few other prominent African American women met to consider plans for registering Richmond's African American women to vote. There they planned mass meetings to prepare women to register, and in the weeks that followed they flooded city hall with willing applicants.[32] In northern Virginia, local NAACP leaders called meetings in different parts of Fairfax County in order to encourage African American women to vote and instruct them in methods most likely to result in successful registration.[33] The NAACP was active in Birmingham as well, where "Citizenship Schools," conducted to prepare the city's African American women to register and cast their ballots "intelligently," mobilized thousands of black women to attempt to register.[34] Even in Mississippi, organized African American women reported that they were "urging . . . women to pay their poll tax and qualify in every way they can for registration and as citizens of this country."[35]

In Nashville, the efforts of African American women organizers brought thousands of new voters to the polls. Just six weeks after the ratification of the Nineteenth Amendment, African American women had established a Negro Women's League of Voters in that city and had addressed more than twenty different women's clubs. Voters' leagues for black women had been established in a number of "county districts" outside the city as well. The league sponsored voter mobilization meetings in churches and organized dozens of black women to assist others in registering. Local Republican

Party leaders sponsored a "school of instruction" for black women voters to provide "technical instructions with regard to the use of the ballot." Classes were held daily during the week prior to the election.[36]

Savannah's black clubwomen were similarly well organized. The Savannah Federation of Negro Women's Clubs spearheaded an effort to enroll black women voters, and it spent "considerable money on literature" encouraging voter registration.[37] In addition to hosting mass meetings and night schools, African American clubwomen in Savannah printed leaflets listing "Ten Reasons Why Negro Women Should Vote."[38] Determined to "push registration" among as many black women as possible, clubwomen distributed these leaflets by sending them home with black children attending Savannah's segregated public schools.[39] The women's efforts were so successful that by early October 1920, black women's registration in Savannah nearly equaled that of white women. Stunned by the voter mobilization efforts staged by black clubwomen in the city, leaders of the city's all-white League of Women Voters publicly charged that the registrar had failed to enforce the voting qualifications by registering black women. "We do not believe," they insisted, "that there are one thousand educated negro women in Chatham county, who can sign their names, who own property, who understand the laws, or who are descendants of Confederate veterans."[40] Despite the opposition of white women voters, 2,700 African American women succeeded in registering by the summer of 1921.[41]

In North Carolina, Charlotte Hawkins Brown organized a massive statewide campaign to register black women. Working with the NAACP and the state Association of Colored Women's Clubs, Brown distributed information about registration and voting and then instructed African American women to take registrars by surprise by waiting until the last two days of the registration period to enroll. Local registrars in most places were, as in South Carolina, unprepared for such a well-coordinated effort, and, according to historian Glenda Gilmore, white southern Democrats "stood by incredulously on that day as black women passed the literacy test and entered their names on the books."[42]

To be sure, Democratic Party elites did not stand idly by as African Americans worked to take advantage of the Nineteenth Amendment and return to southern polls. As one Texas newspaper described it, the "outpouring of colored women" at the polls "made the Democrats flash the S.O.S. signal."[43] Party leaders across the region provided registrars with instructions on how to prevent the registration of African American women and even threatened to disqualify registrars who did not maintain strict racial lines at the polls.[44] Of course, many Democratic functionaries needed no such instruction. When "a number" of African American women attempted to register at the Jefferson County Courthouse in Birmingham, for example, the registrar refused, insisting that "the State of Alabama doesn't want you."[45]

Black southerners and white newspapers alike commented on the ways in which the region's disfranchisement laws were being used to prevent African American women from voting. A Mississippi woman described the obstacles that black women faced in exercising their right to vote: "We have some good women that would make leaders but they do not want their names published because they are in sc[h]ools and payed [sic] by the state of Miss." She continued, "Embarrisment [sic] kept a lot of our race from registering. They asked a lot of silly questions or have them read something written across two pages in stead of reading to the end and going back it read across they would say *you can't read* even teachers who had taught for years in city schools are told the same."[46] Black women from Alabama reported that "they would be allowed to register [only] if they could tell how many drops of water there is in the Mississippi River."[47]

Such arbitrary and racist use of the literacy qualifications by southern registrars was quite common. From North Carolina, the Raleigh *News and Courier* reassured its white readers that the state's literacy requirements would disfranchise black women as effectively as black men:

> It is well known that since the passage of this law, no Negro has been allowed to register, unless the registrar, under the wide discretion given him, permitted him to do so. The registrar can refuse to be satisfied, and generally does refuse to be satisfied with a Negro man's ability to read and write the constitution to the registrar's satisfaction. . . . Negro women will be placed in the same statute as the Negro men. When she applies for registration, she will not be able to satisfy the registrar of her ability to read and write the Constitution, certainly not to his "satisfaction."[48]

In the *Virginian Pilot*, Representative Henry Flood, leader of the Democratic Party, insisted that Virginia's registration requirements would "enable all the white women in the state to be registered and would practically exclude all the Negro women."[49]

Yet in the face of these unsurprising efforts by white political leaders to use disfranchisement laws to exclude black women from the polls, African Americans not only continued to make application to vote, but they also sought relief in the courts and from Congress when southern political leaders prevented black women from voting. In October 1920, following unsuccessful efforts to register to vote, African Americans in Anniston, Alabama, echoed the sentiments of many black southerners when they contacted the NAACP for help, declaring, "We want to make cases."[50] In Savannah, those black women who were registered but were refused ballots in November 1920 had a lawyer accompany them to the polls.[51]

In Columbia, South Carolina, the African American women who were refused enrollment after that first successful day of registration took their cases to court, charging that the actions of local registrars violated their right to vote as guaranteed by the Nineteenth Amendment.[52] As the president of the local NAACP branch described it, "It was unpleasant, to put it mildly, to know that graduates, College women, and many teachers were rejected on the basis that they could not 'explain' . . . the passage which they had just read, when the law does not require them to explain."[53] Despite the merits of their case, these women remained disfranchised, as Judge Marcellus Whaley of the Richland County Court dismissed their claims, insisting that his court had no jurisdiction in the matter.[54] Black women in Orange, Texas, also found little protection from the courts. Though they had been "told at their church on Sunday that they would be registered," black women who "proceeded to the Court house" found the sheriff (who also served as registrar) "very insulting." "Indignant" at the registrar's refusal to enroll them as voters, the African American women hired an attorney and took their cases to court. Their efforts to "mandamus the sheriff" ended in vain, however, as the judge dismissed the case.[55]

African American women appealing their disfranchisement in Virginia had greater success. Like many black southern women, Mrs. Emma V. Kelly, Mrs. Rebecca Bowling, and Miss Bessie Morris were refused enrollment in the city of Norfolk when they failed to answer the questions posed to them by the registrar, Mr. Ritter. Refusing to submit to the unfair practices of the registrar, these women took their case to court and succeeded not only in winning their franchise but also in publicly humiliating the city's registrar. To prove the merits of the case, attorneys for the women called the registrar to the stand and submitted him to the same questions he had posed to the would-be women voters. In the opening salvo, African American attorney J. Eugene Diggs asked the registrar when the Constitution of the United States was adopted. The registrar "emphatically" replied, "1787." Diggs responded, "Then you would consider a person who answered that question as you have done as being qualified to vote?" The registrar replied, "Certainly," whereupon "the test ended." As the *Norfolk Journal and Guide* reported, "Having thus demonstrated either a failing memory, or a lack of information, the women began to wonder whether Mr. Ritter or his deputies really knew when they had answered a question correctly." The judge in the case ordered the three women registered.[56] Similarly, an African American woman who had been twice refused enrollment by the registrar in Hampton, Virginia, was admitted to the voter rolls by a circuit judge after taking her case to the courts.[57]

In addition to seeking justice through the courts, African American women sought the assistance of Republican Party leaders to challenge their disfranchisement. In Birmingham, thousands of African American women applied for registration in the months immediately following the ratification of the Nineteenth Amendment. When all but 100 were denied enrollment, African American leaders allied with defeated Republican candidates, "demanding a Congressional investigation of the election laws of Ala[bama]."[58] Six years later, Birmingham's African Americans were still actively protesting their disfranchisement, calling on the U.S. Department of Justice to investigate charges that the city's black residents were "being denied their rights under the Fourteenth Amendment through a conspiracy of Klan leaders and county officials."[59] From Graham, Virginia, an African American contacted the Republican Party for assistance when the registrar and Democratic county chairman denied African American women access to the polls, declaring, "No more damn niggers should register."[60]

In a private letter, one Greensboro man articulated the frustration that African Americans felt when black women were denied the rights accorded by the Nineteenth Amendment and he defiantly proclaimed their determination to take advantage of the opportunity that the new federal amendment provided. Referring to the white supremacist campaign and race riot that followed the last major effort of black North Carolinians to engage in a vigorous electoral politics, he declared, "No one wants any Red Shirt exhibitions and I feel safe in saying that if it should start any of its 1898 actions when the smoke clears away they won[']t have a whole Red Shirt to lay away for future use as they did twenty years ago."[61] With equal determination, however, a white newspaper in that state insisted, "North Carolina is going to continue a white people's State if it takes red shirts and shot guns."[62]

In the face of white southerners' determination to maintain the franchise for whites only, African Americans called for a congressional investigation of the disfranchisement of black southerners in the 1920 elections. African American women were persistent advocates of a federal probe of their disfranchisement, and they called on the leaders of the former suffrage organizations to join them in protesting the violations of the Nineteenth Amendment that had occurred in the South. In their appeals to the National Woman's Party and the National League of Women Voters, African American women highlighted "the disfranchisement of women *of both races* in the Southern States . . . by evasion and perversions of the state election laws."[63] These activists warned that "the anti-suffragist neither slumbers nor sleeps" and insisted that the disfranchisement of southern women, black or white, nullified the Nineteenth Amendment victory.[64]

The delegation of black women who sought support from their white sisters in the National Woman's Party was met, however, with "evasion, then discourtesy, and finally open hostility."[65] As one woman reported, "the Woman's Party used every conceivable tactic and fought with great vehemence for the passage of the Suffrage Amendment. It adopted the same method at its convention to prevent the question of the disfranchisement of colored women from coming before its body."[66] In support of the demands of black women, Florence Kelley of the National Consumers League insisted, "If burning men at the stake when they try to show women how to vote is not a feminist question, I don't know what is."[67] Her calls, too, fell on deaf ears. Though met with more courtesy by the leaders of the League of Women Voters, African American women found this organization no more willing to assist black women voters in their legislative cause. After meeting with their "careless white sisters," African American activists lamented, "Wherever white women were not allowed the ballot it was counted worth while to relinquish it in order that it might be denied colored women."[68]

Nevertheless, African Americans continued to call on Republican leaders to reduce the South's congressional representation. Spurred by reports of the disfranchisement of black voters that followed the ratification of the Nineteenth Amendment, Representative George Holden Tinkham, a Republican from Massachusetts, introduced legislation to use the number of votes cast rather than total population as the basis for congressional reapportionment in 1921.[69] Black southerners submitted detailed accounts of the discrimination they faced at southern polls for use in lobbying efforts on behalf of the bill, and many black newspapers voiced their support for the legislation.[70] Armed with countless examples of discrimination against black voters by white southern officials, leaders of the NAACP testified before Congress that the pervasive disfranchisement of black voters in the South resulted in one white man in the South having four to ten times the voting power of a northern voter.[71]

Southern congressmen responded by denying the existence of racial discrimination at southern polls. Representative Aswell of Louisiana declared that "no discrimination was practiced in the South," and Representative Larson of Georgia pointed to "1,365 negroes . . . registered in his home town" as evidence of the fair administration of southern election laws.[72] Senator McKellar of Tennessee went so far as to declare that the election laws of his state were less restrictive than Tinkham's own Massachusetts.[73] Southern congressmen referred to reports of racial discrimination as "hearsay," and they had the word "nigger" inserted repeatedly into the printed report of the hearings, though they "had not dared" use that word in addressing African American witnesses.[74] The efforts by Tinkham and a small band of Republicans to address the disfranchisement of African Americans in the South did not worry white southerners. Indeed, one North Carolina newspaper responded defiantly, "Let Southerners, regardless of party, say to the rest of the country: 'We are resolved that the majority of the colored people shall not vote. Reduce, if you will our congressional representation; or, if you are wise, join us in modifying the suffrage amendments to the Constitution.'"[75]

Though congressional Republicans were apparently unwilling to go so far as to "modify the suffrage amendments," few white leaders in the party were committed to enforcing them. Tinkham's legislative attack on disfranchisement ended quickly in defeat. Less than one month after Tinkham called on Congress to investigate the extent of disfranchisement in the South, the House Committee on the Census voted to increase the South's representation rather than reduce it.[76] Despite renewed attempts when a Republican-led Congress reconvened, Tinkham and his supporters were unsuccessful. As the *Savannah Tribune* put it, "Congress, Republican or Democratic, does not propose to tackle the subject of disfranchisement, and if it is brought close to the front, it will be blocked at every stage of the game."[77]

With the support of white Republicans, white southerners once again effectively prevented enforcement of the Fourteenth and Fifteenth Amendments. Nevertheless, when white political leaders in the South began to turn the machinery of disfranchisement against black women, as well as black men, African Americans in the region insisted that the "legitimacy," the "legality" of disfranchisement was not a settled question. They took their cases to court. They called on the Justice Department to intervene. They demanded that the Republican Party do something, and they petitioned Congress to reduce the congressional representation of the South to reflect the disfranchisement of voters in the region. The political activities of African American women in the South thus posed a significant challenge to politics-as-usual in the region. Beneath the seemingly set surface of the "Solid South," black women contested their exclusion from the body politic. In response, white men were forced to shore up their work of disfranchisement and of Jim Crow.

MUCH TO THEIR DISMAY, white southern leaders found that the region's white women were weak allies in this cause. Though they expressed no desire to open the polls to black voters, southern white women were determined to expand the southern electorate. Like African American women, they organized "citizenship schools," called meetings, and sponsored house-to-house canvasses to ensure that after their years of struggle to obtain the vote, the region's women would be prepared to cast their first ballots. State and local branches of the National American Woman Suffrage Association became Leagues of Women Voters following the ratification of the Nineteenth Amendment. These leagues used the existing organizational structure and membership lists as the foundation for a new force in American politics. Established as a nonpartisan organization with a mission of "training for citizenship, improved legislation, efficient government, and international cooperation," the League of Women Voters was designed to give meaning to the Nineteenth Amendment by facilitating the entrance of women into electoral politics.[78] In the South, and throughout most of the nation, membership in the league was limited to white women, and in the years that followed its creation, the league became the most visible organization of politically active white women in the region and a focal point for women's political activism. Although the state and local leagues were involved in many different kinds of activities, their primary goal was the creation of an expansive and informed electorate, an objective that, despite their adherence to the region's white supremacist ideals, put these women at odds with Democratic Party leaders who for decades had worked to achieve just the opposite.

Southern Democrats had long relied on complicated registration requirements and confusing balloting rules to control the electorate. Throughout the region Leagues of Women Voters challenged the work of disfranchisers by organizing citizenship schools to provide newly enfranchised women with the information necessary to cast their first ballots. These schools offered seminars on a broad range of topics, from how a bill becomes a law and state and local election procedures to legislative issues affecting women and children and the role of political parties.[79] While these citizenship schools often lasted for two days or more and were aimed at white clubwomen with time to spare, league leaders also provided shorter lectures on citizenship at club meetings and opened the doors of their citizenship schools to men and women alike.[80] In a letter to Virginia's director of citizenship education, one citizenship school alumna described the effects of this league program. A number of citizenship school students, she wrote, "have said that it gave them a new insight into political parties" and, in words that must have had an ominous ring to Democratic Party leaders, "inspired them with a desire to use the privilege of suffrage in a way not before thought of."[81]

In order to ensure that these ballots, cast in ways "not before thought of," were actually counted by election officials, politically active white women also staged ballot-marking classes.[82] Disfranchisers, determined to establish their control over the region's political system, not only had enacted registration procedures that barred many poor, uneducated, and African American men from voting, but also had passed measures that made it easy for election officials to disqualify the ballots of dissident voters. In North and South Carolina, for example, voters faced a multiple-box system, under which they had to complete separate ballots for the different contests and place each contest's ballot in the corresponding ballot box. Moreover, in those two states the parties also issued separate ballots, which made it easier for Democratic election officials to identify dissident votes and prevent them from being cast into the correct box. In Arkansas, Georgia, Texas, and Virginia, voters had to mark their ballots not by selecting the candidates they did support but by scratching through the names of the candidates they opposed. Many southern states also had time limits for the completion of ballots, which discriminated against semiliterate voters and which could be enforced in discriminatory ways against other known dissident voters.[83] Ballot-marking classes were designed to ensure that voters were not only able to register but that they also understood how to cast their ballots properly and could cast their votes "according to [their] conscience."[84] In Texas, organized white women specifically indicated that such classes were "not for members [only] but for [the] general public."[85] Consequently, women in that state held ballot-marking classes in "booths in stores, and near polls at election time," as well as in meetings of women's clubs.[86] Through these classes, as with their citizenship schools, politically active white women challenged aspects of disfranchisement that concealed fraud and made it less likely that dissident votes would be counted.

For those who could not attend citizenship schools, league lectures, or ballot-marking classes, leaders of the state and local League of Women Voters worked to gather and publicize election laws and registration procedures.[87] Immediately following the ratification of the Nineteenth Amendment, suffragist Eulalie Salley contacted South Carolina's attorney general "for an opinion as to the prerequisites for voting" and then relayed the attorney general's response to the newspapers so that women would be able to exercise their new political privileges.[88] White women in Alabama recognized that "not all voters are conversant with these laws [governing elections]" and made plans to issue a "popular digest of the election laws of Alabama."[89] In Texas, the League of Women Voters issued "The Voters Calendar," which listed poll tax deadlines and election dates alongside relevant voting information each month.[90] Leagues thus became informal authorities on state and local election laws, and ordinary women from around the region called on them for information about how to qualify to vote.[91]

Politically active white women also publicized registration and poll tax payment deadlines in league-sponsored publications and pressured political parties and white newspapers to do the same. The first edition of *The Woman Voter* promised to provide Mississippi women with "instructions as to how to qualify as a citizen, how to obtain the right to vote, how to register, in fact how to go thru every minute detail to the depositing of the ballot in the box.

So that the women may be as well posted on all the procedure as a man."[92] Similarly, politically active white women in Norfolk, Virginia, "prepared and distributed minute directions for registering—WHO, WHERE, WHEN and HOW." In a telling remark, these women observed that the instructions "were greatly in demand, especially by the men. To qualify in Virginia is not a simple thing."[93]

AS SOUTHERN WHITE WOMEN worked to expand the electorate, the first order of business was convincing other women to engage in electoral politics. Many activists expressed frustration at the difficulty of their task. A league organizer working in Winder, Georgia, reported that "the old idea still prevails here that women must keep out of politics. I was asked not to speak about politics or the League, I talked on Citizenship generally and wound up with what the League was doing. . . . Winder is not encouraging."[94] In North Carolina a league organizer reported on conditions in Edenton and noted that one woman, a former antisuffragist, "said she is not interested because 'she is not that kind of a woman'!!"[95] Antisuffragists had long argued that "unclean politics" was not a suitable arena for real southern ladies, and cultural proscriptions about the proper role of southern white women proved an obstacle to the mobilization of white women voters. Organizers found that opposition to their efforts came from both men and women. As a woman in Virginia reported, one of her town's most prominent men "was and is opposed to much freedom of thought or action for women" and "the women are not awfully interested anyway."[96] Reports from South Carolina highlighted similar troubles: "Every line of work that we undertook naturally aroused opposition in a new quarter and with it much ridicule and unfavorable criticism. The majority of the women began impulsively and as soon as they found unpopularity ensued, gradually fell away."[97] Tennessee League of Women Voters leaders urged organizers not to become discouraged, but one Virginian captured the attitude of many: "I am disgusted with the apathy of the womankind."[98]

While politically active white women worked hard to refute the assertion so often made by southern white men that southern ladies did not want the vote, Democratic Party leaders in the region must have considered the problem of women voters' apathy with some ambivalence. On the one hand, their firm grip on the region's politics was based on their control of a tiny electorate; thus more voters meant a greater threat to their power. On the other hand, if white clubwomen, former antisuffragists, and good southern ladies failed to vote, who would?

The first targets of white women's political organizing were most often white clubwomen. In Terrell, Texas, league organizers "spoke at five church societies" to encourage these rural women to register and vote.[99] In North Carolina, league leaders called on women "from patriotic organizations and from civic betterment organizations and from religious organizations" to use their votes to further their aims.[100] Gertrude Weil addressed a convention of the Daughters of the American Revolution in Raleigh where she urged members to participate in government, "form their own opinions" about political matters, and resist "the orders of the bosses higher up."[101] Determined to increase voter participation and make "every citizen an intelligent voter," these league leaders first targeted other women like themselves: educated, materially comfortable, white clubwomen.[102]

Even without prompting from these former suffragists, women's clubs throughout the South focused increased attention on the civic duties of women following the ratification of the Nineteenth Amendment. Some of these clubs, like the Thursday Afternoon Book Club in St. George, South Carolina, and the Woman's Club of Blacksburg, Virginia, contacted league leaders for information and lecturers to guide their studies of citizenship.[103] Others, like Atlanta's Wednesday Morning Study Club, chose "Citizenship for Women" as their study topic for the year and worked to prepare themselves for the ballot independent of female political organizers.[104] These efforts by women's clubs energized some of the most apolitical white women in the region, women who would not otherwise attend a meeting of political organizers. For example, the Wilmington YWCA offered a program on women's "duties as citizens, [and] as voters" but asked the speaker to tailor her message to a broad audience, "since so many dislike the words 'Women in Politics' or 'Woman Suffrage.'"[105] While many clubwomen had been able to avoid the issue of woman suffrage in the years prior to 1920, the ratification of the Nineteenth Amendment made it inescapable. From the Daughters of the American Revolution and the United Daughters of the Confederacy to Home Demonstration programs and apolitical study clubs, organized white women acknowledged their new status as citizens and worked to prepare themselves as voters.

Existing records from southern Leagues of Women Voters indicate that organizers traveled extensively to encourage white women's participation in politics. In Arkansas, Florence Cotnam traveled to Fordyce, Warren, Arkansas City, Dewitt, Dumas, McGhee, Dardanelle, Adkins, Russellville, and Fort Smith to meet with women and organize them for political action.[106] In just one month, a league organizer working in Alabama visited Montgomery, Calera, Columbiana, Wilsonville, Sylacauga, Anniston, Albany, Decatur, Sheffield, Florence, Tuscombia, Gadsden, Mobile, Selma, and Dothan.[107] As hundreds of thousands of white women placed their names on the voter rolls, it was clear that southern white women were heeding the calls to political action.

Although former antisuffragists, Democratic Party leaders, and their female allies appealed to women voters to buttress white supremacy and the political status quo, many white female activists undermined the work of disfranchisers as they took their message of political participation to a surprising variety of women. Membership in the leagues throughout the South was restricted to whites only, and almost no league members were interested in helping African Americans obtain access to the ballot box. Nevertheless, league leaders and former suffragists consistently held it as their aim to encourage *all* (white) women to vote. Southern disfranchisement efforts had not been aimed at African Americans alone. Registration and poll tax requirements had worked for decades to limit the participation of many poor and disaffected white voters, as well, and the South's politically active white women seemed untroubled about welcoming these people back into the political system.

These activists were particularly determined to reach rural white women. At a meeting of the Wake County League of Women Voters, North Carolina members discussed a plan to reach farm women by providing them with regular bulletins about voting and other political information but requiring no attendance at meetings, which were seen as an obstacle to organization in rural sections.[108] In Virginia, the league cut the membership fee by half for women in rural sections in order to encourage membership, because, as one member put it, "country people have no money to join anything."[109] Politically active white women in Clarksville, Georgia, worked to tailor their voter registration message to rural women, and they redoubled their efforts when it became clear that country women were being dropped from the registration books to avoid payment of the poll tax.[110] Even in Moncks Corner, South Carolina, an area "so thinly settled" that it had "only about four miles of local telephone lines in the whole county," one newly enfranchised white woman worked to ensure that her rural neighbors went to the polls. When she discovered that the local registrars "had not been notified to keep the books open . . . in order to give all the women a chance to register," she promptly contacted each member of the board of registration, and she asked Governor Cooper "to please notify them also, as I thought it would be more forceful." She also put a notice in the county paper "so that a majority of the folks will know that they can still register."[111]

Other rural women received registration and voter information from home demonstration agents or other rural organizations.[112] In South Carolina, the state Council of Farm Women and the Union County home demonstration agent worked with the League of Women Voters to mobilize rural women voters and to pursue common legislative goals.[113] In Alabama, the director of home demonstration agents served on the league's board of directors. She used the "opportunity" of "being in touch with so many rural women" to promote the electoral mobilization of the state's farm women.[114] In Columbia, South Carolina, farm women took advantage of "plant exchange day," when they came to town to sell butter and eggs, to obtain information on the League of Women Voters and, more importantly, to register to vote.[115] Similarly, "Trade Day" in Russellville, Alabama, provided an opportunity to reach rural white women who "shied away from" citizenship schools the league had held in nearby towns.[116]

County fairs were another popular means of encouraging rural women to become politically active.[117] There, league members set up booths encouraging women to register and vote. They decorated the blackboards with slogans such as "Do you care for your children's future? VOTE!" and "The food your husband eats does not feed you. When he votes, can he vote for two?"[118] The league distributed bulletins on such topics as how to register and candidates' attitudes toward specific issues and one titled "Six Reasons Why Farmers' Wives Should Vote."[119] In Spruce Pine, North Carolina, politically active white women also used leaflets to encourage local women to vote, but because "reading is none too easy for some of our people," they were careful "to use just a few forceful arguments in simple words."[120]

Clearly, politically active white women were not merely interested in organizing white clubwomen to vote or even organizing educated farm women. Efforts to reach even semiliterate women suggest that activists did not share the commitment of Democratic Party leaders to an electorate tightly limited by formal education or even means. As the South Carolina League of Women Voters declared in response to those who questioned the need for such an organization, "No group of men or women has ever before undertaken to train the masses in the proper use of the ballot."[121] Indeed, the actions of Democratic Party leaders for years had demonstrated their preference that the masses need not use the ballot at all.

Politically active white women worked to take their message to working-class white women as well. When the Atlanta League of Women Voters staged its spectacular week-long voter registration drive, for example, the Coca Cola plant in ward six was among the many places visited by the movable registration booth. Though the records do not reveal precisely who was registered during this stop, it seems likely that female and male workers from the plant were the league's targets here. Moreover, the league publicized their get-out-the-vote efforts not only in the city's white daily newspapers but also in the *Journal of Labor*. League members described their efforts: "We tried not only to stop at the business sections, but to go thru' the big plants and factories, and found generally splendid cooperation."[122]

In Alabama, white women directed their voter mobilization efforts not only at fellow clubwomen but also at the state's industrial workers. During its 1923 poll tax campaign, the local League of Women Voters worked directly with the Birmingham Trades Council to encourage organized workers to pay their poll taxes.[123] While Birmingham was "something of a labor town" in the 1920s, white women's encouragement of the labor vote through the Trades Council was significant.[124] As historian Liette Gidlow has argued, "the Trades Council addressed explicitly and forcefully the radical potential of full voter turnout."[125] That organization promoted voter registration among its members by urging them to "Vote For Your Kind Of People, And Then Evil Legislation Against You Will Cease."[126] By reaching out to organized laborers through the Trades Council and encouraging them to qualify to vote, league leaders signaled their determination to include these workers among the "public spirited voters" of the city.[127]

The mobilization of industrial workers was not limited to Birmingham. During that same poll tax campaign, one Alabama activist noted that there were "a large number of women needing education in citizenship" in Sylacauga, the home of Avondale Cotton Mills.[128] While this comment certainly reveals the upper-class bias of many white clubwomen, it also demonstrates their belief that working-class women should be the targets of their political mobilization efforts. Even before they obtained the right to vote, suffragists in Alabama supported the rights of workers to unionize and opened their headquarters as a place for working women to have lunch.[129] Once suffrage had been achieved, these female political leaders worked to ensure that working-class women would use their newly acquired right and cast their votes.

Throughout the South, white women activists carried their message of voter registration into the streets and movie houses in an attempt to reach out to working-class voters. At a meeting of southern league leaders, the region's most politically active white women discussed "how to reach factory women when the managers object," and it was determined that "women should reach this class of their sex outside of the factory if they could not reach them through it."[130] Conditions of women in industry were a primary concern of all southern leagues, and at least some female activists viewed working-class women as legitimate targets of their political mobilization efforts. Undoubtedly mill owners and Democratic Party leaders would have been happier if these politically active women had focused their attentions elsewhere.

The most subversive work of white political women, however, may have occurred when they did not focus their voter information at all. Through their publications and political stunts, organized white women distributed information about election laws in ways that made voting more accessible to the masses. Not content simply to mobilize voters who were already registered, these activists focused their activities on increasing the number of southerners who were qualified to vote.[131] One Virginia activist recalled that "our rural women had a lot of trouble running all over the county trying to catch the registrars, who were out plowing or fishing or doing various things."[132] In response, league leaders publicized the requirements for registration, as well as the dates and times for enrollment.[133] League leaders in Norfolk even distributed letters to apartment houses assuring residents that "if you cannot go to the Registrar, we will send him to your neighborhood."[134] Thus, Virginia registrars were forced to open up the process, and once "Registration Days" were publicized, neither the registrars nor the league leaders themselves could control who might attempt to enroll.[135]

White women in Dallas organized a massive voter mobilization drive in the weeks preceding the poll tax deadline. Poll tax payments were due on the last day of January, and politically active white women recognized that get-out-the-vote activities were useless unless women qualified themselves to vote. Through an "active campaign," Dallas's League of Women Voters worked to increase the number of poll tax payers to new levels. Some of this activity was aimed at white women members of the state's Federation of Women's Clubs. Activists gave talks about the importance of poll tax payment to the Parent Teachers' Council, the City Federation, and the Woman's Forum. They contacted female church members by telephone. Other voter mobilization efforts were less focused, however, as local radio stations broadcast reminders about the importance of poll tax payment and local theaters ran a short league film about the importance of voting at each screening. During the last ten days of the campaign, female activists gave "three-minute" talks every evening in local movie houses, and newspapers devoted space to the league's message. According to the league's president, the poll tax payment campaign "was the talk of Dallas."[136] By making registration information transparent and ubiquitous, white women's voter mobilization efforts seemed designed to bring unpredictable, to some even undesirable, new voters to the polls.

In Kentucky, organized white women staged a massive voter mobilization drive in advance of the statewide elections in November 1923. In the absence of restrictive registration and poll tax requirements, Kentucky women focused on county and precinct-level efforts to get voters to the polls.[137] Like white women in Dallas and elsewhere, leaders in the Kentucky League of Women

Kentucky women doing voter mobilization work in the 1920s (courtesy Library of Congress)

Voters coordinated their efforts with the Woman's Christian Temperance Union (WCTU), Parent Teacher Associations, the Chamber of Commerce, and other women's clubs and civic organizations.[138] In Jefferson County, the Louisville League of Women Voters made an "appeal to every minister" to remind his congregants of their duty to vote.[139] They also secured the use of "property on Fourth Street" to conduct demonstrations "on the use of the ballot" and arranged for slides encouraging voter participation to be run in fifteen movie houses in the city.[140] Women in smaller localities conducted house-to-house canvasses.[141] In Fayette County, white women took their voter mobilization efforts to the streets in a dramatic way, conducting their get-out-the-vote activities from a car decorated with nonpartisan campaign slogans.[142]

Similarly, the Atlanta League of Women Voters' movable registration booth provided a vivid reminder to register, and the booth brought the enrollment books directly to the voters.[143] People need not make special trips to the courthouse and city hall; instead, they could just step outside their office or home and enroll. Since enrollment closed before the campaigns heated up and voters were required to register for city elections annually, it was easy for Atlanta voters to become disqualified. After 1920, the city's politically active women worked to ensure that city fathers would not be able to control municipal elections so easily. In the months that followed their first movable registration booth efforts, critics claimed that those registered during the campaign "were not properly qualified."[144] If these objections are any indication, Atlanta's women not only succeeded in getting out the vote but also rattled party leaders who did not approve of the new voters that the women had mobilized.

League leaders did their best to circulate their voter mobilization messages widely, and they encouraged the distribution of registration and poll tax information in white newspapers, at movie theaters, on sidewalks, and on the radio, as well as in churches and club meetings.[145] In cities and towns throughout the South, politically active white women staged house-to-house canvasses to encourage voters to register and vote, and Boy Scouts were enlisted to distribute handbills to members explaining how and where to register. In Kentucky, members of the Louisville League of Women Voters worked with "retail merchants, grocers, laundrymen, and druggists" to distribute "150,000 pamphlets giving vital information necessary to the unregistered voter."[146] Such widespread distribution meant that detailed information about election laws was available in places to which any dissident voter — even African American voters — might have access.

By casting ballots, acting as election officials, and participating in public politics, white women declared that they no longer needed the protection of white men. Moreover, their voter mobilization activities indicated that they did not always share white men's concerns about the vulnerability of the racial order. In Jackson, Tennessee, white women distributed posters in African American neighborhoods announcing the time and place for registration, and the local chapter of the United Daughters of the Confederacy promoted voter registration by offering a badge with the national colors to both black and white registrants.[147] As one activist insisted, "Although white men and women and negro men and women were found at various registration booths (voting precincts) south of the Mason and Dixon line, no race riot resulted, no presumption of social equality will follow, no woman was insulted, none was contaminated. The work was done properly and in orderly fashion, and if any revolution comes, it will be only a change of heart and mind upon the question of how far women can safely exercise the duties of citizenship."[148] Such sentiments stand in stark contrast to the vigilance of disfranchisers who saw threats to white supremacy in even the slightest assertions by black southerners.

While the vast majority of organized white women supported the disfranchisement of African Americans, at least one Texan acknowledged the subversive implications of women's voter mobilization efforts. The most effective work for African American rights, she argued, would result from "going at it from one end on Education and from the other on Clean Elections and simple, understandable election laws."[149] Indeed, league leaders in South Carolina decided not to publish their citizenship course material "on account of the negro women," fearful that African Americans would make use of the voter education information to register and vote.[150] The actions of these South Carolina women were the exception that proved the rule, however. As white female activists in all of the other southern states worked hard to distribute full and accurate information about how to qualify to vote, they directly challenged the work of disfranchisers who depended on confusing procedures to keep the electoral system closed.

IN ADDITION TO THEIR registration and voter mobilization efforts, which were designed to bring new people to polls within the confines of existing laws, politically active white women also pressed for electoral reforms that directly challenged the legal framework of the Democrats' closed system. In Tennessee, the League of Women Voters called for "simplified registration laws" as a "practical need for the voter."[151] Alabama women publicly announced their support for the "revision of registration and poll tax laws" among their top four legislative priorities in 1926.[152] Throughout the region, southern Leagues of Women Voters endorsed the "liberalization of primary and election laws in order to increase the number of qualified voters," legislative changes that posed a frontal assault to the institutional structure of disfranchisement.[153]

Throughout the decade, white women worked to secure permanent registration where it did not exist and prevent the purging of poll books that would require all voters to reregister.[154] Determined to increase voter participation rates in the South, politically active white women did not want to have to fight the same battles twice. They wanted voters, once registered, to remain registered. In a battle typical of those waged throughout the region, Virginia white women fought Democratic leaders in Norfolk who, just three years after women were enfranchised, declared a crisis of voter fraud and sought to clean up local politics by forcing all voters to reregister. Leading white women denounced this proposal, which would have reversed their years of determined voter mobilization. Skeptical of the motives of Democratic politicians, one woman declared, "The trouble is the men do not want to come up to the summer primaries with 5500 or 6000 women on the books and an unknown (as yet) number of men."[155] Another woman responded acerbically, "If we have been nineteen years without any cleaning at all in the poll-book house, I can't see that cleanliness can be such a necessity . . . as to reguire [sic] the scrubbing of the new-born babe."[156] She continued, "If dead men have been voting nineteen years it is just and prpoer [sic] to let the dead women vote for three."[157]

In North Carolina, which had no secret ballot system, and in the localities of some other states where voting was not a private affair, white women also battled for the Australian ballot, to remove what they viewed as opportunities for fraud and intimidation. The Australian, or secret, ballot had been an early device of southern disfranchisers, used in many states in the late nineteenth century to limit the electorate to literate voters. By 1920, however, southern Democrats had much more powerful disqualifying laws, including robust literacy requirements in many states. As historian Michael Perman has shown, the secret ballot was "not the ultimate remedy" sought by southern disfranchisers, because "it did not disfranchise thoroughly enough to be relied on exclusively."[158] While the secret ballot no doubt "deter[ed] the illiterate and the uninitiated" upon its introduction, by 1920 southern Democrats throughout the region had embraced much more powerful weapons to keep voters from the polls.[159] With a thoroughgoing system of disfranchisement in place, secret ballot laws in the 1920s served primarily as a limit on electoral corruption.[160]

The absence of ballot secrecy in some areas of the South created opportunities, as political scientist V. O. Key described it, "for intimidation, for bribery, [and] for reprisal."[161] In particular, the "separate party tickets" used for balloting in several states forced voters to announce their party preference to election officials, as well as onlookers. A Democratic Party leader in Alabama reported in 1930 that "it is no trouble to tell who votes for the Republican ticket in the general election, and in this county a list was made of them at the time the election was going on."[162] In his 1932 survey of African American political participation in the South, Paul Lewinson described the ways in which nonsecret balloting disenfranchised black Republicans who were "told that there were no Republican tickets available; it took a courageous citizen," Lewinson continued, "to demand that the enemy party's ballot be produced for him, the unwanted voter."[163] North Carolina, South Carolina, and rural areas of Tennessee all relied on separate party balloting, with the attendant opportunities for corruption and intimidation. Moreover, local and municipal elections, as well as primaries, were subject to different rules in most states, which left the secrecy of those balloting procedures to the discretion of local officials. Consequently, organizations of white women often fought for the adoption of a secret ballot in states where the battle seemed to have been won. In Savannah, for example, members of the League of Women Voters worked to persuade city officials to adopt a secret ballot after a "shameful primary disgraced by vote buying and ringing and slugging."[164] In short, female activists in the South advocated the Australian ballot as a way of enhancing political competition, not eliminating the political voices of those with whom they disagreed.

A prominent North Carolina woman echoed the demands of many political women who argued the need for a secret ballot to combat Democrats' "control of the election machinery."[165] Among North Carolina white women, this fight for a secret ballot became a decade-long crusade, as they challenged party "henchmen" who were "panic[ked]" by the prospect of free and fair elections.[166] Indeed, opposition to the measure was so great among Democratic Party operatives that in 1927 members of county Democratic committees from around the state descended on the capitol to remind wavering lawmakers of the threat that a secret ballot posed to the party's success and their own political futures.[167] Like their efforts to secure permanent registration, activists' support for the Australian ballot epitomized the kinds of challenges that politically active white women posed to Democratic stalwarts. Opening the system to more voters and working to ensure fair elections encouraged the very political competition that Democratic Party leaders had worked so hard to suppress.

DESPITE THEIR EFFORTS to expand the electorate, organizations of white women did not actively challenge the region's literacy requirements or poll taxes in the 1920s, and they offered no resistance to the white primary. Their lack of opposition to these voting requirements reveals the limits of their vision for inclusive government. In their correspondence and reports regarding registration drives, these white women did not mention literacy requirements or understanding clauses as an impediment to white voters. Registrars exercised so much discretion in the application of literacy tests and understanding clauses that they seem rarely to have been enforced among white women voters. Moreover, given their concern for "intelligent" voting and "education for citizenship," these politically active white women, like many other Progressives, may have viewed such requirements as a useful mechanism for ensuring better government. Thus, in stark contrast to African American women in the region, who often found literacy requirements the main obstacle to successful enrollment, white women did not even think these literacy requirements worthy of mention.

All voters in poll tax states had to pay to vote, however, and white female activists recognized that tax deadlines and the financial burdens of the taxes made it more difficult to expand the electorate. Indeed, several scholars have noted the disproportionate disfranchisement experienced by women as a result of the poll tax.[168] Poll taxes ranged from $1 to $2 annually during the 1920s, and those fees could rise in states that authorized localities to levy additional taxes. In 1929, the average per capita income in Arkansas was $310 per year, and the poll tax was set at $1 annually.[169] During the 1930s, white women's wages in Alabama averaged $8.31 per week.[170] Moreover, African American women working for cash wages in the 1920s "earned as little as two dollars a week."[171] As one woman from rural Georgia put it, "A dollar ain't much if you've got it."[172] Southern women often controlled no money of their own and were dependent upon husbands or other male relatives to pay their poll taxes. While black men seemed open to the possibility of black women going to the polls in their stead, when money was tight in white households, it was the women whose poll taxes went unpaid.[173]

Women in Kentucky and the Carolinas did not face the poll tax, but in the remaining southern states, poll tax payment proved a substantial burden to political participation. The contrast between the 1920 and 1924 presidential elections in Alabama was telling. In 1920, Alabama women were exempted from the poll tax requirements, as the poll tax books had closed before the ratification of the Nineteenth Amendment. After that election, however, Alabama's women had until 1 February 1921 to pay their poll taxes. "Many failed to do so," resulting in 85,000 fewer votes cast in 1924 than in 1920.[174] As the president of the Alabama League of Women Voters explained, "The large vote in 1920 was due to the fact that women were allowed to register and vote without paying poll tax."[175] In Tennessee, as well, newly enfranchised women could vote in the 1920 presidential election without paying poll taxes, and according to one observer, "almost as many women as men voted in the state elections" that year. With the extension of poll tax requirement to women in 1921, however, "the little $2 tax . . . nullified the Nineteenth Amendment before the constitutional change could be noted in the textbooks."[176]

White female activists in the region objected to these disfranchising effects of the poll tax, and they made poll tax drives an important component of their voter mobilization efforts. Nevertheless, no major organization of southern white women opposed the poll tax in the 1920s.[177] In response to a survey distributed by the National League of Women Voters, both the Georgia and Virginia leagues listed the poll tax as one of the major structural obstacles to voting in their states.[178] The cumulative feature of the tax in those states proved a prohibitive burden to many voters, but abolition of the poll tax did not appear on white clubwomen's extensive lists of legislative goals. In Clarksville, Georgia, where league leaders became particularly concerned about the effects of poll taxes when scores of women were removed from the enrollment lists for nonpayment, white women did not demand an end to the poll tax. Instead they worked to persuade women that the poll tax was money well spent.[179] Similarly, members of the Baldwin County League of Women Voters reminded Alabama women that "all of the despised poll-tax is devoted to the schools."[180]

Activists throughout the region made poll tax collection part of their get-out-the-vote efforts, and in Louisiana, organized women collected $30,000 in just sixty days as they worked to mobilize white women voters.[181] Determined to expand the electorate, white clubwomen worked hard to ameliorate the effects of the poll tax without challenging it directly. They advertised poll tax deadlines, raised money, and worked to convince women that the money that they spent on the poll tax not only enabled them to vote but also provided vital resources for state services. Though they clearly identified the poll tax as a key obstacle, white women chose not to make abolition of the poll tax a legislative priority during the first years of their enfranchisement. By the late 1930s, however, white women's organizations in Alabama and Tennessee and individual women from across the region would play central roles in the state and national campaigns to end the poll tax. Perhaps their experiences in the 1920s proved to white women activists that as long as the poll tax remained, they would never be able to open the polls quite far enough.

For the vast majority of white women, however, this determination to expand the electorate clearly did not include black voters. Thus, even as they objected to the disfranchising effects of the poll tax and worked to increase voter participation, white political women never challenged one of the most important pillars of disfranchisement in their region: the white primary. Although most black southerners who could vote remained loyal to the Republican Party in the early 1920s, organized African Americans began in that decade to challenge the constitutionality of barring black southerners from Democratic primary elections. As one historian has noted, the white primary was "the most effective scheme used in southern states to strip blacks of the vote and render them politically impotent."[182] Yet, unsurprisingly, white female activists never mentioned the white primary as an obstacle to increased voter participation. Even as growing numbers of African American women attempted to participate in Democratic primaries and looked to the Democratic Party as a way to leverage their ballots more effectively by the late 1920s, organized white women remained unconcerned about the disfranchising effects of the white primary. Through their voter outreach efforts, poll tax drives, and information campaigns, organized white women encouraged urban workers, uneducated southerners, women, and the poor to join their fellow citizens at the polls. The efforts of these activists opened up the system to voters with unpredictable political loyalties, and they occasionally, often unintentionally, assisted African Americans as they attempted to take their place at the polls. Nevertheless, white female activists did not object to the white primary; it did not affect them or the voters they targeted.

Thus, during their first decade with the vote, white women left major structural impediments to voting unchallenged, despite their determination to increase voter participation rates. While they staged elaborate voter mobilization efforts, attacked electoral fraud, taught voters how to cast complicated ballots in ways that were sure to be counted, and even lobbied for permanent registration and a secret ballot, white women did not completely reject the political system that they had just entered. They did not reject the notion that some people were more fit to vote than others. Rather, they hoped to improve the workings of democracy by preparing more southerners to vote and by making sure that the process was "clean."

THE EXTENT OF THEIR challenge was reflected in the number of new voters who went to the polls in 1920. In the South in November 1916, 2.3 million voters cast ballots. Four years later, in the wake of woman suffrage, 3.4 million voters crowded southern polls. But the South had 26.5 million residents in 1920, more than half of whom were voting age. The proportion of new voters at the polls in 1920 varied widely across the region, from a 7 percent decline in Georgia to an 86 percent increase in voters in North Carolina.[183] Those discrepancies were a reflection of each state's political culture and a measure of the obstacles that faced southern women as they worked to get out the vote.

Registration and poll tax barriers provided the most formidable obstacles to voter participation. Mississippi and Georgia, which suffered declines in voter turnout in 1920, did not allow women to vote at all in elections of that year. Both states had registration deadlines that had long passed by the time the Nineteenth Amendment was ratified, and neither state's leading men were willing to bend the rules to allow newly enfranchised women to vote in November 1920. For one final election the men of those states went to the polls without women. By contrast, Alabama, Kentucky, North Carolina, and Tennessee, the states that posted the largest increase in voter strength during the 1920 election, welcomed women to the polls. Instead of adhering to the deadlines that Mississippi and Georgia used as an excuse to bar women from the polls one last time, these states waived their deadlines, and parties and women's clubs worked hard to get new women enrolled as voters. Moreover, none of these states imposed a poll tax on the newly enfranchised women. Kentucky did not have a poll tax, and North Carolinians repealed that state's poll tax in the same election that women cast their first ballots. Alabama and Tennessee both had poll tax requirements but waived them for the newly enfranchised women in 1920. Thus would-be women voters in these states sought enrollment free of the registration and poll tax obligations that prevented so many southerners from voting. As a consequence, Tennessee witnessed a nearly 60 percent increase in voters in 1920, and the other three states saw increases above 75 percent.

In states where women were subject to a poll tax in their first election, new voter turnout was not as impressive. For example, Arkansas, a ratification state, boasted a measly 8 percent gain. There women not only faced a poll tax requirement, but the deadline for the payment of taxes had passed before the Nineteenth Amendment was ratified. Because the women of that state had achieved primary suffrage in 1917, women were fully subject to Arkansas's registration laws, and some women were registered and able to vote in November 1920. Indeed, those who were registered had helped to choose the parties' nominees in primary elections that year. By the time the women of the state knew that they would be allowed to participate in the general election of 1920, however, the deadlines for poll tax payment had long passed. In Texas, the poll tax requirement was compounded by the legal uncertainty of women's registration requirements following the Nineteenth Amendment. When state courts finally ruled on the registration requirements for new women voters, would-be registrants were left with just three days to pay their poll taxes.[184] Moreover, the poll taxes that women paid to vote in the general election of 1920 would not entitle them to participation in the next Democratic primary or general election. Under these circumstances, it is little wonder that many women in poll tax states chose to sit out their first presidential election.

Political competition also played a crucial role in voter mobilization. As party leaders and political women staged voter registration campaigns in the wake of the Nineteenth Amendment, vigorous political battles encouraged women that their new ballots would matter in some states. Kentucky, North Carolina, and Tennessee had in common a competitive general election in 1920. North Carolina and Tennessee had heated gubernatorial races on that first ballot, and the presidential race in Kentucky was determined by fewer than 6,000 votes out of more than 900,000 cast. The close presidential race in Tennessee resulted in a Republican victory. In both Kentucky and North Carolina, half of the congressional races were competitive as well, factors that encouraged new voters to participate in this first election. Though the presidential race in Alabama was a foregone conclusion, there were other compelling races for Alabama's new women voters to participate in. Both the Seventh and the Tenth Congressional Districts witnessed spirited general election campaigns; the winner was determined by fewer than 2,000 votes in each case. Many of the counties that saw the largest increases in voter turnout were located in the competitive Seventh and Tenth Districts.

By contrast, Arkansas, Louisiana, South Carolina, and Texas faced anemic challenges in the general election. Heated Democratic primaries had chosen the party's nominees for state and local offices, and in most counties those nominees ran virtually unopposed in the general election. In South Carolina no Republican congressional candidate won more than 8 percent of the vote, and in the absence of partisan competition in the general election, few white women in that state organized voter registration campaigns in advance of the fall elections. South Carolina's only political battles occurred in the primaries, and organized white women saved their voter registration activities for the primary season when their votes would matter. Once they registered, however, South Carolina's white women made an impressive showing. During the 1922 gubernatorial primary in that state, more than 77,000 new voters crowded the polls for the runoff election, a 71 percent increase over the last all-male primary runoff.[185]

In short, southern women, both white and black, faced substantial structural obstacles as they worked to take advantage of their new ballots. The mobilization of women voters did not map onto a divide between ratification states and nonratification states, nor does it provide any obvious measure of white men's reactions to woman suffrage. Rather, female voting was part of a larger political and power structure in which registration obstacles had quashed political dissent and the absence of political competition had stifled political participation.

FOR DIFFERENT REASONS and in different ways, newly enfranchised white and black women staged the first substantial challenges to this closed system since the passage of disfranchisement laws at the turn of the century. Black women, undeterred by the use of disfranchisement laws to prevent them from casting ballots, insisted that the legitimacy of disfranchisement was not settled. They called on the courts, the Republican Party, Congress, and the federal government to help ensure their right to vote. White women, by contrast, challenged the legal structure of disfranchisement in an effort to open elections to more white voters and to make the political process more responsive. Through citizenship schools, publicity campaigns, and voter mobilization drives, both white and black women subverted disfranchisement by providing would-be voters with the information they needed to enroll successfully. Consequently, for the first time in decades, the region's political leaders faced a growing number of voters. More than one million new voters went to the polls for the first time after 1920, in no small measure because of the work of newly enfranchised female activists. As southern Democrats struggled to manage this new political reality, they confronted not only new faces at the polls but also a new political force that valued an expanded electorate and did not fear political dissent.

Chapter Three

Making Their Bow to the Ladies
Southern Party Leaders and the
Fight for New Women Voters

I t must have been quite a sight, in the summer and fall of 1920, as male candidates and party officials worked to woo new white women voters whom they had just recently denounced as "he-women" and supporters of "Negro Domination."[1] In mass mailings, in their stump speeches, and in their sudden solicitousness of advice from female leaders, the South's leading men pursued women voters in a new political ritual that visibly symbolized the transformations that woman suffrage had wrought. Of course, women had been active in party politics long before they had the right to vote.[2] Even in the antebellum period they had embraced partisan identities, made public presentations of their support, and attended campaign rallies. Never before, however, had southern women been the voters being rallied. Faced with long lines of women registering to vote and the prospect of hundreds of thousands of new voters at the polls, southern politicians in the fall of 1920 confronted the most substantial change in southern politics since the Populist revolt of the late nineteenth century. And unlike the growing force of discontent that characterized Populism, woman suffrage transformed an incredibly stable political status quo to a great political contest in just a few short weeks, as more than a million new voters suddenly took to southern polls.

Although most of the South's political leaders had resisted woman suffrage to the bitter end, their public attitudes changed swiftly once they stood before women voters as candidates. As one Virginian noted, "We (the women) are the most popular people ever. The candidates all *think* they have always wanted the women to have the vote and have always worked hard to attain this end."[3] In North Carolina's Republican mountain district, Buncombe County Democratic leaders seemed unabashed by their election-eve about-face as they welcomed women into the party: "Although I do not claim any credit for bringing you here, for I was against you," one party stalwart an-

Political cartoon depicting the new political courtship of enfranchised women (courtesy Tennessee State Library and Archives)

nounced, "now that the agony is over, I welcome you heartily and extend to you the glad hand of fellowship."[4] In Tennessee, a cartoon appeared in local newspapers that captured this sudden change in southern politics. Titled "In the Spring the Young Man's Fancy — ," it pictured politicians queued in front of the house of "Miss Suffrage," each bearing gifts of flowers or candy.[5] This depiction of politicians as suitors vividly illustrates the importance southern politicians suddenly placed on courting women's votes. Confronted with a doubling of the electorate, candidates had no choice but to search for ways to ingratiate themselves among new women voters. Those who could touted their long-standing advocacy for woman suffrage. Others tried to romance the voters with promises to support legislation for women and children and bouquets of newfound dedication to "clean politics."

Perhaps the most conspicuous evidence of men's efforts to court women voters appeared in newspaper advertisements and campaign broadsides. Candidates for state and local offices campaigned vigorously in the weeks before election day, and after 1920 many of their advertisements specifically targeted women voters. One broadside on behalf of U.S. Senate candidate Hubert D. Stephens was addressed, "To the White Women of Mississippi."[6] Lamar Jeffers, a candidate for Congress from Alabama, published a campaign handbill that included a letter of endorsement from Mrs. E. M. Fuller urging that "each mother" of a serviceman "should do all in their power to send him to Congress."[7] Even the Klan-sponsored newspaper made a special "appeal to Protestant Women of Atlanta" to register and vote for

Klan-supported candidates: "Remember Protestants Your Ballots Are Your Bullets."[8]

Candidates looking to target their appeals even more directly to women often turned to the bulletins and programs issued by state Leagues of Women Voters. There they placed advertisements that were sure to be seen by the state's most politically active white women — women who not only voted but who also had influence over the votes of others. Though the 1920 convention of the Tennessee League of Women Voters was held several months before Tennessee ratified the Nineteenth Amendment, both the Democratic and Republican Parties proudly claimed credit for the woman suffrage amendment in the league's program. Hopeful presidential candidates also placed advertisements in the bulletin, convinced that 1920 would be the year in which women's votes would turn the tide. And the entire back cover was devoted to an advertisement supporting the reelection of prosuffrage candidate, Governor A. H. Roberts. On each page of the program readers were encouraged to "Please Patronize the Concerns Whose Ads Appear in This Program," an instruction that candidates hoped would be heeded.[9] In the *Woman Voter*, a publication with statewide circulation among organized white women in Mississippi, candidates for U.S. Senate squared off in dueling advertisements, each challenging the other's credentials as a supporter of women's concerns.[10] In the *Pilgrim*, the bulletin of the Georgia League of Women Voters, candidates for mayor, governor, U.S. Senate, Congress, commissioner of agriculture, superintendent of schools, and other offices paid to have their political advertisements included alongside the league's own calls for women to vote.[11]

Many candidates sought the direct assistance of leading white clubwomen. In preparation for the campaign of 1922, for example, Governor Hardwick asked Mrs. Lamar Lipscomb whether she would lend her name to "a State Campaign Committee made up of some of the representative women of Georgia."[12] Congressman Butler Hare of South Carolina subscribed to the League of Women Voters bulletin in order to better understand the woman voter and ingratiate himself with league leaders.[13] In Virginia, Congressman C. Bascom Slemp invited the state's most prominent suffragist to be his guest at the Republican state convention, adding, "We will give you wonderful receptions."[14] The Alabama State Democratic Executive Committee solicited women to serve as stump speakers in their 1922 campaign efforts.[15] To increase his standing among women voters, one member of the LaGrange, Georgia, town council even "made [his wife] join" the League of Women Voters.[16]

As campaigns for state and local offices in Virginia got under way in early 1921, candidates from both parties running for governor, lieutenant governor, and the General Assembly contacted the League of Women Voters requesting endorsements, campaign assistance, lists of women voters, and introductions to important women around the state.[17] Politicians recognized that new women voters could turn the tide in these elections, and they looked to the women voters, as one candidate put it, "to stand back of me in this fight of my life."[18] Even candidates who had previously opposed suffrage or other legislation of concern to women contacted prominent white women in an effort to redeem themselves with women voters. For example, C. R. Warren, a member of the Virginia House of Delegates, wrote a letter to the League of Women Voters congressional district director in his area attempting to repair his reputation among women voters. He apologized profusely for his votes against woman suffrage: "I realize the fact that the ladies in some sections have concluded that I am their enemy and have no patience with their demand for recognition in politics. In this they are mistaken as much as it is possible for them to be."[19] In Alabama, Congressman Tom Heflin "boldly" sought the support of new women voters at a gathering of the local league. As a longtime opponent of woman suffrage, Heflin insisted that he had "no apologies to make" for his previous stance, but he did confess, "My view has been modified somewhat . . . by subsequent events."[20]

To the extent possible, candidates promoted themselves as the champions of women's issues. Lamar Jeffers, for example, solicited the support of Alabama's leading white women by highlighting his support for legislation to create a federal bureau of education that prominent women's organizations had endorsed.[21] Supporters of James K. Vardaman recommended him as "the foremost champion of prohibition, education and other questions in which [Mississippi's] women are vitally interested."[22] In the *Arkansas Gazette*, candidates for U.S. Senate sparred over their suffrage credentials, convinced that new women voters would reward suffrage's friends and punish its enemies at the polls. Candidate T. H. Caraway excerpted letters from prominent suffragists to create an ad titled "When Suffrage Needed a Friend Congressman Caraway Responded Loyally." Much to his chagrin, one of those suffragists shot back in an advertisement that revealed Caraway's limited support for woman suffrage and pledged her support for his opponent.[23]

Southern politicians recognized the new power of organized white women in other ways as well. In Alabama, for example, the governor sought the endorsement of the League of Women Voters to bolster his political capital.[24] A hopeful candidate from South Carolina, "planning to ride in on the women's vote," tried to take advantage of the power of organized white women by asking a prominent member of the League of Women Voters to run on his slate.

"He proposed to turn over to her a certain large number of votes which he 'carried in his vest pocket,' provided she throw the league's vote to him," but she declined, insisting that "she had but one vote at her command, and that would not go to him."[25] In North Carolina, the state legislature recognized the power of enfranchised white women lobbyists by inviting the honorary president of the National League of Women Voters to address the session.[26] Endorsements of the legislative work of organized white clubwomen, such as that offered by the governor of Arkansas in 1922, were common.[27] By seeking their endorsements and inviting them to address state legislative bodies, leading southern Democrats recognized the voting potential of white women's organizations.

While some candidates worked to secure the support of the region's newly enfranchised white women, other southern white men occasionally found it advantageous to help white women win. As Democratic and Republican Party leaders scrambled to curry favor among white women voters, some party leaders offered the nomination of female candidates as proof of their party's commitment to white women's concerns. Immediately following the ratification of the Nineteenth Amendment, Republicans in North Carolina and Arkansas courted white women voters by nominating women for the post of superintendent of public instruction. In Norfolk, Virginia, Republicans challenged the incumbent Democratic state legislator Sarah Lee Fain with another woman, Frances G. Ellis, but their efforts were unsuccessful.[28] Republicans in Arkansas also worked to recruit white women for state legislative races, with one party leader reminding himself to "ask Mrs. Moody if Mrs. Markwell will run for legislature."[29]

Democrats employed this tactic as well, offering Annie Webb Blanton as a Democratic candidate for state superintendent of education the year that Texas women were granted primary suffrage.[30] As one partisan strategist put it, "A woman candidate can bring out more women's votes than anything else."[31] Although female candidates were often nominated as members of the minority party and never had much hope for election, certain defeat was not always a prerequisite for a white woman's nomination. In Henry County, Virginia, the Democratic county committee unanimously nominated Sallie Cook Booker to the House of Delegates even though they knew she would face little or no Republican opposition.[32] In competitive Buncombe County, Democrats nominated Lillian Clement for the North Carolina state legislature in 1920 before the Nineteenth Amendment had even been ratified.[33] She went on to serve as the state's first woman legislator. Party leaders hoping to secure the loyalty of newly enfranchised women recognized the political utility of supporting an occasional female for public office. The symbolic value of such nominations was great, and partisans in Kentucky went so far as to comment publicly on the need for "the next Democratic State ticket [to] have a woman on it."[34]

After 1920, southern Democrats also frequently appointed white women to serve out the unexpired terms of male officeholders. The most famous of these "widow appointments" was Rebecca Latimer Felton's elevation to the U.S. Senate. Her service for a few hours as Tom Watson's successor entitled her to the honor of being the first woman senator. Her service also exemplified what many party leaders hoped to gain by the appointment of white women to unexpired terms. By honoring one of the state's most politically active white women with a seat in the U.S. Senate, party leaders in Georgia courted white women voters, but they did so without having to contend with her service for long. Felton had to fight hard even to be sworn in, and Tom Watson's "real" successor, a male senator, was waiting in the wings. Similarly, Arkansas Democrats twice sent widows to the U.S. House of Representatives in the 1920s. Effigene Wingo and Pearle Peden Oldfield both filled out the unexpired terms of their husbands, and both dutifully stepped down, returning the real political power to the men.[35] In Texas, Miriam "Ma" Ferguson served as governor for her husband, who was not dead but whose illegal conduct had resulted in his impeachment. "Ma" Ferguson had to fight hard to win the Democratic nomination, but once in office, she served her party's faction faithfully, with her husband's desk right next to her own in the executive office of the capitol.[36]

Party officeholding served as another important means by which party leaders hoped to enhance their party's standing among white women voters. Sue Shelton White, a Democratic partisan from Tennessee, conducted a survey of women in public and party office in part to remind party leaders that "if the rank and file of the women do not have before them some evidence of a more concrete appreciation" for their party loyalty, "it will become increasingly difficult to interest women in party affiliations."[37] Another southern partisan warned the men of her state, "The party half organized is like a crippled man in a race. Women represent approximately one half of what should be the democratic strength. In order to organize this vote so that it may be reached readily and effectually women must be represented upon the State and County committees."[38]

Both Republicans eager to take advantage of the Nineteenth Amendment and Democrats determined to curtail the threat posed by woman suffrage recognized that the limited inclusion of white women in party councils, like the occasional nomination of white women to political office, was to the advantage of male party leaders. In every part of the South, white women were appointed (or elected) in token numbers to serve on county and state party councils. In 1924, one North Carolina Democrat proudly reported to an influential woman in his state that "we are sending four women delegates at-large from this State, which was a full recognition of their desires at the State Convention."[39] Desiring that his party obtain the full political benefit for its action, this partisan added that the request by his party's women "was granted not only without reservation on the part of the Convention, but was done cheerfully as the whole Convention atmosphere disclosed."[40] When the Alabama State Democratic Executive Committee opened its membership to white women and temporarily added ten female members, party leaders issued a statement "of their desire to have women members and the counsel of women" and worked to advertise "this fact to the Democrats of the state."[41] Southern party leaders, many of the very men who had so vigorously opposed woman suffrage, did not invite white women into party councils for their wisdom. They did it to court white women voters, and they advertised white women's appointments to make sure that they got the credit.

They also consulted influential white women and key organizations of white women for advice, to make sure that they picked the right women for their councils. In Alabama, Democratic leaders called on the League of Women Voters to suggest a woman to serve on the state's Democratic Executive Committee.[42] In Richmond, Virginia, Democratic Party leaders simply chose the chair of the state's league as the first woman member of their city executive committee.[43] The Tennessee League of Women Voters reported that "the executive members of the two parties' state committees were made up almost entirely from our roster of officers" and that both the Republican and the Democratic Women's Clubs were chaired by league members.[44] Despite the substantial disagreements between party leaders and the state leagues on policy grounds, male party leaders recognized that their political advantage lay not only in appointing white women to party councils but also in associating the party with the most politically influential white women in their state. One southern Democrat summed up his party's selection process this way: "The men will be naturally inclined to favor the woman for that position who is favored by the women delegates."[45]

The nomination and appointment of token women to positions of real authority were not without risks, however. After serving eight years in the Georgia legislature, Bessie Kempton was remembered for her "militant sponsorship of progressive legislation" by one of the state's leading dailies.[46] Another Georgia representative, Viola Ross Napier, was described as "vot[ing] with the insurgents all down the line."[47] In North Carolina, Democratic Party leaders supported the appointment of Kate Burr Johnson to the position of commissioner of public welfare, motivated in part by the hope that this action would endear them to Johnson's clubwomen supporters. Once in office, however, Johnson's exercise of her authority "put her at odds with machine politicians."[48] In just one example of her political independence, Johnson supported a Republican for Surry County superintendent of public welfare, rather than offering that patronage plum to a Democratic loyalist.[49]

Even widows and female stand-ins were not always the submissive tokens that party leaders had hoped for. Anne Worley, for example, succeeded her antisuffragist husband in the Tennessee state senate and promptly used her new powers to sponsor legislation to remove civil disabilities against Tennessee's women.[50] Hattie Wyatt Caraway, the first woman elected to the U.S. Senate, also proved to be a troublesome political placeholder. In 1931, Hattie Caraway was appointed to serve out her husband's unexpired term in the Senate because she seemed a "harmless innocuous compromise" with Arkansas's regular Democratic primary just a few months away.[51] From the moment that Caraway's name was first mentioned as a successor to her husband, Democratic Party leaders were attracted to her candidacy as a way of ensuring that all the men who wanted the Senate seat would compete on an even footing in the state's August primary. Nearly everyone assumed that she would step down at the end of her husband's term, leaving the field open for a fight among the state's leading men. Yet on 10 May 1932, the last day to file for candidacy in the August primary, Caraway submitted her filing fee and party pledge, sending shock waves through Arkansas's political establishment.[52] Although few observers at the time gave her any chance of winning, Caraway turned Governor Parnell's "gesture of Southern chivalry" into a thirteen-year career in the U.S. Senate.[53] Caraway's refusal to serve as a benchwarmer defied expectations and demonstrated, as she once noted, that "chivalry's all right in the parlor, but mighty dangerous when carried into politics."[54]

Through partisan appointments and other means, candidates of both parties appealed to prominent white women as a way of reaching the mass of newly enfranchised women voters. A South Carolina woman reveled in her new position as political power broker when the son of an antisuffragist legislator decided to run for the legislature himself. Unpersuaded by the son's explanation of his father's antisuffragism, the woman reported that he "probably thinks he may need a few of the women's votes to get [his seat in the legislature]. Oh my dear our fun is just beginning."[55]

Indeed, not only did male candidates solicit white women's support, to the amusement of many longtime suffragists, but they also engaged in completely new types of campaigning, devised by white women, in order to woo women voters. The League of Women Voters in every southern state organized mass meetings to which they invited all the candidates to address the voters and listen to their concerns. Yet these meetings were a far cry from the partisan rallies staged by candidates in the past. At these meetings candidates shared the stage with their opponents, and women ran the event, often forcing candidates to confront difficult policy issues or simply to sit quietly as women voiced their concerns. The *Hanover Herald* indicated the meaning of this new political ritual in its headline, "Candidates to Make their Bow to the Ladies."[56] Local papers provided extensive coverage of these meetings, and candidates rarely declined invitations to appear before voters. As one Virginia league representative reported in 1923, "At our July meeting we invited them all to come and nine responded with their presence, the others with regrets (Shows they notice us)."[57]

Democrats and Republicans alike continued to stage partisan events after 1920, but once women were enfranchised, these candidates found that they could not do all their campaigning at partisan rallies if they wanted to win. A candidate meeting sponsored by the Wake County League of Women Voters garnered front-page attention as the *Raleigh News and Observer* noted, "Candidates Present But Not Asked to Talk."[58] With the power of the ballot to command men's attention, the white women voters of Raleigh summoned their candidates and demanded their attention as the women announced their legislative priorities for the coming year. In a similar meeting, according to one newspaper, "women voters of Mecklenberg County . . . reversed the usual order of things" when they invited candidates not to speak but to listen to women's demands. These invited guests were described in the newspaper as "Meek as Women Voters Opine What's What."[59] "Meek," "silent," "bowing to the ladies" in the wake of woman suffrage, southern white men found themselves in these unfamiliar, deferential positions. Accustomed to their status atop the southern social order, white men after 1920 found that the Nineteenth Amendment made politics look different and forced them to confront the power of white women's ballots.

In 1922, a cartoon in the *Woman Voter*, a bulletin for Mississippi's white clubwomen, captured the dilemma of southern Democrats. Titled "The Politicians' Worried Dream," it pictured a man asleep, dreaming of "The Womens' [sic] Vote."[60] Even in Mississippi, where partisan competition had been ruthlessly eliminated decades before, white southern men worried that white women might not follow party leaders. And, according to one Virginian, the politicians had reason to worry. As this prominent suffragist recalled, "They were dreadfully afraid we were going to organize a woman's party. And also they were very much afraid that a number of us were going to become Republicans, which we had, for gratitude, every reason to be."[61] Similarly, a South Carolina suffragist contended that southern politicians

Political cartoon depicting Democrats' fears of unpredictable southern women voters (courtesy Mississippi Department of Archives and History)

opposed woman suffrage because they "fear[ed] that they might not know what to do with the women if their [*sic*] consented to this thing. They feared they could not manage them, which was a well founded fear."[62]

Having for years rejected the appeals of women for enfranchisement, Democratic Party leaders had reason to worry about how this massive new group of voters might cast their ballots. Throughout the South, indeed throughout the nation, professional politicians, journalists, and ordinary men and women speculated about the changes woman suffrage would bring. In an editorial titled "Potential Force Behind Senator Mapp," the *Sunday Journal* pointed to the powerful new force in Virginia politics: "How many male voters realize that thirty-six thousand women are enrolled on the lists of the Equal Suffrage League of Virginia, one-third of whom live in Richmond? What a potential force to rally behind any candidate for office lucky enough to enlist their support!"[63] In Tennessee, a newspaper headline read: "Women's Vote May Decide It, Primary of June 10 Will Have This Unknown Quantity."[64] The assistant editor of the *Columbia Record* wrote to the Democratic presidential nominee, speculating about the effects of woman suffrage on the traditionally "solid Democratic vote of South Carolina."[65]

Suffragists had long contended that women's ballots would provide American politics with a thorough housecleaning, while opponents had forecast political cataclysm and the end of the American family. Yet in the absence of polling data, politicians had no way of predicting how these new voters would really behave. A wire story that ran in southern newspapers warned, "Party Chiefs Puzzled Over Women's Vote" and focused on women's indeterminate voting habits and their peculiar lack of party loyalty.[66] The *Richmond Times Dispatch* editorialized ominously about "campaign novelties in Virginia," highlighting both a "full-fledged Republican State ticket" and "the appearance of women [of both parties] on the hustings," a combination that could not have comforted Democratic Party leaders.[67]

As party leaders were puzzling over how women might vote, reports from across the South suggested that women might be in the majority at the polls. In Macon, Georgia, a newspaper reported that "at times new voters far outnumber men in lines waiting to cast ballots," and the *Richmond Times Dispatch* warned that "unless the white men of Virginia look to their spurs, the women will dominate the field of politics. . . . From all over the state come indications that women are qualifying themselves for the ballot, and in many localities they are already in the majority among qualified voters."[68] When a woman from Princeton, Kentucky, reminded the men of her community that women were in "the majority in registration," the men "look[ed] a little sober over the facts."[69] Even in Alabama, the home of the Southern Women's League for the Rejection of the Susan B. Anthony Amendment, "more women than men registered in some sections."[70] As a prominent antisuffragist from that state faced defeat in his home precinct, one observer suggested a connection between women's registration figures and the election returns in Alabama: "Mr. Calhoun is still saying that the women of the South don't want [the vote], and his home box is going against him. What next shall he say?"[71] As if in warning to party leaders, a newspaper article in Tennessee confidently declared that women voters, "if sticking together, will be capable of swinging the result any way desired."[72]

It was more than just the sheer number of women voters that troubled southern Democrats, however. It was white women's lack of party loyalty — or rather white southern Democrats' lack of faith in white women's party loyalty — that fueled their fears. While many southern Democrats tried to take comfort in the notion that women would vote as their husbands did, newspapers warned that "if the opinions of the women themselves are accurate, the male politicians are all wrong. . . . Women will be 'independents' in politics. They will not stay in one party for a lifetime, as men are accustomed to do. They will vote their convictions . . . and when it comes to voting, women are more likely to influence men than men are to influence women."[73] The editor of a Virginia newspaper drew a similar conclusion: "I am convinced that the women will revolt at the attempt to pledge their votes in advance to any boss-ridden ticket. I see in the advent of woman suffrage more independence for the electorate in Virginia than could otherwise have been obtained."[74] Another article that ran in southern newspapers warned simply, "Three Suffragists Say Women Will Not Vote as Husbands Do."[75]

While historians have demonstrated the ways in which white southern Democratic men relied on southern white women as symbols to bolster both party hegemony and white supremacy in the region, the partisan leaders had no confidence that they could rely on southern white women as voters to do the same.[76] Perhaps it was their belief in woman's fickle nature, or perhaps it was a more pragmatic fear that women so long denied the ballot would not care to reward their opponents at the ballot box. Whatever the cause, one North Carolina woman put it simply, "The effect of women in politics has been, in part, to create uneasiness in the minds of the professional politicians."[77]

SOUTHERN DEMOCRATS evidenced this uneasiness in their public pronouncements and their frantic efforts to endear themselves to the newly enfranchised women. In South Carolina, Major J. F. J. Caldwell exhorted the men of his state, "It is the duty of men, not to demand that the women about them shall follow their lead implicitly and vote as they do . . . but to assist them" in their duties of voting. Highlighting the "infirmities of mind and disposition thought to be characteristic of that sex," he urged men not to "stand aloof and leave them to the management of ill informed, excitable, and excited leaders of their sex."[78] Clearly, this southerner did not want former suffragists, so recently scorned by the Democrats of their state, to be the ones instructing the mass of the state's women in the use of their new ballots. In Alabama, a leading Democratic official pleaded with his state's women "not to use the franchise in spite."[79] Opting for the stick rather than the carrot, nervous Democratic Party leaders in Virginia threatened newly enfranchised women voters that they would not be permitted to vote in the 1921 Democratic primary if they failed to vote a straight ticket in their first election.[80]

With the Nineteenth Amendment no longer in question, southern Democratic leaders worked to incorporate white women into the party fold. As one handbill sponsored by Kentucky Democrats, featuring a long line of African American women voters, suggests, race-baiting characterized many party appeals to white women.[81] Many Democrats assumed that black women would vote, and would vote Republican. Partisan men feared that the line of black women waiting to cast ballots for Harding would stretch into the

horizon. Hysterical headlines and editorials in white southern newspapers
decried black women's attempts to register and called on white women to
defend white supremacy with their ballots. Yet as black women purportedly
lined up to do "their duty," Democratic Party leaders worried that white
women would fail to vote, or even worse, fail to vote Democratic. Consequently, Democratic leaders cast the Republican Party as the party of African Americans, urging white women not to let the South be governed by
"them."

A notice to the party faithful in Lunenburg County, Virginia, was characteristic of southern Democrats' appeal: "It is not a question now whether
women shall be permitted to vote or not. That part is already settled. . . .
A few days ago a republican leader in Richmond declared that five thousand colored women would register in Richmond alone. One hundred and
twenty eight registered there in one day. We must look to the good women
of Virginia, whether they favored Equal Suffrage or not, to uphold the honor
and traditions of this state."[82] A prominent South Carolinian called on the
women of his state using similar language: "I hope that every good woman

will promptly avail herself of the opportunity to discharge the moral obligation of voting . . . whether they want to or not out of a sense of duty."[83] In Virginia's "Fightin' Ninth" Congressional District, where party competition was fierce and a Republican represented local voters in Congress, an editorial in the Democratic *Bristol Herald Courier* referred to voting as "women's plain duty" and argued that "suffrage may prove a curse to state and nation" if good women failed to vote.[84]

Democratic Party leaders in Texas combined race-baiting with threats of violence to manage the new political realities of woman suffrage. In McKinney, two articles demonstrating these approaches ran in the Democratic newspaper, just days before the 1920 election. One called on white women to perform their civic duties in support of white supremacy. "Quite a number of negro women have been paying their poll tax at Fort Worth," the paper decried. "Will white women please take notice?"[85] The other article reported, "A negress, Mattie Henry, aged 32 years, paid her poll tax here Thursday."[86] That sentence was followed ominously by Henry's full local address.

The presence of black women at the polls generated "hysteria" among many Democrats in the South.[87] In the weeks following the ratification of the Nineteenth Amendment, white newspapers highlighted the activities of these would-be voters with headlines such as "More Negro Women Register Than White" and "Outnumber White Women In Ward 3."[88] The historian of the Kennesaw chapter of the United Daughters of the Confederacy (UDC) urged white women to respond to the crisis of woman suffrage by registering "at once." Like many other white southerners who were startled by the determination of black women to vote, this Georgia UDC leader reported "stacks of registration papers registered by the Negro women" and declared, "For every evil vote there must be one on the other side, the side of truth and honesty to counteract the evil."[89] In Glasgow, Kentucky, the headline in a white newspaper declared, "Whites must vote in Negro homes."[90] Faced with black women at the polls, albeit in numbers much smaller than the dramatic headlines would suggest, white southern political leaders shifted their race-baiting away from attacks on suffragists and leveled them squarely on Republicans and black women voters. The participation of white women in politics was no longer characterized as scandalous. Instead, as Congressman Thomas Bell of Georgia put it, white women's registration was "of the utmost importance in maintaining white supremacy."[91] In Chattanooga, however, one white antisuffragist expressed frustration with suffragists for their inability to anticipate this political crisis. "What else did those women who have been energizing for suffrage . . . expect of colored women," he demanded, "than that they should manifest a desire to vote?"[92]

Although southern Democrats' long-standing opposition to woman suffrage signaled party leaders' reluctance to share political power with the region's white women, those men immediately worked to create space in the party organization for loyal women once the Nineteenth Amendment was ratified.[93] From the national Democratic Party organization down to individual campaigns, politicians sought the loyalty of these new voters by creating structures in which women could participate as partisans. In North Carolina, for example, Democratic Party leaders specified that "Democratic voters, both men and women," would be welcome at the party convention.[94] In Alabama, one woman from each congressional district was added to the state Democratic Executive Committee.[95] And in Richmond, Virginia, white women were admitted as members of the city Democratic Committee before they even cast their first ballots.[96] In Kentucky, where partisan competition was fierce, male Democratic leaders worked "promptly" to "provide for the participation of women in the councils . . . of [their] party."[97] As soon as the Nineteenth Amendment was ratified, Kentucky Democrats called on loyal men across the state to recommend "an energetic, capable, popular Democratic woman, who could be depended upon to effect a strong organization of women" in each county.[98] From Banner County, one Democratic partisan wrote to the party's leading female organizer requesting assistance "as to our women."[99] Men and women alike believed that women voters would be more successfully mobilized by other women, and this local party operative worried that "some of our best women speakers have been influenced . . . to vote prohi[bition]."[100] He called for help from state headquarters to encourage "influential women" to help bring their sisters "into the democratic camp."[101]

A photograph from Richmond, Virginia, featuring partisan women engaged in voter registration activities, captured what Democrats hoped to gain from partisan women. They wanted white women voters to be loyal to the Democratic Party and to encourage other white women to register and vote loyally. Nevertheless, as historian Kimberly Brodkin found, "men's interest in capturing women's votes did not necessarily produce any greater willingness to give women power in the parties."[102] Democrats opened their party institutions to women in an attempt to secure women's partisan loyalty, but they were not eager to share real political authority with these new women voters. Consequently, political leaders frequently created new Democratic women's clubs rather than welcome women into existing decision-making bodies. In Louisiana, Tennessee, and Texas, Democratic women's demands for equal representation on party committees were dismissed by party leaders and state legislators.[103] In Alabama, state party leaders increasingly relied on a system of Democratic women's auxiliaries, rather than mobilizing women through full inclusion in party decision-making.[104] Even in Ken-

Democratic women in Virginia helping to mobilize other partisan women in the 1920s (courtesy Cook Collection, Valentine Richmond History Center)

tucky, where the Republican threat was imminent and the Democratic Party had moved swiftly to mobilize Democratic women, the party's female leader complained privately that "there is not provision yet made for us [women] in the party com[mittee]s."[105]

Though not eager to share real political authority with women, Democrats worked to bind white women voters to the party so as to render them no longer dangerous. As one southern white woman insisted, "The way politicians have of depriving women voters of their power is to get them once safely enlisted in a faction, where they can be instructed how to vote, where they can be so fired with partisan zeal that they are no longer capable of unprejudiced decision."[106] Through advertisements and race-baiting, party membership and Democratic women's clubs, direct courting of women voters and threats against party bolters, Democrats worked to inculcate the region's white women with just such partisan zeal. Party leaders worked to manage the threat posed by woman suffrage by encouraging the region's white women to adopt the loyalties of their husbands and brothers. After the ratification of the Nineteenth Amendment, one southern suffragist reported, "the sentiment of the politicians [is] changing and they are all, or nearly all, doing all they can to help us with the registration."[107] Of course, faced with a small number of newly registered black voters, who would presumably vote Republican, and a much larger number of unpredictable new white women voters, Democratic Party leaders had little choice.

LIKE NERVOUS DEMOCRATS, Republican Party leaders also worked to secure the loyalty of these new women voters. While Democrats saw women voters as a potential threat, however, Republicans viewed woman suffrage as an opportunity to revive their party's fortunes in the region. In Virginia the secretary of the Republican State Executive Committee wrote a letter "To the Women of Virginia" to provide information and offer assistance in registering to vote, "regardless of [their] political affiliations."[108] Despite the nonpartisan magnanimity of this offer, the Republican Party official wasted no time in reminding Virginia's women that their enfranchisement had come "despite the efforts of the Democratic Party in this state to keep it from you." In Georgia, Republicans staged a massive drive to register women voters and offered a full slate of candidates the first year that women were able to vote in statewide races.[109] The efforts of the Republican Party to woo newly enfranchised women voters in Arkansas exemplified the spirit of Republicans throughout the region as they opened their 1920 campaign with a rally to "Welcome the Ladies to the Ballot."[110]

In Alabama, Republican Party leaders targeted women voters with appeals to fair play and good government. When Democratic Party leaders threatened to expel all party bolters, Alabama Republicans called on women voters to "profit by the political serfdom of the men in our State, and not permit their hands to be manacled by the political chains of Democratic slavery."[111] In words hardly distinguishable from the broadsides issued by the League of Women Voters, Alabama Republicans declared their party's commitment "to the untrammeled right of franchise, to vote for whomsoever the dictates of conscience would direct, and the desire for good government would demand."[112]

In North Carolina, Republicans seized upon the virulent opposition of the state's leading Democrats to woman suffrage in their efforts to woo new women voters. They staged aggressive voter registration drives, publicly condemned the Democratic Party's treatment of the state's women, and nominated a white woman for superintendent of public instruction.[113] Democrats throughout the state worried as prominent white women proclaimed their nonpartisanship and prepared to split their ballots, voting for the Democratic presidential nominee as the candidate for peace and the Republican gubernatorial nominee as the supporter of woman suffrage.[114] In one of the state's largest daily newspapers, a Democratic man publicly lamented, "My wife and four daughters are going to vote for him [the Republican gubernatorial candidate] in spite of all I can do."[115] For those southern white women who could not bring themselves to vote for a Republican, instructions on how to "scratch" antisuffragist Democrats from their ballots were made available at local citizenship schools.[116] Democrats scrambled to maintain their control over the state's politics, employing loyal Democratic women to stump for the ticket and insisting that white supremacy was at stake at the polls.[117] In the midst of this heated battle, a prominent newspaper editor publicly warned the Democratic leadership that "the women are unattached at this writing. They may join the Democracy but it will do well to understand that the Democracy will do the courtship from now on."[118]

As Republicans courted women's votes, they welcomed the ladies to the ballot with more than rallies, registration drives, and reminders of Democratic Party intransigence. Southern Republicans also welcomed white women with lily-whitism. At the same time that former suffragists called on new women voters to cast independent ballots, white party leaders worked to make the Republican Party an attractive alternative for these new voters by ousting the party's traditional black allies. Southern Democrats continued to invoke white supremacy and fears of "Negro Domination" to secure the loyalty of white women voters, but white Republicans in the region embraced lily-whitism as a way to neutralize the race issue in the contest for these new voters. As one historian put it, Republicans appealed to newly enfranchised white women by promising that "for the first time . . . there would be no black Republicans: now or ever."[119]

In Virginia, Republicans began their "lily-white" appeals to women voters with the presidential election of 1920. While Virginia's Democratic leaders struggled to swallow "the bitter pill" of woman suffrage, newspapers commented on the opportunity that woman suffrage offered to Republicans and the way that the state's opposition party "hope[d] to gain."[120] Fearful Democrats worried that these lily-white appeals to women voters were helping to breathe new life into the state's Republican Party. In a campaign rally in Norfolk, one Democratic leader admonished the region's white women: "If the white women of the South don't know whether they are Democrats or not, it is high time they were learning, for the white women of the South will be the first to suffer humiliation if Democracy is defeated. And if the women don't hurry up and decide whether they prefer white or black supremacy, the Republicans will have the battle won before the women get through being advised as to what they are politically."[121] Indeed, Republicans' racist appeals to white women seemed to have had their intended effect. As one Virginia newspaper reported, "Not all of the women who voted this morning voted for Cox and the league of nations, regardless of the view taken by their husbands."[122]

In 1921, the first year that women could vote in state and local races, Republicans in Virginia made their "first campaign as a white man's party" with a full slate of candidates.[123] Having barred African Americans from the state's Republican nominating convention, Virginia's white Republicans hoped that strong support from women in 1921 would "swell [the] vote" for their gubernatorial nominee, Col. H. W. Anderson.[124] White Republican leaders courted white women voters by "preaching a doctrine of eternal repression for the Negro" and, as one black newspaper editorialized, "going even further than the Democrats have gone" in championing white supremacy.[125] Democratic leaders did not allow these lily-white appeals to go unchallenged, however. White newspapers denounced Republican attempts to "rid itself of the incubus it has borne ever since the war between the States."[126] And the state's Democratic campaign headquarters issued a press release linking Republican attempts to court white women voters with that party's support for the "promiscuous participation" of African American men and women in the electoral process.[127] Although it was the Democrats who had stood steadfastly against the enfranchisement of the state's women, Democrats nevertheless denounced the expediency of Republican appeals to "the white women of Virginia for assistance."[128] While Republican Party leaders courted white women voters by attacking African Americans and nominating a white woman for superintendent of public instruction, Democrats publicly insisted that Republican appeals to these newly enfranchised women were "an insult to . . . Southern womanhood and to the State at large."[129] Despite these time-honored references to white supremacy and southern womanhood, woman suffrage and lily-whitism had decidedly changed the state's political landscape. Even Democratic leaders publicly predicted that "the Republican vote throughout Virginia in the November election will set a new record."[130]

In North Carolina as well, Republicans looked to woo white women voters with pledges "to keep [the] Negro entirely out of politics."[131] Hoping to capitalize on the Democratic Party's opposition to woman suffrage, John Parker campaigned vigorously to become the state's first Republican governor in decades. He stumped the state reminding voters of his support for woman suffrage and assuring white voters that neither he nor his party would "bring back the Negro into politics."[132] As in Virginia, Democratic leaders in North Carolina responded by calling on white women to defend white supremacy with their Democratic votes. Indeed, desperate Democrats even went so far as to fabricate a letter, which they falsely attributed to the Republicans, urging black women to register and vote.[133] In response to the "Negro Woman Letter," the chairman of the state's Republican Party issued an open letter denouncing the Democratic tactics and assuring "the women of North Carolina that if we carry the state in this election, you will have a strictly white government, honorable and decent."[134] He further pledged to "the good women of North Carolina that if they assist us in breaking the hold of democracy, which has held North Carolina like the grip of a vise for the past quarter of a century, nothing will transpire in a republican administration that will cause any woman who voted for our cause to be ashamed of what she did."[135] On the campaign trail, Republican candidate Parker continued to denounce his party's former black allies and attack the Democratic Party. Before a crowd in Gastonia he declared, "The false cry of Negro domination was made to frighten the white women, whom the democratic machine had done its best to keep from voting. . . . Not a single instance can be shown where the republican party has tried to register a Negro."[136] Indeed, much to the dismay of African American women, the actions of the lily-whites matched their rhetoric. When an unidentified black woman contacted Republican Party officials for assistance in registering African American women in Kannapolis and Salisbury, white party leaders refused and "told the woman frankly that they didn't want Negroes to get into politics."[137]

In Arkansas, lily-white Republicans seized control of the state party machinery in 1920. Hoping to build a new Republican Party with the help of white women, party leaders courted women voters with a lily-white slate of nominees, including a white woman candidate for superintendent of public instruction.[138] Although Arkansas's Democratic leaders had not fought woman suffrage with the dogged determination of some other southern politicians, new women voters seemed nonetheless attracted to the new face of Republicanism. In 1916, when election days in Arkansas remained an all-male affair, the Democrats polled 25,637 votes in the Fourth District of Arkansas. The Republican vote was zero. In 1920, the Democratic total shrank to 19,722 while the Republicans polled more than 11,000.[139]

In Texas, too, the lily-whitism of the state's Republican Party reached new heights with the enfranchisement of women. In 1920, white Republican leaders in that state seized control of the state's party machinery; the new lily-whitism of the party was so pronounced that African Americans bolted the party for a full slate of "black and tan" nominees of their own. Among the lily-whites, Mrs. Myron A. Kesner, former president of the state's Housewives Chamber of Commerce, led the party's efforts to recruit white women voters. In words that echoed the fears of Democratic Party leaders, Kesner contended that "the vast majority of women voters of Texas are not bound to any particular political party."[140] She encouraged the state's white women to cast their first ballots for Harding, insisting that support for the Republican nominee did not require, or even imply, membership in the Republican Party.[141] While male party leaders denounced African American voters and stripped them of participation in party councils, Kesner appealed to white Texas women by encouraging them to resist unthinking partisanship.

Even in Georgia, Republican leaders looked to reverse their fortunes by enlisting white women voters. Democratic Party leaders in that state had fought woman suffrage to the bitter end, and even after the ratification of the Nineteenth Amendment, they had refused to permit the state's women to vote in the November 1920 elections. Thus, Georgia's women voted in statewide races for the first time in 1922. Meeting nine months before the election, white Republicans hoped to capitalize on the anger and frustration that attended the delay. Led by Mrs. W. J. Wilson, Republicans planned to organize "G.O.P. feminine forces in every section of Georgia," and the meeting site itself provided clues to the new Republican strategy. Gathering at the Georgian Terrace Hotel in Atlanta, Republicans held their first rally at an establishment "where colored women cannot go."[142] As white Republican leaders sought to build a viable opposition party in the state, they worked diligently "to interest a number of prominent women" in "build[ing] a white party in Georgia."[143]

Although the lily-white movement had begun among white Republicans in the years before 1920, it took on a new urgency after women were enfranchised, as white southern Republicans attempted to cast themselves as a legitimate political alternative for white women voters, one that would not jeopardize white supremacy. Democrats throughout the region denounced the political expediency of Republicans who suddenly broke ties with African Americans and called on white women for support. Democratic Party leaders insisted that the only way to safeguard white supremacy was for new white women voters to join their fathers and husbands in the party of Redemption. Nevertheless, these heated denunciations and shrill cries of white supremacy reveal the very real threat that lily-whitism and woman suffrage posed to Democratic control.

In Kentucky, Democrats recognized immediately that the strong partisan competition in the state made woman suffrage all the more threatening. Even before the enfranchisement of women, Kentucky supported a viable Republican Party. Once the Nineteenth Amendment was ratified, Republicans in the state worked quickly to bolster their party's strength with new women voters. In Frankfort, for example, Mrs. John G. South spoke to a packed audience of women on the topic "Why I am a Republican." Like Republicans elsewhere in the region, she highlighted the party's achievements, denounced the Democratic Party's "mismanagement of public affairs," and appealed directly to women voters by declaring that it was the Republican Party that "had given suffrage to the women."[144] Republican women throughout the state were "working hard" for the party, and the female Republican chairman in Scott County baited her Democratic counterpart that Republican women would outnumber Democrats "two to one" on election day.[145]

Republican leaders in Kentucky, however, were not so quick as other southerners to abandon their black allies. In many parts of Kentucky, African Americans were able to register and cast ballots without substantial interference, and reports from around the state in 1920 indicated that "the colored Republican women seem to be better organized than the white Republican women."[146] Consequently, when Mrs. South made her Republican pitch to women voters, her audience was composed predominantly of black women, with "as many white women and men as could crowd their way into the church."[147] But just as Republicans in other states feared, the activism of black Republicans in Kentucky made the race-baiting appeals of Democrats all the more effective. Throughout the state Democrats insisted that "if the white women fail to vote . . . negresses shall decide the balance of political power."[148] Newspaper headlines contended that the "aggressiveness of negroes" was "hurting Republicans" and many Democratic women were not hesitant to "holler 'Nigger' if that will make them win."[149] While African Americans in Kentucky, particularly in Louisville, protested racial discrimination by members of their own party, Kentucky Republicans did not rely on lily-whitism to appeal to white women.[150] Instead, they mobilized black and white women alike to organize women voters for their party.

CONFRONTED WITH NEW WOMEN voters and Republican Party efforts at renewal, southern Democratic leaders faced the elections of 1920 with trepidation. The results of those elections did little to assuage their fears. Throughout the region, the increase in voter turnout alone suggested to political leaders that women were a force to be reckoned with. The sudden introduction of more than a million new voters to the polls defied Democrats' traditional means of controlling politics. Moreover, the fact that voter turnout declined in the two southern states where women remained unenfranchised in 1920 due to registration laws suggested that these new people at the polls were unpredictable women voters.

Even more frightening to Democratic Party leaders, a comparison of election results from 1916 and 1920 suggests that women's votes helped the opposition.[151] In every southern state except South Carolina, Republicans increased their showing over the 1916 presidential election results. In Mississippi and Georgia, where women remained unable to cast ballots in 1920, these results heightened the anxiety of Democratic Party leaders who would be forced to face women's ballots in the next election amid increasing Republican competition. As figure 2 and table 2 illustrate, Republicans not only increased their statewide totals but also increased their voting strength in nearly every county in the South. Moreover, in every southern state, the gains of the Republican Party proportionally outstripped the overall change in turnout. For example, in Alabama the number of voters casting ballots in the presidential election increased 79 percent between 1916 and 1920, but the number of Republican ballots cast increased 159 percent. Indeed, in Arkansas, Kentucky, Louisiana, Tennessee, and Texas, the total increase in Republican votes exceeded the increase in Democratic votes. In the absence of voter survey data or exit polls, the most obvious, and worrisome, explanation for this was that a majority of new voters had cast ballots for Republicans.

As Republicans had hoped, the party of Lincoln made impressive gains in the region during the first elections in which women voted. In Tennessee, Democratic Party leaders surveyed the new political landscape with dread as that state tallied Republican majorities for president in the wake of woman suffrage and antisuffragist women claimed credit for defeating the incumbent Democratic governor who had opposed their cause.[152] Voters in Tennessee, Texas, and Virginia elected seven Republican congressmen, four more than in the previous Congress.[153] Even in Alabama, the incumbent Tenth District congressman faced a tough challenge from his Republican rival, and a Republican lost the state's Seventh District congressional seat by only 730 votes out of more than 45,000 cast.[154]

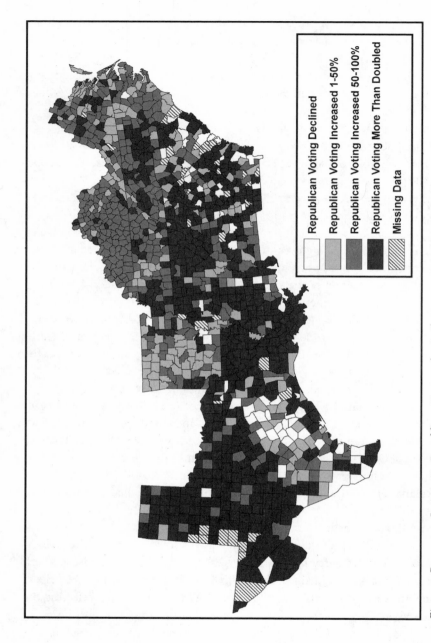

Figure 2. *Percentage Increase in Republican Voting after Suffrage, 1920 Presidential Election*

Legend:
- Republican Voting Declined
- Republican Voting Increased 1–50%
- Republican Voting Increased 50–100%
- Republican Voting More Than Doubled
- Missing Data

Table 2. Change in Republican Party Strength, 1916–1920

State	Change in No. Repub. Voters	Change in No. Dem. Voters	% Change in Repub. Voters	% Change in Dem. Voters	% Change in Voter Turnout
Alabama	46,057	56,948	161%	57%	79%
Arkansas	22,228	–4,805	45%	–4%	8%
Georgia	31,687	–21,642	281%	–17%	–7%
Kentucky	209,626	187,213	87%	69%	77%
Louisiana	32,073	7,480	496%	9%	36%
Mississippi	7,274	–11,170	171%	–14%	–4%
North Carolina	111,929	136,984	93%	81%	86%
South Carolina	694	2,325	45%	4%	4%
Tennessee	103,006	53,278	89%	35%	57%
Texas	49,385	1,518	76%	1%	30%
Virginia	39,072	39,830	81%	39%	52%

In the weeks and months that followed the 1920 presidential election, Republicans pointed to presidential and congressional election returns from southern states as evidence of "the changes at hand."[155] The newly elected Republican congressman from Texas viewed his own victory as the vanguard of a new politics in the region, in which southern states would become "bitterly contested battleground between the two parties."[156] Republican congressman Bascom Slemp of Virginia echoed the optimism of many Republicans when he confidently predicted that "in 1922 some of the most spirited congressional contests in the nation will be waged in these North Carolina, Alabama, Arkansas, Texas, and other southern districts. And I believe that for the first time in more than half a century some of these districts are going to elect Republicans to the next Congress."[157]

In North Carolina, Democratic Executive Committee members studied these same presidential and congressional election returns in an attempt to discern the future of their party and the effects of woman suffrage. In the absence of separate tallies of men's and women's ballots or exit polling data, political leaders relied on comparisons of election returns before and after the ratification of the Nineteenth Amendment to determine how women's ballots affected party competitiveness. In North Carolina, Democratic Party leaders found in these numbers a warning. Not only did Republicans enjoy a greater proportionate increase in the number of votes cast for their presidential nominee, but Republicans gained ground in five of the state's ten congressional races as well.[158]

Consequently, North Carolina Democrats felt compelled to issue instructions to local party leaders, advising them on the need to mobilize women voters. In a pamphlet titled "The Woman Voter of North Carolina: Where She Votes and Where She Does Not!," Democratic Party leaders used 1920 election returns to provide party operatives with a "guide to the potential woman vote still *unregistered* in many counties."[159] The message from party leaders was clear: Democrats must do a better job of getting loyal women to the polls, because Republicans were gaining ground. No Republican revolution had followed the enfranchisement of women, but Democratic leaders saw a threat looming to the brittle machinery of partisan domination. As North Carolina's Democrats put it, "Our greatly increased Democratic majority is most gratifying, but it should not blind us to the percentage of increase of our wide awake Republican opponents."[160]

In Virginia, the potential force of women's voting strength was worthy of similar editorial admonition in 1921: "If the women choose to exercise the ballot that has been placed in their hands they are potentially as strong as the men in determining the candidates to be elected and the administrative and legislative policies to be pursued. If they refuse to jump at the crack of the party whip and stand together for a given set of policies, it is absolutely within their power to decide which party shall come into control of the government in the next election."[161] As politically active white women exacerbated the political uncertainty of southern politicians by organizing voter mobilization drives, denouncing party loyalty, and encouraging political competition, Democratic leaders occasionally lashed out. In South Carolina, one Democratic partisan called on southern men to provide guidance for women voters: "If we would secure efficient, rational and fair government let us guard against the seesawing between a man's party and a woman's party. The League of Women Voters in the South already threaten a course of sweeping activities not at all pleasant to contemplate."[162] Fearful of the effects that the formation of a local league might have on party fortunes in her area, the leader of the Rutherford County Democratic Women's Party spearheaded the opposition to a local league in Murfreesboro, Tennessee.[163] A white activist in North Carolina reported that her efforts to organize women into Leagues of Women Voters were "handicapped by the positive opposition of the politicians to a 'non-partisan' organization tending to encourage independence."[164] In Kentucky, Democratic partisans accused the League of Women Voters of serving as "an adjunct to the Republican party."[165] More ominously, at least one observer contended that the extension of the poll tax to Tennessee's women in 1922 was an attempt to disfranchise these new women voters who were tending Republican.[166]

Party leaders in Alabama, unused to partisan rivalry, discussed the problem of women voters specifically when a subcommittee of the Democratic State Executive Committee met to make plans for the 1922 elections. Julius Jones, chairman of the Coosa County Executive Committee, pleaded with the state committee for campaign funds to redeem his county from Republican officeholders, and in his description of the forces arrayed against Democrats in his area, he noted that "the woman vote is a little uncertain."[167] When asked about the vote of Republican women in his county, the Chilton County representative, L. F. Gerald, declared, "They qualified 100% two years ago, and they are still that way. They paid their poll tax after that." Insisting that local Democrats had worked to get their women to the polls in 1920, Gerald conceded, "We qualified fully six hundred voters last February, about that number. We have got to get out and get them to the polls this time. That is where the main fight that we have lies."[168] While Chilton was a Republican stronghold in the state, and Coosa County had seen Republican victories for four years prior to the enfranchisement of women, Clay County lost its first local election to a Republican in 1920, "on account of some peculiar circumstances . . . one of which was the failure to get all of our women registered like we should."[169]

After the 1920 elections, Democratic Party leaders faced a Republican Party that had made successful inroads in the Upper South. In Kentucky, North Carolina, Tennessee, Virginia, and even parts of northern Alabama, Republican candidates were competitive in the general election. As figure 3 demonstrates, Republicans had taken advantage of the influx of new women voters to build on their historical strength in the Upper South.[170]

To be sure, Republican strategies to woo white women voters were more successful in states like Kentucky, North Carolina, Tennessee, and Virginia than they were in Mississippi or South Carolina. Even the 45 percent increase in the number of Republican voters in 1920 amounted to only a few hundred Republican votes in South Carolina. Nevertheless, in election outcomes, as well as in the voting behavior of individual women, political leaders increasingly recognized that enfranchised white women did not always vote like white men. When one Democratic man discovered that his wife planned to cast her ballot for the Republican nominee for president, he confessed to a friend, "We are all badly split up."[171] He and his wife were not alone. A Democratic activist from North Carolina reported that the most common excuse for nonvoting by women in her county was that "the husband voted 'the other way.'"[172] As antisuffragists had feared, white women did not always share the political views of the men in their households. As a consequence, some failed to vote. But as hundreds of thousands of other women successfully tackled the voting restrictions in the region and cast their ballots, they gave voice to the separate opinions in their households.

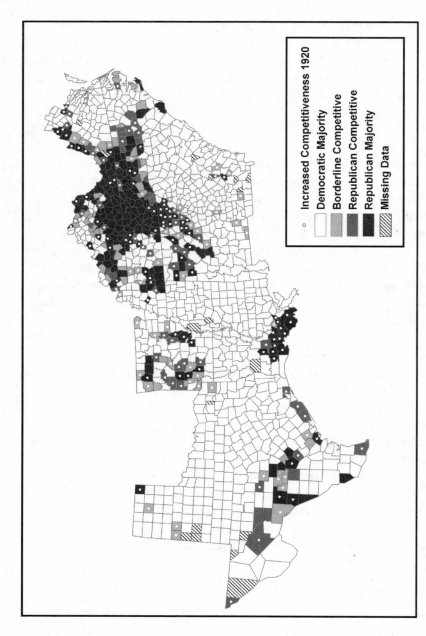

Figure 3. Change in Republican Competitiveness after Suffrage, 1920 Presidential Election

In most cases, those separate opinions found expression in Democratic primary contests, rather than in general elections. In many parts of the South, Democrats routinely ran unopposed in general election contests, but intraparty competition posed a threat to Democrats throughout the region. Throughout the 1920s, the proportion of the primary vote received by the leading gubernatorial candidate in the South was generally less than 50 percent.[173] In Texas and Mississippi, the Democratic primaries were so competitive that the winner of the first primary for governor typically earned the support of a mere third of primary voters. In 1924, J. T. Duncan won the Democratic nomination for governor in South Carolina by fewer than 2,000 votes; in 1930, Ira Blackwood edged out his opponent for the same office by just 969 votes. Even in Virginia, where gubernatorial primaries were often uncompetitive, General Assembly races were won and lost by small margins. Throughout the 1920s, only 60 percent of the members of Virginia's House of Delegates retained their seats from election to election.[174]

Disfranchisement ensured that only a minority of southerners participated in state primary elections, but the competition for those votes was fierce. With just a few thousand (or a few hundred) votes separating the Democratic nominee from an also-ran, the introduction of hundreds of thousands of new women voters into the primaries sent shock waves through the Democratic Party. In Mississippi, the number of voters participating in the gubernatorial primary increased by 71 percent once women were enfranchised.[175] That year more than 100,000 new voters cast ballots in the August Democratic primary, and observers credited Henry Whitfield's victory to the votes of women, as he defeated Theodore Bilbo and three other candidates to become governor.[176] In Alabama, the number of voters participating in the state's Democratic primary for U.S. Senate increased by nearly two-thirds after women were enfranchised; that first contest was so competitive that the victorious Democrat earned just 33 percent of the total primary vote. In Louisiana the story was much the same: primary vote totals increased by more than 67 percent after women were enfranchised, far outstripping the increase in general election voters. Across the region women voters took to the polls, and they recognized that the most important contest in most states occurred in the Democratic primary.

As the voting habits and voter mobilization activities of newly enfranchised white women expanded intraparty competition in the region, Democratic politicians in many southern states responded by attempting to eliminate the primary altogether. As one Mississippi suffragist explained, "Having lost their fight against woman suffrage, they made a move to destroy the effectiveness of the woman vote."[177] In North Carolina, members of the Democratic "Old Guard" sought "to put women out of state politics by abolishing the state wide primary law."[178] These efforts were thwarted by the state's organized women voters, however, and league leaders proudly announced that "this coup-d'etat was frustrated by the League's Legislative Committee in a spectacular but effective way."[179] Similarly, newly enfranchised women in Tennessee successfully fought a 1921 attempt to "abolish the Primary law of the state," which would have "practically disfranchis[ed] all the women and the working classes."[180]

With their efforts to eliminate the primary largely unsuccessful, Democratic Party leaders across the region found that they had reason to fear the region's "Democratic" women voters. In Atlanta, for example, newly enfranchised white women defeated every member of the city's Democratic Executive Committee in the first municipal election in which women cast ballots.[181] Even in the absence of separately tallied ballots, many Democratic Party leaders were well aware of the independence of women voters. Atlanta's white women exacted their electoral revenge after Democratic Executive Committee members reneged on their agreement to allow the city's white women to determine how their poll taxes would be spent.

In Memphis, the Citizens' Non-Partisan League was created to oppose machine rule in that city. Newly enfranchised women "worked early and late" for the reform candidates, opening their homes for registration drives and getting out the antimachine vote. At least one woman faced opposition from her own husband, as he insisted on voting the machine ticket "for business reasons." In a marked departure from the presuffrage era, when men represented their families with a "household vote" on election day and wives stayed away from the polls, this woman responded to her husband by insisting, "I must vote against that ticket for other than business reasons." On election day in 1919, they each went to the polls to cast a ballot that canceled the other one out.[182] The Democratic machine was defeated, however, as the reform ticket was propelled to victory by new women voters.

In Texas, too, newly enfranchised women immediately put their votes to work to defeat a longtime enemy in his bid for governor. Former senator Joseph W. Bailey had vigorously opposed the federal suffrage amendment and stood in opposition to many of the legislative priorities that organized white women endorsed. Throughout the heated primary season in the summer of 1920, the Texas League of Women Voters issued candidate profiles and publicized information about the candidates' voting records that were designed "to teach the women how to vote against Mr. Joseph Weldon Bailey."[183] In a competitive primary field, Bailey was challenged by two men with strong ties to the newly enfranchised voters. Robert Thomason, Speaker of the Texas House of Representatives, had been a longtime supporter of white clubwomen's causes, including suffrage. He had the support of Minnie

Fisher Cunningham, one of the state's most influential suffragists, who referred to his candidacy as "one of the first fruits of women's participation in affairs of government."[184] Pat Neff, though no ally of suffrage, was a staunch prohibitionist who consequently attracted many white women voters. On election day, more than 450,000 Texans went to the polls, and their ballots forced Neff and Bailey into a runoff. Faced with the determined opposition of many former suffragists and white clubwomen, Bailey lost his bid for governor in the runoff primary by 80,000 votes.[185] Competitive southern primary elections offered newly enfranchised women voters an opportunity to cast meaningful ballots and hold their lawmakers accountable. In the first gubernatorial primary in which they voted, Texas women thus demonstrated their new power as voters by helping to defeat a former U.S. Senator and powerful Democratic politician in his bid for governor.[186]

In Mississippi as well, enfranchised southern white women posed a challenge to Democratic machine candidates. In public pronouncements and private behavior, organized white women in Mississippi warned party leaders that they would not fall lockstep behind one faction or the other. As the president of the state League of Women Voters explained, "The moment we ally ourselves with either faction we cease to be the balance of power and so lose our one and only opportunity to make good our promise that the enfranchisement of women would make for the moral and social welfare of our state."[187] And in the primaries that followed their enfranchisement, Mississippi's women made good on that warning. In 1922, for example, Mississippi's white women voters were credited with defeating the Vardaman political machine when Belle Kearney, the unsuccessful female candidate, urged her supporters to throw their votes behind Hubert D. Stephens, James K. Vardaman's opponent in the runoff primary contest for U.S. Senate.[188] Just two years later, a former suffragist challenged the Democratic Party machine in her Mississippi county by staging a separate nominating convention, and she successfully unseated Washington County's machine delegates at the 1924 state convention.[189] Just as some politically active white women mocked the region's political orthodoxy by supporting Republicans, other white women challenged the party machinery from within, supporting independent Democrats and defying the party bosses.

ELECTION RETURNS early in the decade, the efforts of white Republicans to court white women voters, and the political activities of women themselves gave southern Democrats throughout the region reason to worry. As Republicans built on their traditional strength in the Upper South, new women voters played active, and at times decisive, roles in southern primaries. The limited electorate that was the foundation of Democratic Party control had been greatly expanded in 1920, and party leaders scrambled to maintain their footing in this new political terrain. As Mrs. John McNeel, the national Democratic committeewoman from Alabama, warned Democratic Party leaders in her state, "If the Democratic party wants them [the women] they must go and get them. The Republican Party is getting them. The League of Women Voters is getting them, and the Democratic Party must be up and doing."[190]

Chapter Four

Not Bound to Any Party
The Problem of Women Voters
in the Solid South

An absolute menace to Democratic supremacy."[1] That is how one white southerner described woman suffrage. Like the antisuffragists who warned that woman suffrage was an affront to southern manhood and that votes for women would subvert traditional gender roles, this observer recognized the potential power of women's ballots to transform party politics in the New South. Even small numbers of black voters and dissident white voters had long terrified southern Democratic men, spurring disfranchisement in the first place. And the Nineteenth Amendment introduced not just a few but more than a million new voters to the polls.

As they eagerly embraced their new political status and worked feverishly to expand the voter rolls, newly enfranchised women not only undermined disfranchisement but also directly challenged the Democratic stranglehold in the region. On the eve of woman suffrage, white southern Democrats stood in command of a political system in which few men voted and even fewer men maintained any real influence in political life. Yet as these political elites well knew, with so few southerners voting, it would not take many disloyal votes to threaten Democratic supremacy in the region. For more than a decade, literacy tests, property requirements, poll taxes, and complicated registration and balloting procedures had prevented all but a small minority of southern men from casting ballots. Such tight control of the electorate had eliminated real partisan competition from nearly every corner of the South and depressed voter turnout even among those who could qualify for the franchise. After 1920, southern women worked to open up this closed system. As they brought new voters to the polls, these women threatened to revitalize not only partisan competition in the region but intraparty competition as well. With Democrats in many southern states divided by faction, the ballots of a few new voters could tip the balance in many primary elections, and with voter turnout in many states below 20 percent, Republicans needed only to win the support of a small number of new voters to cast off the yoke of Democratic Party hegemony in the region. For Democratic Party elites, then, woman suffrage posed not only a psychological challenge to their sense of manhood but a tangible threat to their control over southern politics.

THE NASHVILLE CITY elections of 1919 offered southern Democratic Party leaders perhaps the first glimpse of just how profoundly woman suffrage could challenge their control over the region's political system. In April of that year, the Tennessee state legislature granted women the right to vote in municipal and presidential elections, and suffragists immediately set about organizing newly enfranchised women to cast their first ballots. In a pattern that would be repeated by women throughout the region after the ratification of the Nineteenth Amendment, Tennessee suffragists in 1919 publicized their cities' registration requirements, canvassed neighborhoods to register women voters, spoke to women's clubs about the importance of voting, and worked tirelessly to get out the woman vote. In Nashville, however, these efforts took on special significance as white suffragists joined with African American suffragists and clubwomen to elect a slate of reform candidates to the city government.

White suffragists throughout the South had long denounced corrupt machine politics, and they staked their claim to the ballot, at least in part, on the idea that women would use their votes to clean up politics.[2] Thus, it is no surprise that Tennessee's white suffragists worked fervently to elect reformers in the 1919 city elections. African Americans, however, had a more ambiguous relationship with Tennessee's urban political machines. While white southern Progressives had long believed African Americans to be the tools of corrupt city bosses, willing to sell their votes for a few "treats," African Americans often had compelling reasons to support the machine candidates. For example, Mayor Edward Crump of Memphis promised African American voters that he would protect them from abusive treatment by the county justices, and Mayor Hilary Howse of Nashville occasionally placed African Americans on his slate of candidates. Both men wooed African American voters with individual handouts, but they also used government resources to fund services that benefited African American neighborhoods, such as schools, libraries, and parks. Thus, for African American women to support reform candidates on the Democratic ticket meant opposing elected leaders who had provided needed services to their communities, as well as rejecting their own Republican partisan loyalties.[3]

Moreover, it was an inauspicious time for interracial cooperation at the polls. White southerners used legal and extralegal means to keep African American men from the polls, and Jim Crow statutes ensured that African Americans received only the barest access to inferior public services. As many African Americans sought escape from the oppression of southern society by moving to the North, white southerners increasingly resorted to violence and intimidation in response to perceived threats to their authority. In fact, just the year before Nashville's women forged their historic alliance, a lynching in a nearby community had prompted 2,000 of the city's African American citizens to march in silent protest.[4]

Despite these obstacles, both prominent African American clubwomen and leading white suffragists in Nashville saw political advantage in uniting the votes of their supporters. For white women, the benefit could be simply calculated: more votes for their reform candidates. For African American women, their cooperation came in exchange for an explicit promise that if the reformers won, specific demands of African Americans for city services would be met. Once this bargain had been struck, Catherine Kenny, chair of the Ratification Committee of the Tennessee League of Women Voters, appointed two prominent African American clubwomen, Dr. Mattie E. Coleman and J. Frankie Pierce, as "state negro organizer" and "secretary of colored suffrage work," respectively.[5]

Though the white and black women worked through segregated ward organizations to register voters and get them to the polls on election day, their alliance amounted to more than separate trains running along parallel tracks. Kenny and her assistant in the campaign, Della Dortch, addressed meetings of African American women, urging them to register to vote and to cast their ballots for the reformers. Kenny even called on "the common bond of womanhood and motherhood" in her appeals to African American women voters.[6] Likewise, Coleman and Pierce were invited to address meetings of white women voters, where they reiterated their commitment to "the same moral uplift of the community in which we live as you are. . . . We are asking only one thing—a square deal."[7] While limited interracial work among women's organizations was not uncommon in southern cities in this period, the union between African American clubwomen and white suffragists in pursuit of electoral victory was unprecedented in the South.[8] Indeed, white men looking to Nashville for indication of what woman suffrage might bring must have been shocked by the spectacle of "maids and cooks . . . taken to the polls by their mistresses in automobiles."[9] Contrary to the bitter racial antagonisms of the time and even the arguments of some white suffragists who contended that white women's votes would help bolster white supremacy, these women in Nashville reached across the racial divide to use their votes collectively against white Democratic men in power.

On election day, the reform slate won, and Kenny publicly credited her African American allies with the impressive African American voter turnout. According to one estimate, fully 22 percent of the women who cast ballots in Nashville that day were African American.[10] In the months that followed, reform candidates, now city officials who owed their positions to the unusual alliance of Nashville's women, quickly fulfilled many of the promises made to the city's black clubwomen. In 1919 the South's leading white men could look to Tennessee as a harbinger of the effects of woman suffrage in their region, and they could not have been comforted by what they saw. Women crossing racial boundaries, expanding the electorate, defeating Democratic machine candidates, and demanding policy changes in exchange for their votes — these were precisely the things that Democratic Party leaders feared most as the Nineteenth Amendment loomed on the horizon.

WHILE DEMOCRATIC AND Republican Party leaders worked to secure the loyalty of new white women voters, southern women themselves insisted on crafting more nuanced relationships with political parties. As many scholars have pointed out, women entered the political system in 1920 with a strong tradition of nonpartisanship.[11] Although gender infused partisan politics and women embraced partisan identities long before the ratification of the Nineteenth Amendment, the expansion of women's sphere to include politics and policy-making in the presuffrage era was justified in part by women's claims to a higher morality, in contrast to the base political calculations that supposedly motivated men. As one historian put it, women "were viewed and presented themselves as motivated by issues not elections, and by principles not a search for power."[12] With the ratification of the Nineteenth Amendment, political parties sought to erase this "gendered border of politics" to make loyal partisans of these newly enfranchised women, even as leaders resisted the full inclusion of women in party decision-making.[13]

Political women responded ambivalently to these overtures. Some scholars have attributed the persistence of nonpartisan activity by women in the 1920s to a distinct female political culture that prevented women's organizations from moving effectively from their nonpartisan traditions into the world of electoral politics.[14] The interaction of southern women with political parties, however, suggests that newly enfranchised women were neither trapped by notions of appropriate female behavior nor incapable of playing partisan politics. Rather, they recognized that political power existed on both sides of this "gendered border."[15] Thus, even as they worked for full inclusion in party decision-making, many southern women publicly denounced strict party loyalty.

In the debates over woman suffrage, and in the frantic efforts to wed newly enfranchised women to one political party or the other, the political loyalty of African American women was largely assumed — or ignored. Antisuffragists based their most hysterical claims on the "fact" that the African American women who would flood the polls would be opponents of the Democratic status quo. White southern Republicans, likewise, believed that African American women would be loyal partisans, but they pinned their party's hopes instead on the uncertain ability to win over the votes of white women, for whom disfranchisement laws posed a less daunting obstacle.

For African American women themselves, the issue of party loyalty was not so clear-cut. To be sure, black women voters had no reason to support the party of Redemption. Indeed, they faced predictable hostility from these proponents of white supremacy, as well as organized Democratic efforts to prevent African American women from participating in the region's political life. Perhaps even more discouraging to black southerners, however, was that as Republican leaders in the South worked to build a viable opposition party in the region, they pursued a strategy that was based on creating a whites-only Republican Party.

At the same time that they courted white women's votes, white Republicans, at the state and national level, refused to protect the rights of black women to cast their ballots. Immediately following the election of 1920, African Americans implored the Republican Party and members of Congress to enforce the Nineteenth Amendment or reduce the representation of southern states in Congress until they permitted black citizens to vote. But their pleadings largely fell on deaf ears. Throughout the decade the *Crisis* ran stories and editorials condemning Republicans for "kicking us [African Americans] out" of the party and documenting the refusal of Republicans in power to pass the Dyer antilynching bill or enforce the Fourteenth, Fifteenth, and Nineteenth Amendments.[16] Thus, as historian Glenda Gilmore has suggested, black women entered the political system with Republican "roots far more shallow than those that black men had planted in Emancipation."[17] Like the southern white women who announced that they had no Democratic Party loyalty, southern black women also entered electoral politics with limited commitment to partisan identity. After all, the Republican Party had enfranchised black *men*, not black women.[18]

Nevertheless, African American women recognized that their plight in the South was made all the more difficult by the absence of political competition in the region. And so they organized. Throughout the region, African American women went to the polls singly and in groups. They worked through the Republican Party, the NAACP, and women's clubs. African American women were convinced that only with the vote would they be able to protect their rights as citizens, earn a living wage, and obtain equal access to public services. Following the ratification of the Nineteenth Amendment, they tenaciously fought for access to the polls, and they did so for the most part as Republicans, determined to cast their ballots against the party of Redemption and white supremacy.

Despite the increasing lily-whitism of the Republican Party, many of these political women were convinced that the Republican Party—the party of Lincoln—represented their best hope. As Ella Elm, a black migrant from Arkansas explained, "When I was a little girl my daddy used to say to me. Ella you is a little girl now but when you grow up to twenty-one and can vote don't never vote a democratic ticket."[19] Long before his daughter could vote, this black father warned her of the dangerous white supremacist ideology of the Democratic Party. More than ten years after women were enfranchised, this African American woman proudly insisted that "to this day" she had "never" cast a Democratic ballot.[20] Moreover, many southern black women did more than simply vote Republican. They created partisan organizations to mobilize African American women *as Republicans*. In Tennessee, for example, leaders of the Republican Party's "Colored Women's Bureau" organized African American women on behalf of the Republican Party, provided speakers to their civic groups, and enlisted African American women to work the polls on election day.[21] In Georgia, African American women staged a "thrilling" campaign to mobilize their sisters to vote for Republican candidates.[22] In Kentucky, hundreds of African American women formed the "Christine Bradley South" club to promote the aims of the Republican Party. In New Orleans, Louise J. Ross, Mrs. Sylvester Bete, Lottie McDonald, Virginia Thompson, and Mrs. Tropas organized themselves into a branch of the National League of Republican Colored Women, determined to defy disfranchisement and directly challenge the Democratic Party in the region.[23] As they organized like-minded voters and helped African American women gain access to the polls, these partisan clubs signaled a bold defiance of disfranchisement and Democratic Party dominance in the region.

Yet, even as they determinedly sought access to southern polls, African American women did not unwaveringly support the Republican Party. While partisan organizations of Republican black women were not uncommon in the South, many black women chose to fight disfranchisement through nonpartisan, rather than partisan, organizations. Black women worked with the NAACP, for example, establishing citizenship schools and staging registration drives that added thousands of African American women to the rolls. In Birmingham, nearly 100 African American women gathered in April 1921 to "interest the women citizens in the franchise" and to spearhead voter registration campaigns. Although Birmingham was home to "a well defined Republican Party," the Colored Women's Voters' League was decidedly nonpartisan.[24] As they worked to reach "thousands of colored women throughout the county and inform them along the lines of good citizenship," these African American activists worked "on their own initiative," making reference to "no party or section."[25] Similarly, in Virginia, members of the Women's Non-Partisan Political Club welcomed representatives of both the Democratic and Republican Parties to address their meeting in preparation for the general election.[26] Across the region, southern black women staged registration drives, provided citizenship information to would-be voters, and encouraged African Americans to make application at the polls without any reference to partisan politics or assistance from the Republican Party.

Indeed, when the ratification of the Nineteenth Amendment confronted black clubwomen with the issue of partisanship for the first time, many resisted the Republican Party. Just a few months after the ratification of the Nineteenth Amendment, and before any women in Georgia had enjoyed the opportunity to cast a ballot, the report of the retiring president of the Savannah Federation of Negro Women's Clubs reflected the ongoing debate. A loyal partisan, Rebecca Stiles Taylor urged black clubwomen to "stand together" in the Republican Party, denouncing "whoever attempts to lead otherwise" as a "traitor to his race."[27] Taylor's shrill rhetoric suggested the extent of black women's dissatisfaction with the Republican Party. When she warned that "Negro men and women must, must stand together" in the absence of "some other party . . . which gives us more protection," she acknowledged both the root of the problem and the gendered divide among black southerners.[28] Determined to use their ballots to the benefit of the race, and frustrated by the Republican Party's refusal to protect their rights, many black women voters refused to bind themselves to any party, even the party of Lincoln.

Indeed, leaders of the National Association of Colored Women (NACW) repeatedly insisted that their members should "be non-partisan."[29] While state and local affiliates of the NACW sponsored citizenship education and worked to ensure that "every woman exercise the right of suffrage and see that her neighbor does also," they carried out this work as nonpartisans and encouraged would-be voters to "vote [their] convictions."[30] And when some black Republican women sought to organize African American clubwomen for partisan ends, leaders of the National Association of Colored Women insisted that they form their own organization. Founding members of the National League of Republican Colored Women, including Mrs. George Williams and Mrs. Rebecca Stiles Taylor of Georgia, and Mrs. Mary C. Booze of Mississippi, played prominent roles in the NACW. Nevertheless, the creation of these two separate organizations signaled the importance that many African American clubwomen attached to nonpartisanship. Even as they worked to make the Nineteenth Amendment a reality for black women and a force for improved legislation in their communities, many black clubwomen were not ready to commit themselves fully to the Republican Party.

When mobilizing voters and speaking before groups of women, politically active African American women focused on the vote as a mechanism for solving problems and emphasized the importance of voting for issues rather than parties. Even before they cast their first ballots for president, African American women in Nashville were encouraged "to ignore parties and vote their convictions."[31] NAACP leaders urged newly enfranchised black women to "unite to defeat all candidates for office who are unfavorable, and to support those who can be depended upon to deal justly" and address the problems of African Americans.[32] Even as speakers called on black women to "uphold prohibition with their vote[s]," prominent black clubwomen insisted that "a new day had liberated the race from the traditional ideas, and we now had the right to exercise perfect freedom in the choice of our political candidates."[33] Clearly, newly enfranchised black women privileged issues above partisanship. As one leading clubwoman reported, while African American women "are always Republicans in a national election," they cast their ballots in state and local races for the candidate who is "just to all citizens without regard to race or color . . . no matter to what political party he belongs."[34]

While some black political women insisted that "Negro women cannot be non-partisan," many southern women insisted that they would not mechanically "line up with their Negro men" in the Republican Party.[35] Instead, they demanded that the Republican Party earn their loyalty by promoting the interests of African Americans. Indeed, even before southern women cast their first votes, representatives to the National Association of Colored Women's Clubs meeting in Tuskegee, Alabama, refused to endorse the Republican Party platform because "it did not take a bold enough stand against lynching."[36] In Richmond, at the same mass meeting in which plans were laid to assist African American women in qualifying to vote, the city's black men and women also protested against the lily-whitism of the state's Republican Party. From the moment of their enfranchisement, African American women looked to use their votes "for the betterment of conditions affecting colored people."[37] As the Republican Party increasingly adhered to a policy of lily-whitism and ignored the demands of its black allies, newly enfranchised African American women insisted that "their duty in politics" was to cast their ballots "for men who will uphold the Constitution . . . and who stand for justice and fair play to all."[38] As one prominent black clubwoman put it, "Organize, organize, and again organize. Then vote for men who are friends to the race, irrespective of party or political superstition."[39]

African American women voters provided more than rhetorical support for their thoughtful nonpartisanship. They also worked against southern Republicans when the party rejected their concerns. On election day 1920, for example, reports circulated that African American voters were voting for the Democratic presidential nominee, James Cox, "as a rebuke to 'lily-whitism' in Virginia."[40] Despite African Americans' historic loyalty to the Republican Party, Christia Adair's experience may have been more common than scholars have thought. When Warren G. Harding's campaign train made a stop in Kingsville, Texas, in 1920, this African American woman escorted "11 or 12" black children to the campaign stop to meet the Republican nominee for president. As she recalled, "All Negroes were Republicans" then "because Abraham Lincoln was a Republican." When the train pulled in, Adair and her young black charges were "right at the steps," but "Mr. Harding reached over my children's heads to shake hands with the white children." The president never acknowledged the African American supporters right in front of him. Faced with such a personal example of the Republican Party's increasing lily-whitism, Adair decided at that moment, "If that's what Republicans do, I cannot be a Republican. . . . From here on out I'll have to work for Democratic presidents."[41]

In 1921, Virginia's black women joined black men in support of a separate "lily black" ticket, in opposition to both the Democratic and white Republican Party slates. Maggie Lena Walker, a leading Richmond clubwoman, was the nominee for superintendent of public instruction, and she campaigned tirelessly for the "lily black" ticket. At local churches, a meeting of the Council of Colored Women, and in notices distributed by black clubwomen, Walker touted the benefits of the all-black slate of candidates.[42] Following a parade in Richmond, on the eve of the election, Walker and another female activist, Mrs. Mildred Cross, joined prominent African American men in addressing the crowd of supporters.[43]

On election day, the "lily blacks" lost, of course, but Walker polled well over 20,000 votes as the first African American woman in Virginia to run for statewide office. Even more important, in publicly rebelling against the party of Lincoln, black southerners demonstrated their political power, since white Republicans could count the number of votes they had lost as a result of the party's lily-whitism. Indeed, when white Republicans renewed their efforts in 1922, black Virginians "won their point," as "Democrats for the first time in years carried every District in Virginia."[44] In particular, African Americans rejoiced at the defeat of Republican congressman C. Bascom Slemp, "the leader of Lily Whitism" in the state.[45] His seat, in the Ninth Congressional District, had not been held by a Democrat for more than a decade before the African American electoral revolt. As the African American newspaper the *Richmond Planet* crowed, "The election last Tuesday has ended the hopes of the 'Lily white' contingent of the Republican Party in the Southland. . . . The promised 'land-slide' for Republicans did not develop."[46]

In Texas, too, the resurgence of lily-whitism in the wake of woman suffrage led many African American women to cast their new ballots in opposition to the party of Lincoln. Driven out of party councils and denounced by white party leaders, Texas's black Republicans in 1920 offered a slate of nominees for statewide office, as well as nominees for Congress and even state legislature in several districts. These "black and tan" nominees included two women: one nominee for the General Assembly and another for state superintendent of public instruction.[47] While the presence of black women on the ticket signaled their new status in political life, they made their most important contributions at the ballot box. The *Houston Informer* declared that "the colored women of Harris County saved the day for genuine republicanism and undefiled Americanism" by mobilizing "every qualified voter to go to the polls and cast a vote for the entire black and tan republican ticket."[48] In Dallas, newly enfranchised black women "left no election judge ignorant of the fact that they intended to vote the Black and Tan ticket."[49] While African American women in Texas used their first ballots to rebuke the party of Lincoln for failing to represent them, black newspapers took note that not all the male leaders in their communities were so willing "to stand up for the principles of justice and equity."[50] African American observers condemned the men who supported the lily-white ticket as "race traitors" and contrasted the bravery of black women at the polls to the men who "take cold feet at the least flurry and semblance of high-handedness."[51] Indeed, the *Houston Informer* demanded, how can such an individual "call himself a man."[52]

It was not only the masses of newly enfranchised black women who seemed willing to set aside Republican partisanship. Even the African American women who seemed to be the most loyal Republicans were willing to question their party. Members of the Republican League of Women Voters in Savannah, Georgia, "urged the women to vote in accordance with their honest convictions," even as they "directed a vigorous campaign" to get newly enfranchised African American women to the polls.[53] African American women working for the Republican Party in Kentucky resigned their posts and publicly denounced the party after the secretary of the state party attacked black partisans and repeatedly referred to them as "damn nigger[s]."[54]

As one observer described it, the party leader "not only laid bare his own prejudiced heart, but . . . the lily white, anti-Negro heart of the whole Republican organization."[55]

By mid-decade, black Republican women complained openly of the discrimination they felt from white members of their own party. Ora Stokes of Richmond, Virginia, was exasperated with white Republican leaders who ignored black partisans. Despite her own efforts and those of other African American women to support Virginia's Republican ticket in the last campaign, she explained, "We could never get in touch with the Central Committee. . . . They met in Murphy's Hotel where no colored person, except for help, is allowed. . . . We financed ourselves, worked to get out our own literature, had nothing sent ot [sic] us to give out. The White Republicans, with one exception were not to be found."[56] Although her comments were made at a gathering of partisan women determined to advance the cause of the Republican Party, Stokes captured the sentiment of many black political women when she lamented, "It is not the attitude of the Democrats," which she found unsurprising, "but the attitude of the Republicans that discourages us, or makes us fighting mad."[57]

On the eve of the 1924 presidential election, less than a month after black women had formed the National League of Republican Colored Women to further the aims of the Republican Party, the members of that organization publicly condemned uncritical partisan loyalty. Instead, these partisan black women encouraged their followers to "put men and measures above parties and pockets."[58] Black Republican women objected to their party's policy of lily-whitism and resented the way Republican leaders expected African American votes while simultaneously ignoring African Americans' policy concerns. Increasingly, even these partisan women supported Republican candidates only when those candidates seemed genuinely committed to upholding the Constitution. At the very moment that the federal government began to reassert its power to open southern polls, the Republican Party was increasingly abandoning its commitment to black voters and citizens, a fact that did not go unnoticed by African American women. Consequently, as they planned their political futures, African American women, like southern white women whose loyalties to party were supposedly so fixed, were open to political alternatives.

WHILE AFRICAN AMERICAN women struggled to take advantage of the Nineteenth Amendment without acquiescing to the increasing lily-whitism of the Republican Party, many southern white women expressed a similar reluctance to become instruments of the Democratic Party. In the weeks and months immediately preceding the ratification of the Nineteenth Amendment, southern Democratic men had not endeared themselves to female suffrage leaders with their rejection of the Nineteenth Amendment, and bitterness encouraged many former suffragists to consider Republican alternatives. Moreover, after years of lobbying their state lawmakers, many white clubwomen were skeptical of the Democratic Party's support for their concerns. As newly enfranchised white women surveyed the field of candidates, they were willing to consider the Republicans who endorsed education reform, prohibition enforcement, and social welfare programs. Even more important, newly enfranchised white women recognized the strategic value in their nonpartisanship, and they publicly predicted that women voters, once enfranchised, would not mechanically toe the Democratic Party line. In South Carolina, a prominent suffragist took issue with an editorial on woman suffrage, responding publicly, "He takes occasion to speak of the 'Democratic women' of South Carolina. There are no 'Democratic women' in South Carolina. The women of South Carolina have no political rights, and belong to no party." She went on to warn the men of her state, "The women resent it bitterly; there is an end of patience even among women, and . . . they have lost confidence in the men who are pretending to represent the state and the Democratic party."[59] Abby Milton, president of the newly formed Tennessee League of Women Voters, announced before a crowd of women voters and the state press that "Party Lines Will Not Bind Women." She warned that, unlike men who will "vote for any candidate their party puts up," women would base their decisions on the qualities of the candidates, not partisan loyalty.[60] As Democratic Party leaders well knew, these strong statements were not idle threats. They came from white suffragists, the very women who were most likely to vote and who were most actively involved in mobilizing other women voters.

Indeed, while southern Democratic leaders invoked white supremacy and fears of a "black menace" to secure the loyalty of white women voters, they were increasingly confronted by political women who refused to march obediently into the party of their fathers.[61] On the eve of ratification, Mrs. W. P. Nesbitt of Birmingham wrote to Governor Thomas Kirby urging him to endorse the Nineteenth Amendment. Though she was active in Democratic Party circles, she warned, "If Alabama fails to ratify, I hope I may be able to move in some good Republican State where they are progressive and up-to-date."[62] Furious with the Democratic men of her state for their rejection of women's demands for political participation, a South Carolina activist angrily declared, "I am sure I am not going to *stump* the state, and you are not, and who will?"[63] Even "loyal" Democratic women, on whom party leaders hoped to rely, seemed to lack true partisan commitment. One Democrat wrote from Dry Ridge, Kentucky, to express concern that the female party organizer chosen for the county "is about to turn Republican."[64] When a Democratic leader in Virginia wrote to Jessie Townsend of Norfolk to advise her of her appointment to the local Democratic Campaign Fund Committee, he assumed that Townsend and the other twelve members would automatically respond to the call of the party. Instead, she declined the "honor," informing the party leader, "Until I know more I cannot be bound to any party."[65]

The wife of a former state senator in Kentucky seemed to know plenty about southern politics, but her knowledge (and her husband's political position) did little to secure her partisan loyalty. In the rural district where she lived, she worked with other women to nominate men "of principle" in both the Republican convention and the Democratic primary. As she put it, "The women have the balance of power in the state, and now is a good time to show the old parties that they must do right if they want us with them."[66] Abby Crawford Milton, who not only came from a Democratic family but also served as one of Tennessee's delegates to the Democratic National Convention, denounced party regularity in an address to more than 200 clubwomen. She cautioned the women in her audience, "If you are going into politics to be the shadow or echo of men you had better stay home and knit."[67]

While these startling examples of anti-Democratic sentiment surely unnerved party leaders, the refusal of white women's organizations to promote party loyalty signaled the enormity of the Democratic dilemma. In a typical appeal, the honorary president of the North Carolina Federation of Women's Clubs called on women to go to the polls, "not to save any party, but to save our constitution upon which the republic is founded."[68] With the ratification of the Nineteenth Amendment, southern white women went to the polls by the hundreds of thousands. Democratic Party leaders reached out to women voters as part of an electoral strategy, but, as one scholar put it, "neither party had a superb track record in organizing its women."[69] By contrast, women's organizations had a commitment to keeping their members informed, and many southern white women received their most consistent and detailed political information through women's clubs. Through meetings and club bulletins, women's organizations provided information about the progress of clubs' legislative agendas and reminded women to register and vote. The Leagues of Women Voters took the lead in this work, and league efforts reached well beyond the committed cadre of political women who were dues-paying members. Leagues of Women Voters in the region not only had their own meetings (which were almost always open to nonmembers as well as members), but they also regularly sent speakers to provide political information to meetings of other women's organizations. The leagues in Georgia, Kentucky, North Carolina, South Carolina, and Virginia issued regular bulletins, and league news was a frequent feature of white newspapers. Voter registration drives and get-out-the-vote efforts were regularly sponsored by southern leagues. Yet, to the chagrin of Democratic Party leaders, these efforts by women to expand the electorate and provide political information were marked by a determined nonpartisanship.

As a matter of national policy and local practice, the League of Women Voters was a nonpartisan body that publicly encouraged women to "enroll in the parties of their choice."[70] Throughout the Solid South, league leaders hailed from both political parties and politically active white women often employed explicitly antipartisan rhetoric. In southern states, publications distributed by the league urged women to exercise good citizenship by "never voting a straight ticket from party expediency."[71] In a regular newspaper column, South Carolina league leaders reminded women that "a citizen's duty is to country first and to party second. The women of the League do not believe in giving their consciences into the keeping of a political party."[72] Such antipartisan rhetoric must have seemed downright heretical to white southern Democrats who had hoped that prominent southern ladies would use their ballots to bolster the party of Redemption and white supremacy. Instead, these men found influential white women publicly urging wives not just to vote as "hubby" does: "It is fine if he will vote like you do, but if you just have to 'kill' his vote, why, you just have to, that's all."[73]

During campaign seasons, the league's candidate questionnaires, get-out-the-vote drives, and other voter mobilization efforts often rivaled the activities of political parties in their contact with the electorate, but the league did not encourage Democratic fealty. Rather, league members denounced the men "who bitterly opposed woman suffrage by every trick and device within their power and when it came in spite of them they determined if possible to induct women in to the parties in blind obedience to the powers that be and complete surrender to the system that they find—hence the cry, party loyalty—party regularity."[74] Newly enfranchised women voters and women newly interested in voting often turned to their local league for information about voting, and this condemnation of party loyalty was contrary to the message that Democratic leaders hoped to send. Instead of party operatives and male relatives guiding women directly into the Democratic fold, party stalwarts found that through newspapers, league publications, citizenship schools, club meetings, and get-out-the-vote efforts, nonpartisan female activists were encouraging new voters to cast their ballots without regard to partisanship.

It was more than just nonpartisan rhetoric that worried Democratic Party stalwarts. Even more frightening were white women's interactions with the Republican Party. An important part of the league's mission was making sure that voters had the information they needed to cast their votes intelligently. As a result, leagues throughout the region distributed information from both the Republican and Democratic parties about their candidates and platforms. In a region where Democrats had maintained political control by limiting the franchise and eliminating partisan competition, league forums that invited women to explain "Why I am a Democrat," "Why I am a Republican," and "Why I am a Progressive" seemed designed to revive opposition party fortunes. In Tennessee, the league's eighth annual convention and citizenship school followed this popular format, offering two sessions in which a Republican and a Democrat explained their party loyalty.[75] In Baldwin County, Alabama, the local League of Women Voters held a public forum that featured speakers from the Democratic, Republican, and Progressive Parties discussing their candidates and platforms.[76] Newspaper coverage of league meetings provided opposition parties with an even wider audience for their message.[77]

Just six weeks before the November 1924 elections, the Mecklenburg County league held a meeting using this format, and newspaper coverage of the event ensured that the women's endorsement of open-minded debate was not limited to those who attended the meeting.[78] In strident tones, one newspaper reported, Miss Clara Cox, the Republican, "stated that the domination of one party in a state did not foster good government. She spoke against 'machine rule' and asserted that the best thing for the South would be to have its solidarity broken."[79] As the meeting sponsors had hoped, the full extent of her denunciation of the Democratic Party and her rationale for her Republican partisanship were detailed in newspaper accounts. While the Democratic speaker responded with a defense of the progressive measures enacted by North Carolina under Democratic rule, which were also covered in the paper, this league meeting and others like it provided a forum for Republican candidates to reach out to voters.

Such bipartisan voter mobilization was not limited to clubwomen, nor even to literate southerners who experienced these events through local newspapers. In Alabama, for example, politically active white women sponsored a program for the rural women of Gumtersville just weeks before the 1924 election. Before a small group of farm women who "shy at the term school," local speakers gave talks, "one on the history and principles of the democratic party, one on the republican."[80] The next day, a member of the League of Women Voters spoke to an assembled crowd of "between four and five hundred farmers." As part of their "Trade Day" activities, these rural white men spent twenty minutes listening to a woman exhort them to vote, in nonpartisan terms. When her speech was concluded, the activist reported a "very gratifying" response from these "horny handed sons of toil."[81]

During campaign seasons, local leagues throughout the South also sponsored mass meetings of men and women in which all candidates for a given office were invited to speak. Like other nonpartisan events sponsored by the league, these mass meetings offered minority parties and candidates the opportunity to take their message to a wide audience. The Louisville League of Women Voters sponsored just such a meeting on the eve of the 1928 general election. There a Republican, a Democrat, and a Socialist stood before women voters and explained their positions on five issues of concern to women, including prohibition enforcement and Sheppard-Towner programs. Three newspapers provided coverage of the event, and the women organizers reported "wide interest in the meeting."[82] For party leaders, however, the subversive potential of such gatherings was plain, as the women titled their preelection meeting "How Shall I Vote?"[83] In a direct challenge to notions of party loyalty, such gatherings assumed that women voters would choose among the parties represented.

While these mass meetings, particularly those that offered a day-long picnic with the political message, seemed reminiscent of energetic and enthusiastic Gilded Age political meetings, the nonpartisan events were the very antithesis of the masculine and militaristic displays of partisan loyalty that had characterized late-nineteenth-century mass politics. These mass meetings, and the questionnaires that league leaders distributed to candidates to determine their policy positions, provided a venue for voters to "inquire diligently into the qualifications and purposes of all candidates, regardless of party lines, before casting a ballot."[84] While league leaders and many Progressive southern white women believed the region's politics could be purified through such nonpartisan deliberation, the region's Democratic Party leaders had maintained control of the system for decades by assuring southern voters that they need not think twice.

Many historians have contended that this rise of "educational politics" and the transformation of politics into a "domesticated space" contributed to the declining voter turnout that characterized the early twentieth century.[85] In the South, however, these changes may have had quite the opposite effect, as the purification of politics and elite support for casting independent ballots threatened to revive inter- or at least intraparty competition in the region. Instead of the exciting partisan battles that had once attracted voters to the polls in overwhelming numbers, the elections of the first decades of the twentieth century offered voters lopsided competitions staged increasingly by state officials rather than partisan boosters. Scholars agree that new registration and voting laws narrowed the scope of the electorate and that the absence of vigorous partisan competition spurred electoral demobilization. Although woman suffrage was not the primary cause of declining voter turnouts, political scientist Paul Kleppner has demonstrated that the entry of women into electoral politics "coincided with the onset of political conditions that served to deflate turnout . . . creat[ing] a political environment that retarded the mobilization of newly enfranchised women."[86] Nevertheless, in the South it was the newly enfranchised women who worked to increase voter turnout for the first time since disfranchisement. They organized to help potential voters register and cast their ballots, and their nonpartisan rallies and meetings offered the possibility of a revival of partisan competition. Far from contributing to electoral demobilization in the South, the feminization of the polls and women's demands for electoral reforms cracked opened the door to vigorous political competition in the region.

In fact, southern league leaders deliberately and publicly flirted with the Republican Party in many of their voter outreach activities. For example, in Tennessee, a league organizer visited headquarters of both the Republican and the Democratic state central committees in order to solicit support for the league's activities, and the chairmen of both parties' women's organizations were invited to an organizational meeting of the league.[87] In Texas, each congressional district was represented in the state League of Women Voters by two women — one Republican, and one Democrat.[88] In Alabama, the most successful voter mobilization drive in 1924 was conducted by the Chilton County League of Women Voters, which helped to boost voter turnout to 84 percent in that staunchly Republican county.[89] Many of the league members in Charlotte and Mecklenburg, North Carolina, who "began 'shelling the woods'" to enroll new voters were themselves Republicans.[90]

In Kentucky, which supported competitive Republican and Democratic Parties, partisans on both sides saw the league's nonpartisan voter mobilization activities as a threat. The league in that state was "composed of members of all political faiths," and both Republican and Democratic women served as officers.[91] League leaders regularly invited representatives from the two major parties to share space at their meetings, not only in candidate forums, but also in meetings devoted to discussions of legislative matters.[92] The Kentucky league worked closely with the Democratic and Republican state committees during their voter mobilization drives, going so far as to ask each party for a "list of the women who are serving at the polls on election day."[93] Activists then contacted those partisan women and asked them to assist the league in its effort to get "all the women who are eligible out to register this fall."[94] In the face of such nonpartisan (or bipartisan) efforts, Kentucky league leaders found their organization accused by partisans of being an "adjunct" of one party or the other.[95] Democrats objected to the organization's willingness to work with Republicans, and as one white club-woman explained, "Republicans regard the L.W.V. as an attempt to wean Republican women from their party allegiance."[96]

With very few exceptions, southern leagues remained committed to the merits of nonpartisanship, and to the dismay of many Democratic men, nonpartisanship meant encouraging the votes of Republicans and Demo-crats alike. In Pittsylvania County, Virginia, politically active white women contacted Democratic *and* Republican Party leaders for assistance in staging a countywide voter registration drive. If this solicitation of Republican Party assistance were not enough to convey the message, one woman made the point clear: "I do not want the Democratic Party to feel that we are binding ourselves in the least to them."[97] In a response that undoubtedly resembled that of Pittsylvania County Republicans, the chairman of the Republican Ex-ecutive Committee for Wake County, North Carolina, said he would "gladly accept" the offer of his county League of Women Voters to work together "in getting the women registered and in seeing that the opportunity to vote just as they please, without solicitation or interference, is theirs on the day of election."[98]

Even in Mississippi, league leaders refused to toe the Democratic Party line: they devoted a front-page story in their bulletin to the candidacy of a Republican for the state's Third Congressional District seat. As the women put it, "If Mr. Montgomery condemns himself in the eyes of time-honored Democrats by being on the Republican side of the fence, let us at least say for him that he is an out-and-out clean man — honest, conscientious, scrupulous in all dealings with his fellow man."[99] While the league's nonpartisanship prevented the organization from issuing candidate endorsements, Mont-gomery and Democrats alike must have thought that the Mississippi women came quite close in their praise for the candidate.[100] In a tone hardly distin-guishable from an endorsement, they commended Montgomery's honesty, his southern heritage, and his support for prohibition, "a single standard of morality for men and women" and an "equal deal for men and women in all walks of life."[101] In South Carolina, league leaders publicly endorsed the revival of two-party politics, declaring, "If one party is always sure to win no matter what candidates they put up, they have little incentive to live up to a high standard."[102] Through all these activities, many ordinary white women received tacit encouragement to vote Republican from the same influential women who first engaged them in the political system.

Occasionally, the encouragement to vote Republican was more than tacit. In Virginia, one of the state's founding suffragists abandoned her Demo-cratic Party ties altogether and declared her opposition to the Solid South, campaigning for the state's Republican nominee for governor in 1921.[103] In Texas, Minnie Fisher Cunningham joined forces with other anti-Ferguson Democrats when she bolted the party and campaigned for the Republican candidate for governor in 1924. Although the Republican failed to win, he polled "four times the vote that the GOP candidate had mustered in 1922," and women were widely credited with providing his support.[104] One Texas activist condemned the unquestioning loyalty of white men to the Democratic Party, lamenting that "the party collar was too firmly fixed around their own necks for them to join with their independent spouses."[105] But the ease with which many "Democratic" women bolted the ticket unnerved party leaders. Sue Shelton White, a prominent Democratic woman in Tennessee, set a frightening political example as she worked with the National Woman's Party to support the election of a Republican woman to Congress.[106] Though she kept a low profile in the fight, White helped facilitate political coordination between the woman candidate and the National Woman's Party, and she refused to work on behalf of the candidate's Democratic opponent. Such public displays of partisan disloyalty on the part of Democratic women were rare, but they only served to reinforce the notion held by Democratic men that white women's party loyalty could not be trusted.

Of course, some white women were loyal partisans. Despite their long exclusion from the ballot box, many women had adopted strong partisan identities, and those historic loyalties guided them once they joined men at the polls.[107] Other women committed themselves to the Democratic Party because they believed it best suited their policy priorities, particularly in its safeguarding of states' rights and white supremacy. Former antisuffragists like Marie Bankhead Owen were often especially active in their displays of partisan loyalty.[108] Partisan women offered counsel to male party leaders about the voting habits of other white women, and they often warned Democratic leaders of the threat that white women voters posed to the party.[109] In this regard, white partisan women offered southern Democrats precisely what they had hoped for when women were enfranchised — more loyal Democratic white voters. But the behavior of other white southern clubwomen (and occasionally even "loyal" Democratic women themselves) suggested that there were far fewer partisan women than party leaders might have expected.

Partisan and nonpartisan women alike recognized that much political power in the region rested in the Democratic Party, and both types of women sought access to this power. In Louisiana, Tennessee, and Texas, organized white women called for legislative action to ensure equal representation on political party committees.[110] And many of the white women who sat on party councils in the South were also members of the nonpartisan League of Women Voters. The North Carolina League of Women Voters boasted in 1924 that both the Democratic and the Republican Committeewomen, as well as all four of the female delegates-at-large to the Democratic National Convention, had league connections.[111] While league leaders worked hard to ensure that the partisanship of their members did not call into question the credibility of the league's nonpartisan stance, the willingness of "Democratic" women to work alongside Republican women in the electoral activities of the league must have given party leaders some pause.[112]

Within the parties, Democratic women worked to leverage their constituency for specific policy choices. For example, in North Carolina, female Democratic leaders met "soon after every election." "We get together," one woman explained, "and decide what we will ask of the party, in return for our work."[113] In Mississippi, WCTU member and state legislator Nellie Nugent Somerville staged an alternate convention and challenged the legitimacy of the ruling Democrats in Washington County. After months of fighting and a climactic final battle before the state's Democratic Executive Committee, the state party leaders "recognized her faction to handle affairs of the party in her county."[114] Although a number of issues were at stake, including a reputed dispute between Klan and anti-Klan forces, Somerville and her followers claimed that their victory was "one of right against might — of prohibition enforcement against alleged wet tendencies."[115] As she seized control of the party committee in her part of the state, Somerville signaled the threat that even partisan women posed to the power long held by Democratic men.

EVEN IN THOSE PLACES, like Louisiana, Mississippi, and South Carolina, where Republican opposition was not a credible threat, white women challenged the control of Democratic Party leaders through the primary system. Politically active white women recognized that primaries offered the most important political competition in many parts of the region, and during primary election seasons, white clubwomen articulated their nonpartisanship as a refusal to ally with any one faction or candidate. Throughout the South, Leagues of Women Voters used the same kinds of voter mobilization techniques to encourage primary participation as they did to get voters to the polls in November, and they publicized information on primary candidates' policy positions so that voters could make informed choices. They staged mass meetings of all the primary candidates, issued candidate questionnaires, and met with candidates individually to determine their positions on issues of concern to organized women. State and local leagues extended their nonpartisanship to primary battles by refusing to endorse primary candidates, and these activists encouraged citizens to vote without regard to

whom they might vote for. One disgusted Democrat in South Carolina registered his dismay as he "spied a woman joyriding to the polls with a carload
of women voters," two of whom were supporting a candidate not endorsed
by the woman driver or the disgusted observer. When confronted with her
political heresy, the woman driver responded, "They are members of the
League of Women Voters and I am helping to get out the woman vote!"[116] As
this poor party stalwart realized, women voters could be a disruptive force,
with or without real interparty competition. Activists in Mississippi urged
new women voters to resist alliances with Democratic factions and instead
cast their ballots as independents. In the weekly bulletin of the Mississippi
League of Women Voters, the league's president bluntly assessed the political
scene, "The women voters of Mississippi are at the crossroads. Two ways lie
before them. One way is alliance with one of the two factions of the state. The
other is political independence. . . . They will take the way of independence,
which women have discovered to be the only way by which they can make
their vote count."[117]

The region's white female political leaders were determined that women's
ballots would count for something, and they consistently fought the Democratic Party's use of nominating conventions to control politics. Nominating
conventions enabled party leaders to select nominees without regard to the
wishes of women voters, or any other constituents. White women throughout the South fought to preserve the power of their ballots by demanding
that party leaders hold primaries for the selection of the party's nominees.
These women reformers recognized that candidates seeking nomination in
a direct primary system would have to court voters, not party leaders, and
would therefore be more easily persuaded to endorse policy positions favored by organized white women. Moreover, the direct primary deprived
parties of the power to nominate candidates, "the single most important
source of their authority," in the opinion of one historian.[118] Shorn of this
power, politically active white women believed, the Democratic Party would
become more responsive to the wishes of voters.

To be sure, the direct primary system, particularly in the South, had its
antidemocratic elements. First and foremost, the direct primary in the South
was restricted to whites only, barring even those few African Americans
who remained eligible to vote in general elections. Moreover, as historian J.
Morgan Kousser has pointed out, the white primary was designed by Democratic Party leaders in the South to "substitute intra- for interparty competition."[119] By settling policy differences or party squabbles before the general
election and barring defeated candidates from opposing the party's nominee
in November, the white primary allowed southern Democrats to present a
united front and further stifle partisan competition in the region. In some

southern states, like Virginia, primary voters could lose their right to participate in future primary elections if they voted against the party's nominee in the general election. Clearly, the white primary was a system that was designed to serve the southern Democratic Party and white supremacy.

By 1920, however, disfranchisement laws and the subsequent decimation of the Republican Party in most of the region had left the Democrats decidedly in control. By the time newly enfranchised women entered the political fray, the white primary had become the sole venue for political competition in many parts of the region. Organized southern white women recognized that "the politicians do not want the women to have the power of deciding elections and issues."[120] As one Mississippi clubwoman announced to her readers, "By staying outside we shall be free to support the faction or factional candidate that is the most nearly right."[121] An Atlanta woman explained, "Primary nominations are the actual elections, the general ticket regular election being only a ratification proceeding."[122] Under the circumstances, many white women were convinced that the use of nominating conventions to select Democratic candidates would essentially nullify the Nineteenth Amendment, robbing them of the opportunity to participate in the only election that mattered.

Indeed, the experience of white women in Claremont, Virginia, suggested that Democratic political leaders hoped to do just that. In 1924 local Democratic bosses in Claremont, Virginia, rejected the results of a party caucus attended by women and instead staged a secret nominating convention attended exclusively by male members of the machine. A woman from Claremont wrote to leaders of the League of Women Voters in her state, looking for redress. In the absence of a primary system, however, women voters were powerless. In response to the incident, league leaders instructed the Claremont woman that prompt protest through party channels or a write-in campaign might have allowed the women to "beat the 'ring' at its own game."[123] But politically active white women recognized that primary elections were the only way to ensure their participation in the nominating process.

Thus, throughout the region, white women worked with sympathetic party leaders to "urg[e] localities to arrange primaries."[124] They publicly denounced the use of conventions in place of primary elections. They distributed information on the merits of the direct primary. And they worked hard not only to open the nominating process to primary voters but to get those voters to the polls. They staged car pools, house-to-house canvasses, and publicity campaigns to register new voters and get them to the polls on primary day. In Atlanta, organized women voters went further, demanding that the date of the primary elections be changed "in order that more people will be in town at the time of the primary than are here in the summer."[125] Although they never challenged the racial exclusiveness of the region's white primary, politically active southern white women nevertheless saw the primary as an essential element of a more democratic, more responsive politics. As one Virginia activist explained, "There is nothing the professional politician respects and fears so much as a large vote."[126]

Through the pamphlets and broadsides they used to motivate reluctant women voters, league leaders called on women to use their ballots to fix a political system that was broken. One campaign-season slogan used by the league warned that "minority vote is really a controlled vote, it puts the power in the hands of the machine rather than of the people."[127] Another typical slogan read, "Are you willing for a few self appointed bosses to decide on your taxes, your schools, your roads?"[128] In North Carolina, a prominent white woman gave a speech in 1927 denouncing "the methods of the Grandole [sic] Democratic Party" in her state.[129] As she put it, "Nowhere are machine politics very savory. They stink in North Carolina as elsewhere."[130] On the front page of the Woman Voter, Mississippi women attacked factional politics, bossism, bribery, and machine politics, urging the women of the state to use their ballots to "clean up politics."[131] Through these appeals white women called on voters to challenge the status quo.

White female activists coupled these demands for political change with a determination to battle election fraud. Throughout the decade, political women demanded that white women be appointed as registrars, poll watchers, and election clerks, and they denounced the partisan administration of these civic duties. The league's efforts to place women in the polls as judges and clerks not only served to change the social drama of politics but also threatened the prerogatives of machine men who were used to counting their own votes. As one league member wrote in 1921, "Haven't heard whether you were successful in getting Mrs. Jobson on the Electoral Board, but I certainly hope so — it would be the beginning of the death blow to some of the gentlemen's manoeuvres."[132] Another southern woman reported that league members in her county opposed the use of absentee ballots and worked to "keep some of the people from being voted two or three times."[133] In North Carolina, Gertrude Weil simply marched in to her Wayne County polling place and eliminated the corruption herself, destroying all of the ballots that local Democratic bosses had marked for the machine candidate.[134]

White women in Alabama, disgusted with the conditions they found as poll watchers in Mobile, took their case to court, contesting the election of county officials in the November 1920 elections. According to white women activists, party leaders issued instructions to voters, candidates enjoyed unrestricted access to polling places, and, most egregiously, party operatives allowed ballots to be removed from the precinct and marked elsewhere.

Despite what the women believed to be compelling evidence, a grand jury dismissed these charges. Nevertheless, these white women did gain a victory of sorts as city leaders restructured election day practices and these activists found no evidence of fraud in the 1921 elections.[135] From Gertrude Weil's destruction of marked ballots in North Carolina to the contestation of election results by the women of Mobile, politically active white women worked to ensure that Democratic Party leaders could no longer rely on fraud to guarantee their party's — or their preferred candidate's — victory.

PERHAPS MOST STRIKING, rare coalitions of black and white women voters allied against the Democratic machine suggested that party leaders could not rely entirely on white supremacy either. In Savannah, white reformers called on black voters to help them oust a "corrupt machine" government that reforming Democrats could not defeat on their own.[136] In the Democratic primary election in December 1922, the incumbent mayor, M. M. Stewart, confronted challenger James M. Rogers, who represented prohibition and reform forces in the city.[137] Newspapers described the primary election as "the bitterest and closest municipal fight ever waged in Savannah" and reported widespread fighting and other "old-time scenes . . . despite the presence of hundreds of women" at the polls.[138] When the ballots were counted, the incumbent had won by a majority of just ten votes.[139] Election day had been marred by voting irregularities, including illegal voting and missing ballot boxes, and Rogers supporters challenged the election results.[140] When the local Democratic Executive Committee upheld Stewart's renomination, the "Rogers Faction" bolted the party. Because of the loyalty pledge required of all Democratic candidates for office, Rogers was barred from running as an Independent in the general municipal election. His supporters recruited Judge Paul Seabrook to stand for the reform forces in the general election, and reformers "invoked the aid of leading Negro citizens who brought out the full Negro vote."[141] With the aid of African Americans, white reformers defeated the incumbent mayor by a considerable margin.[142]

It was no coincidence that this success came in a community in which nearly a dozen black women were members of the National League of Republican Colored Women.[143] Savannah was also home to the state's Republican National Committeewoman, a prominent black clubwoman by the name of Mrs. George S. Williams. Despite threats of violence, these politically active black clubwomen worked to mobilize black voters in their community in support of the anti-administration forces.[144] While some black women voters may have been influenced by their "white mistresses," as one observer contended, the *Crisis* characterized the election as one in which black voters exercised this "balance of power" in pursuit of "their own interests."[145]

Successful biracial alliances of women voters like that forged in 1919 by Nashville's women, or even the less unified coalition in Savannah, were exceedingly rare. Nevertheless, there were scattered reports of politically active white women working with black women to open up southern polls to African Americans. Former suffrage leader Lulu Reese waged an unsuccessful campaign to unite black and white working-class women in Memphis in opposition to the city's reform candidates.[146] In Chattanooga as well, a biracial coalition of voters failed to materialize, but former suffragist Abby Milton worked hard in the weeks prior to the election to encourage African American women to register and vote. She had hoped they would vote Democratic, but when their votes were credited with the Republican victory in the city, she became an ardent proponent of the poll tax.[147]

While Milton encouraged African American women to vote in a misguided attempt to bolster the Democratic Party, most of the southern white women who worked to increase African American voter participation did so fully aware that African Americans would likely cast their ballots for Republicans. Just as they did in the white community, these politically active white women provided African American clubwomen with information on voting or materials for citizenship education regardless of party affiliation. For example, Republicans in Georgia who contacted the NAACP for information on voting and citizenship education were provided with League of Women Voters publications.[148] In Atlanta, the League of Women Voters appointed a committee to consult with African American leaders about citizenship education for the city's black residents.[149] Viola Ross Napier, a league member and one of Georgia's Democratic state legislators, was routinely asked by African American church groups for information on voting.[150] Even in South Carolina, organized white women helped African Americans in Charleston organize a Colored Civic League.[151] While these scattered reports do not suggest that white women led a charge for the full enfranchisement of African Americans, they do indicate that some of the region's most politically active white women and prominent political organizations of white women were surprisingly unconcerned about maintaining the polls for whites only.

According to the National Association of Colored Women's Clubs, local Leagues of Women Voters sponsored citizenship classes for African American women in all the southern states where black women could vote; Tennessee and Virginia were singled out for praise as states where the leagues and African American women's clubs had particularly close working relationships.[152] White women in Louisville, Kentucky, asked permission to organize an affiliated "league for colored women voters" in their city.[153] In their voter mobilization efforts, too, white women occasionally included black women. In 1924, as Birmingham's white women organized for a massive voter registration campaign, they invited several representatives of the Alabama Federation of Colored Women's Clubs to participate in a meeting concerning local get-out-the-vote activities.[154] In North Carolina as well, historian Sarah Wilkerson-Freeman has found that white women conducted voter mobilization activities in "black and white neighborhoods" alike.[155]

In Virginia, Adéle Clark, the president of the Virginia League of Women Voters, offered her support to black clubwomen who were organizing voter registration efforts in Richmond. Maggie Lena Walker and other African American women had already worked to bring thousands of African American women voters to the polls by the time that Clark called, offering assistance with citizenship study.[156] On election day, Clark and several other white women drove to the polling places in African American neighborhoods "just to see if everything was going quietly." As she described it years later, despite the "threats of bloodshed and riot and everything else . . . the Negro women went up quietly and voted, but I think they were very much heartened by the fact that there were four or five white women that went to the polls to give them their backing."[157] No doubt African American women were even more heartened when Adéle Clark publicly announced her support for black women's registration. When asked by a reporter about "the negro issue," this prominent white suffragist responded, "Many negro women are entitled to register and will be placed on the books." She went on to defend these black women voters by characterizing them as good Progressive women, insisting, "During the World War, Richmond negro women did fine work. They are interested in the schools."[158]

In Hampton and Phoebus, Virginia, scores of well-educated African American women, many of whom were associated with Hampton College, faced humiliation and rejection as they attempted to register to vote. As black men and women sought assistance from Republican Party leaders, the NAACP, and local lawyers to exercise their rights of suffrage, a white woman who had long been involved in the suffrage movement happened to arrive in town on other matters. Upon discovering the situation among African American women, she "missed a train to Richmond in order to go to the registrar with a colored woman who had been refused," but, the report continued, "she was able to do nothing."[159] She may not have been able to force the registration of any black women, and there is no indication that she or any other politically active white women pursued this injustice any further, but her presence escorting an African American woman to the polls must have shocked the registrar. Her efforts were, undoubtedly, soon well known to

Democratic Party leaders. Certainly these were isolated incidents, but they signaled to Democratic Party leaders that for at least some white women, the determination to expand the electorate did not end at the color line.

For most white women, to be sure, the desire to expand the electorate did clearly end at the color line. League membership throughout the region was restricted to whites only, and newspapers undoubtedly would have taken note if white women's organizations had worked consistently to register black women. While there were scattered instances of white women's support for black women's voting rights, there were many more occasions when southern white women supported efforts to disfranchise their black sisters. An Alabama woman wrote to national league leaders to apologize for her failure to appoint someone to the Committee to Study Negro Problems, and her words captured the racial attitudes of most politically active southern white women: "Unfortunately, many of our women do not see the responsibility or feel the obligation to work at this."[160]

Nevertheless, the mere presence of African American women and white women casting ballots in newly decorous public polling places demonstrated that white southern Democrats would not be able to control elections in the same ways that they had in the past. Certainly, disfranchisement methods would continue to keep the vast majority of African Americans from casting ballots, and violence would remain a threat to black voters in many parts of the South for decades. Yet with their emphasis on clean politics, transparency in election laws, nonpartisanship, and an expanded electorate, white women signaled their distance from the party of Redemption and disfranchisement.

WITH THE RATIFICATION of the Nineteenth Amendment, southern women — white and black — set about to take advantage of their rights as voters. To the chagrin of many party leaders, they consistently resisted efforts to bind them to one party or the other. Certainly, women voters did not make the South a competitive two-party region during the 1920s. Women, and most frighteningly to Democratic leaders, *white women*, did, however, pose a credible threat to the party's power. Black women, whenever they could vote, mobilized to challenge the party of Redemption, and even the party of Lincoln, when the Republican Party failed to serve them. White women worked to expand the electorate, advocated that voters *not* toe the Democratic Party line, and mobilized women to vote against the Democratic Party's chosen candidates if those men failed to heed women's demands. Nonpartisanship itself and white women's repeated attacks on machine politics and party corruption made being something other than a Democrat seem plausible. In the

1920s, for the first time since the Populist revolt, white women voters made it acceptable to *not* be a rabid Democrat but rather a discerning, nonpartisan voter who might split her ticket. Politically active white women did these things in part out of a philosophical conviction that government would be less corrupt and the people better served if inter- or at least intraparty competition kept political leaders attentive to voters' demands. But they also had more utilitarian motives. Organized white women conscientiously protected their nonpartisan credentials and publicly encouraged party competition in order to enhance their own power as voters and as lobbyists. Faced with this threat, southern Democrats in the 1920s had to contain the challenges that women voters posed by changing their campaign styles, making policy concessions, and offering white women some access to political power.

Chapter Five

The Best Weapon for Reform
Women Lobbying with the Vote

On 16 October 1923, clubwomen from across Kentucky met in Louisville for a conference of state women's organizations. Before the assembled women, the Republican and Democratic nominees for governor stood for questioning. The state's League of Women Voters, Parent Teacher Association (PTA), Home Economics Association, Consumers League, Woman's Christian Temperance Union (WCTU), Business and Professional Women, Girls' Friendly Society, Daughters of Isabella, and Social Hygiene Association were coordinating their work through a joint legislative council, and the issues that the gubernatorial candidates faced reflected the council's agenda. The women asked pointed questions about the candidates' commitment to prohibition enforcement and adequate appropriations for the state's Board of Corrections and Charities. They asked the candidates to "pledge" their "utmost support" and "agree, if elected," to advance the legislative agenda presented that day. Just three weeks before election day, both of Kentucky's candidates for governor spent precious time campaigning — side by side — before a group of demanding women. They did not send surrogates, and they did not decline the women's invitation. When the men were done, the assembled women transcribed the candidates' responses for distribution to other women and for future reference.[1]

As this episode demonstrates, activist white women recognized that the Nineteenth Amendment marked an important turning point in southern politics. It changed not only who cast ballots but also who counted as a constituent. With their votes, women commanded the attention of political candidates, and they used that opportunity to make politicians respond to legislative demands. White women reformers, who had long lobbied the political leaders of their region in support of legislative reform, understood the way their position had changed as a result of enfranchisement, and they embraced the vote as a powerful new weapon in their persuasive arsenal. Immediately upon their enfranchisement they adopted innovative and sophisticated lobbying techniques based on the power of women as voters. While they certainly continued to argue the merits of their legislative proposals, organized white women increasingly confronted their legislators with an electoral threat. No longer did they go to legislators as supplicants, requesting their support for legislation simply because it was the right thing to do. After 1920, southern white women approached their representatives as constituents and lobbied their legislators armed with the vote.

Organized African American women, by contrast, remained largely unarmed. As much or more than white women, they recognized the potential of the ballot as a weapon for reform. Despite their widespread and concerted efforts to seize the opportunities offered by the Nineteenth Amendment, however, African American women were largely unsuccessful in obtaining access to southern polls. Thus, as white women's political power surged in this period, the inability of organized African American women to obtain increased support from the state testified both to the racism of the region's white leaders and to the power of the ballots denied African Americans.

A cartoon published in the *Woman Voter*, a bulletin for Mississippi clubwomen, expressed the optimism that southern white women shared for the power of the ballot.[2] The caption, "He'll Have to 'Kiss the Baby' Now," signaled southern white women's belief that elected officials would be forced to offer legislative reforms in exchange for women's votes. Female political leaders in Virginia echoed that sentiment when they called on newly enfranchised women "to endorse with their votes the measures they have hitherto been unable to support effectively."[3] A South Carolina activist declared that woman "is no longer a supplicant" and warned that "the ballot is a powerful weapon built for striking."[4] The Georgia League of Women Voters similarly described the vote as "The Best Weapon for Reform," and the president of the North Carolina Federation of Women's Clubs reminded clubwomen that "there is only one way actually to achieve progress and reform and that is through the ballot."[5] Throughout the region, in private correspondence and public pronouncements, southern white women expressed faith that their ballots would bolster their demands for reform. Clubwomen and suffragists alike were convinced that women would be able to "take advantage of enfranchisement as a means of securing the reforms for which they formerly worked indirectly."[6]

Most scholars have contended that after their long struggle for the vote had ended, women were unable to leverage their ballots in the ways that they had hoped.[7] Some studies have suggested that having pursued reform for so long as outsiders to the formal political system, organized women found it difficult to craft lobbying strategies that effectively capitalized on their new

HE'LL HAVE TO "KISS THE BABY" NOW!

Cartoon depicting new policy outcomes that white clubwomen expected from legislators as a consequence of enfranchisement (courtesy Mississippi Department of Archives and History)

position as voters.[8] Indeed, sociologist Elisabeth Clemens has argued that "having mobilized around identities and organizational forms defined in opposition to party politics, women activists found it difficult to mobilize as a bloc within the electoral system" once the vote was won.[9] Moreover, scholarly emphasis on the continuities in women's pre- and postsuffrage reform activity suggests that women's political behavior was essentially unchanged by enfranchisement.[10] Yet the experiences of organized southern white women demonstrate that both the meaning and the consequences of their lobbying strategies changed as a result of the Nineteenth Amendment.

IT IS TRUE that having lobbied for decades on behalf of social welfare and good government reforms, newly enfranchised women were not strangers to the political arena. As recent studies have shown, southern white women served their "political apprenticeship" in Progressive Era reform organizations and found ways to win legislative victories even without suffrage.[11] The lobbying tactics they developed before 1920 had served them well, and women reformers did not abandon them with the arrival of suffrage. As they had before enfranchisement, white women continued to make well-reasoned arguments on behalf of the legislation they sponsored. They visited with their legislators, sent them long and thoughtful missives, wrote persuasive letters to the editor, and testified at hearings on the merits of legislation. But they also approached their representatives with something to bargain with: women's votes. Thus, while there were great similarities between white women's lobbying efforts in the pre- and postsuffrage periods, even apparently similar tactics differed in key ways as a result of enfranchisement.

White clubwomen recognized that "it is always easier for a man to fight for a measure when there is a general interest manifested in it," and they crafted their lobbying strategies — before and after 1920 — to demonstrate the strength of that interest.[12] Before they were enfranchised, white women demonstrated the public interest in their legislative priorities by using publicity to arouse public opinion. As Theda Skocpol has explained, unenfranchised clubwomen effectively used "moralistic publicity and talk to reshape public opinion and the opinions of well-placed male citizens as well as officials."[13] Through "educational tactics" that ranged "from conversations with husbands to the orchestration of national and local publicity," unenfranchised women pressed the merits of their legislative proposals.[14] The success of these campaigns, however, depended upon white women's ability to persuade *men* of the rightness, and righteousness, of their cause. Once enfranchised, white clubwomen no longer had to rely on their ability to persuade male voters to support their cause; women's political opinions carried weight of their own. The contrast between southern women's lobbying tactics before and after 1920 illustrate the change. During one of their most successful legislative campaigns before 1920, Alabama's women fought for child labor regulation in their state. And one of their central lobbying activities during that 1903 session of the legislature was "to give to each member of the legislature . . . a pamphlet . . . listing the arguments for and against child labor."[15] Twenty years later, Virginia's enfranchised clubwomen made a point of placing "a brief mimeographed letter . . . on the desk of each legislator, asking his support" for the legislation they endorsed. These enfranchised lobbyists insisted that the letter include "the names of the organizations they represent," but "brief arguments for the bill" were only to be included "if practicable."[16] Reasoned arguments still mattered, of course, but during a legislative floor fight, *enfranchised* white clubwomen presented their legislators not with a pamphlet to persuade but with a letter that indicated the electoral strength of the bill's supporters.

Petitions and letter-writing campaigns were a staple of white women's lobbying techniques by the time the Nineteenth Amendment was ratified. Clubwomen seeking prison reform, prohibition laws, mothers' pensions, and suffrage itself sent letters to public officials to "let [their] wants be made known."[17] Nevertheless, as historian Stacey Horstmann has demonstrated, even as they expressed faith in the importance of this correspondence, white women confessed that "letters, cards and telegrams *from voters* are what really count."[18] Consequently, once women became voters, the nature of these letter-writing campaigns changed. In a letter to Senators Glass and Swanson in 1921, Josephine E. Houston wrote, "Your *constituents* are thoroughly in sympathy with sanitary and economic provisions set forth in this bill."[19] After enfranchisement, white women leaders consciously employed a rhetoric of women as voters in these appeals. Writing to urge passage of the same bill, another Virginian advised, "This measure has endorsement of *women voters* in all sections of [the] State."[20] In Atlanta, organized white women called on the governor to protect the Department of Public Welfare, insisting that "it is considered absolutely essential by the *women voters*."[21] Even in its name, the League of Women Voters called attention to the new political position occupied by women. When league leaders wrote to their representatives to say "we were sorry to note that you did not feel justified in supporting" our legislation, or "we ask that you vote for Demonstration Work appropriations," elected officials well knew that "we" signified a group of women who were paying attention and would go to the polls.[22]

This marked an important departure from the letter-writing campaigns of the presuffrage era. Despite obvious similarities in their calls for cards and telegrams, women reformers in the postsuffrage era did not have to enlist men in their letter-writing campaigns. Before 1920, white clubwomen recognized the importance in having men sign their petitions or send letters to their representatives, "as they are voters."[23] After 1920, however, white clubwomen did not have to find men willing to sign on to their demands. They could rely on their well-organized female club memberships to generate pressure on legislators, without worrying that the missives were "only signed by a 'bunch of women.'"[24] Consequently, the lobbying directives from white women's clubs after 1920 no longer emphasized the need for women to "'use their influence' with the men in their lives."[25] Instead, they frequently encouraged women to write their own letters and to encourage other women to do the same.

In this new era of lobbying, the sheer volume of calls or letters from women to their legislators also took on added significance. Before enfranchisement, when women's lobbying efforts were devoted to changing public opinion, one well-reasoned argument might be worth more than a dozen letters from women that simply implored elected officials for their support. Once women were enfranchised, however, each letter from a woman represented a vote. For that reason, leaders of women's organizations throughout the South routinely called on their members to contact their representatives on behalf of specific legislation. Activist women in Kentucky, for example, mailed 12,000 letters to "fellow voter[s]" calling on "the women of the state" to "wire or write" to their representatives "immediately" in support of the state Board of Health.[26] In Texas, the leader of the WCTU called on its members to contact their representatives in support of a minimum wage bill, and she asked local leaders to "report the number of letters" that women in their district sent in.[27] In Alabama white clubwomen organized a massive letter-writing campaign to persuade Congressman George Huddleston "of the tremendous sentiment back of the Maternity bill."[28] The plan for that campaign specifically encouraged women to set "a goal of so many letters from influential people daily."[29] Female political leaders believed that legislators would find it hard to ignore a "constant stream of requests" from women voters in their district.[30] Once they were enfranchised, organized white women pursued their policy goals by ensuring that elected officials "realize what their Woman constituents want and how strongly they want it."[31]

The Nineteenth Amendment not only changed whose letters mattered, but it also changed the content of the letters themselves. In the presuffrage era, women reformers focused on crafting compelling arguments for the legislative reforms they demanded. As one historian put it, unenfranchised women "seemed to understand that as non-voters, they needed to do more than express their opinion, they needed to make an argument."[32] After 1920, just being a woman with an opinion was enough to matter. In a letter to North Carolina women, the Mecklenburg League of Women Voters merely listed its legislative program, noted that the Woman's Club, the PTA, the Business and Professional Women, and the WCTU were all supporting the same platform and urged the state's women to "write your legislators how you stand on them."[33] No supporting information was provided about the items on the legislative agenda, and no suggestion was made that women include such reasoning in their own letters to their legislators. South Carolina women were urged to "appoint a committee to go before your county delegation when it meets and have as many women as possible talk to the legislators after their meeting."[34] Female political activists did not encourage local women to send one particularly well-informed and articulate woman to persuade state legislators of the merits of their legislative agenda. Rather, they recommended sending "as many women as possible."

While these entreaties undoubtedly contained some reasoned arguments in support of the desired legislation, female political leaders were unselfconscious in their focus on the volume of letters women could generate. "Eloquence, reason, and appeals to chivalry," which had served as the foundation of southern white women's lobbying efforts before 1920, were immediately augmented (and often superseded) by a focus on organized women's electoral strength.[35] As one prominent Georgia woman put it, "When a representative is deluged with letters and telegrams from his district or state he is apt to step carefully and not go against what his constituents want."[36] Another activist explained, "If the solicitor is persuaded that to refuse to help . . . will lose him the women's vote it might have weight with him. Of course we could not tell him that in plain English, but if enough women would approach him on the subject he could come to that conclusion himself."[37]

In these appeals, female political leaders were always careful to encourage their members to contact representatives from their own district. The North Carolina League of Women Voters made the point clearly: "Nothing holds so much weight with a Legislator as the wishes of his constituents. Nothing will be so likely to win the support of YOUR Legislators for these measures as YOUR request for their support."[38] An activist in Georgia reminded white clubwomen of the need for support from the women "'back home,' because," she explained, "the man you send wants to do the things that will please the greatest number of his constituents."[39] These grassroots campaigns demonstrated to legislators that their own constituents wanted them to vote a certain way and that those constituents were watching to make sure that they did.

In addition to encouraging as many women as possible to write letters of their own, white female political leaders emphasized the large number of voters they represented when they wrote or wired public officials. For example, in a letter to Congressman William Harris of Georgia, the Clarksville League of Women Voters made sure that their representative knew exactly how many women voters cared about the Newton Bill by listing each member's name individually.[40] Similarly, the Birmingham Council of Women's Clubs sent a telegram to the governor that focused exclusively on the number of constituents who opposed the measure rather than the failings of the legislation itself: "The B'ham Council of Women's Clubs composed of 53 organizations and representing over 2500 women earnestly request you to veto the bill permitting the election of County Superintendents of Education by the people."[41] In a letter to members of the General Assembly, the president of the Georgia Federation of Women's Clubs made very clear the electoral weight that backed her legislative demands: "No action of the General Assembly could please the thousands of women represented by the Georgia Federation [more] than to have the word go out to every club in the state that the Children's Code had passed."[42]

The honorary president of the North Carolina Federation of Women's Clubs put the matter simply: "A club has as many votes as it has members."[43] It was a message the politicians apparently understood. In Arkansas, state legislators initially dismissed white women's demands for an increase in the age of consent, but, according to one report, "then the women organized into the League of Women Voters, and got what they wanted."[44] In Kentucky, the Women's City Club president highlighted the group's membership of "between seven hundred and eight hundred women" when she called on lawmakers to defeat the Blanket Equality Bill.[45] Another activist urged fellow women to "get in as many letters and telegrams as possible."[46] By encouraging local women to inundate their representatives with letters and telegrams and by highlighting the number of women represented by sponsoring organizations, white southern clubwomen worked to quantify women's support and thereby encourage legislators to vote as they requested.

Female political leaders also sought to maximize their political leverage by establishing women's councils or legislative councils, which brought together representatives from as many white women's clubs as possible to pursue common legislative goals. White southern clubwomen had long participated in the General Federation of Women's Clubs, but after 1920 white women in nearly every southern state formed these new councils in order to leverage the greatest number of women's votes in support of a single legislative agenda. The councils represented women's groups ranging from the United Daughters of the Confederacy (UDC) to the YWCA, and the Council of Jewish Women to the American Legion Auxiliary.[47] The purpose of the councils was to coordinate the lobbying efforts of such disparate women's organizations and to articulate more clearly the policy concerns of this new political constituency. In Alabama, the legislative council represented the state's farm women, clubwomen, business and professional women, church women, prohibitionists, teachers, mothers, labor organizers, and members of both the League of Women Voters and the National Woman's Party. According to their annual report, these widely varying groups of white women petitioned the state's legislators "with one heart and mind."[48]

Of course, not all white women, not even all politically active white women, were of "one mind." They had different views on the important issues of the day. They had different educational and employment backgrounds. They had different reform priorities, and some even had different opinions about the South's racial order. They were Republicans and Democrats, loyal partisans and independents, committed activists and occasional volunteers, farm women and city dwellers. Their private letters reveal occasional differences of opinion about policy issues and political strategy, as well as personal quibbles. Nevertheless, politically active white women worked hard to "present to the people a unified opinion of the women of the State."[49] The very public divisions among politically active women at the national level over protective legislation and the Equal Rights Amendment were noticeably absent in the southern states. In Alabama, members of the National Woman's Party went so far as to denounce "blanket legislation" to address the legal status of women in their state, instead joining Legislative Council members in support of measures that would consider "each legislature [sic] matter separately."[50] Although white clubwomen pursued legislative reforms with varying degrees of enthusiasm, public disagreement among politically active women over any legislative matter was quite rare.

Through the legislative councils, in particular, organized white women in the South worked through their differences and shaped a political agenda that they could all agree on. Across the region, the legislative demands of white clubwomen focused on eliminating the legal discriminations against women that remained in the law, improving working conditions for women and children, providing protections for some of the region's most vulnerable citizens, and enacting "good government" reforms designed to make southern politics more efficient and more fair.[51] In the years before their enfranchisement, major organizations of southern white women had worked together for legislative reform with surprising infrequency.[52] After woman suffrage, however, such disparate groups as the UDC and the League of Women Voters recognized the political utility of presenting a united front. For nervous politicians looking for ways to ingratiate themselves among women voters, the ability of a single organization to speak for thousands or tens of thousands of organized white women voters carried great weight.

LIKE THEIR PETITIONS and letters to elected representatives, the nonpartisanship of women's organizations after 1920 was not new. In the years prior to enfranchisement, organized women had used their position as political outsiders to make appeals to both political parties. Although recent studies have shown that women adopted partisan identities and participated in partisan activities long before they obtained the right to vote, a "strong logic of appropriateness" demanded that unenfranchised women reformers maintain a nonpartisan stance as they sought to persuade male politicians of the rightness of their cause.[53] Women's organizational nonpartisanship before 1920 signaled their deference to the gender boundaries that excluded them from formal politics. After 1920, however, both Democrats and Republicans courted white women voters, inviting them to become party members and even to hold voting positions in party councils. Faced with the direct participation of white women in the electoral process, men from both parties hoped that newly enfranchised women would abandon their nonpartisan traditions. Nevertheless, most white women's organizations found new reasons to maintain an independent stance.

The League of Women Voters, in particular, jealously guarded its nonpartisanship, even though that stance, from its inception, bred dissent. Some suffragists opposed the league, believing that women, once enfranchised, should work in politics alongside men in the parties. Mary Johnston, a prominent novelist and member of the Equal Suffrage League of Virginia, refused to serve on the League of Women Voters' organizing committee because she was opposed to "any re-segregation of women in the political and social life of the country."[54] Other women found league policy frustrating to their partisan goals. Many men feared that a nonpartisan political organization of women would pose a threat to established party politics. Party leaders and candidates also realized, however, that the League of Women Voters was an organization of the very women whose votes they now needed, and thus could not be ignored. Reflecting this ambivalence toward the league, the *Richmond News Leader* ran an editorial in May 1921 praising the platform of the league for exhibiting such "political insight and practical common sense" that it "might be taken over almost in its entirety by the Democratic Party," while questioning "the wisdom of maintaining a bi-partisan organization of women voters."[55]

The discomfort that this editorial revealed was precisely what league leaders had in mind when they guarded their nonpartisan status. Female political leaders recognized that much of the league's strength as a lobbying organization came from its refusal to commit itself to any one party. During campaign seasons, the leagues worked tirelessly to help voters register and get them to the polls, but these organizations did not work on behalf of any party or candidate. In a direct challenge to the work of southern Democratic leaders who had relied on disfranchisement to maintain control over the region's politics, activist white women brought new people to the polls without regard to their party affiliations and fought to provide greater access to the franchise. Without polling data or separately tallied ballots, Democrats could not know how these new voters would cast their ballots, and in the face of this electoral uncertainty, politicians were forced to court the new voters. As the "He'll Have to 'Kiss the Baby' Now" cartoon from the *Woman Voter* made clear, organized white women expected to be courted with legislative goodies.

Although many individual women joined political parties and worked on behalf of candidates, white activists understood that the ability of their organizations to gain access and policy concessions hinged on their use of an independent ballot. As one league publication put it, reforms "may be accomplished within the party providing the woman's vote remains an uncertain quantity at each election. The party, in order to secure the woman's vote, which may now be the determining factor at any election, will see to it that the demands of women are fulfilled."[56] In South Carolina, the chairman of the League of Women Voters declared, "The Women Hold the Balance of Power," and women voters were advised, "If one party is always sure to win, no matter what candidates they put up, they have little incentive to live up to a high standard."[57] "Politicians pay little attention to their settled followers," the president of the Mississippi League of Women Voters explained. "They devote their best efforts to the independent voters. The unsettled, irregular, independent, and, if you like, fickle voter is the person for whom the whole fight is conducted."[58]

Clearly nonpartisanship was more than a holdover from presuffrage days.[59] Before the ratification of the Nineteenth Amendment, the nonpartisanship of women's organizations indicated their pursuit of reform through nonelectoral means. By contrast, organized white women after 1920 embraced nonpartisanship precisely for its value as an electoral strategy. By constantly reaffirming the independence of their ballots, in both primaries and general elections, organized white women exacerbated politicians' fears about reelection and were able to demand the attention of all candidates.

In Virginia, organized white women explicitly used their nonpartisanship to play on Democratic fears of a Republican insurgency. For example, in 1921 the legislative chairman of the Virginia League of Women Voters wrote a letter to members of the state Democratic Committee urging the committee to include in its platform the legislative agenda proposed by the league. In making this appeal, however, the league did not rely on sophisticated arguments regarding the merits of the platform. Rather, the league warned nervous Democrats that "this program was presented to the Republican Convention by Republican members of the league and the Republican platform contains in favor of nearly all of its points."[60] The league employed this threat again in 1924 as it encouraged league members to meet with their local delegates to the Democratic National Convention to obtain their support for the league's agenda in the party platform. Specifically, the legislative chairman suggested that organized women "call [the delegates'] attention to the planks adopted by the Republican Convention that are favorable to the wishes of the league."[61] Not all organized white women were so blatant in their use of nonpartisanship as a lobbying strategy, but white female political leaders recognized that their power as voters was enhanced by remaining politically uncommitted. Politicians would have little incentive to promote women's proposals if they believed that they were already assured of women's support, or if they believed that white women voters would only support their opponents. Virginia's political women put it simply: "There is no other way for dem[ocratic] forms of gov[ernment] to function but by opposing parties."[62] Nonpartisanship, thus, was a key element in leveraging white women's voting power. It enabled white women to play both sides of the street, pledging their support to whichever candidate would best represent their policy interests, regardless of party or faction.

THE NINETEENTH AMENDMENT did not only transform the way southern white women used familiar, presuffrage-era lobbying tactics. It also encouraged them to develop new lobbying strategies based on women's new position as constituents. Female reformers had worked for decades to shape public opinion and frame public issues using publicity and persuasion. After 1920, however, leaders of white women's organizations also worked to achieve their legislative goals by rewarding their friends and punishing their enemies at the ballot box. Many political scientists who study interest groups contend that the ability of interest groups to gain access and policy concessions is directly related to the number of voters they represent and their ability to convince politicians that the policies being advocated will have an effect on the next election.[63] Female interest groups understood this as well in the 1920s; thus, organized white women tailored their lobbying strategies in the 1920s to emphasize both the size of their constituency and the salience of their agenda.

Fully aware that politicians are motivated by their desire for election, organized white women publicly announced their legislative demands during campaign seasons and staged new political rituals designed to extract policy concessions from candidates when they were most vulnerable. At public meetings sponsored by organized white women, candidates were asked to present their platforms and respond to policy concerns raised by the audience. Once enfranchised, white women could command the attention of hopeful candidates. Organized white women used these opportunities to determine which candidates deserved their support and to put all candidates on the record.

In Alabama, a correspondent for the *Birmingham Age-Herald* blasted these new tactics in an article that revealed the power of organized white women voters: "An invitation from a unit of the league for a candidate to speak before it is nothing less than a royal command, disobeyed at the peril of his political life. . . . Popping questions at candidates for office is something out of which league members get a lot of cruel enjoyment. And they are not always satisfied with mere verbal and evasive replies."[64] Other observers commended the league's political innovations, and as candidates for office were described as having to "Make Their Bow to the Ladies" or "reply to their quizzing," the power of this lobbying strategy was clear.[65] Convinced that "votes are the only things that count with politicians," organized white women demanded that candidates do more than "just kiss the babies [and] hand out a few platitudes about the weather."[66] "No longer content to charm and be charmed," newly enfranchised white women insisted that politicians make policy promises in exchange for women's votes.[67] As one North Carolina woman put it, "The women have the ballot, and they mean for the candidates to take notice."[68]

In addition to these "command" performances, organized white women pioneered what has become a staple of interest group politics: the candidate questionnaire. Before each election, state and local Leagues of Women Voters distributed questionnaires to each candidate inquiring as to his (or her) position on the league's platform. Candidates gave careful attention to these surveys, and local leagues not only published the candidate responses in their own bulletins but they also provided copies of these completed questionnaires to local papers, which often printed candidates' responses in full.

Organized white women, like those in Louisville, Kentucky, characterized these candidate questionnaires as "an aid for voters," but they served as an aid for politicians as well.[69] In the league's legislative strategy, questionnaires and the publication of candidate responses contained an implied quid pro quo. As a representative of unpredictable white women voters, the league, with its questionnaire, offered candidates a road map to electoral success. If you endorse these policies, the league seemed to suggest to candidates, we will make sure white women know of your support and get out to vote. As one league member announced in a South Carolina newspaper, "We get out a platform of what is just and right and good and the candidate that can come the nearest to matching with us gets our support."[70] The response of Thomas Bailee to the Virginia league's questionnaire suggests that candidates were well aware of this political bargain. He wrote in 1923, "You will note that I have incorporated a great many if not all of the issues suggested in your recent circular, and if elected I assure your association that I will be at your service and will use every legislative effort in securing legislation in their behalf. I would appreciate a letter from your League, that I may use for publication in 'The Chronicle,' which I am satisfied would result in a great deal of good."[71]

Throughout the decade, leaders of white women's organizations reminded their members to discuss their policy concerns with candidates *before* election day. As the secretary of the Virginia Women's Council explained, "This will further show to candidates the extended interest in these matters, which exists among their own constituents."[72] Given the realities of Democratic Party dominance in most areas of the region, organized white women emphasized the need to seek politicians' endorsements during the primary campaign. "In Democratic districts," the Virginia Women's Council advised, "such work done before the primary will be ten times as valuable as work done afterward when candidates are practically assured of their election."[73] Similarly, activists in South Carolina worked to obtain information from their congressional candidates and declared it "very inportant [*sic*] that we . . . publish it before the primaries."[74] This attention to the electoral cycle in the timing of their lobbying activities marked another departure from women's presuffrage lobbying tactics. For obvious reasons, unenfranchised white women could do little to command the loyalties of political candidates. Consequently, white clubwomen's lobbying activities before 1920 tended to focus on the meetings of the state legislatures rather than primary or general election campaigns. They visited with legislators during the session, testified at hearings, and made themselves a presence in legislative galleries. They were politically savvy enough to "make use of favorable political situations," but it was not until they had their own votes that they could make use of the elections that were the most favorable situations of all.[75]

Once enfranchised, organized southern white women devised new lobbying strategies to take advantage of their new power as voters, and as these women well knew, candidates would be most receptive to women's demands when they were most in need of votes. The experience of Savannah's white women was typical. In the heated municipal campaign of 1923, the local League of Women Voters prepared questionnaires "for ascertaining the attitude of the candidates . . . on fundamental policies." While party leaders initially scoffed at the women's efforts, two candidates for mayor and all but one of the twenty-four candidates for alderman responded to the women's questioning. The questionnaires and their responses "proved to be no laughing matter" when the answers submitted were "read aloud" at a mass meeting featuring the two mayoral candidates. At that public meeting, "the hall was packed to the doors and several hundred people were turned away." There, the two candidates fought for their political lives, and they did so on women's terms, in a nonpartisan context, amid friends and political enemies, forced to court the city's voters by debating the issues that white women cared about.[76]

Organized white women could mobilize large numbers of voters, and candidates recognized the power of these nonpartisan interest groups to influence the outcome of elections.[77] Thus, in responding to the questionnaires, candidates worked hard to demonstrate their support for the league platform.[78] Candidates who supported the league agenda proudly endorsed the league's legislative proposals and detailed their voting records. At least one Virginia candidate who failed to receive a questionnaire felt that it was important enough to write to the league for one so that he might respond.[79] Candidates who were not in complete sympathy with the league's platform often wrote that they supported a particular issue "in principle" but would have to see the legislation as written before they committed.[80] Even those who could not obscure their opposition to white clubwomen's policy interests routinely wrote lengthy explanations of their positions. One candidate admitted, "While I know that these answers will not please many and if you propose to take an active part in the campaign will cost me many votes, I have given these problems much study and shall be guided by what in my opinion is the wiser course to pursue and not by what is the wise plan to get votes."[81] The responses to league questionnaires and candidate forums indicate more than just a pro forma acceptance of white women in politics. Candidates needed white women's votes, and office-seekers had to serve white women's interests and work with white women's organizations to obtain them.

At the same time they made legislative demands of politicians through public forums and candidate questionnaires, organized white women also staged massive voter registration drives and get-out-the-vote efforts that served to heighten the electoral threat that stood behind their legislative demands. At movie houses and at churches, on sidewalks and on the radio, organized white women urged their fellow citizens to register and vote. They staged car pools, gave speeches, made posters, and did virtually anything else they could think of to bring new people, male and female, to the polls. By simultaneously enhancing the nonpartisan image of southern white women and expanding the electorate, these voter mobilization efforts heightened the reelection fears of southern Democratic leaders who had long relied on a tightly controlled electorate to maintain their political power. Moreover, these get-out-the-vote activities, coupled with their policy demands, assured politicians that organized white women would use their ballots to back their policy concerns.

Throughout the South, female political leaders worked to register new women voters by encouraging them that voting had important policy implications. One League of Women Voters handbill asserted that by voting women could do everything from ensuring "wholesome amusements" for their children to protecting their "families from the contagion that lurks in sweatshop clothing."[82] The Georgia branch of the WCTU used its bulletin to urge women to register and vote. Calling on women to "cast a clean, patriotic, God-honoring ballot," WCTU leaders contended, "If we can not enforce and preserve the [prohibition] law by helping . . . to elect those who are able and willing to enforce it, we have failed our children our country and our God."[83] Similarly, a representative from the South Carolina WCTU "outlined to the women voters the part they may take in pushing [the work of the WCTU], and especially in enforcing prohibition."[84] White clubwomen from several North Carolina organizations met to discuss women's lobbying efforts and focused on women's voting habits as key to the success of their legislative agenda. In particular, the group called on women to "work from now on to elect men and women who are for the measures. . . . Concentrate against opposing leadership and for friendly leadership. Realize the importance of the presiding officers and vote with this in view."[85] The United Daughters of the Confederacy in that state made voter registration a requirement for membership.[86] Even the Birmingham Council of Women's Clubs, whose work more typically involved charity fund-raising and honoring the city's longest-serving domestic servant, urged women to use their ballots to ensure public ownership of the Port of Mobile.[87] Organized women had found ways to work for civic reforms long before they obtained the right to vote, but once the weapon was at hand, white women's organizations of all varieties mobilized their members as voters to achieve their political goals.

For politically active southern white women, get-out-the-vote efforts, candidate forums, questionnaires, letter-writing campaigns, and all their other lobbying tactics were complementary means to the same end — achieving reform.[88] Southern women reformers may have regarded their get-out-the-vote efforts as beneficial in their own right, but they also served an important purpose in quantifying the electoral threat that stood behind the legislative demands of organized white women. Their voter mobilization projects were designed to demonstrate that their electoral strength was not limited to the number of members in their clubs. As they mobilized members of the Daughters of the American Revolution and teachers, farmers' wives and factory workers, men and women, Republicans and Democrats, these activist white women signaled to politicians that their policy concerns were shared by a wide cross section of the region's voters. Thus, get-out-the-vote drives enabled organized white women to request policy concessions not only on behalf of the members of their own organizations but also on behalf of all of those voters they helped get to the polls. As the *Woman Voter of Virginia* explained, "In political work, remember that men are doubtful about the guidance of women in politics, but have great respect for women's votes. These two truths may be used to advantage."[89]

Once elections were over, white women's organizations kept track of how legislators voted on issues of interest to women. Moreover, they distributed that information in an effort to keep up the electoral pressure and try to hold legislators to their promises. The Alabama League of Women Voters described its role as "to indorse measures rather than candidates" and "to provide a political memory for the community by keeping candidates' records and campaign pledges."[90] Leagues, Women's Councils, and federated clubs throughout the South issued bulletins and held meetings to inform organized women of the actions of their elected representatives. In case there was any doubt as to how organized white women planned to use this information, one South Carolina activist declared that the league would "educate its members" and "turn out . . . 100 per cent women who know just where to place their ballots to do the most good for the state."[91] Kentucky women put it plainly; they kept track of how lawmakers voted so that they could "compare the records with the answers to our questionnaire submitted to legislative candidates last fall."[92] Female political leaders were determined that white women voters use their new electoral power to demand legislative action, and when southern Democrats refused to make policy concessions, their female constituents were for the first time able to insist, "Our legislator has got some explaining to do when he comes home."[93]

Of course, suffragists had kept similar records in their battle to obtain the vote, but, as Elisabeth Clemens found in her study of interest group politics, "women's use of roll-call tabulation and file-card records on individual legislators rang hollow in the absence of a politically meaningful constituency."[94] Once enfranchised, organized white women could build that constituency and use such information to reward their friends and punish their enemies at the ballot box. In its statewide publication, the North Carolina League of Women Voters published information on the fate of legislative council bills in the 1927 General Assembly and demanded of its readers, "What will you do in the next primaries? Will you vote for men who voted against the honest election law proposed?"[95] League leaders targeted the Speaker of the North Carolina House of Representatives in particular and promised to provide "material to have a campaign to force Harry Nettles to fight for his election or vote for a state wide Australian Ballot."[96] The women never did persuade Nettles to endorse the "honest election law" they had proposed, but they surely played a role in his early retirement from politics. Nettles, a powerful Democrat, was defeated in 1928, part of a Republican insurgency in the region that was widely blamed on women voters.

In Atlanta, the information provided by the League of Women Voters about the candidates for commissioners of Fulton County "constituted so damaging an indictment of certain candidates tha[t] the mere statement was sufficient to brand the League as partisan."[97] On another occasion, Atlanta league members bragged that "simply by giving out nonpartisan information on candidates, 23 out of a possible 28 who endorsed changes sponsored by the League were elected to the Democratic Executive Committee."[98] Throughout the South, women voters called on the league for information about not only the qualifications for voting but also "the *right* way to vote."[99] Despite league protests that they did not endorse candidates and that it was not their place to influence elections, their dissemination of candidate records was designed to do just that.[100]

Not only did organized women closely monitor legislators' votes, but they also made sure their representatives knew it. "The members of the Legislative Council recognize the purposes for which this Special Session has been called," one Women's Council letter to members of the Virginia General Assembly read, and are "watching with interest your program."[101] On occasion, organized white women even sent thank-you notes to demonstrate their gratitude and, as important, their attentiveness. In February 1922, for example, the league's legislative chairman mailed a letter to the presidents of all the local leagues, with information as to how each member of the Virginia General Assembly had voted on Senate Bill Number 85. She encouraged all league presidents to write a letter to "each one from your congressional district, as well as the delegate and senator from your county, thanking him for his vote" and urging his support of the nine-hour day for women.[102] In Alabama, the secretary of the League of Women Voters wrote to Congressman George Huddleston to commend him for his support of the Sheppard-Towner bill and noted that his letter of support for the bill was read before all the members of the league.[103]

When an Alabama legislator broke his promise to white women voters to support the abolition of the convict lease system, he received letters of another kind. Activist white women, with the political currency to demand policy concessions, insisted that he "be called to account."[104] Mrs. Brenton Fisk urged politically active white women in the legislator's district to "see him and send delegations to see him and have as many protesting letters written to him as possible. Make it very plain to him that the women of his district are not at all pleased with his action."[105] Similarly, in North Carolina, Gertrude Weil wrote her congressman: "We were sorry to note that you did not feel justified in supporting the Sheppard-Towner Maternity Bill when it came to a vote in the House last month. When I spoke to you on the subject last spring in Washington you seemed sympathetically inclined toward its purpose and provisions."[106] In this letter Weil used "we" to indicate that she spoke for a number of women voters, and she made sure the congressman knew those voters were aware of his opposition to their legislation.

Such tactics were bold innovations in the 1920s. As John Mark Hansen found in his study of the farm lobby, American Farm Bureau Federation lobbyist Gray Silver was hauled before the House Banking and Currency Committee in 1921 for asking all House members to report how they had voted on a Farm Bureau measure that was defeated on a voice vote.[107] Clearly, politicians did not always want their constituents to know how they voted. Nevertheless, they knew that, whatever their wishes, white women's organizations were monitoring their performances and that these organizations did so as representatives of constituents who could vote in the next election.

Southern white women undertook sophisticated pressure group tactics in pursuit of their legislative objectives. They devised new strategies for putting candidates on the record in support of legislation and worked hard to provide voters with information about candidates' policy positions and to get those voters to the polls. Organized women's tradition of nonpartisanship took on new importance in the postsuffrage era as female political leaders used the independence of their ballots to command the attention of all politicians. Moreover, their grassroots lobbying activities, in their references to numbers of women voters supporting a particular bill or in their attempts to deluge politicians with mail, suggest not merely an appeal based on logical persuasion or calls on leaders to join the bandwagon of popular opinion. Rather, these references to volume of support were actually reminders to politicians of the many *voters* who were keenly interested in a particular issue. In these lobbying tactics white women used their position as voters and constituents, not just as mothers or members of the supposedly more moral sex, to make their case for improved legislation. In a press release prepared for the *Hanover Progress*, the Virginia League of Women Voters asserted that newly enfranchised women occupied "an entirely new angle, that of the voter whose opinion is backed by the weight of her ballot."[108] Despite the apparent continuity in women's reform activities both before and after 1920, the vote significantly altered the meaning and consequences of white women's lobbying strategies. No longer did they go to lawmakers armed only with persuasion. After 1920 organized white women approached their representatives as constituents and lobbied with a weapon that they were not afraid to use — the vote.

LIKE WHITE CLUBWOMEN, organized African American women also believed in the power of the vote to achieve reform. In fact, given the experiences of disenfranchised black men in the South, African American women
may have had an even greater appreciation for the potential of the Nineteenth Amendment than white women. In the absence of meaningful political participation, African Americans in the South obtained only the barest
access to inferior public services. As the *Birmingham Reporter* explained,
"Political administrations have but little time to give to subject citizens. . . .
They must hear the voice and follow the dictates of voters only."[109] Like other
African American suffragists, Charlotte Hawkins Brown of North Carolina
looked to woman suffrage as a means of "emancipation of the race from this
political thraldom" and described the vote as "our only hope."[110] The official
magazine of the National Association of Colored Women's Clubs optimis-
tically declared, "There is no doubt that some of the disadvantages under
which the colored women labor may be removed by their votes."[111] Similarly,
before an audience of both black and white clubwomen in Birmingham,
Mrs. George Williams urged her fellow African American women "to organize in precinct schools and to teach each and every woman the value of her
vote, to pay their poll taxes for the ballot is their only salvation. A voteless
people is a voiceless people."[112] African American reformers in the South
believed that if they could cast their ballots, they would be able to leverage
their votes in exchange for services for their communities. In an appeal to
black women, the *Atlanta Independent* put it simply, "You have the remedy
in your hands — use it. The ballot can build you school houses, raise the
salaries of your teachers, . . . get your streets fixed, . . . will give you light in
front of your house."[113]

In pursuit of those goals, African American women throughout the region
and the nation worked to take advantage of the Nineteenth Amendment by
going to the polls. By voting, African American women clearly intended
to influence policy and help determine election outcomes. The national
chairman for legislation of the National Association of Colored Women's
Clubs "urged" black women to "work like Trojans to put good men into
office."[114] She encouraged women to "hold meetings. Go after indifferent
women, educate them," and to cast their votes "wisely."[115] She even encouraged black women to write their senators and congressmen and to vote in
primaries. While she insisted that "it will be a terrible reflection upon us, if
we do not use our ballots to promote the welfare of our race," her national
message bore little resemblance to the local realities under which southern
clubwomen labored.[116]

This juxtaposition between the national and the local was pronounced in
the May 1921 edition of *The Kentucky Club Woman*. In this "official organ of

the state federation of colored women's clubs," the president of the National Association of Colored Women called for the "passage of the maternity bill," enforcement of the Nineteenth Amendment, "abolition of Jim Crow cars[,] . . . enfranchisement," and "complete equality before the law." Nowhere did she suggest how these goals should be achieved, however, and her comments stood in stark contrast to the content of the rest of the bulletin. The publication was filled with reports from the state's black clubwomen about their goals and accomplishments. The report from Maysville, Kentucky, was typical, with news of "charity church work" and efforts to "purchase a piano for each school." On that same page, the president of the state federation addressed the state's black clubwomen, urging them that "paramount" among the club's work was the Scholarship Loan Fund. She encouraged Kentucky women to give this fund their full attention and to make themselves "felt in the religious, racial, social and civil activities at our various homes, cities, and towns." Kentucky's black clubwomen did not denounce the goals of the national organization or even disagree with them, but they did not — and could not — embrace them as projects for work. Indeed, even the organization's national president failed to suggest the political tactics that southern black clubwomen might use to achieve these goals. While white clubwomen's bulletins in this period were filled with demands for southern legislators, southern black clubwomen rarely mentioned state legislation. Unable to secure full access to the polls, southern black women asked little from the state, and their organizational tactics seemed largely unchanged by the Nineteenth Amendment.[117]

Despite their faith in the ballot, southern black women were unable to rely on the sophisticated lobbying techniques that newly enfranchised white women employed to leverage their votes during the 1920s. Faced with poll taxes, literacy tests, white primaries, and the "shotgun quarantine" around many polling places, black women in the South recognized the limits of their electoral leverage.[118] Consequently, southern black women did not adopt the candidate forums and questionnaires that were the most powerful innovations of enfranchised white women lobbyists. In the absence of ballots, southern black women could not "command" candidates to speak before black clubwomen or address their demands. Indeed, most southern political candidates avoided appearances before black audiences just as assiduously as they sought invitations from white women's groups. Paternalistic race relations notwithstanding, southern Democrats spoke in friendly terms before black audiences *after* they had been elected, not during the heated campaign seasons when references to white supremacy were more useful politically.[119] In the Jim Crow South, African American women dared not issue questionnaires asserting their legislative demands, and politicians would have had no incentive to respond positively had they done so. In contrast to the experiences of white women, who found politicians eager to support white clubwomen's issues in exchange for their votes, African Americans found that even their white allies wanted no public acknowledgment of black southerners' support.

In this context, the letter-writing campaigns that were a staple of white women's efforts offered little strategic value to black clubwomen. Consequently, even as black clubwomen staged voter registration drives and worked for (and against) legislation, they did not urge their members to send letters and telegrams to their legislators. Club leaders did not contact legislators enumerating the hundreds or thousands of African American women who supported legislative action. Indeed, there is no evidence that southern black women pointed to their status as voters or even constituents as they sought support for their legislative aims. As one historian described the situation in the South, "Although white clubwomen . . . struggled to get legislators to listen to them, with rare exception black women's clubs in the state did not even bother trying."[120]

The fight against Virginia's Racial Integrity Bill is illustrative. In 1926, the National Association of Colored Women's Clubs called on Virginia's black clubwomen to fight the state's proposed Racial Integrity Bill.[121] The bill, an outgrowth of the eugenics movement, proposed a legal definition of "whiteness" designed to strengthen Virginia's already draconian laws against miscegenation.[122] Politically active African American women denounced the bill as "destined to widen the gap between the races, and bring on uncalled for friction, produce race hatred and cause a spirit of unrest." They urged Virginia's black clubwomen to "do what lines [sic] within our power to prevent its passage."[123] This call to action suggested no specific legislative strategy, however. In contrast to letters issued by white women's organizations, which instructed members to deluge their senators and representatives with mail and "let the candidates know [how] you are expecting them to vote," this letter made no mention of contacting state legislators.[124] Without real access to the polls, African American women could not approach the state's politicians as constituents. In the absence of an electoral threat, they were left to fight the racism of the South's political leaders with simple persuasion.

This same lack of political clout hampered the efforts of southern black women to obtain state support for African American institutions. In nearly every southern state, organized African American women founded homes for delinquent black girls that, in the 1920s, they looked to the state to support. Many state institutions for white southerners originated in similar efforts successfully pursued by white clubwomen before the ratification of the Nineteenth Amendment. In one of the few examples of interracial cooperation in the political arena, organized white women often joined black clubwomen in their calls for state support of these African American institutions. Nevertheless, white clubwomen and black clubwomen employed strikingly different reform strategies as a result of woman suffrage. Empowered by their ballots, politically active white women added their support for these African American institutions to their lists of legislative demands. They included them in their candidate questionnaires, and they wrote to their legislators as constituents to request adequate funding. In South Carolina, for example, the legislative chairman of the League of Women Voters wrote to Representative McKendrick Barr to request his support for state funding of the Fairwold School for Negro Girls, as well as for two other bills supported by the state's organized white women.[125] When South Carolina's organized African American women initiated this effort to obtain state aid for Fairwold, they too "wrote a stirring appeal for aid."[126] But in the absence of their own ballots to leverage, they addressed their appeal to the state's white clubwomen. Decades later, leaders of the South Carolina Federation of Negro Women continued to express "gratitude . . . to a committee of [white] supporters who verified facts to the Legislature concerning our needs."[127]

In North Carolina, the Federation of Colored Women's Clubs began urging the need for a "home for maladjusted Negro girls" in 1911.[128] Charlotte Hawkins Brown, the organization's president, spent more than two decades raising money and support for the Efland Home, which was founded and initially operated with private philanthropy. By the early 1920s, the state's Federation of Colored Women's Clubs sought to make Efland a state institution. As her "first step" in obtaining legislative support for this proposal, Charlotte Hawkins Brown wrote to a white woman, asking her to "accept the chairmanship of our board" and to "select a group of [white] women interested in the colored people in the state who would serve with her."[129] Though Brown had helped to orchestrate the registration of thousands of African American women in North Carolina in the weeks following the ratification of the Nineteenth Amendment, she recognized that those few votes gave the federation little leverage with the state's legislators. Instead, she appointed a legislative committee to "contact the Federation of White Women's Clubs . . . in an effort to properly present to the North Carolina Assembly the need for establishing" Efland as a state institution.[130]

With the support of organized white women, Efland did receive state appropriations beginning in the 1920s, but the contrast between the lobbying tools available to enfranchised white women and those available to disfranchised black women was stark. The Legislative Council of North Carolina Women, an alliance of white women's organizations from across the state, included support for Efland among the five bills "introduced by the Council" in 1925.[131] The white women wrote directly to legislators to seek support for the bill, and they encouraged other women to contact their legislators about it by featuring it in the official publication of the state's League of Women Voters.[132] When the General Assembly provided appropriations for Efland in 1927, Gertrude Weil, the president of the legislative council, wrote to thank one of her state's political leaders for his "help in the work for the appropriation for the Industrial School for Negro Girls," noting, "We know that many considered the measure 'one of the women's' only."[133] Years later, however, Charlotte Hawkins Brown decried the political system that denied African American women the political power to be included in that group of "women" constituents to whom Weil referred. "The Negro woman has built and financed homes for delinquent Negro boys and girls," Brown insisted, "[and yet] she has endured ignominy and insult and shame as she almost stood at the back door of legislative halls."[134]

In contrast to organized white women who immediately and dramatically transformed their lobbying strategies to take advantage of their new power as voters, organized black women pursued their reform efforts in the 1920s much as they had in the decades before—raising money and awareness within their own communities and working to persuade the region's white leaders that their reform priorities should be adopted on their merits. Because African American women in the South fought unsuccessfully to achieve full access to the polls, they were unable to reap the same power that white women did from the ballot. The experiences of African American women in the South thus stood as an important counterpoint to the experiences of white women in the region. While black clubwomen sought the assistance of white reformers just as they had before the ratification of the Nineteenth Amendment, newly enfranchised white women had new tools with which to build legislative support. And as white women occasionally helped to shepherd legislation sought by black clubwomen, the differences in their lobbying tactics highlighted the power of the vote.

WITH THE RATIFICATION of the Nineteenth Amendment, white women reformers rejoiced that their political influence would no longer be indirect. As one Georgia woman put it, "It is all very well to say that the women should be the power behind the throne, but let me tell you that one woman on the throne is worth dozens of women behind the throne."[135] Every southern state except Louisiana elected at least one woman to serve in the state legislature during the 1920s.[136] Southern white women served on party executive committees, as convention delegates, and as candidates for office at every level. Southern white men were forced to contend with white female legislators, mayors, aldermen, sheriffs, clerks, registrars, and election judges. To the white men who viewed a few African Americans serving in public office during Reconstruction as "Negro Domination," the spectacle of female officeholding in the 1920s might have seemed like "petticoat rule."[137]

Certainly, many politically active southern white women reveled in the idea of women officeholders. Even before the ratification of the Nineteenth Amendment, a woman in Silverstreet, South Carolina, wrote to one of the state's most prominent suffragists, urging her to run for office: "I trust you will enter the race against Williams opportunely and will 'beat the sox' off him."[138] In Macon, Georgia, a white woman wrote to a local activist, "It was a delightful pleasure to read in the paper that you will invade even the legislature if given an opportunity. . . . We need such women as you in the halls of government."[139]

Throughout the region, female legislators served as sponsors and as supportive voters for the legislative reforms promoted by organized white women. In Arkansas, for example, the state's female representatives cosponsored legislation to provide matching funds for the federal Sheppard-Towner program, one of the first legislative priorities of women after the ratification of the Nineteenth Amendment.[140] Many female legislators were members of the League of Women Voters, and nearly all held memberships in the white women's clubs that annually urged passage of reform legislation in their state assemblies.[141] Belle Kearney, who had begun her public career as a leader in the WCTU, continued to press the concerns of that prohibitionist organization when she served as Mississippi's first female state senator.[142] In the Georgia House of Representatives, Viola Ross Napier introduced a number of the bills sponsored by the state's organized white women, including compulsory education legislation, child labor legislation, and the legislative recommendations of the Children's Code Commission, which was itself requested by the state League of Women Voters.[143] At the conclusion of Napier's first term in the legislature, the president of the Atlanta Federation of Women's Clubs wrote to express her appreciation for the solon's efforts: "We are proud of you and of the distinct place you have made for yourself in the Legislature, a place of honor and dignity. I hope we will have more women like you in the next Legislature."[144]

Occasionally, white women activists even blamed the defeat of their measures on the lack of female representation in state legislatures. Disgusted with the resistance of the state's political leadership to white women's reform priorities, South Carolina women in 1926 publicly announced, "The confidence of women is being shaken in the ability of the men we are sending to fill these responsible places to legislate intelligently for the home and its inmates, and the realization will eventually sink in that if they want it done right they must do it themselves."[145] A North Carolina woman, frustrated at the failure of her legislators to equalize the property laws in her state, lamented to a friend, "I wish we had a good sensible married woman in the legislature, one who has felt some of the pangs of our most unjust laws to present the bill."[146] In the absence of women legislators to represent their interests, she continued, "public spirited women . . . will have to continue to beg and plead with the men to let us have some of our own toys."[147] In South Carolina, a white activist described her frustrating experiences lobbying in the state senate: "As I sat there looking at those men I could not help but think what a vast difference the presence of even a few women might have made."[148] Another exasperated southerner put it simply, "Oh for more women on the floor."[149]

Yet, as white men fretted about women's increasingly assertive role in politics, and white women applauded the policy priorities of their sister solons, organized southern white women did not actively pursue the election of women to public office. Southern white women carried out sophisticated voter mobilization programs during the 1920s, but they did not use these get-out-the-vote drives to elect women to public office. Certainly, female candidates, like male candidates, could benefit from the mass meetings and candidate questionnaires sponsored by women's organizations, but electing female candidates per se was not a goal of the league or other prominent women's organizations in the South. In their newsletters, southern Leagues of Women Voters rarely mentioned the need for women in public office, and their annual "Programs for Work and Study" never included electing women to office. In their assessments of what women had accomplished during their first ten years with the ballot, white women in Virginia and Atlanta did not even mention the election of women to office.[150] The explicit purpose of white women's candidate meetings and questionnaires was to elect public officials who supported their agenda, irrespective of gender. In fact, the North Carolina League of Women Voters specifically encouraged its members to "work from now on to elect men *and* women who are for the measures."[151]

In part, this decision not to focus on electing women to office was driven by social reality. The southern white men who fought so vigorously to prevent women from casting ballots were unlikely to turn the reins of power over to women officeholders without a fight. The men of Winslow might have seen little downside to letting the women "take a turn" in unpaid local office, but the power and prestige associated with state and federal offices were another matter. While leaders from both political parties occasionally found it politically advantageous to support white women's candidacies, women's access to public office was extremely limited. In a public condemnation of the treatment of South Carolina's white women, one activist offered this analysis: "It is clear that the bars are up, the probability of women being elected to office is slim. The dominant parties so far will not nominate women if there is a chance for winning. Political offices are too valuable to be given to women, they need them to pay debts — they do not owe women anything; that is — not yet."[152]

During the first decade after the ratification of the Nineteenth Amendment, the number of women serving in southern state legislatures grew from just three in 1921 to a high of fourteen in 1926, and every state except Louisiana elected at least one female state legislator during the 1920s. The number of house and senate members serving in southern legislatures, however, was well over 100 in each state. Although there were more women legislators at the end of the decade than there had been in 1921 or 1922, there was little pattern to their election. As was true in the rest of the nation, female representation in southern legislatures rarely topped 2 percent.[153] While white women did occasionally break inside the halls of power, their presence was always rare and noteworthy.

Nevertheless, a letter from a Virginia woman suggests that the failure of organized white women to push for women in public office was more than a simple acquiescence to cultural norms. In 1926, Sarah Matthews wrote to a friend to inquire whether two Richmond women were really planning to run for an open U.S. Senate seat or was "it only newspaper talk?" She continued, "Between you and me, while I am keen for advancement of women generally, I doubt if Mrs. M. would add any great light to Senatorial deliberations. But if Adele went in, we would have the comforting assurance that it added one mind, lots of information, one honest purpose, and one sense of humor."[154] Like the majority of politically active white women, Matthews was not interested in electing just any woman to office. She wanted a woman who would contribute substantively to policy deliberations. In response to a request that she run for the Virginia House of Delegates, a prominent southern activist denounced the identity politics that would promote women officeholders on the basis of gender alone. Instead, she endorsed a politics of interest: "I hope women will not rush into politics feeling they can do as well as the men have done — but stay out rather, a few years longer, studying and preparing until they are sure they can do much better. . . . I can not fill that bill now and my principles would not let me even vote for one so inexperienced."[155] In a comment that expressed both personal animosity and a decided lack of identity politics, Nellie Nugent Somerville of Mississippi wrote to a friend that fellow suffragist Belle Kearney "would never get my vote," noting that Kearney had "worried and hindered legislative work."[156]

In North Carolina, an editorial called for more women to serve in the state legislature, but in a phrase that was common in the writings of many politically active white women, the author cautioned that "the test should always be efficiency and not sex."[157] Organizations of white women publicly endorsed the idea of women in office very rarely, and those rare endorsements were motivated not by a demand for gender representation but by a belief in female officeholders as useful means to legislative ends. At the annual convention of the North Carolina Federation of Women's Clubs, for example, the suggestion that Mrs. C. C. Hook, the federation president, might run for state legislature produced a "wave of excitement" among delegates who hoped she could thereby "carry out the legislative program of the federation."[158] In a report of its work, the Tennessee League of Women Voters issued one of the rare calls for female officeholding, lamenting, "One thing in particular is necessary if we would secure legislation — we must have women in the legislature."[159]

Such calls for female officeholding as a legislative solution were extremely rare, and the candidacy of Miriam "Ma" Ferguson once again demonstrated white clubwomen's preference for representation of their policy priorities rather than representation by their gender. In 1924, "Ma" Ferguson was a stand-in for her disgraced husband, former Texas governor Jim Ferguson, whose unlawful exercise of power had been so egregious that he was removed from office. In the eyes of many white clubwomen, Jim Ferguson was more than corrupt; he had led the charge against women's Progressive reforms, including woman suffrage. "Ma" Ferguson had never signaled any allegiance to the legislative priorities of the state's white clubwomen, and when she ran for the state's highest office in 1924, many vowed to defeat her. As one activist later wrote, "She has never been the choice of the women, and if we can only get them to the polls she will be defeated."[160] Although some of Ferguson's enemies supported her in the Democratic primary when she squared off against the Klan candidate Felix Robertson, many Democratic women cast their ballots for the Republican candidate in the general election.[161] Faced with a choice between loyalty to gender and loyalty to issues or principles, organized white women resisted calls to identity politics, even if it meant bolting the party.

While gender solidarity and issue politics were only occasionally in conflict, support for female candidates always jeopardized nonpartisanship. Organizational support for candidates — male or female — risked the nonpartisanship that lay at the heart of white clubwomen's electoral threat. Over and over again, politically active white women touted their use of an independent ballot as the best means of achieving their legislative goals. Pledged to no candidate or party, organized southern white women could use their ballots to demand the attention of all politicians. Throughout the region, state and local Leagues of Women Voters specifically prohibited their officers from running for public office or actively participating in political campaigns. Enforcement of the prohibition against campaign work perplexed leagues across the country, given their avowed mission of encouraging women to engage in partisan politics, and individual league women worked on the campaigns of men and women alike. Nevertheless, leagues were insistent that their own officers not stand for public office. There were rare reports of local leagues encouraging women to run for public office, but the official policies and the rarity of such occasions testified to the political strategy of southern white women. They had limited political capital, and they specifically chose not to spend it on women candidates.

Despite the likemindedness of many female candidates, organizations of white women never saw the election of female candidates as a goal or even a significant strategy. They were politically savvy enough to work with women politicians when they were present, but they also recognized that female officeholders were likely to remain isolated and rare. Moreover, they did not need to elect women to office to enact their agenda. The success of their legislative priorities, as they well knew, was based on electoral threat that organized white women posed to *all* legislators, not on whether they had one or two particularly friendly women in office. Thus, politically active white women focused their energies on lobbying their representatives, protecting their nonpartisanship, and getting out the vote.

THE ORGANIZATIONAL innovations of women lobbyists in the South after 1920 signaled the power of the vote. In the years following their enfranchisement, white clubwomen in the region increasingly pointed to their electoral strength, as well as the merits of their demands, as they pressed for legislative change. Long before candidate surveys and election scorecards became fixtures of American politics, organized white women in the South demanded that their local politicians respond to policy questionnaires and tracked their representatives' voting records so that constituents could hold their leaders accountable. Political leaders, in turn, responded by acquiescing in white women's new political rituals and by accepting white women reformers as partners (however unequal) in the legislative and electoral processes. For the first time, politicians could conceive of supporting controversial or expensive legislation because white women wanted it and would back them at the polls. And after 1920, southern political leaders were forced to consider the election-day implications of policy choices that contradicted the expressed wishes of organized white women.

If the contrast between white women's pre- and postenfranchisement lobbying tactics demonstrated the value of the vote, so too did the contrast between black and white women's reform strategies. In the absence of a meaningful electoral threat, southern black clubwomen generally were unable to press their demands more effectively after the ratification of the Nineteenth Amendment. Indeed, the continuities in black women's experiences as reformers in the 1920s serve to highlight the changes in white clubwomen's tactics and effectiveness. Although the Nineteenth Amendment did not provide white women with unbounded political authority or equal representation in politics, it did provide some southern women with a powerful new weapon in their political arsenal. As newly enfranchised southern women made increasing demands of the political system, male political leaders worked to maintain their control over the region's politics, carefully negotiating the new political landscape posed by woman suffrage by appeasing this new constituency with policy concessions when they had to and courting them rhetorically when that would suffice.

Chapter Six

No Longer Treated Lightly

Southern Legislators and
New Women Voters

In 1920, an aide to South Carolina's Governor Cooper wrote to one of his state's most prominent women for advice. He had received a request from an organization of women, and in contrast to years past, he was unsure how to respond. Letters from women's organizations had once been of no consequence. When women were enfranchised, however, such letters came to represent groups of constituents. Faced with the electoral uncertainties posed by woman suffrage that year, he confessed, "Letters from women's organizations, you know, can no longer be treated lightly!"[1] In the years following the ratification of the Nineteenth Amendment, Democratic Party leaders throughout the South looked upon the demands of organized white women with a newfound respect. Faced with a large and unpredictable bloc of new voters at the polls, nervous Democrats worked furiously to bring the region's white women into the party fold. They addressed women's club meetings, targeted women directly in campaign literature, and moved the locations of polling places and party meetings to accommodate the ladies' sensibilities. They called on female political leaders for help in winning the votes of women, and they grumbled among themselves as election returns and the efforts of organized women demonstrated that white women's partisan loyalties would not be easily won. Perhaps most important, these Democratic men were forced to consider the political implications of policy choices that contradicted the expressed wishes of organized white women.

While Democratic political leaders in the South had long touted the influence of white women on the political process, white women recognized "the change of atmosphere in the politicians after [they] had got the vote."[2] As suffragists had anticipated, southern politicians responded to white women's new electoral power with unprecedented concern for their legislative priorities. Backed by the weight of their votes, white women in Georgia found "the

Legislature very polite and very anxious to meet the wishes of the 'ladies.'"[3] A newspaper article declared: "Nothing legislative will be done in North Carolina that arouses the active antagonism of these women . . . and nothing will be long denied which they really demand."[4] Confronted with the demands of organized white women who were keeping track of candidates' records and going to the polls, southern politicians were forced not only to court women voters on the campaign trail but also to follow through on their promises once in office. "With those little official slips of paper right in the women's hands," a white Mississippi clubwoman explained, "it is not so easy for case-hardened politicians to smile and smile and be villains still."[5]

EVEN IN THE SIMPLEST things, like politicians' responses to women's correspondence, southern white women found that their enfranchisement made a tremendous difference. As the aide to Governor Cooper made clear, letters sent by unenfranchised women reformers had often gone unheeded. Once white women received the vote, however, their petitions received more deferential treatment. Faced with white women "raising sand from all parts of the state," South Carolina legislators in 1921 heeded their demands for an increase in the age of consent.[6] In a testament to the new lobbying strategy of enfranchised white women, one politician confessed that "every mail overwhelms him, he couldn't think of answering all the letters he gets!"[7] A suffragist from North Carolina explained the transformation simply when she challenged state legislators at a public hearing, "If you *know* many officials who pay more attention to a constituent without a vote than a constituent *with* one, I'd like to meet the gentlemen."[8] Like organized white women from around the region, Virginia's newly enfranchised white women noticed a significant "change in the nature of a response receive[d] to these letters from the promises of careful consideration of the old days to a definite advocacy of plank after plank of the platform."[9]

Southern politicians recognized the new power of organized white women in ways that were more than just rhetorical. After the ratification of the Nineteenth Amendment, politicians could for the first time imagine supporting controversial causes that white women favored with the understanding that white women would back them at the polls. In an exceptionally blatant example of this type of understanding, Congressman T. W. Harrison from Virginia's Seventh District contacted the legislative chairman of the League of Women Voters less than a month before the 1924 general election with a request. Harrison had supported the national child labor amendment in the recent session of Congress, which prompted the league, as he reminded her, to write "me a letter in which you commended my stand." Suddenly, just weeks before the general election, an independent Democrat decided to challenge Harrison in a campaign based almost exclusively on Harrison's support for the child labor amendment. "I am therefore writing to you," Harrison addressed the league, "and to other prominent leaders who favor my attitude on this bill, asking you to do anything that you can towards aiding my candidacy on this issue. I realize that the National League of Women Voters has many members in my district, and I would appreciate greatly anything you could do towards interesting the members of this organization th[r]oughout my district in my candidacy." In short, Harrison wrote, I sponsored this legislation at your request, and now I need your help at the ballot box. This kind of exchange would have been unimaginable in the presuffrage era, and Harrison's victory on election day testified to the value of supporting women's legislative priorities and courting women voters.[10]

In Georgia, Representative Hamilton McWhorter Jr. also recognized that organized white women used their ballots to back their policy concerns, and when asked by a woman's club in his district to discuss his stewardship of the bills they had endorsed, he eagerly accepted. He knew that he had supported their bills, but he confessed to a fellow legislator, "I do not recall in detail just what they were."[11] In fact, he not only could not remember "in detail" the nature of the bills, his letter revealed that he had no idea what the bills were, nor if they had passed. It seems clear that he had supported the bills because the white women of his district demanded them, and he most certainly wanted those women to give credit for his support — if only he could figure out what it was he had supported.

Southern politicians did not always give organized white women what they wanted, of course, but after 1920 they certainly seemed to think twice before they defied white women's wishes. In December 1921, Congressman J. T. Deal delivered a long speech before a meeting of the Virginia League of Women Voters, defending his opposition to the Sheppard-Towner Infancy and Maternity Protection Act. After detailing his reasons for rejecting the bill, Deal noted, "[My] district has a population of 300,000 and I received perhaps twelve or fifteen letters asking me to support this bill."[12] He also made a point of noting that he had been "urged by the Chamber of Commerce and other individuals to oppose the bill."[13] These comments reveal Deal's belief that he was safe (from a reelection standpoint) in voting against Sheppard-Towner because few women in his district had contacted him in support of this bill. At the same time, these comments suggest the power of white women's lobbying strategy, even if the women of Deal's district had failed to make effective use of it. Deal paid attention to the number of voters in his district who expressed concern about this issue, and the volume of support for Sheppard-Towner from his constituents was insufficiently persuasive. Deal's reference to the opposition of the chamber of commerce is also significant; even a demand broadly shared by women had to be weighed against the power and votes of those in opposition. Finally, Deal's presence before the league to defend his vote demonstrates the power of organized voters. While Deal had comfortably cast his ballot against Sheppard-Towner, he was not comfortable allowing the league to remain in opposition to him. Politicians knew that white women organized in special interest groups, like white men organized in special interest groups, could be a powerful force at the polls. Before the end of the decade, that force would result in his early retirement from politics.

Congressman Deal was not the only candidate who felt the need to explain himself to the organized white women of his district. Just two months before women in Mississippi cast their first ballots in a general election, one of the state's legislators requested to speak before the League of Women Voters of his county in "defense of his acting in opposing the league bill in the Mississippi Legislature."[14] Clearly he did not want to face his female constituents at the polls without having explained his vote against their bill. Even the Ku Klux Klan, which held unprecedented political power in Georgia in the 1920s, seemed to take the policy concerns of organized white women quite seriously. Not only did the KKK encourage Klan women to vote in support of like-minded candidates, but it also reached out to clubwomen whose policy agendas differed from its own. A Klan candidate for Georgia legislature, recognizing that his position on city manager form of government "would cost him their votes," sought a hearing before his local League of Women Voters to explain his position and plead his case.[15]

AS THESE SOUTHERN politicians recognized, the fate of white clubwomen's legislative reforms was perhaps the most important measure of the new political stature of enfranchised white women. The wide variety of white women's organizations that had lobbied legislators in the presuffrage era continued to do so after 1920, and regardless of clubwomen's previous attitudes toward woman suffrage, their ballots helped to make the case for reform. As they had before suffrage, white clubwomen's concerns touched many policy areas, but men and women alike believed that moral reform, education, health, and children's issues were of particular interest to women. Moreover, state legislative councils presented comprehensive agendas that reflected the specific concerns of many white women's organizations. By organizing in this way and appearing to speak with one voice, legislative councils were able credibly to represent these policy demands as the wishes of white women voters. Although the priorities of these legislative councils were hardly representative of the concerns of all women, or even all women voters, the fact that they were presented to legislators as such makes them good measures of the responsiveness of policy-makers to newly enfranchised women.[16] More than one million new voters demonstrated the magnitude of woman suffrage in November 1920, and in the legislative sessions that followed, nearly every legislature in the region responded to the enfranchisement of women with the passage of white women's legislative priorities.

In Arkansas, for example, the 1921 session of the General Assembly granted women equal guardianship of their children and raised the age of consent.[17] Just two months after the passage of the Sheppard-Towner Infancy and Maternity Protection Act, Governor Thomas McRae accepted the provisions of this federal legislation to provide funding for maternal and child health programs in his state.[18] In 1923, the Arkansas General Assembly appropriated matching funds for the Sheppard-Towner program, the first state monies ever made available for child-hygiene work in Arkansas.[19] At the request of the Arkansas Federation of Women's Clubs, legislators also provided $4,000 to be used for traveling libraries in the state, "the first State appropriation for a free library service."[20]

In Georgia, legislators welcomed the white women of their state to the ballot with an impressive array of legislative victories in 1921 and 1922. At the request of organized white women, the legislature passed a bill in 1921 providing women with "the same privileges of office holding as men," with the exception of jury, military, and road service.[21] According to a white suffragist who monitored the workings of that first postsuffrage legislative session, "These legislators were so courteous and obliging the women could scarcely believe it was a Georgia Legislature." She continued incredulously, "They gave everything [we] asked for and inquired, 'Is there anything else we can do for you?'"[22] Of the nine items included in the Georgia League of Women Voters' legislative program for 1922, five were adopted immediately by the state legislature. They included the creation of a children's code commission to propose legislative changes for the benefit of the state's children, a bill to regulate the placement of children in foster homes, and a law to give married women "full power to act as a guardian of a minor."[23] They also included increased appropriations for the Georgia Training School for Girls and an appropriation of matching funds for the Sheppard-Towner program.[24] In 1920, Georgia's women reformers faced a legislature so hostile to women's presence in politics that it refused to permit women to vote in the presidential election, even after the ratification of the Nineteenth Amendment. One year later, state legislators responded to newly enfranchised white women by enacting more than half of their legislative agenda. While organized white women undoubtedly pressed the merits of their legislative priorities, the about-face of their state representatives could only have been the result of newly felt electoral pressures.

After a hard-fought election in which nearly 400,000 new voters crowded the polls, Kentucky legislators responded to these new electoral pressures by immediately enacting several bills that increased the legal authority of women. During that first legislative session after women could vote, the state legislature granted Kentucky women the right to serve on the board of the state university and the power to serve as executor, administratrix, guardian, trustee, curator, and any other judicial capacity then allowed men.[25] These southern men also offered women an increase in the age of consent that year.[26] Hoping to endear themselves to these new constituents before they again faced the state's women voters at the polls, Kentucky legislators provided full matching funds to support Sheppard-Towner activities in the state and nearly tripled the budget for the Board of Charities and Corrections.[27]

Under pressure from their new female constituents, Louisiana legislators eliminated "thirteen important discriminations against women in the laws of Louisiana" during the first postenfranchisement session of the General Assembly.[28] Among the "new rights gained for women through this campaign" were the right to be consulted before the sale or mortgage of their family home; equal rights and obligations in terms of public officeholding; the right to become arbitrators, notaries public, administrators, executors, and "witnesses assisting at public inventories"; the right to retain guardianship of their children after remarriage; equal rights with fathers in the guardianship of children after a spouse's death; equal rights with men to be appointed guardian; and equal rights with grandfathers for grandmothers to act as guardians. Women were legally determined "capable of all kinds of engagements and functions," whereas previously the law held them incapable unless specifically declared otherwise.[29] In 1921, Louisiana's leading politicians recognized the new political position occupied by white women by striking from the books more than a dozen laws that had made the subjugation of women a legal reality.[30]

The New York Times described the influence of "women voters in the Bayou State" as "very great," evidenced by "the adoption of some legislation designed for the benefit of 'the home.'"[31] In the first legislative session following the ratification of the Nineteenth Amendment, men who had refused to grant the franchise to women approved Mississippi's participation in the Sheppard-Towner program and appropriated full matching funds for that purpose. Heeding the demands of organized white women, these representatives also enacted legislation that made women equal with their husbands as guardians of their children and provided funding for the state college for women that exceeded the state's funding of the flagship state university,

Ole Miss.[32] After the ratification of the Nineteenth Amendment, the Mississippi *Woman Voter* announced to its readers and to the state's wary politicians, "The men of Mississippi did not give us the ballot and so we come into the electorate bound by no ties of gratitude."[33] Determined that these new white women voters would not remain unattached for long, the state's leading Democrats immediately worked to bind these women to the party by attending to their legislative concerns.

North Carolina's organized white women outlined six legislative priorities before the 1921 legislative session, all but one of which they achieved by 1923.[34] Like nearly all other southern state legislatures, North Carolina's leading politicians had rejected women's demands for suffrage until it was forced upon them by the federal government. In 1921, faced for the first time by enfranchised women in the halls of the legislature, North Carolina's politicians responded with state resources for the programs white women supported. They passed "unusually liberal appropriations" for the state's educational and child-caring institutions that year, including full matching funds to support Sheppard-Towner programs in North Carolina.[35] A majority of legislators also granted white women's requests for the establishment of a training school for delinquent African American boys.[36] In 1923, state legislators increased the age of consent to sixteen after more than forty years of agitation.[37] That year, legislators also established the state's first program for mothers' pensions and again provided full funding for the state's portion of the Sheppard-Towner programs.[38] Just three years after they were enfranchised, North Carolina's white women had achieved all but one of their initial legislative goals, including demands that "the women of the State have been bringing before each successive Legislature for many years."[39]

In South Carolina, a former suffragist wrote in 1921, "I am happy to report that we have carried out our program and passed every bill we undertook to see through."[40] Like their counterparts in other southern states, South Carolina's white women reformers found unprecedented legislative success once they had won the vote. Although the state's leading politicians had repeatedly rejected women's demands for the ballot, once women were enfranchised, these politicians immediately granted white women's demands to raise the age of consent to sixteen, to establish a children's code commission, and to defeat a "blanket" equal rights bill, which activists believed would threaten protective legislation for women.[41] In the next legislative session, organized white women again found their representatives in a generous mood, granting women joint guardianship of their children and providing for full funding of Sheppard-Towner work in the state.[42] South Carolina's legislators capped these legislative reforms by passing a "resolution of thanks" honoring the chairman of the Legislative Steering Committee of the women's organizations of that state. The resolution commended Mrs. Richard Williams for giving them "reliable and trustworthy information in an amiable, tactful, and dignified manner on the progressive and important legislation sponsored by the women."[43] This about-face from legislators who had for so long opposed the presence of women in politics prompted one observer to comment that the actions of the South Carolina legislature "may sound incredible" to the organized women reformers "whose efforts and sacrifices have not always received the approbation of the law-makers."[44]

In Tennessee, too, former suffragists might have found the actions of their legislators incredible as they granted numerous policy concessions in the face of demands by newly enfranchised white women. Just months after the bruising ratification fight, the Tennessee League of Women Voters reported, "The women for the first time had an extensive legislative program which we pushed successfully."[45] Among those early successes were measures that equalized women's status in the law. At the request of the state's organized women, legislators granted women the right to hold public office and pay poll taxes equal to that of men. They also repealed the right of a father to deed or will away his child from the mother. Legislators extended mothers' pensions to all counties in the state and enacted "several important school laws" and "social hygiene laws" advocated by the League of Women Voters.[46] Tennessee's legislators also provided appropriations for programs that white women demanded, including funding for a vocational school for African American girls and an institution for the "feeble-minded."[47] By 1923, organized white women in Tennessee had secured matching funds for the Sheppard-Towner program, an equal guardianship law, equal representation on political party committees, and a children's code commission.[48]

In Virginia, too, enfranchised white women had impressive early legislative accomplishments. The Virginia League of Women Voters was organized in November 1920, and one of its first lobbying efforts was a request to Governor Westmoreland Davis for the establishment of a children's code commission to propose legislative changes for the benefit of Virginia's children. Davis responded favorably to this request from the league, and in April 1921 he appointed a commission of five men and four women, two of whom were members of the league. After nine months of work, the commission proposed twenty-six bills, ranging from mothers' pensions to the establishment of a state board of public welfare, from compulsory school attendance to the regulation of child labor.[49] Of the twenty-six bills, seventeen passed both houses of the General Assembly and were signed by the governor that year.[50] In that same session, white women also secured full matching funds for the Sheppard-Towner Act programs, legislation equalizing property rights in dower and curtesy, and legislation equalizing laws of descent.[51] It certainly cannot have been mere coincidence that state legislators who had been so hostile to woman suffrage enacted nearly two dozen pieces of legislation advocated by white women immediately following their enfranchisement. Writing in 1921, the *Richmond Times Dispatch* explained legislators' sudden attentiveness to white women's demands: "Their protests now carry with them the weight of their votes, whereas formerly they were at the most persuasive."[52]

ON THOSE RARE OCCASIONS when southern black women were able to cast ballots in sufficient numbers, they, too, found that their demands carried greater weight with lawmakers. The types of policies that African American clubwomen sought by their use of the ballot varied. At the national level, through the NAACP, the National Association of Colored Women, the National League of Colored Republican Women, and other organizations, these women voters demanded that Congress and Republican presidents pass federal antilynching legislation and provide African Americans in the South with the rights afforded them by the Thirteenth, Fourteenth, and Fifteenth Amendments. As one woman from Louisiana put it, African Americans should demand their "Constitutional rights [and] that national elections be controlled by U.S. Marshalls in the South."[53] In their local and state political activities, however, African American women put their political voices to more tangible, and less controversial, ends. Indeed, black clubwomen in the South rarely issued anything that could be construed as legislative demands or even a legislative agenda. When they did clearly articulate demands of the state, black women voters generally sought provision of basic public services: paved streets, access to city water lines, street lights, high schools, and appropriations for homes for delinquent boys and girls. The experience of one poor and illiterate black woman in Nashville is telling. When women were granted the right to vote, one observer reported, this "old ignorant Negro woman went to see one of the suffrage leaders. She had heard that the women were going to vote . . . and she wanted to know if she could vote and how to do it so that she could help elect the right men to office." Having lived nearly two decades in the same home, on an alley with no street lights and no access to city water services, she wanted to cast her vote to, as she put it, "see her town 'cleaned up.'"[54]

Those occasions when black southerners were able to vote in substantial numbers demonstrated the political potency of the vote. In Nashville, for example, black clubwomen worked with white clubwomen to elect a slate of reformers to the city council in 1919. In exchange for their support, African American women demanded and obtained the appointment of an African

American probation officer, the appointment of an African American to the city's movie censorship board, and the employment of African American nurses in city hospitals to care for black patients.[55] Like the League of Women Voters, who sent questionnaires to policy-makers that offered white women's votes in exchange for specific policy concessions, Nashville's black women leaders negotiated for specific municipal improvements before the election and got their voters to the polls in fulfillment of their end of the political bargain.

After the ratification of the Nineteenth Amendment, Atlanta's newly enfranchised African American women were able to leverage their new ballots in exchange for a long-sought high school for the city's black children. In 1919, city fathers had attempted to pass a bond for city improvements that excluded any appropriations for Atlanta's African American schools. In response, African Americans organized to defeat the bond issue. According to city law, two-thirds of all registered voters had to cast ballots in the municipal election for the election results to be valid. Fully aware of the law's provisions, African American leaders staged a massive voter registration campaign in 1919 and then urged those newly registered voters to boycott the polls on election day. Their efforts were successful in defeating the bond measure, thus denying white Atlantans their civic improvements until the needs of the city's African Americans were addressed.

Two years later, in the wake of woman suffrage, the city's white political leaders, male and female, recognized that they would need African American votes to pass a bond issue. As one historian put it, "For the first time, white leaders found themselves in the position of encouraging African American men and women to vote."[56] Aware of the need to obtain the support of newly enfranchised African American women, the mayor called a meeting of leading black clubwomen to enlist their support for the bond campaign. These clubwomen, who had long pressed city fathers for reform, demanded that the city fulfill many of their decades-old demands, including a new high school with an African American planning committee, in exchange for their electoral support. Consequently, the bond proposal in 1921 provided that one-third of the funds would go to support improvements in African American schools and other services for African American neighborhoods. Having successfully leveraged their votes, African American women, working separately from white clubwomen and other white supporters of the bond issue, mobilized Atlanta's black voters in support of the bond campaign. As a result of the decisive victory, African Americans won the city's first public high school for black students, as well as funding for two new elementary schools.[57]

In Kentucky, a bond election provided the opportunity for African American voters to register their objection to Jim Crow education. In November

1920, the same election in which Kentucky women went to the polls for the first time, voters in Louisville faced a million dollar bond initiative for the benefit of the University of Louisville. Early in the summer, however, local NAACP leaders began to register their concerns about the bond initiative because the university excluded "men and women of African descent."[58] In an extended correspondence with the dean of the university, Wilson Lovett, the local NAACP leader, condemned segregation and the resulting educational inequality. In response to calls by the dean for black Kentuckians to support the bond issue, Lovett challenged him to identify "one single institution in all this vast city, for the advanced education of colored boys and girls or men and women, supported by taxation of any kind."[59] African American leaders in Louisville framed the issue as one of basic fairness; taxation levied upon the entire community, they argued, should benefit all citizens, white and black alike.[60] Under the proposed bond issue, Lovett charged, "the colored are to get exactly nothing."[61] Consequently, the NAACP branch undertook a massive voter registration campaign to enroll black voters "who will vote against the issuing of the bond."[62] In the weeks before the election, university officials responded to the growing electoral revolt by offering "extension courses" to local African Americans.[63] The majority of black voters in Louisville rejected these "makeshift" offers, however, insisting instead that their numerical strength in the city entitled them to at least $250,000 in benefits.[64] On election day, black voters defeated the bond initiative by a margin of 4,000 votes.[65] On their first foray to the polls, black women in Louisville joined black men in a forceful demonstration of the power of the vote, denying white Kentuckians additional public resources to support a segregated system of higher education.

Where they voted in substantial numbers, African Americans were able to leverage their ballots to obtain services for their communities, a fact that testifies to the power of lobbying with the vote. But as one observer put it, "There were not many cities in which, like Atlanta, the Negro vote was large and active enough to make demands before delivering its ballots."[66] Those elections in which black southerners were able to vote in sufficient numbers were a function both of geography and of Progressive politics. Clearly, Kentucky and Tennessee provided more hospitable environments for African American political participation than states in the Deep South. Neither Kentucky nor Tennessee forced would-be voters to pass any literacy tests. In Kentucky, African Americans in many parts of the state voted without difficulty, as the state had neither a white primary nor a poll tax. Nevertheless, the amount of leverage black women were able to exert was not exclusively a function of differences between Upper South and Lower South, or even rural and urban. As Paul Lewinson observed in 1932, across the region "there were many fewer [black voters] than an Abolitionist might hope, but rather more than even Southerners suspected."[67]

In particular, black southerners often found important opportunities to vote in nonpartisan municipal and bond elections because of the absence of the white primary. In 1927, black voters in Raleigh, North Carolina, were "the deciding factor" in a heated contest for municipal offices.[68] The incumbent Democratic administration provided for "unprecedented" registration of African American voters in the city, insisting, "We have as law-abiding colored citizens as any city in the State and if colored people desire to take part in the city election that is their privilege given under our form of government."[69] By contrast, their opponents railed against the participation of black voters "in a white man's election," and editorials from around the state denounced the return of African Americans to politics.[70] In response to reports that white supporters of the administration had "haul[ed] Negroes to the polls," one Smithfield, North Carolina, editorial warned that there could be no "issue of sufficient importance to cause the electorate to resort to the Negro vote."[71] Yet, as African Americans reveled in this exercise of political authority and white southerners warned against reopening the "Pandora's box" of black voting, one newspaper called attention to the broader lesson of the election.[72] "The election in Raleigh," the *News and Observer* warned, "convinced every Democrat of the danger of non-partisan city elections."[73]

In Raleigh, Atlanta, Louisville, and Nashville, the votes of black southerners could determine the outcome of local elections because the usual white primary bar did not prevail. As the *News and Observer* recognized, black voters crowded the polls in Raleigh only because city offices were determined through nonpartisan contests. In his survey of political conditions in the South, Paul Lewinson found that nonpartisan municipal elections also "made the Negro vote important" in Norfolk, Portsmouth, and Newport News, Virginia, as well as Dallas, Fort Worth, Galveston, Houston, and San Antonio, Texas.[74] Lewinson also discovered that African American voters exercised considerable leverage in nonpartisan referendums in Augusta, Savannah, Durham, Greensboro, and Raleigh, in addition to the Texas cities already named.[75] In short, disfranchisement had not entirely robbed black southerners of the ability to cast effective ballots. Moreover, given the opportunities that nonpartisan elections afforded to black voters, white women's support of nonpartisanship and Progressive electoral reforms took on new meaning. Not only did these efforts challenge Democratic Party hegemony, but they also subverted disfranchisement by offering opportunities for black southerners to cast and leverage their votes.

Nevertheless, violence, disfranchisement laws, and the white primary barred the vast majority of black southerners from the polls. Despite these rare occasions in which newly enfranchised African American women were able to use their ballots to demand specific, tangible reforms, African American clubwomen in the South found that the ratification of the Nineteenth Amendment did not mark the beginning of a new era of black women's political power. Instead, while organized white women continued to build on their successful first forays into electoral politics, the region's African American women recognized that disfranchisement sharply curtailed their political power. The experiences of African American women in Atlanta, Louisville, and Nashville were the exceptions that proved the rule. The vote truly was a powerful weapon in the hands of reformers, but clubwomen had to be able to use those votes on election day in order to leverage them.

OF COURSE, even white women did not get everything they asked for once they were enfranchised. Despite the state's ratification of the Nineteenth Amendment, white women in Texas found their legislators particularly unresponsive to white clubwomen's legislative priorities during their first session as enfranchised lobbyists. That year, newly enfranchised women, organized through the League of Women Voters, called on state legislators to support five specific measures.[76] Two of the provisions called on lawmakers to accord women equal status by permitting them to serve on juries and providing for equal representation in state political party organizations.[77] Others called for "an effective minimum wage law," a survey of state prison conditions, and a state constitutional convention.[78] All five measures were defeated.[79]

Similarly, Alabama's state legislators greeted new women voters with as many defeats as victories in their first postenfranchisement legislative session. White women in that state, organized through the state legislative council, pressed for twenty specific measures when Alabama legislators gathered in Montgomery in 1923.[80] The Alabama legislature met only once every four years in the 1920s, and the last time the legislature had been in session was 1919, before women were enfranchised. By 1923, white women in the state were well organized and the council represented fifteen different women's organizations, including the state Federation of Women's Clubs, the state's home demonstration agents, the League of Women Voters, members of the WCTU, the PTA, business and professional women, and the National Woman's Party.[81] Together they called on legislators to establish an eight-hour day for women workers, to increase the age of consent to eighteen, to make fathers financially responsible for their illegitimate children, and to make mothers equal guardians of their children.[82] They also called for the establishment of a home for "delinquent negro girls" and a home and reformatory for "fallen women."[83] They opposed "blanket legislation" to equalize the rights of men and women in the law, they called for women members of state boards related to the welfare of women and children, and they asked for a variety of appropriations.[84] They reserved most of their energies, however, for a battle to abolish the convict lease system.[85] "Yet with all our effort," the council's president lamented, "we have little of concrete attainment to show."[86]

Of all the nearly two dozen measures supported by white women through the legislative council, only three won anything like a victory in the Alabama General Assembly. The legislature accepted the provisions of the Sheppard-Towner program and provided appropriations for it. The council also succeeded in securing a small appropriation for home economics work and defeating a measure that would have changed the way county superintendents were selected. Nearly every other bill they sponsored, however, went down in defeat. The legislators "denied" all of the women's requests "having to do especially with the legal status or protection of women," and "all constructive legislation calling for any appropriation was brought to final disaster in the last days" of the legislative session. Indeed, the state's white women had been hopeful that the measure establishing a home for African American girls would pass "until panic struck the legislators for fear that the eight thousand called for annually would bankrupt the state." Finally, despite the determined opposition of the state's organized white women, Alabama legislators granted an extension of the convict lease system for four more years.[87]

Armed for the first time with ballots, enfranchised women in Alabama and Texas failed to persuade state legislators to enact their legislative agendas. At one level, these failures call into question suffragists' claims about the power of the ballot. Clearly, the ballot alone was not sufficient to secure expensive programs, such as the new institutions endorsed by Alabama's clubwomen, or legislation that radically challenged white men's political power, like the proposal for equal representation on party committees in Texas. At the same time, however, these legislative defeats underscore the responsiveness of politicians in other southern states who gave newly enfranchised white women nearly everything they asked for. As the resistance of legislators from Texas and Alabama demonstrates, the legislative victories granted by southern politicians in the 1920s were not empty concessions to women. Newly enfranchised white women added ballots to their arsenal for reform, but their legislative demands still contrasted sharply with the priorities of their states' leading men.

As southern legislators confronted enfranchised women lobbyists for the first time in the 1920s, the legislation they enacted both testified and contributed to the erosion of their own power. Organized white women in

Arkansas, Kentucky, North Carolina, South Carolina, and Virginia counted increases in the age of consent among their first legislative victories after enfranchisement.[88] For decades white women reformers had lobbied lawmakers to improve the morality of their communities by making sexual relations with young women a criminal offense.[89] Nevertheless, when the Nineteenth Amendment was ratified, the legal ages of consent in the South remained low, fourteen in many states. Faced with new electoral pressures after 1920, lawmakers in these five states immediately raised the age of consent to sixteen. Yet the campaigns by organized white women to raise the age of consent, establish "equal guilt" laws for sexual offenses, or make fathers financially responsible for their illegitimate children all challenged the sexual freedom of white men. North Carolina white women, who fought for forty years before achieving an increase in that state's age of consent, faced opposition from state legislators who jealously guarded their own sexual prerogatives and asked, "What are you going to do with our boys?"[90] In South Carolina, activist white women decried the actions of state legislators that left "a girl of 14 . . . the prey of any ravaging wolf in men's clothes that happens along."[91] Alabama women lamented that their legislators, "while individually courteous and kind to us, . . . collectively seemed to be on the defense for the rights, still, left to mere man."[92] Just as the presence of white women casting ballots and campaigning in public challenged the notion that white women needed the protection of white men, white women's legislative demands insisted that they needed protection *from* white men. When legislators enacted these laws because "women were raising sand from all parts of the state," they acknowledged the power of white women's votes at the same time that they legislated new limits on their own sexual freedom.[93]

Similarly, when white women reformers successfully demanded equal property rights or equal guardianship of their children or equal representation on party committees, they used their ballots to limit the authority of men per se. Throughout the region, white women fought to remove the legal privileges enjoyed by men, and male legislators fought just as hard to defend them. Although organized white women throughout the region opposed "blanket" legislation to remove women's legal disabilities, they all demanded changes to remove the specific discriminations against women in laws pertaining to property rights, guardianship, and laws of inheritance. Leading white female activists used their publications and other forums to arouse the ire of ordinary women voters about the injustices of laws that permitted fathers to will their children away from their mothers or to seize a wife's wages. Faced with the antagonism of such a large class of voters, legislators in southern states immediately agreed to reforms in at least some of those laws. No longer in sole command of the family property or legally capable of willing a child away from his own mother, white men enjoyed fewer privileges as a result of the ways organized white women used their ballots.

Lawmakers also had less money to spend. If legislative concessions are the best measure of women's new electoral power, appropriations demonstrate the extent of politicians' fears. While it might be argued that increasing the age of consent was a small price to pay for the loyalty of white women voters, legislators in every southern state also provided substantial increases in the public funding they allocated to white women's priorities. Funding for Sheppard-Towner activities provided a case in point. Long promoted by Progressive reformers and agents of the Children's Bureau, the Sheppard-Towner program was designed to address the nation's alarming maternal and infant mortality rates. It was the first federal measure to receive strong backing from organized clubwomen after the ratification of the Nineteenth Amendment, and upon its enactment in 1921, it provided federal funds for states to support maternal and infant health care. In addition to small direct grants, states were eligible for increased matching funds, based on population. In every southern state except Louisiana, legislators immediately began appropriating tens of thousands of dollars annually for child hygiene work as soon as the federal Sheppard-Towner legislation passed. In every southern state, these appropriations marked an increase in state allocations for maternal and infant health; for some states, this was the first time public resources had ever been allocated to such programs.[94] And these sums were not insubstantial in the context of southern state budgets. In fiscal year 1923, the first year that full matching funds were available from the federal government, Kentucky's spending on child hygiene work was $55,613.35, an amount that exceeded the state's spending for the Agricultural Bureau and compared favorably to the $300,000 that the state spent on Confederate pensions.[95] That same year, Mississippi spent more than $39,000 on Sheppard-Towner activities and South Carolina spent more than $37,000.[96]

Moreover, Sheppard-Towner activities were not the only programs that received increased state support in the wake of woman suffrage. Throughout the region departments of public welfare represented the institutionalization of many white clubwomen's priorities, and newly enfranchised women voters provided an important new constituency in support of public welfare programs. Consequently, these departments provided both a symbolic representation of white women's priorities and a measure of how much southern legislators were willing to pay in order to support programs sponsored by women. Throughout the decade, southern white women requested increases in the state appropriations for public welfare programs, and they found that their legislators were often willing to oblige. In fiscal year 1923, the Virginia General Assembly increased the funding for the state board of public welfare by 26 percent, although the total state outlays increased by only 8 percent that year. State funding for the placement of children in foster care was also increased by 45 percent in that first budget drafted after women could vote. Under pressure from women constituents, state legislators created a new appropriation in the Bureau of Labor and Industry to focus exclusively on the employment of women and children and increased the funding for industrial homes for boys and girls, both white and black, by more than $65,000.[97]

Just as legislators supported public welfare appropriations in part to court organized white women, attacks on these state institutions represented an aggressive rejection of white women's new political authority. In Georgia and North Carolina, for example, some legislators took aim at the state departments of public welfare as a way of challenging the new political authority of enfranchised women. The legislators who were willing to reject the priorities of their new constituents so boldly were a minority, however. In both states, the majority of legislators rejected proposals to abolish boards of public welfare — proposals that had faced "emphatic protest" from organized and newly enfranchised women.[98] In Georgia, legislators not only rejected these attacks on the state board of public welfare but also responded to the demands of the state's legislative council by increasing the appropriations for the state board by $5,000. Although this was not as much as the women had requested, it constituted a 25 percent increase in the funding for the board. Moreover, in the next biennial budget, women's full demands were met, and $30,000 was appropriated annually for the board.[99] As southern states increased their budgets in the 1920s, newly enfranchised white women insisted that some of that spending should go to the education, public health, and social welfare programs they had long championed. When southern legislators appropriated funds for new programs or dramatically increased the public resources available for white women's priorities after 1920, their generosity testified to the power of women's votes.

As the defeats in Alabama demonstrated, southern legislators considered public resource allocation a zero-sum game. Increases in health and welfare programs necessarily demanded reductions in other types of spending. As one frustrated clubwoman from Alabama put it, "The entire aim of the lawmakers, apparently, has been to pass laws for raising funds and to deny all legislation, no matter what phase of Alabama's needs it might deal with, which does not promise immediate returns in dollars and cents to the state treasury."[100] Throughout the 1920s, the demands by enfranchised women for specific public appropriations challenged southern lawmakers' efforts to limit the size of the government and maintain control over the public purse. Moreover, in times of fiscal crisis there was little discretionary money available to lawmakers.[101] That organized white women were often successful in their demands for state appropriations is testament to the electoral pressure they brought to bear. Although members of the state's legislative council of women asked for more, when Alabama legislators granted appropriations for Sheppard-Towner programs during that 1923 legislative session, they believed that they had given their new white women constituents enough.

While the electoral strength of organized white women forced southern legislators to acquiesce to at least some of white women's spending priorities, the lobbying pressure from organized women in support of labor reforms was more than matched by the opposition of manufacturing interests. In the first decade after their enfranchisement, organized white women allied with labor interests to demand the regulation of child labor and protective labor legislation for women. Despite the fact that female political activists rarely hailed from working-class backgrounds, these southern white women decried the exploitation of laborers — especially women and children — by men of their own class.[102] As Elna Green has pointed out, mill owners and other manufacturing interests had long opposed woman suffrage because they "feared that suffragists would make good on their promises to vote in various reform measures and, in effect, change their world."[103] In the years after 1920, many white clubwomen worked to do just that.

Throughout the decade, organized southern white women placed labor legislation on their reform agenda. Repeatedly, their demands were met with weak reforms and outright resistance. In Texas, for example, legislators rejected the demands of white women for the establishment of a minimum wage for women and children workers in that first postenfranchisement legislative session. Faced with the determined opposition of business leaders, as well as the hostility of the governor eager to eliminate state bureaucracy, newly enfranchised women failed to exert the electoral pressure necessary to effectively challenge these powerful interests.[104] In Alabama, white women's efforts to abolish the convict lease system were opposed by the state's influential mine owners who relied on convict leasing for a cheap and expendable workforce. In 1923, mine owners' support for the program was enough to secure an extension of the convict lease system in Alabama over the expressed opposition of women reformers. Even the Georgia legislature, which granted the majority of the demands of enfranchised clubwomen in 1921, refused to make changes to the state's labor regulations. Indeed, when Georgia women joined with the Federation of Labor to demand maximum-hours legislation for working women, "every cotton mill man in Georgia" descended on the state legislature in protest.[105] As they fought for legislative reforms in the 1920s, southern white women had a new weapon with which to fight, but their enemies remained powerful. For the first time, state legislators had to balance the electoral pressure of white women reformers against that of manufacturing interests when they considered the merits of reform, but white clubwomen frequently lamented that manufacturers retained the upper hand.

Some of that influence was a function of existing political structures, and Democratic leaders worked throughout the decade to minimize women's threat to the political status quo. Indeed, some southern legislators showed their antipathy for woman suffrage by immediately introducing legislation to limit white women's political authority in other ways. In North Carolina and Tennessee, some members of the "Old Guard" responded to the enfranchisement of women by attempting to abolish the states' primary laws in 1921.[106] Having failed in their efforts to keep women from voting, these legislators hoped to limit the effects of woman suffrage by returning to a convention system for party nominations. As these men well knew, women's voices would be more easily excluded from conventions. The president of the Mississippi League of Women Voters framed the issue as a battle between nervous Democratic Party officials and newly enfranchised white women: "It is highly significant that the nation wide attack on the primary system began just about the time that the women of the country were enfranchised. The machine politicians had done their best to keep the women from getting the vote, but they had failed. However, machine politicians never say die. Beaten in one way they try another. . . . Having lost their fight against woman suffrage, they made a move to destroy the effectiveness of the woman vote."[107]

Determined that their voting would not be reduced to "a mere formality," organized white women fought hard to preserve the primary.[108] White clubwomen recognized that the primaries offered the only real competition in many districts and that men nominated without the support of women would be less responsive to the demands of these new constituents. Faced with growing opposition to the primary system, activist white women in South Carolina publicly denounced the convention system as one that "makes the political machines get as active as sparrows before a rain."[109] In North Carolina and Tennessee, politically active white women organized "very strong protest[s]" against lawmakers' efforts to abolish the statewide primary laws.[110] Faced with the opposition of their states' newly enfranchised women, "the more thoughtful political leaders" in both Tennessee and North Carolina "decide[d] that it would be a most unwise step to estrange the new electorate" by passing this legislation.[111]

State lawmakers were not always so reluctant to limit the political authority of organized white women. As one female activist in North Carolina confessed, she "did not, at any time, expect" that the Australian ballot bill would pass in the 1921 session.[112] When they pressed for changes in the laws that governed state elections and political parties, white women challenged the political authority of the state's leading men at the same time that they worked to increase the influence of white women's organizations. North Carolina's legislative council battled throughout the decade to secure the secret ballot law they first demanded in 1921. In Louisiana, Tennessee, and Texas, organized white women called for legislative action to ensure equal representation on political party committees. Organized white women in Louisiana insisted that, in the absence of equal representation on the Democratic State Central Committee, "the equal representation for all citizens guaranteed by our laws is a farce and a mere delusion."[113] While disfranchisement and segregation laws ensured that "equal representation for all citizens" would long remain a "farce," politically active white women recognized that their exclusion from party councils significantly limited their political power. In the states where political party rules were set by legislative enactment, enfranchised white women worked to leverage their ballots for power within the party. Although party leaders and legislators recognized the utility of female partisans and the necessity of courting women voters, they resisted efforts to invest women with real party authority.[114] The determination with which men fought "fifty-fifty" legislation signaled the challenge it posed to the political status quo. Legislators in all three states initially rejected equal representation bills, and a Texas legislator cautioned representatives of the women's legislative council to "quit asking for so much."[115]

In the legislative battles of the early 1920s, organized southern white women tested the limits of their new political authority and signaled their distance from the views of white men of their race and class. This was nowhere more evident than in their requests made on behalf of African Americans. Despite their general support for the disfranchisement of black voters and the system of Jim Crow, white southern clubwomen routinely included appropriations for African American institutions in their legislative requests. Since its establishment, legalized segregation had served as a vehicle for relegating African Americans to inferior physical spaces. Having thus separated the races, southern legislators allocated public resources with extreme prejudice, ensuring that those public facilities available to black southerners remained underfunded and inadequate. In their appropriations requests, however, white clubwomen resisted this pattern of public resource allocation by demanding state support for African American institutions. In particular, white clubwomen in the South frequently embraced the priorities originally championed by their black sisters, lobbying for state funding for homes for delinquent black boys and girls.[116] In 1928 the legislative agenda of the Richmond League of Women Voters included demands for park and playground facilities. Remarkably, these white women requested that "the first step in this direction should be the provision of a park and a swimming pool convenient to the congested colored sections of the city." That year, Richmond's politically active white women also called for increased teacher salaries "in both white and colored schools."[117]

On rare occasions, white clubwomen in the region also used their status as voters to demand better treatment for African Americans in the law. In 1926, for example, the Virginia Women's Council, whose member organizations included the United Daughters of the Confederacy and the Daughters of the American Revolution, as well as the more liberal League of Women Voters and YWCA, protested legislation that would have excluded some African American women from legal limits on women's hours of work. The bill proposed an exemption for "a certain industry in tobacco drying" from the labor laws that regulated women in industry, and legislators insisted that "this only affects a few colored women." In a hearing before the committee of the General Assembly that had responsibility for the bill, the white Women's Council members stood their ground, "saying out strongly that it made no difference to the women interested in defeating this measure whether these working women were white or colored, they did not want women overworked." Faced with the protests of organized white women, the bill died in committee.[118] Both the actions of Virginia's white clubwomen in challenging the racial status quo and the response of the General Assembly were unusual. Nevertheless, this episode demonstrated what was possible when organized white women were willing to use their ballots on behalf of African Americans.

Despite these tentative efforts, organized southern white women did not use their ballots to demand any sweeping amelioration of conditions for African Americans. No organizations of southern white women called for an end to Jim Crow in the 1920s. Despite organized white women's occasional resolutions of protest and their appropriations requests, their actions did not suggest to white Democrats that their candidacies were at risk if they opposed the measures that African Americans advocated. If southern legislators had believed that white women's votes hinged on their support of African American institutions or anti-Klan legislation, then the efforts of the Virginia's Women's Council would not have been noteworthy. Black women and men who were unable to leverage their own ballots could have worked effectively to leverage the ballots of white women in support of their own causes. Instead, however, the predictions of Annie Blackwell came true. In contrast to the optimistic views of some African American suffragists for the power of the ballot, this African American woman from North Carolina concluded that white women reformers, once enfranchised, would use their ballots to further white supremacy. As she put it, "If the women of the dominant race had a broader and clearer vision of the Fatherhood of God and the Brotherhood of man, they would exert that influence now in the legislative halls and criminal courts."[119]

Despite the important role of women in the region's early interracial movement, most organized southern white women did not view racial justice as a priority—or even a legitimate goal.[120] They did not question the idea that some people in society were more worthy than others. The same white women reformers who urged the end of the convict lease system or worked to expand the electorate or condemned lynching also supported eugenics legislation and worked to make sure that the poll tax was applied to women, as well as men. They did not oppose the restrictions that kept African Americans from the ballot, and they did not work to ensure that African American schools received equal funding or that Sheppard-Towner funds were used to help African American mothers and babies. The organized white women who used their ballots to demand a more equal place in southern society and greater protections for some of the region's weakest members did not use their new ballots to demand a change in the system of white supremacy.

Nevertheless, the legislative requests that white clubwomen did make on behalf of African Americans demonstrate that there were some things that they privileged above white supremacy. In their support for African American institutions, playgrounds for African American children, raises for African American teachers, and labor standards for African American employees, these activist white women indicated their support not for racial equality but for reforms that they believed would benefit their communities, white and black. By advocating these reforms, white women also signaled that they did not think that white supremacy was as vulnerable as many white men seemed to believe.

In contrast to many of the men of their own race and class who were sensitive to the slightest risks posed to their privileged place in southern society, many of these white female activists wanted political power and public authority to be more widely distributed. They did not dream of challenging the system of racial oppression from which they greatly benefited, but they had tired of politicians who resorted to "that bugaboo that inflames the people" in order to maintain their hold on power.[121] In the Norfolk, Virginia, *Housewife*, one southern woman denounced the political system in which candidates persisted in "rattling the dry bones of the spectre of 'negro domination.'" Women, she said, "came to the franchise too late to be blinded by these memories."[122] Although hers was perhaps not the sentiment shared by most politically active white women, another activist's explanation of white women's support for African American institutions suggests how far these women were from the mainstream views of white southern men. "In advocating state support for the institution for delinquent girls established at Efland by the N.C. Federation of Colored Women's Clubs," she contended, "the white women showed admirable breadth of sympathy and liberality." They also "realized that the aspersions cast in this region upon the morality of the Negro woman and the Negro girl are, certainly to a large extent, a racial prejudice fostered by white men for their own convenience."[123]

AS THIS QUOTE SUGGESTS, woman suffrage posed real challenges to the authority of white men in the region. Like all interest groups, white women's organizations suffered defeats, as well as victories, at the hands of state legislators. Their demands for the reallocation of public resources, labor reforms, and an expansion of women's public and private authority under the law were often rejected by southern legislatures. Nevertheless, as constituents, these white women could not be completely ignored. They forced onto the political agenda issues that threatened southern patriarchy, the economic status quo, and, occasionally, white supremacy itself.

The ratification of the Nineteenth Amendment did not immediately make southern women as politically powerful as southern men, but the ballot did make them more powerful than they had ever been before. Enfranchisement put organized white women — and occasionally even organized African American women — on a more equal footing with white men who also based their claims for legislation on the number of voters they could represent. Despite their lack of experience with the ballot, both black and white women took advantage of political opportunities in the 1920s to use their votes, and the political strategies they had honed over the decades, to shape the southern political system and southern society more to their liking. Even in the Solid South, where contemporary observers and scholars have assumed that women's votes failed to offer any political leverage, organized white women — and occasionally even black women — were able to use their votes successfully to make demands from the political system.

Chapter Seven

To Hold the Lady Votes
Southern Politics Ten Years after Suffrage

In June 1930, the candidates for state office appeared before the voters in Edgefield, South Carolina. There, one of the office-seekers announced his support for women jurors. Just ten years before, "candidates would have preferred the guillotine to a suspicion that they favored" jury service for women. On that hot summer afternoon, however, the candidate's announcement received little attention from the assembled voters, who were more focused on the issues of prohibition and taxes. In fact, only one unusual thing happened at the rally that day. In his speech to the crowd, another candidate "forgot the 'ladies,'" failing to acknowledge these important voters or to mention their concerns. The activist who recounted this event in the newspaper assured her readers that she "took note of it, and shall forget him when my time comes."[1]

Ten years after the ratification of the Nineteenth Amendment, southern politicians had grown accustomed to white women's participation in formal politics. They knew that they needed the votes of white women at election time, and they generally did not have to be reminded to pay attention to the concerns of these constituents. The candidate meetings that had been pioneered by newly enfranchised white women were no longer considered "novel stunts."[2] Candidates recognized the opportunity that these rallies offered, and office-seekers routinely pledged their support for issues of concern to women. Nevertheless, scholars have since concluded that the threat women voters posed to policy-makers was fleeting. According to historian Alan Lichtman, "By the late 1920s, male politicians surely realized that the female voter posed no threat to business as usual and need not be granted any special concessions."[3] "Putative leaders of the rank and file of American women," Lichtman contended, "could not use the political clout of their sisters as a bargaining chip in support of their demands."[4] Over time, scholars have shifted the "blame" for the ultimate failure of women's policy demands, but nearly all agree that the ability of women reformers to extract policy concessions waned as the 1920s wore on.[5] Far from the legislative "reign of terror" that antisuffragists had feared, enfranchised women "became neither an independent force in American politics nor an interest group within the parties whose loyalty had to be preserved."[6]

Yet in the face of ongoing efforts of women, both white and black, to undermine the system that southern Democrats had set in place, party leaders continued to express concern about the electoral threat posed by woman suffrage long after the region's women had cast their first ballots. It is true that by 1930 newspapers took little note of the presence of white women at the polls, but the seismic expansion of the electorate that began in 1920 reverberated throughout the decade. As figure 4 demonstrates, the hundreds of thousands of voters who had rocked the region's political system in 1920 continued to go to the polls in the years that followed.[7]

In Kentucky and North Carolina, the dramatic increase in presidential election voters that began in 1920 was sustained throughout the decade. In Alabama, 79 percent more voters crowded the polls after woman suffrage, and by 1928 that figure had climbed to 91 percent, despite the imposition of the poll tax on women after 1920. In Texas, the number of voters participating in presidential elections steadily increased after women became eligible to vote; by 1928 the number of Texans at the polls was nearly double that in 1916. In Louisiana and Virginia, the upsurge in new voters after woman suffrage was sustained through 1924, and by 1928 more than twice as many voters cast ballots in those states than had done so in 1916. While it is true that these states experienced substantial population growth during the 1920s, in nearly every state the proportional increase in voters from 1920 to 1932 exceeded the percentage increase in state population.[8] In short, the increase in voters during the 1920s was not simply attributable to population growth. Instead, registration figures from Louisiana suggest that the South's new voters were predominantly white women. Louisiana was the only southern state to keep registration data by race and gender in the 1920s, and those figures show a steady increase in white women's voter registration, both as a raw number and as a percentage of the total.[9] In Georgia and Mississippi, women were not permitted to participate in the 1920 elections, but the years that followed witnessed a slow, steady increase in total turnout, despite small incentives for participating in presidential elections in those states. Although voter turnout never increased significantly in Arkansas, and the dramatic increases in voter turnout in Tennessee were reversed once women faced the burden of the poll tax, the general trends indicate the persistent strength of women voters. After decades of declining voter participation, the increasing

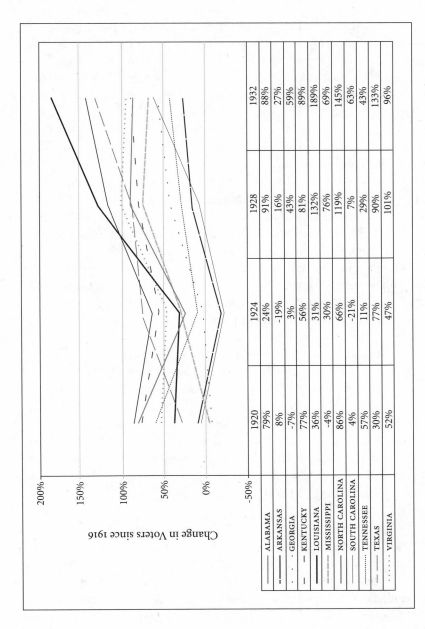

	1920	1924	1928	1932
ALABAMA	79%	24%	91%	88%
ARKANSAS	8%	-19%	16%	27%
GEORGIA	-7%	3%	43%	59%
KENTUCKY	77%	56%	81%	89%
LOUISIANA	36%	31%	132%	189%
MISSISSIPPI	-4%	30%	76%	69%
NORTH CAROLINA	86%	66%	119%	145%
SOUTH CAROLINA	4%	-21%	7%	63%
TENNESSEE	57%	11%	29%	43%
TEXAS	30%	77%	90%	133%
VIRGINIA	52%	47%	101%	96%

Change in Voters since 1916

200% — 150% — 100% — 50% — 0% — -50%

Figure 4. Trends in Voter Turnout in Presidential Elections, 1920–1932

number of voters at the polls in the 1920s signaled that women voters were in politics to stay.[10]

While there were important variations across the states, election statistics suggest that the southern women who first voted in 1920 continued to go to the polls in the years that followed. Perhaps even more important, female activists continued to work throughout the decade to qualify new people to vote. A 1929 report from Texas was typical: "The GET OUT THE VOTE Campaign was a splendid success," the league advised, "Dodgers and placards had been distributed, urging people to vote. Merchants put on their statements, 'Vote as you please, but please vote.' Radio talks were made and other methods were used to urge people to vote."[11] Women in Alabama "worked all summer from one end of the state to the other" to register new voters in 1928.[12] And while Atlanta's women no longer worked from a NuGrape truck, their voter mobilization efforts continued throughout the twenties.[13] In rural areas and urban centers, in movie houses and at county fairs, activist white women further refined the already sophisticated get-out-the-vote efforts that they had pioneered early in the decade. As historian Liette Gidlow has found, the League of Women Voters "sustained a serious commitment to GOTV throughout the period," and these local efforts no doubt encouraged the increasing number of voters that most southern states enjoyed.[14] In the South, these voter mobilization campaigns were white women's most persistent and effective challenge to disfranchisement. Through voter registration campaigns and citizenship schools, white clubwomen continued to disseminate information that made increased voter participation possible. Democratic Party leaders had long relied on complicated registration procedures to secure disfranchisement. Throughout the twenties, organized white women regularly pulled back the veil, revealing the labyrinthine requirements disfranchisers had put in place and showing would-be voters how to navigate them.

As white women continued to pry open the closed system of southern politics by bringing new voters to the polls, they also persisted in challenging Democratic Party control of the region. In contrast to the southern men who were the architects of disfranchisement, many organized white women abhorred the lack of political competition in their region. Through their candidate meetings and questionnaires, white clubwomen continued to offer Republicans and independent Democrats a regular venue and audience for their messages. By decade's end these events had become commonplace, and the state legislative councils and Leagues of Women Voters had established their nonpartisanship. Southern white women also persisted in their more explicit overtures to the Republican Party. Richmond league members, frustrated with the lack of electoral competition in their city, publicly called on

Republican leaders in 1927 to field candidates for all public offices, instead of ceding Virginia's elections to Democrats without a fight.[15] A prominent North Carolina woman, disgusted with the multiple box system of voting in her state, the absence of a secret ballot, and the poor field of candidates offered by the Democratic Party, denounced the political status quo in 1926 and "before a group of interested spectators" she refused to "vote — 'er straight."[16] She then spread the news of her political heresy through the bulletin of her state's League of Women Voters, thereby setting a political example. Just as Democratic Party leaders had suspected, women's votes could not be counted upon; indeed, long after women cast their first ballots in the region, some white women persisted in publicly challenging Democratic Party hegemony. Just weeks before election day in 1924, one "Democratic" woman in Kentucky wrote to party headquarters to explain why she would not vote for the party's nominee for senate. "I should never have been put in the position of having to choose between a wet Democrat and a dry Republican," she insisted, "but since I have been put in that position, I have made my choice." In an election-eve threat that captured the sentiment of many voting women, she continued, "It is for women to call out, get behind, and elect the best men we have. Until they do this, I will scratch my ticket whenever I think the cause of righteousness would be served by my so doing."[17]

That willingness to "scratch" one's ticket whenever "the cause of righteousness" might be served is precisely what white women's organizations worked to cultivate in their members during the twenties. Through women's councils, PTAs, federated women's clubs, and the League of Women Voters, white clubwomen in the twenties continued to leverage their ballots for specific policy goals by demonstrating the independence of their votes and the size of their electoral threat. In a call to members to register to vote in 1930, the president of the Georgia PTA reaffirmed the nonpartisan lobbying strategy of enfranchised women. "We have 45,527 members," the president declared. "If the men who aspire to high political office in the state realized that every member of the Georgia Congress of Parent-Teacher association is a potential voter and may be influenced in his or her choice of a candidate by the aspirant's attitude to the welfare of Georgia's children, it might and in all probability will contribute to the success of salutary legislation."[18] Determined that the region's white women would "vote with their eyes wide open," white women's organizations established their legislative agendas in advance of the primaries and called on candidates to publicly articulate their positions.[19] Like many women in the region, rural white women organized in South Carolina's Council of Farm Women endorsed five legislative measures in advance of the 1926 elections and urged their members to "carry these questions to your county campaign meeting and find out how your candidates stand on these subjects."[20] Enfranchised white women were politically savvy; they recognized that "the public men whose policy is to give their constituents what they want . . . will always continue in public life in large numbers."[21] Consequently, these clubwomen worked to remind "public men" of women's status as constituents and make it clear what women wanted.

In most southern states, women's legislative councils increased their membership during the 1920s, which enhanced their ability to speak on behalf of what "women" wanted. In nearly every southern state, the federation of women's clubs joined the legislative council, which enabled lobbyists to claim grassroots support from all white clubwomen.[22] Moreover, there was little evidence at the state level of the public acrimony that characterized the divisions among some national women's clubs.[23] Throughout the decade legislative council membership in southern states remained wide-ranging, with the state's Interracial Commission working alongside the United Daughters of the Confederacy in Georgia, and members of the League of Women Voters and the YWCA working alongside Daughters of the American Revolution in Virginia.[24] Despite growing skepticism about "what women have done with the vote," southern white women remained convinced that their ballots could be used to achieve policy ends.[25] As they increasingly joined forces and adopted similar tactics, organized white women worked to hone the electoral threat that their new ballots afforded them.

GIVEN THE VOTING STRENGTH of their new constituents, southern politicians had no choice but to maintain an ongoing courtship with these enfranchised white women. Despite the apparent continuity in Democratic supremacy before and after 1920, the Nineteenth Amendment posed a substantial challenge to the Solid South. To remain in power in the postsuffrage era, Democratic Party leaders had to attract white women voters. In the years that followed the enfranchisement of women, the political courtship that seemed so novel in the fall of 1920 became commonplace and, significantly, expected. Organized white women continued to submit policy questionnaires to candidates for office, and in election cycle after election cycle, those candidates made the effort to meet white women's demands, not only responding to the questionnaires, but also working to characterize their own policy positions in ways that would be favorable to white clubwomen. They also continued to make their "bow to the ladies" by appearing before women's organizations and participating in the League of Women Voters's candidate meetings. They did so not out of a sense of chivalry or commitment to public service but because these organizations represented groups of voters. And any good politician knew that a woman who took the time to write for information or compile candidate scorecards would certainly make her appearance at the polls.

In addition to accepting invitations to speak before women's organizations and responding to women's questionnaires, Democratic Party leaders continued to target white women voters for special appeals. In 1924, for example, the vice chairman of the Democratic National Committee addressed the Third Regional Conference of Democratic Women. There she urged the need for "Schools of Democracy," especially among the women of the South. As she put it, southern women "vote the Democratic ticket from habit and the trouble with that is that any habit, however good or bad, can be broken."[26] That same year, members of the Charleston (South Carolina) Democratic Executive Committee moved the location of Democratic club meetings to locales more likely to attract women voters, noting, "It is important for the best interest of the Democratic Party that these new voters be urged to take an active part in the affairs of the Party."[27] In Kentucky, the Democratic state party targeted appeals to women in a monthly *Democratic Woman's Journal*.[28] Certainly party leaders would not have wasted time or money on voter outreach efforts for women if their votes were not to some degree in question.

Southern candidates campaigned vigorously for the votes of white women, and they targeted their messages to women in increasingly sophisticated ways by decade's end. In 1930, one Alabama partisan outlined "the campaign literature most needed by the women," insisting that white women's persistent independence at the polls must be met with literature "giving the fundamental principles of the Democratic Party, explaining the difference between independent voting and party voting, party allegiance, explaining the party system of government . . . and answering the contention that a vote for the party is a vote for the return of open saloons."[29] Loathe to target all Kentucky women with a single message, one candidate for governor in 1927 called on women from across the state to help him devise local appeals "to interest the women voters" in his election.[30] In a creative, if patronizing, attempt to win support from women in his primary fight for U.S. Senate in 1928, Texan Alvin Owsley distributed souvenir thimbles to women supporters.[31]

Just as candidates targeted "women's" issues to appeal to white women voters, they also continued to rely on prominent white women to reach key groups of voters. It was demeaning for white southern men to seek the assistance of women in politics, and they undoubtedly humbled themselves before women only to the extent necessary to ensure political victory. Yet southern politicians continued to call on white women for help throughout the 1920s. In Kentucky, a man considering a run for governor contacted the state League of Women Voters in 1926 "and asked for all the speeches, etc. that had been used and made at [their] Convention."[32] After he had looked the materials over, he returned them to the league and asked what the women "wanted of him as a candidate."[33] In contrast to 1920, when candidates looked to women leaders merely for introductions to other women, politicians by the end of the decade recognized the need to look to leading clubwomen for strategic policy advice. As the Kentucky League of Women Voters reported in 1926, politicians were "just a little bit afraid of the women."[34]

Leaders of white women's organizations represented themselves as spokesmen for "women voters" when they lobbied for legislative change; consequently, hopeful candidates called on these clubwomen for assistance during the hot campaign seasons. G. Walter Mapp, of Virginia, was no exception. He devoted considerable effort to the organization of white women on behalf of his 1925 gubernatorial campaign. Determined to effectively target women voters in his state, he wrote to friends and supporters asking them to "kindly send at your earliest convenience a list of the . . . key women, in your section."[35] Similarly, a campaign coordinator for Senator Furnifold McLendl Simmons contacted a prominent North Carolina woman in 1930 to ask if she would be willing to take charge of organizing women on behalf of his reelection.[36] Democratic candidates throughout the decade called on prominent women to assist their campaigns, made election-eve speeches before women's clubs, and addressed campaign literature specifically to women voters. If southern white men believed that the threat of women's ballots had faded by the end of the decade, this solicitousness of white women voters certainly did not reflect it.

Party leaders did not always respond to the threat of women's votes with such consideration, however. Occasionally white women's election-season activities provoked attacks by southern Democrats, and in those rare moments, politicians' frustration with the political fallout from woman suffrage was clear. In 1926, for example, the Richmond City Democratic Committee warned the local League of Women Voters to "stop meddling" in party affairs by holding mass meetings of Democratic primary candidates.[37] In a direct attack on the league's voter mobilization efforts, the News Leader just one year later declared that "too many questionnaires confuse" and "too much discussion is apt to carry the argument into abstrusities that confirm indifference."[38] While they couched their objections in the democratic rhetoric of concern for voter participation, Democratic Party leaders in Richmond simply objected to having to court women voters. They did not want to fill out more questionnaires. Perhaps they had grown tired of having to stipulate their campaign promises so specifically, and in writing. To be sure, party leaders longed for the days when they could choose their party nominees without women "meddling" in party affairs.

Politicians in Richmond were not alone. In Alabama as well, Democratic Party leaders attacked the state league for its election-season questionnaires and mass meetings. League leaders there saw clearly the reason for party leaders' opposition and responded: "Those who would try criticizing the LWV for seeking information and seeking it from the candidate himself is [*sic*] lacking in just plain everyday common sense. Some claim the league has made enemies by this procedure and the league realizes it. It always will make enemies of certain groups who do not want their way disturbed."[39] A North Carolina woman described the situation in her state simply: "'The powers that be' are, and always have been very antagonistical [*sic*] toward our league."[40]

By mid-decade, it seems, many southern Democrats had had enough. While they justified their critiques of the league by arguing that the organization's style of political mobilization contributed to voter apathy, the vehemence of party leaders' denunciations (and the growing number of voters at the polls) suggest another reason for their concerns. Perhaps they had grown tired of "bowing to the ladies" at league political meetings, or perhaps they objected to the league's providing a forum for Republicans and independent Democrats.[41] The essential problem for these southern Democrats, however, was the power of women's votes. After 1920, politicians knew that they could not simply ignore organized white women voters. Instead, politicians courted white women, addressed women's clubs and answered their questionnaires, and, occasionally, when frustration boiled over, denounced women, publicly and in private. Politically active white women seemed to recognize that all of these forms of attention were indicative of women's political power. As the Georgia League of Women Voters noted when it described its role in the bruising primary battle of 1926, "We have gained confidence. We have gained self-respect. We have gained strength. We have gained the notable privilege of having men write us anonymous letters to threaten and revile us. And thereby we know they fear us!"[42]

Indeed, many southern Democrats found that they had reason to fear women voters at the polls. In the absence of meaningful partisan competition in most southern states, Democratic primaries offered voters their only real choice among candidates. State and local races were often hotly contested in the primaries, and the addition of women voters only exacerbated the competition. In Mississippi, for example, more than 100,000 new voters crowded the polls for the first gubernatorial primary in which women were allowed to vote. This surge in voters marked a 71 percent increase in the

electorate since 1919. Over the course of the decade, primary voter participation continued to increase, with nearly 60,000 additional voters helping
to select the state's gubernatorial nominee in 1931.[43] While party leaders in
Mississippi could be reasonably certain that new women voters would not
vote Republican, they could not always control—or reliably predict—the
ways in which the increasing numbers of new voters would align themselves
in the primaries.

The extent to which women's presence undermined Democratic Party
leaders' control was underscored by men's efforts throughout the region to
abolish the primary system in favor of conventions. Unsuccessful attempts
to eliminate the primary in North Carolina and Tennessee in 1921 signaled
the desire of some party leaders to quickly remove the political uncertainty
that the Nineteenth Amendment had introduced.[44] Although these earliest
attempts to nullify the effects of the Nineteenth Amendment failed, party
leaders expressed their continuing concerns through their repeated attacks
on the primary. North Carolina Democrats tried again to repeal the primary
in 1924, and Tennessee lawmakers introduced legislation to abolish that
state's primary in 1929.[45] In 1924, Virginia lawmakers attempted to provide
for reregistration of voters in the state. Due to a law providing for permanent registration of men "who were registered before a certain year," activist
women recognized this proposal as an attack "upon the women voters" and
successfully defeated it.[46] In 1923 and again in 1927, Texas women lobbied
successfully in opposition to changes in the primary system.[47] In 1927, the
proposed change in the primary system was opposed not only by the League
of Women Voters but also by the Texas Women's Democratic Association,
women who despite their loyal partisanship recognized that a return to conventions would rob them of the power they had obtained within the party.[48]
By sponsoring the return to a male-dominated convention system for determining the party's nominees, Democratic leaders attempted to lock women
out of politics in the same way that the white primary system had systematically excluded African Americans from the only elections that mattered.
Unlike black southerners who had been unable to prevent the establishment
of white primaries, however, white southern women were adamant—and
successful—in their opposition to a return to convention systems. Nevertheless, the determination with which party leaders fought, and refought,
these primary battles was an acknowledgment of white women's ongoing
threat to party control.

During Virginia's 1925 gubernatorial primary fight, the Democratic machine candidate, Harry Byrd, was greeted with an unexpected display of the
independence of women voters at a mass meeting sponsored by the League
of Women Voters. When Byrd stood to give his speech before the assembled

crowd, he opened his remarks by noting, "My opponent is saying that everything is wrong in Va., and the only way to set it right is to elect him governor."[49] From the back of the room, a man shouted, "And he's right!" whereupon the women in the audience erupted into applause and "absolutely took the speech out of Harry Byrd's hands entirely."[50] During that primary campaign, Byrd was so concerned about the opposition of white women voters that one of his operatives removed copies of the *Winchester Star* from the state library in order to conceal an antisuffrage editorial Byrd had written in 1918.[51] Byrd survived that fight, but efforts by white women to expand intraparty competition remained troublesome to the state's Democrats, as their admonition to women to "stop meddling" made clear.

In Hot Springs, Arkansas, it was not merely women voters but black voters who used their ballots to defeat the regular Democratic nominee for mayor in favor of an independent Democrat who promised African Americans "a square deal."[52] In 1927, when the incumbent mayor of that resort town declined to run for reelection, local Democrats nominated Sidney McNutt in the Democratic primary. McNutt was a "wealthy theatre owner" in the city who had rebuffed African American requests that he provide a separate balcony for black patrons in his theater. Under state law, African Americans could not enter the theater at all in the absence of segregated seating, and McNutt was rumored to have responded that "he did not want Negro patronage."[53] He had also opposed efforts to rebuild the black Union Baptist Church on its original site, insisting that the neighborhood be reserved for white residential use. Black Arkansans had reason to fear McNutt as their mayor, and they "lined up behind" the independent Democrat Leo McLaughlin.[54] "Using the Vote Effectively," more than 3,000 African Americans in Hot Springs cast their ballots for McLaughlin, providing him the margin of victory.[55] Although the press accounts made no mention of black women voters specifically, their votes proved just as crucial as black men's in this "bitterly fought election," as fewer than 1,500 votes separated the two candidates.[56] As "white men and women carried Negroes to the polls" in support of the independent Democrat, the threat that woman suffrage posed to politics-as-usual in the South was clear.[57]

IN PRIMARY CAMPAIGNS and even general elections in some southern counties, Democrats seemed as uncertain of the woman vote at the end of the decade as they had been on the eve of ratification. In October 1924, one newspaper headline read, "Democrats Are None Too Sure of Tennessee," and the article described Democrats as having "the scare of their lives."[58] That same year, partisans in Kentucky fretted about Democratic Party bolters, particularly prohibitionist women. "The 'drys' are on the rampage," one concerned Democrat reported, "and no doubt, other blazes will be kindled by the WCTU which meets here next week."[59] As it turned out, this partisan's fears were well-founded; Democratic candidates in Kentucky that year lost not only the presidential race but many state races as well.[60] As one Mississippi observer explained, "The woman voter was somewhat more inclined to defy the Democratic Party whip than were the men. The women had not been schooled in party loyalty and were not inclined to attach so much importance to that question as were the men."[61] Writing in 1930, a political leader in Alabama contacted the chairman of the state Democratic Executive Committee "to say to [him] that in [his] opinion the Democratic Party is facing a most serious situation — far more serious than many seem to think."[62] Another Alabama partisan suggested that the party's predicament was the result of "having neglected non-partisan Democratic rallies and speakings."[63] Congressman A. J. Montague of Virginia predicted in 1929 that if Democrats did not "win the Governorship this fall . . . [the Democratic Party] is likely to lose control of Virginia for many years."[64]

Of course, Democrats in Virginia would maintain their control for many years after Montague's fateful prediction, but the number of counties in which Republicans received at least 45 percent of the vote increased significantly when women cast their first votes for president. And in Alabama, Kentucky, and Texas, the number of counties in which the Republican presidential nominee was competitive remained above the pre–Nineteenth Amendment level in 1924. After women were enfranchised, the fortunes of Republican congressional candidates improved as well. In every election in the 1920s, Republican congressional candidates in Alabama, Arkansas, Tennessee, and Texas were competitive in more counties than they had been in 1918. Similarly, in all but the 1926 election, Republican congressional candidates in Virginia were more successful in the decade after women were enfranchised than they had been before women were granted the right to vote. Republicans did not make steady increases, but the volatility of the election results suggests that each time Democrats may have believed they had the Republican challenge contained, Republican votes climbed again.[65]

To be sure, the ballots of new Republican voters did not bring real partisan competition to most parts of the South, but the increasing Republican competition did bolster organized women's claims to nonpartisanship and made the threat of female ticket-splitters more apparent. In the absence of separately counted ballots or sophisticated exit polling there was little way for men to know how women voted, even after they had cast ballots in 1920. There was anecdotal evidence and speculation, but the raw election results could only tell party leaders so much, and in most states those election results suggested that women's votes helped Republicans at least as much as they helped Democrats. Moreover, white men's belief in women's fickle nature was not eliminated by the 1920 election results. In fact, politically active white women cultivated their image as independent voters. Thus, while white women may have cast their first ballots for Democrats, Democratic leaders were not convinced that those women would remain loyal. In short, even after 1920 southern political elites had reason to worry that woman suffrage would critically undermine the Democratic structure of political control, particularly when nearly every effort of politically active southern women seemed designed to do just that.

In 1928, at a meeting sponsored by the Norfolk, Virginia, League of Women Voters, Democratic congressman J. T. Deal appeared alongside his Republican rival, seeking the support of his district's white women. Congressman Deal had been in this spot before. Since their enfranchisement, the South's politically active white women had pioneered the use of candidate meetings and questionnaires that were designed to ferret out the candidates most likely to support their legislative agendas. Deal had faced the women's questioning in previous elections, and he had sought a hearing from them after he voted against the Sheppard-Towner Act, one of their legislative priorities.[66] On this afternoon, however, Deal was preaching party loyalty. As one woman described it, he "gave a strong . . . plea to the women to save [the] Democratic party by being loyal to their life-long party affiliations." In response, a woman rose from the audience to remind her congressman that "women had no life-long party affiliations."[67] Congressman Deal's response was not noted, but he was one of three Democratic congressional candidates defeated by their Republican opponents in Virginia that year, part of a Republican insurgency that was widely blamed on women voters.

Through their voter mobilization efforts, their denunciations of party loyalty, and the way they cast their ballots, organized white women posed a persistent threat to Democratic control of southern politics. Eight years after their enfranchisement, the election of 1928 seemed to many to be the inevitable manifestation of women's electoral threat. In 1928, the Republican Party won more votes in the South than it had at any time since Reconstruction. Herbert Hoover, the Republican presidential nominee, won a majority of votes in Kentucky, North Carolina, Tennessee, Texas, and Virginia. In Alabama, almost 49 percent of voters cast their ballots for Hoover, and Virginia sent three Republican congressmen to Washington as a result of the elections that year.

With the nomination of Alfred E. Smith for president in 1928, the Democratic Party released a force that had been growing for some time in the South. A Catholic, a New Yorker, and a "wet" Smith aroused the prejudices of the South's Protestant, rural, and staunchly "dry" population. The choice of Joseph T. Robinson, an Arkansan, as his running mate did little to comfort disgruntled southerners. After the nominating convention, southern Democrats returned to their home states and faced a growing rebellion. While most southern party leaders remained loyal to the nominee and worked to quell the partisan unrest, several of the region's most prominent politicians publicly disavowed the Democratic nominee. In political circles, election-season talk revolved around Smith, Hoover, "Hoovercrats," and how the party would deal with "party bolters."

Although prohibition was not the only issue in this contentious election, it played a central role in driving nominally Democratic voters to support the Republican nominee. And since prohibition was viewed as primarily a "women's issue," party loyalists realized that their main problem lay with white women voters. One of Georgia's Democratic congressmen wrote in July 1928 that "there is considerable opposition to Governor Smith here, principally among the ladies."[68] A party leader gave Smith little chance of defeating Hoover in Virginia, lamenting that "the women and preachers I fear will defeat him."[69] In Alabama, a Democratic organizer declared, "We are going to have a mean fight in this State. The women and the preachers are raising the Devil and you know he is a hard fellow to fight."[70] Even in Arkansas, home of the Democrats' vice presidential nominee, party leaders worried about Smith's fate and accused "women voters" of "bolting."[71] If Democratic leaders had become at all complacent about the threat that woman suffrage posed to Democratic control of politics, the 1928 presidential campaign was a stark reminder of the system's inherent instability.

As they had in 1920, male party leaders turned to Democratic white women to shore up the party structure in 1928. With a renewed enthusiasm born of fear, male party leaders called on loyal white women to organize Democratic women voters and stump the state for Smith. Many white women answered the party's call. In early September, Marie Bankhead Owen, the antisuffragist-turned–Democratic Party organizer from Alabama, was called on by Democratic Party officials in her state. She responded enthusiastically that she was "all cocked and primed to 'knock 'em down' to Al," and she signed her name, "With all good wishes for the success of the Party and assuring you that I will be present at the roll call."[72] Gertrude Weil resigned the presidency of the North Carolina League of Women Voters to campaign actively for Smith.[73] As the Georgia Democratic Party organized for the campaign season, party leaders called on Mrs. Lamar Lipscomb to campaign for Smith not only in her home state but throughout the South. At the party's request, Lipscomb spent the last five weeks before the election on the campaign trail, giving dozens of speeches, each in a different town.[74]

Not all Democratic white women were so willing to lend their efforts to the party's ticket, however. When party leaders called on North Carolina's national Democratic committeewoman to plan for the presidential campaign, headlines announced that "Mrs. James G. Fearing Ignored Mull's Call" and advertised that she "has not yet declared her stand for or against the party's nominee for the presidency."[75] After serving as a Democrat in the Mississippi legislature and working successfully to obtain control of her county's Democratic Executive Committee in 1924, Nellie Nugent Somerville refused to endorse the Democratic ticket in 1928. Instead, she used her position as president of the Mississippi Women's Christian Temperance Union to urge the state's women voters to put the "ideals of Christian citizenship" above party regularity.[76] In her address to the Mississippi WCTU and in other public statements, she called on Mississippi voters to vote for Hoover because "prohibition would be safe in [his] hands."[77] In Texas, two women resigned as Democratic presidential electors when the party nominated Smith.[78] These public acts of defiance confirmed what party leaders had always feared: the loyalty of even the region's most committed female Democrats could not be counted on.

At the same time, Republicans recognized that this revolt by Democratic and independent white women offered them an opportunity to advance the work that they had begun in 1920 of using woman suffrage to bolster Republican opposition in the region. At the national level, Herbert Hoover's campaign pioneered sophisticated political techniques that were designed to target specific segments of the voting population.[79] Under the auspices of the Hoover-Curtis Organization Bureau, Republicans targeted auto salesmen, college students, chiropractors, florists, aviators, lawyers, lumbermen, real estate agents, first-time voters, jewelers, osteopaths, and dozens of other groups of voters for specific campaign appeals. At both the national and local levels, however, Republican organizers seemed particularly interested in targeting their campaign appeals to women voters. Hoover campaign workers established women's divisions composed of state vice chairmen, congressional district vice chairmen, and representatives from every county. These representatives promoted Hoover's candidacy locally and obtained pledge cards from women, which were used to get out the vote on election day. The campaign also recruited women to serve as "Hoover Hostesses" who invited other women to listen to radio shows created by the campaign and specifically targeted to female audiences.[80]

Local Republicans, too, seemed to believe that they could build a viable Republican base with the help of white women voters. In Virginia, a Republican organizer instructed party workers to advertise Hoover campaign rallies by inviting "all persons, and especially ladies, irrespective of party affiliations," to attend.[81] In Georgia, Hoover supporters took out a full-page ad in the bulletin of the League of Women Voters, urging the state's women to cast their ballots for a Republican.[82] In Texas, Republican women appointed "former Democrats" to organize the state's women into "Homemakers" clubs, "first voters" clubs, and other organizations in support of the Hoover-Curtis ticket.[83] A former Democrat who described herself as "a new Republican" recruited support for the Republican ticket in Arkansas through an organization that included women voters active in every county in the state.[84]

Throughout the region, politically active white women exulted in the enthusiasm that surrounded the 1928 elections and continued to extol the virtues of casting independent ballots. In Baldwin County, Alabama, the League of Women Voters praised women's devotion to principle rather than partisanship: "When they go to the polls on Nov. 6th they will vote for Smith or Hoover, not because they have always voted the Democratic or Republican ticket or because their husbands, fathers or brothers tell them which way to vote, but because they believe that the man they choose will most nearly meet their ideas of what the President of the United States should be."[85] In Texas, the state WCTU held its annual convention just weeks before the presidential election and called on prohibitionist women "to elect dry candidates for office, regardless of party affiliations."[86] Even in Mississippi, organized white women defended voters' right not to toe the party line. In an editorial in the *Mississippi Woman's Magazine*, one white clubwoman wrote that no matter who she decided to vote for, "the Mississippi woman can be depended on to vote her honest and intelligent conviction."[87]

The Republican victories that year were only the most obvious expression of the electoral threat that women voters had cultivated since their enfranchisement. Throughout the decade, white women's organizations had urged voters to cast their ballots without regard to party. Their candidate questionnaires and mass meetings were designed to ensure that white women could cast informed ballots, and their lobbying strategy was premised on the notion that issues and conscience, not personal or party loyalty, would guide women at the polls. These messages helped to lay the foundation for the 1928 revolt and, to the "thrill" of female activists, upset party leaders who "just took for granted [women] were born Democrats and had to die that way."[88]

Even more ominously, some loyal Democratic women who had worked determinedly to persuade their sisters to vote for Smith saw a political benefit in the election-day loss. As one Democratic partisan explained, "This situation should be taken as a sort of readjustment to the new order of things. Perhaps even southern democrats will do more strict calculation in the future, on the part that women can and may play in the turning of the scales.

Regrettable, but perhaps it is as well to have the lightning strike and get it over with."[89] Another southern partisan declared that she was "perfectly sick" over the election results, but she nevertheless saw in them an opportunity to build a stronger organization of Democratic women in her state.[90] Referring to another election defeat for the Democrats, one North Carolina observer offered an explanation for the party's uncertain fortunes: "It seemed to the women more important that elections in North Carolina should be honestly conducted, that the voter should be unmolested in casting his ballot than that the Democratic Party should win."[91]

Of course, male Democratic Party leaders in the South disagreed that there was something more important "than that the Democratic party should win." Eight years after southern women obtained the right to vote, the region's politics had been transformed, and the Solid South seemed remarkably unstable. Incumbent Democratic politicians like J. T. Deal had to campaign on white women's terms, and they literally begged white women for their votes. Politically active white women responded with condemnations of party loyalty and demands for legislative change. Southern women, white and black, continued to undermine the system of disfranchisement and welcome new voters to the polls. By no coincidence, Republicans and independent Democrats seemed poised for victory.

Faced with the persistent electoral threat posed by white women voters, southern politicians were forced to acknowledge that the distribution of political power to newly enfranchised white women would not be temporary. To remain in control of the region's political system, southern Democrats would have to continue to grant policy concessions to the region's organized white women voters. Although some Democratic Party leaders, like those in Georgia, responded to women's electoral threat by "intimidat[ing] and heckl[ing] and browbeat[ing]" female party bolters, most southern politicians recognized that the most effective way to secure the loyalty of these constituents was by sponsoring the legislation they demanded.[92] Using this leverage, white clubwomen achieved unprecedented policy outcomes in their states throughout the 1920s.

In contrast to women's lobbying at the federal level, southern white women lobbying at the state level continued to achieve legislative successes throughout the decade. In Alabama, legislators who had rejected nearly every request of organized white women in 1923 credited women with the end of the convict lease system in that state in 1927 and granted other demands that had been rejected in that first postratification session of the General Assembly. In Mississippi, the legislature passed a mothers' pension program in 1928 for the first time, although white women had been demanding it since before the ratification of the Nineteenth Amendment. In Tennessee, white women's demands for a compulsory school attendance law were met in 1925, and, after a decade-long fight for the measure, legislators finally granted a five-day waiting period for marriage in 1929. In Virginia, white women fought to improve the compulsory school law passed in 1922 and finally won the changes they wanted in 1928. It was also not until mid-decade that Virginia's organized white women obtained an increase in the age of consent, and they had to fight for nearly ten years before they obtained joint guardianship of their children.[93] In Kentucky, organized white women staged no similar, decade-long fight for a single policy, but their persistent electoral strength was obvious in 1930 when state legislators granted every single legislative demand of the state League of Women Voters.[94]

In Texas, newly enfranchised women had experienced no initial responsiveness from state legislators. In the legislative session of 1921, all five of the policy demands put forth by the state League of Women Voters were rejected by the General Assembly.[95] Reeling from their postenfranchisement defeat, white women's organizations from around the state formed a legislative coalition in 1922. With the new ability to speak with one voice and articulate a clear set of "women's" demands from Texas legislators, enfranchised white women successfully leveraged their votes for a variety of legislative reforms. In 1923, Texas women secured "prison legislation, prohibition legislation, educational legislation, [and] protection for the professional nurses" under the auspices of the Texas Joint Legislative Council.[96] That year they also secured an enormous appropriation for rural schools, totaling $3 million.[97] As one observer reported, Texas legislators passed all of the measures sponsored by the fledgling Joint Legislative Committee "in almost perfect condition."[98] In the years that followed, the white women organized through the Texas Joint Legislative Committee demonstrated the political efficacy of organized, enfranchised, white women. Despite their inauspicious beginning in the legislative session of 1921, Texas's white women could point to a number of legislative victories by decade's end, including prison reform legislation in 1927, legislation equalizing the property rights of married persons in 1929, and expansion of the compulsory education laws that same year.[99] Indeed, organized white women in Texas were so successful in securing legislation and appropriations after 1920 that one historian has described their "impact on the American political scene" as "profound."[100] At a minimum, their legislative successes indicated the power of the vote to ensure that the "demands of the women's organizations . . . carry any weight."[101]

In North Carolina, the persistent strength of organized white women voters was also obvious. White clubwomen in that state had demanded a secret ballot law throughout the decade, and after years of strenuous opposition from party leaders whose control it threatened, white women won this important victory in 1929. That year North Carolina's legislators also granted the long-standing demands of organized white women for workman's compensation legislation and a five-day notice of marriage. If, as some scholars contend, men and women had come to recognize that women's ballots made little difference at the federal level, the experiences at the state level led one North Carolina white woman to conclude quite the opposite. In the spring of 1928, as organized white women began surveying the primary candidates about their policy positions and preparing their election-year lobbying plans, she wryly noted, "I am happy to find that the men are at last recognizing that women have a vote."[102]

During the 1920s, southern politicians "recognized" white women's votes by enacting a wide array of legislation that protected women and children, limited the power of Democratic officials, and increasingly equalized the civil rights of men and women. The most dramatic measure of enfranchised women's new electoral power, however, came in the appropriations requests granted by state legislators. Throughout the decade, the resource allocations made by southern lawmakers acknowledged the persistent electoral power of their female constituents.

Due in large measure to the lobbying efforts of unenfranchised white women during the first two decades of the twentieth century, Alabama established a Child Welfare Department in 1919.[103] In addition to its broad mandate to protect the children of the state, that agency was responsible for the enforcement of Alabama's child labor and compulsory education laws. When the agency received its first state resources, its annual appropriation was set at just under $11,000.[104] As soon as women were enfranchised, however, the disbursements to the Child Welfare Department more than doubled to $28,000 for fiscal year 1921 and increased to nearly $32,000 for fiscal year 1922.[105] After the state legislature met for its first postenfranchisement session in 1923, the budget for the agency skyrocketed to $50,000 annually.[106] Under pressure from the state's enfranchised women, who made their priorities known through a well-organized legislative council, lawmakers in 1927 increased the department's appropriation to $93,000.[107] Over the course of the decade, funding for the department increased more than 900 percent, substantially outstripping the pace of growth in the budget as a whole. Indeed, even as the state's total budget declined by 11 percent in fiscal year 1930, funding for the Child Welfare Department increased again to more than $97,000.[108] Through two decades of determined effort, Alabama's white women succeeded in convincing lawmakers to create a state agency to care for the state's children, but lawmakers' initial appropriations to this new department reflected the weakness of the agency's unenfranchised promoters. Once white clubwomen began to exercise their ballots, lawmakers responded with substantial and increasing state resources.

In Virginia, organized white clubwomen made appropriations for the state's board of public welfare a top priority beginning in 1924.[109] The state's white women had long supported the work of the board, and appropriations had increased from $11,700 in 1919 to nearly $18,000 in the first three years after women were enfranchised.[110] In 1924, the state's white clubwomen began coordinating their lobbying efforts through a state legislative council, and the member organizations endorsed increased funding for the board of public welfare in each legislative session for the remainder of the decade.[111] In response to this pressure from enfranchised clubwomen, state lawmakers substantially increased funding for the agency in each subsequent biennia, doubling the board's funding in 1925–26 and increasing it an additional 10 percent in 1927–28 to $40,000 annually.[112] These increases for the board of public welfare were notable not only for their rapid growth but also because white women secured them during a period when the state's total budget remained flat. Although the revolt of the state's white women in the November elections could not have been foreseen when General Assembly members met in January 1928 to determine the state's budget, lawmakers nevertheless responded to white clubwomen's continuing demands for public welfare appropriations by increasing the board's allocation by an additional 50 percent for fiscal years 1929 and 1930.[113] By 1931, annual appropriations for the board stood at nearly $90,000.[114]

This strong and consistent growth in state appropriations to the priorities of white clubwomen stands in contrast to southern lawmakers' response to unenfranchised reformers. White clubwomen in Arkansas, Louisiana, Tennessee, Texas, and Virginia all persuaded state lawmakers to enact mothers' pensions in the years preceding the ratification of the Nineteenth Amendment. Scholars have pointed to these legislative victories as evidence of the political power of organized women, even in the absence of the vote.[115] As Theda Skocpol put it, "Where and when organized women took up the cause, they virtually always succeeded."[116] In each of these cases, however, southern lawmakers passed authorizing legislation but refused to provide state appropriations for these public aid programs.[117] To be sure, authorizing legislation was no small victory. The resistance of the remaining southern states testifies to that. Nevertheless, clubwomen's lack of electoral power rendered these victories hollow. Mothers' pension programs were "created" in these five states without any state appropriation; consequently, once women were enfranchised, they had to fight merely to establish state funding for these programs, and in each case lawmakers could point to requirements in the authorizing legislation that made funding the responsibility of the counties.

Underfunding of mothers' pension programs was a national phenomenon.[118] As one scholar explained, "The organized elite and middle-class women who helped to spur the rapid spread of mothers' pension statutes during the 1910s did not have the political clout to achieve adequate levels of funding once the locally varied programs were established."[119] Certainly that was true in the South. Their lack of clout was not simply a misfit between clubwomen's "moralistic, educational style of politics" and the type of politicking necessary to win fiscal battles, however.[120] Their lack of clout was, in substantial measure, due to their lack of voting rights. In the absence of meaningful electoral pressure, the southern clubwomen who sponsored mothers' pensions before 1920 were unable to secure legislation that made mothers' aid the responsibility of the state. At the outset, then, authorizing legislation was crafted in ways that made it difficult to secure funding for the programs. As a result, even after women were enfranchised their ability to leverage their voting strength for state appropriations was constrained by the environment in which the legislation was originally crafted.

By contrast, white clubwomen who fought for the creation of new mothers' aid programs after 1920 were able to leverage their votes for meaningful mothers' pensions, programs that included state appropriations from the outset. Thus, when North Carolina clubwomen secured mothers' pension legislation in 1923, they also secured an immediate appropriation of nearly $30,000 for the program.[121] By the end of the decade, state appropriations had increased to $44,000 annually.[122] Likewise, Kentucky's enfranchised white clubwomen secured a state appropriation for mothers' aid in the same legislation that created the program in 1928.[123] The amount of the initial state funding, just $5,000, was less than the Kentucky Legislative Council had requested, but it came as part of the same state budget that provided sufficient state appropriations to make up for the loss of federal Sheppard-Towner funds. Not all southern clubwomen pursued state appropriations for mothers' pensions once they were enfranchised. In Mississippi, enfranchised white women demanded a mothers' pension program from their state legislators and received it in 1928, but there is no evidence that they asked for state appropriations that year or in the following legislative session.[124] In states where mothers' pension programs had been won before 1920, enfranchised white women found that their earlier "victories" left the hardest battles unfought, and organized white women in some states chose to focus their lobbying efforts elsewhere. Other white women, like those in Virginia, fought throughout the 1920s to obtain state appropriations for the existing mothers' pension program, finally winning a $25,000 annual appropriation in 1932.[125] Having the vote did not ensure adequate state appropriations for mothers' pensions. It did, however, provide white women with the clout to secure something more than the empty enactments they won before 1920, if they chose to spend their political capital that way.

While white clubwomen in different states had different legislative priorities, organized women in nearly every state supported appropriations for the federal Sheppard-Towner program. National women's leaders counted the passage of Sheppard-Towner in Congress as the first major victory for enfranchised womanhood, and the program quickly poured money into public health campaigns to reduce maternal deaths and infant mortality. By decade's end, however, the federal program lay dead as national women's leaders lost their efforts to reauthorize the federal legislation in 1929. The failure of Congress to reauthorize this legislation at the end of the decade should not obscure the ways in which enfranchisement empowered women lobbyists at the state and local level, however. Not only did southern white women continue to obtain legislative concessions and appropriations from their state lawmakers throughout the 1920s, but they also charted a different legislative course for Sheppard-Towner programs at the state level. While national battles raged over the future of the program, southern legislators in every state but Arkansas continued to fund these maternal and infant health programs at steady or increasing levels throughout the decade. Alabama, Kentucky, North Carolina, South Carolina, and Virginia appropriated full matching funds for Sheppard-Towner programs each year from its inception, and Arkansas, Georgia, Louisiana, Mississippi, Tennessee, and Texas all were providing full matching funds by 1928. In fact, Louisiana state legislators did not even agree to participate in the program until 1924, but by 1925 they were investing full matching funds toward the state activities. Thus, as congressional support for the program waned, ostensibly in response to the waning power of organized women, support at the state level — as measured by appropriation levels — remained strong.[126]

Even more impressive, organized women voters proved remarkably successful at obtaining state appropriations for the programs that Sheppard-Towner had supported, even after Congress had eliminated the federal program. During the early 1930s, women in nearly every state persuaded their legislatures to continue appropriations for maternal and infant health work, despite the absence of federal matching funds.[127] Indeed, thirty states appropriated more for state Sheppard-Towner activities in 1930 than they had in 1929. Women in twenty-five states, including Kentucky, North Carolina, Tennessee, Texas, and Virginia, persuaded their legislatures to increase state funds enough to make up for the loss of federal money, despite the growing economic depression.[128] In 1931, Alabama reported that the program in that state "had not been seriously handicapped" by the elimination of federal support.[129] Instead, the state allocated additional resources, including nearly $75,000 for "child hygiene and public-health nursing" in 1929 alone.[130] Like Alabama, Tennessee reported ongoing work in maternal and infant health, confessing that "as our state funds are more flexible than were the Sheppard-Towner funds, we are better able to integrate maternity and infancy work with other services than was the case" when the state was accepting federal support.[131] Women in Arkansas, Mississippi, and South Carolina lamented the elimination of federal support, but publicly funded maternal and infant health work continued in those states.[132] Arkansas even reported a substantial expansion of prenatal and infant health programs once the state's efforts were reorganized following the great flood of 1927.[133] Of all the southern states, only Louisiana abandoned its child hygiene division when federal funds were discontinued, and even there some work continued, though only as a part of the broader public health programs available in selected parishes.[134]

The experiences of organized women at the state level lack the "travail" with which historians have characterized the federal Sheppard-Towner legislation.[135] Despite the elimination of federal funding in the summer of 1929, work and funding continued in the states. At a time of growing pressure on state resources, nearly all southern states increased their appropriations for maternal and infant health programs at the behest of organized white women. While political activists at the national level had fought determinedly to preserve both the appropriations and the bureaucratic structure of the Sheppard-Towner program within the Children's Bureau, organized southern white women did not seem invested in those fights. To be sure, white clubwomen supported the federal program and lamented the loss of federal dollars for women and children. One Mississippi woman captured the sentiment of many as she cursed the nation's "so-called statesmen. . . . God help a country whose congress will do little or nothing for the health and welfare of mothers and children."[136] Nevertheless, her focus on Congress is telling. Newly enfranchised women fought most of their battles at the state level, and there they more often won. Faced with pressure from organized white women constituents, most states' legislators stepped into the breach and provided funding for child hygiene programs that equaled or exceeded the funding they had provided throughout the 1920s. And in the absence of regulations that had accompanied the federal money, some states, like Tennessee, welcomed the opportunity to restructure the way they provided services to mothers and their babies. The elimination of the Sheppard-Towner program may well have been a defeat for the female lobbying organizations that promoted it at the federal level, but it was hardly a renunciation of the power of women's ballots. In many ways the grassroots battle was never joined over the federal legislation, and ordinary women had little stake in the turf war that raged between supporters of the Children's Bureau and the Public Health Service.[137] Southern white women voters simply wanted money for the programs, and when they fought for it in their states, they received what they demanded more often than not.

While an analysis of the Sheppard-Towner appropriations suggests that enfranchised clubwomen's political effectiveness should be measured at the state level, other evidence from the states highlights the importance of the battles that were not fought. White clubwomen were politically savvy, and part of that political acumen included recognizing the legislative battles that were not worth fighting. For example, southern legislators may have balanced the electoral pressure of white women reformers against manufacturing interests in new ways after 1920, but the electoral pressure of white women did not make ratification of the federal child labor amendment a realistic possibility in most southern states. More important, white women voters did not seem interested in a federal solution to the child labor problem. They were, after all, white southerners. As women they endorsed some issues, like increased age of consent and state support for institutions for African Americans, which challenged elements of the regional status quo. But as white southerners they also consistently supported white supremacy and states' rights. Consequently, despite calls from national organizations like the League of Women Voters and the Women's Joint Congressional Committee to wage active fights for the ratification of the child labor amendment, white clubwomen in Mississippi, Tennessee, Texas, and Virginia reported no campaign activity in support of the federal amendment.[138] In South Carolina, the only support for ratification of the amendment from white clubwomen was "a single handed fight" by the president of the state League of Women Voters.[139] State legislatures in Louisiana, Georgia, and North Carolina rejected the amendment quickly, and women in those states staged no active fight on behalf of ratification.[140] Despite the fact that southern white women never pressed their state legislators to ratify this amendment, scholars have cast the failure of ratification, like the failure to reauthorize Sheppard-Towner, as an indication of women's waning power.[141] J. Stanley Lemons pointed to the "rejection of the child labor amendment" as "a cardinal example" of the weakened position of women lobbyists by the late 1920s.[142] Yet in the South it is clear that this was a battle that white women never fought. Moreover, when organized white women did leverage their votes in support of *state* legislation restricting child labor, they were frequently successful.[143]

White women lobbyists preserved their political capital by avoiding some battles, and they maintained their political credibility by ensuring that their initiatives had support at the grass roots. Like other interest groups, white clubwomen recognized that they could not persuasively lobby for things that the majority of women voters opposed, regardless of the policies some female activists would have preferred. Here female jury service serves as a case in point. Contemporary activists and feminist scholars alike have pointed to jury service as a symbol of civic equality and a powerful expression of equal treatment under the law.[144] Once women were granted the right to vote, many activists believed that it was women's right and responsibility to serve as jurors. Some women insisted that jury service was an essential way to check the power of white men and protect vulnerable girls and women. Nevertheless, elected officials in the region proved resistant when some white women declared their fitness to sit in judgment of white men. By the end of the decade, only the women in Arkansas, Kentucky, and Louisiana enjoyed this right, and women in Alabama, Mississippi, and South Carolina would not be permitted to serve on juries until the late 1960s.[145]

This determined opposition to female jury service flowed from two sources and provides insight into the political efficacy of the Nineteenth Amendment. First, female jury service seemed particularly odious to some southern men. As one Texas lawmaker put it, "There are reasons, natural, moral, and domestic which render them wholly unfit for it." He continued, "Who will care for the children during the mother's absence?"[146] A Mississippi legislator concurred, "I don't object to my wife voting—that doesn't take long—but when it comes to neglecting household duties to sit on a jury . . . I am against that form of equal rights."[147] Of course, most southern legislators *had* determinedly objected to their wives voting, but once the Nineteenth Amendment removed that male privilege, southern politicians drew new lines in the sand. They knew that they had to offer some concessions to organized white women voters, but they also hoped they could appease white women voters by enacting their least objectionable demands first.

Even more important, activist white women and leading politicians knew that white women were themselves divided on the issue of jury service. As the North Carolina *Monthly News* sarcastically reported, "Many women distinctly do not wish to serve. In that, at least, they are precisely like men."[148] In Louisiana, another white activist suggested, "Perhaps it is best to leave . . . jury duty to the slow processes of education and time."[149] Throughout the region, organized white women fought successfully for equal property rights and equal guardianship of their children, but they did not work to obtain jury service for women.[150] The Mississippi legislature voted down a bill to provide jury service for women in 1928, but an officer in the state's League of Women Voters, who also happened to be a state senator, had no idea why the bill had been introduced.[151] She confessed that the two female members of the General Assembly may have been responsible for it "by discussing it with several members," but the state's white clubwomen neither asked for the bill nor pushed for its passage.[152]

Despite claims by some scholars that "all the [women's] rights activists supported the jury service campaign," and that the jury service campaign "was a partial measure" of enfranchised women's political efficacy, there is little evidence of state and local activity in support of such legislation in the South.[153] Its failure, then, can hardly be counted as evidence of white women's waning electoral threat. In the legislative contests that pitted the demands of newly enfranchised white women against the legal privileges of southern white men, state legislators granted white women's demands when the electoral pressure was great and the wishes of white women voters were clear. Neither was the case with demands for female jury service. Indeed, in the absence of grassroots support for female jury service, southern white clubwomen in the 1920s focused their legislative demands elsewhere.

Clearly, some of the battles that enfranchised women seemed to lose in the 1920s were really battles not joined. Female political leaders could not effectively press for reforms that the majority of white women voters did not want, and they did not squander their political capital on legislative fights they knew they could not win. At the same time, some of the political battles that enfranchised white women did win have gone unnoticed — or have been intentionally forgotten. In the winter of 1927, for example, the Atlanta Federation of Women's Clubs was hailed in local white newspapers for its successful effort to close white hospitals in the state to disabled black veterans.[154] Congressman W. D. Upshaw himself publicly credited "the fifteen thousand patriotic women citizens for initiating this wholesome and timely movement."[155] In Louisiana, newly enfranchised white women were among the staunchest proponents of racial integrity laws. When the state's new constitution was written, one activist reported that Louisiana's enfranchised women were "successful in securing the enactment of a few fundamental principles into the new constitution," including "the principle of safeguarding racial purity."[156] Although it took them until 1937 to achieve their goal, white women in Georgia working through the state's Federation of Women's Clubs and the Junior League were among the foremost champions of that state's eugenic sterilization law.[157] These policy "victories" are not the sort that scholars like to celebrate, but they are nonetheless expressions of the new political power wielded by enfranchised white women.

OF COURSE WHITE WOMEN voters did not always get what they requested of their legislators. Organized white women in the South, like women in the rest of the nation, experienced frustration in their lobbying efforts after the first rush of postenfranchisement victories. North Carolina's female political leaders commented on the legislative "slump" in their *Monthly News*, noting, "Were it not for the fact that women's legislative programs throughout the country shared practically the same fate that ours did in 1925, your legislative chairman would be somewhat humiliated to report no actual achievement during the past legislature."[158] White women from Georgia reported that more than half of their proposals had been defeated, and South Carolina league members reported no new legislative accomplishments during the legislative sessions at mid-decade.[159] North Carolina women even faced a discouraging reversal as legislators there slashed the appropriations for the new mothers' pensions program in 1925.[160]

Nevertheless, white women lobbyists recognized that legislative change was a process, not an event, and that the battles they fought at mid-decade were harder to win. As early as 1921, a woman in South Carolina remarked, "I am afraid we will have to educate the Legislature gradually and take it in broken doses. . . . Of course, we must ask for more than we expect, in order to anticipate their objections."[161] During the 1927 legislative session, a North Carolina activist made a similar assessment as she plotted legislative strategy: "I believe in 'equal property rights for spouses' all the way through, but as I once heard you remark 'it may take us fifty years to get that.' The question then is, how much can we hope to get as a beginning?"[162]

As in any battle, the outcomes of women's political fights not only were a function of the weapons in organized women's arsenal but were also determined by the strength of the opposition. Some of the strongest opposition came from fiscal conservatives in the South determined that southern states would remain famous for their low taxes and miniscule public spending. Other opposition was staged on gendered grounds. Even when the legislative demands of women cost the state nothing, state legislators did not always surrender their legal privileges in the face of white women's lobbying. For obvious reasons, male legislators resisted white women's demands for equal property rights, and despite their lobbying, women in most southern states still did not have an equal interest in their husband's property at the end of the decade.[163] And, of course, southern manufacturing interests remained an intensely powerful force in southern politics. Wealthy, entrenched, and often male-dominated interests maintained their disproportionate influence in southern politics long after women obtained the right to vote. But after 1920, state legislators for the first time had to balance these entrenched interests against the electoral pressure of white women voters when they considered the merits of reform.

White women lobbyists understood this political landscape. They recognized that in any legislative session, elected representatives would offer the least amount of reform that they could get away with politically. That is not to say that politicians never acted in the interest of the greater good or that they could not be moved by logical arguments. Because politicians were interested in reelection, however, they were unlikely to take political risks — like supporting controversial or expensive legislative changes — unless they felt electoral pressure to do so. White women reformers appreciated that to enact their legislative agenda they had to maintain this electoral pressure, but the ease with which that was accomplished varied considerably by state.

Unsurprisingly, women voters were most powerful where they were well organized and voted with relative ease. For both black and white women in the South, Kentucky offered the most hospitable environment for political organizing. That state demanded neither a poll tax nor a literacy test of voters, and, in part as a consequence of such accessible polls, the state supported healthy partisan competition. White women in Kentucky joined forces in a nonpartisan women's joint legislative council, and throughout the decade the state's clubwomen regularly obtained the legislation and appropriations they requested through that organization.[164] White women in North Carolina also voted with relative ease in the absence of a poll tax. In that state, too, white women organized themselves in a legislative council and thereby presented state legislators with a single list of "women's" legislative priorities. The Republican Party was not as strong in North Carolina as it was in Kentucky in the 1920s, but it was sufficiently viable to make the threat of women party bolters real. Moreover, Democratic primary contests in the state were heated, and the independence of women's organizations in those primary contests encouraged all primary candidates to court women's votes. Although they frequently found themselves at odds with manufacturing interests and Democratic bosses in the state, North Carolina's white women were able to effect consistent electoral pressure, and they consequently won many of the legislative battles they fought.

Like their sisters in Kentucky and North Carolina, white clubwomen in Virginia and Texas organized powerful legislative councils through which they presented "women's" legislative demands. Although the poll tax depressed voting among women in both states, white women's clubs in Virginia and Texas worked effectively to keep their legislative priorities and their voting strength before lawmakers. In Virginia, in particular, annual elections (for federal offices in even years and state offices in odd years) offered white women frequent opportunities to demonstrate their local voting strength. Extremely competitive primaries in Texas and occasional Republican competitiveness in Virginia also contributed to enfranchised women's lobbying strength. In both states the number of women voters was significant and continued to increase across the decade. All of these conditions enabled organized white women to leverage their new ballots for concessions from lawmakers.

In other southern states, suffrage made women more powerful than they had been before, but state and local political structures reduced the effectiveness of their interest group pressure. In Alabama, for example, white clubwomen were well organized and presented a remarkably united front to lawmakers through a statewide legislative council. Like women in Texas and Virginia, Alabama women faced a poll tax, but the imposition of the tax after 1920 did not critically undermine the growth in new voters that followed the Nineteenth Amendment. Nevertheless, the Alabama General Assembly met only once every four years. Given the infrequent opportunities for voters to go to the polls, effective electoral pressure was difficult to sustain. Moreover, Alabama women faced substantial challenges in keeping issues before their members and lawmakers in the absence of frequent opportunities for political debate. Suffrage made a real difference to the political efficacy of Alabama's women, as appropriations levels demonstrate, but between disfranchisement and the structure of legislative activity in the state, even enfranchised white women found it hard to make consistent progress on their reform priorities.

White women in Georgia had a well-organized league and legislative council, and state legislators met and faced reelection on a biennial basis. The enfranchised white clubwomen of Georgia nevertheless "travel[ed] a rocky road."[165] As one activist from that state explained, "There are 207 members of the House, 51 members of the Senate, coming from 161 counties. These men are so occupied with local obligations that they have little time and less inclination to consider state wide measures."[166] Recognizing that electoral pressure for white clubwomen's legislative priorities "must come from the votes of the home county," she lamented that the state's legislative council "faces an almost superhuman task."[167] Competitive primaries offered Georgia's enfranchised white women political leverage, but the county unit system often undermined the effectiveness of women voters organized in urban areas.[168] At the state level, organized white women faced a large legislative body preoccupied with local issues and dominated by rural lawmakers. Consequently, municipal battles in cities like Savannah and Atlanta often provided women with their most important opportunities to achieve their policy goals. As was true throughout the region, enfranchisement made white women more powerful as lobbyists than they had been before, but the structures of politics in Alabama and Georgia constrained the political effectiveness of any organized interest group, including white clubwomen.

While county unit systems and infrequent elections served to limit the effectiveness of women's votes in Alabama and Georgia, disfranchisement statutes stifled meaningful political participation for women in Arkansas and Tennessee. The imposition of the poll tax on Tennessee's women in 1921 decimated voter turnout in that state. More than 155,000 new voters crowded Tennessee's polls in November 1920, but after women became subject to the poll tax, the number of voters at the polls fell by more than 120,000. In Arkansas, women were subject to the poll tax from the outset, and the numbers of voters never increased substantially in the 1920s. Viable partisan competition in Tennessee, competitive primary battles, and frequent election contests should have offered new women voters important leverage in these two states, but surprisingly few women voted. State lawmakers faced a minimal electoral threat from these new constituents, and as a consequence, organized white women from these two states struggled to extract legislative concessions.[169]

Contrary to what one might expect, Mississippi and South Carolina witnessed more substantial increases in new voters than did the ratification states of Arkansas and Tennessee.[170] This was true despite the fact that Arkansas and Tennessee both had larger white populations than did Mississippi and South Carolina. Although neither Mississippi nor South Carolina offered any partisan competition whatsoever, both states experienced competitive white primaries for Democratic nominations, which offered white women an opportunity for electoral leverage. In South Carolina, primary voters cast ballots without being subject to a poll tax, which encouraged the tens of thousands of women who turned out at the polls after 1920. As a consequence of their substantial participation in the primaries, white women posed a real electoral threat in these two states, but in neither case did organized clubwomen seem to capitalize on their leverage for substantial policy outcomes. Although the extant records suggest that white women in these Deep South states received much of what they asked for after 1920, they also seemed to ask very little of their lawmakers.

Louisiana, finally, exemplifies the importance of both voter turnout and nonpartisanship to women's political efficacy. Because voter registration records were separated by race and gender, lawmakers in Louisiana could count exactly how many women were registered to vote in each parish. There, more than in any other state, politicians knew the scope and scale of the electoral threat women posed. As a consequence, when white women voters articulated their policy demands with a clear voice and their votes remained in doubt, they achieved some policy victories. The absence of partisan competition, the presence of a poll tax, and the dominance of machine politics, however, made effective political mobilization an uphill battle. These obstacles were compounded in the early 1920s as the state's League of Women Voters became openly allied with one faction in the state, violating its nonpartisanship to the point that it lost its national charter. With no state organization of women prepared to articulate the policy demands of white women whose votes were in doubt, the political effectiveness of enfranchised white clubwomen waned. In Louisiana, as elsewhere, enfranchisement offered white women an important political tool; by compromising their nonpartisanship, however, the state's white clubwomen failed to make effective use of it.

As the experience of southern clubwomen suggests, access to meaningful political power was not the result of political culture or a state's ratification status. The few states that offered women the right to vote before 1920 did so as a consequence of specific political circumstances, and those circumstances did not always redound to the benefit of enfranchised women.[171] Nor was access to meaningful political participation controlled entirely by parties. Even in the South, where this might seem most obviously the case in the context of Democratic dominance, white clubwomen routinely found ways to exercise electoral pressure in effective ways. Instead, the differences in organized women's effectiveness among the southern states suggest that the ability to cast ballots sufficient to maintain an electoral threat and the existence of a nonpartisan organization that could articulate "women's" policy demands were the two most important determinants of women's political efficacy. As one suffragist from Texas insisted when asked about the "failure" of woman suffrage, "The time has come to dispense with this starry-eyed babes-in-the-wood twaddle about suffragists. We went up against and helped to break the most ruthless and powerful machine that had ever fastened its tentacles on Texas and the United States and we knew what we were about."[172] Indeed, the experience of southern white women suggests that these new voters knew exactly what they were about. Political efficacy, they recognized, was about electoral pressure, the costs of reform, and the strength of the opposition.

Those political dynamics shaped women's legislative outcomes at the federal level, as well as the state level. In both settings organized women lobbyists had to demonstrate that sufficient numbers of voters cared about an issue in order to leverage their new electoral pressure for policy outcomes. They also needed to present a united front. At the federal level this effort was made by the Women's Joint Congressional Committee, a national version of the women's councils that southern white women found so effective. And like white clubwomen at the state level, women lobbyists nationally faced the pressure of the opposition — other organized groups of voters who did not agree with the way they proposed to spend public resources or who flatly opposed the legislation that organized women endorsed.

Despite these similarities, and despite white clubwomen's effectiveness at the state level, newly enfranchised white women found it more difficult to win legislative battles at the federal level. In part, enfranchised women found it harder to maintain the level of electoral pressure needed to win federal concessions. Incumbent congressmen and senators rarely faced meaningful opposition at the polls, and senators faced the voters only once every six years. Moreover, congressmen and senators represented large districts (or states) that made it more difficult for women to gain access, even after they became constituents. Even more important, the divisions among women undermined efforts to present a united claim for legislative change. Although southern women working at the state level recognized the value of narrowing their demands and presenting legislators with a common legislative agenda, women lobbying at the national level had more difficulty reaching consensus on a common set of policy concerns. As scholars like Nancy Cott have demonstrated, "The considerable unity of method among women's organizations contrasted with the diversity — often acrimony — among their specific goals."[173] Despite the efforts of groups like the Women's Joint Congressional Committee, then, federal policy-makers were well aware of the divisions among the nation's women, and they could count on no single women's organization to instruct them in what "women" wanted.

Nevertheless, the experiences of enfranchised women lobbying at the federal level might be taken as a fair measure of woman suffrage if that was where organized women's battles had been waged; but the work of politically active southern women suggests that they focused their energies elsewhere. The legislative agendas issued by state leagues and women's councils focused almost exclusively on issues in the state legislatures. The guests at election-season mass meetings were predominantly candidates for local or statewide office, rather than Congress or the U.S. Senate. And there is no evidence that southern women's legislative councils issued any federal policy demands or coordinated with the national Women's Joint Congressional Council. For the most part, then, the effective grassroots work that laid the foundation for white women's legislative accomplishments at the state level was not mobilized in pursuit of federal legislation. Indeed, in a public talk, one woman in Louisiana insisted that enfranchised women "had best take up matters which may be handled by [their] state legislature" rather than fighting for legislation that "is a matter for Congress."[174]

In short, it seems that the issues that these women voters cared most about were handled at the state and local levels. And as white southerners in the Jim Crow era, most no doubt preferred it that way. Newly enfranchised white women mobilized their votes in support of mothers' pensions, schools, equal property laws, and state institutions for social welfare. But even as they promoted robust mothers' pensions, they endorsed county-level control over such programs and affirmed state support for families, only "if the mother is worthy."[175] They supported state funding for homes for the region's "delinquent" girls, but they remained committed to the Jim Crow structure of those state institutions. In Tennessee, white women even heralded the flexibility of state funds when federal funding for Sheppard-Towner programs was cut off.[176]

Just as the effects of the Nineteenth Amendment must be measured in the policies women actually demanded, so, too, must the effectiveness of women's ballots be tested in the legislative bodies where the battles were waged. At the state and local levels, where newly enfranchised white women did focus their political energies, the record testifies to the power of the vote. Organized southern white women won a number of quick victories after the ratification of the Nineteenth Amendment, prompting one former suffragist to remark that the legislative program "has been carried out with greater success than we had reason to hope for."[177] But southern white women lobbyists were no strangers to bill-signing ceremonies later in the decade. Coalitions of enfranchised southern white women continued to press their legislators with demands throughout the 1920s, and they worked to make sure that new legislation and funding priorities did not jeopardize victories they had already won. During the 1920s, none of their major policy victories was repealed, and funding levels for their legislative priorities generally remained steady or increased, despite the declining economy. Ten years after the ratification of the Nineteenth Amendment, southern white women could confidently say, "We have made some progress."[178]

WHILE A SUSTAINED electoral threat ensured that enfranchised white women would continue to secure policy concessions from their legislators, African American women in the South found few opportunities to exercise any real power within the political system. In contrast to the immediate change in legislators' attitudes enjoyed by southern white women, black women in the region found no such change. Indeed, while the southern Democrats who had opposed woman suffrage went out of their way to court white women voters and enact white women's legislative priorities in the early 1920s, these politicians worked equally vigorously to ban black women from the polls. Republican Party leaders, black women's so-called allies, did nothing to discourage this disfranchisement. When black women challenged discrimination at the polls, their own representatives, far from treating them like constituents, referred to them as "nigger" in the Congressional Record.[179] Southern congressmen and legislators did not seek hearings before black women's groups to explain their opposition to the legislation black clubwomen promoted. To the extent that black clubwomen made legislative demands, southern legislators ignored them with impunity. Southern politicians were free to do so because African American women in the region had almost no access to the ballot.

Violence and the effectiveness of disfranchisement were overwhelming to many black women, and by the end of the decade the energy, enthusiasm, and limited successes of black women's early voter mobilization campaigns had waned.[180] White newspapers no longer ran hysterical headlines about black women at the polls, and antisuffrage publications focused their ire on the actions of other organized white women, apparently no longer concerned about the threat from black women voters. In Louisiana, the only southern state that kept registration statistics by race and gender, the number of black female registrants exemplified this trend. While the number of white women voters continued to grow, African American women's early efforts to gain access to the polls had borne little fruit. By the end of the decade, fewer than 350 black women were registered to vote statewide.[181] And as Paul Lewinson's 1932 study of black voting in the South made clear, those places that did allow black southerners to vote often did so only "with the understanding that there should never be a large enough number to make any difference whatsoever."[182]

As a result of the determined efforts of women like Ora Stokes of Virginia, Elizabeth Little of Alabama, and Charlotte Hawkins Brown of North Carolina, thousands of African American women cast ballots in the South. After the ratification of the Nineteenth Amendment, African Americans demanded the right to vote with new vigor, and the citizenship classes and voter registration drives staged by black women during the 1920s brought new black men, as well as black women, to the polls. Nevertheless, the number of African Americans who were able to cast ballots in the South remained extremely small. Unlike white women, African American women were generally unable to leverage their ballots to extract policy concessions from their representatives, and as it sought to win the votes of white women, even the Republican Party seemed hostile to the concerns of African Americans.

Thus, less than ten years after the ratification of the Nineteenth Amendment, African American women in the South were looking for new political strategies. During the 1928 presidential campaign, the members of the National League of Republican Colored Women adopted a slogan that reflected their growing concerns about the party of Lincoln. The slogan, "Oppose in State and National Campaigns any Candidate who will Not Committ [sic] Him or Herself On the Enforcement of the 13th, 14th and 15th Amendments," was hardly catchy.[183] Nevertheless, it demonstrated the limits of African American women's partisanship. African American women, particularly the southern black women who had been central figures in the creation of this Republican organization, had no illusions about the threat that Democratic Party dominance posed to their interests. They opposed the Democratic nominee because, as one black woman explained, "Smith in the White House means the South in the saddle."[184] At the same time, however, they recognized that Republican victories were of little use to them unless Republican legislators represented the interests of their black constituents. Thus, at the same meeting where they began to map out strategy for Republican victory in the 1928 campaign, these women also drafted a "statement for the enlightenment of the Administration" in which they outlined their concerns "as a result of Party inaction."[185]

Despite the Republican victories at the end of the decade, African American voters could hope to gain little political advantage as a result of the disruption of the Solid South. Although most African Americans in the South were loyal Republicans, party officials recognized that it was not African American votes that had given Hoover his southern victories. Republican Party leaders in the South could afford to ignore this tiny bloc of voters; in fact, their strategy for taking advantage of the Nineteenth Amendment was premised not only on ignoring African American voters but also on driving them from the party. If it had not been obvious before, the race-baiting by Republicans against the Democratic nominee Al Smith provided clear evidence to African American voters that the party of Lincoln did not welcome them. And once in office, President Hoover worked to take advantage of his unprecedented victories to build a viable Republican opposition in the South by attacking the "black and tans" and supporting the "lily-white" movement.

Discouraged by the failure of Republican Party leaders in the South to advocate the cause of African Americans and briefly encouraged by the 1927 U.S. Supreme Court decision in *Nixon v. Herndon* invalidating the white primary in Texas, some African American women voters began to change their party affiliation by the late 1920s. The president of the Southeastern Federation of Colored Women's Clubs called on members to "go to the polls in all primary elections and at least attempt to cast your ballot for the best man running and if you are prevented, fight it out in the courts as a group. . . . Texas has cracked the door, let us press wide the crack until the door swings open upon its hinges."[186] In words that sounded much like the nonpartisan rhetoric of the all-white Leagues of Women Voters, African American men and women called on black voters to cast independent ballots. As one leading clubwoman put it, "What matters it, whether we are Republicans or Democrats, when a vote of ours can put a decent man into office or keep a bad one out?"[187] By November 1929, even Georgia's Republican National

Committeewoman "made public her grievance" with the party. As she issued a "warning to the Republican Party from the White House down," this African American woman insisted, "I am a Republican." Nevertheless, she condemned the party leaders who had turned their backs on the party's traditional principles "of right and justice."[188] Determined to exercise political power, some black southern voters by the late 1920s looked to Democratic partisanship as a way of affecting the elections that really mattered, or as a way of politically punishing the Republican Party that failed to serve them.[189]

The political potency of this strategy was made clear by black Virginians in 1927. That year, African Americans in Arlington County "swung" the county election "into the Democratic column." In a pattern typical among lily-white leaders in the South, Republicans in that county had "ignored the Negroes in the selection of their party candidates." Frustrated by the lily-whitism of the state's Republican leaders, African Americans in Arlington organized in support of the Democratic ticket. Black leaders targeted both male and female voters, with Mrs. Mary Harris and Mrs. Margaret Morton helping to mobilize African American women. Faced with this dissatisfaction among African Americans, a Republican leader from Washington raised "the Ku Klux Klan issue as a bugaboo to scare Negroes into supporting his candidates." Eight hundred black voters in the county rejected these tactics, however, and "turn[ed] the election" for the Democrats. Faced with a Republican Party that increasingly ignored its black allies, growing numbers of black southerners chose to "ignore them at the polls."[190]

The experience of Maggie Lena Walker suggests that frustration, not optimism, lay at the heart of this "realignment" in the late 1920s. Walker spent the early twenties organizing African American women voters in Virginia, and she even ran for statewide office on Virginia's "lily-black" ticket in 1921. On election day in November 1925, however, Walker wrote in her diary, "Out early today — and voted an entire Democratic ticket. Why — no reason — just voted the ticket. One party is as good as the other."[191] By her own account, Walker's realignment seems less the product of political calculation than utter disillusionment. Nevertheless, she was not so disillusioned that she failed to vote. She and other black activists in the South remained committed to the idea that the vote was a very powerful weapon, but they also acknowledged that African Americans needed more of them to make a difference.

ON JUNE 30, 1928, the polling places in Wake County, North Carolina, were busy with voters. At College Court Pharmacy, male and female voters in the first precinct announced themselves to the registrar, Mrs. H. B.

Poindexter. Another woman, Mrs. Tal Stafford, served as the Democratic judge for the precinct.[192] Outside, white women encouraged voters to cast their ballots for Nell Battle Lewis for state legislator.[193] According to supporters, Lewis was a Wake County native and "is well qualified for the position she seeks. Her constituents could present her with pride and feel that she would be a credit not only to the county but to the state as a whole."[194] Female supporters also highlighted Lewis's position as "the only woman seeking office on the Democratic ticket." These partisans were determined that white women's votes would not go unnoticed — or unrewarded. They insisted, "Democratic women have been loyal to the party. They should have consideration in the distribution of offices."[195] By contrast, upon hearing of her candidacy, Lewis's own brother remarked: "Sorry to know you are really going to run for the Legislature. Doubt if you can be elected, and if the running will help you any."[196] When the ballots were counted, Lewis had indeed lost. The Wake County delegation to the North Carolina General Assembly would once more consist entirely of men. Under pressure from their female constituents, however, those men would in 1929 enact the Australian ballot law, which was at the top of Lewis's legislative priorities.

After 1920, scenes such as this one were not uncommon in the South. Male voters and Democratic Party leaders had to face white women as voters, precinct officials, campaign workers, and occasionally even candidates on election day. The Nineteenth Amendment transformed white women's relationship to the state, and election day in Wake County exemplified both the possibilities and the limits of female political participation. After a decade of agitation, the white women of North Carolina won their most hard-fought legislative battle in 1929, as Wake County's newly elected delegation joined a majority of state legislators to enact a statewide secret ballot law. It was just one of the victories for organized white women that year, as North Carolina's state legislature also increased its appropriations for the state's Sheppard-Towner programs. Nevertheless, as the comments of Lewis's brother make clear, the Nineteenth Amendment could not remake southern politics overnight. Not long after they cast their first ballots, southern white women as voters ceased to be a novelty. Newspapers stopped reporting what the polls looked like on election day, and the presence of southern white women casting ballots was no longer worthy of comment. Female officeholding, however, remained uncommon and noteworthy.

Despite the cataclysmic predictions of antisuffragists, leading southern white men *and* white women had a stake in making woman suffrage commonplace after 1920. Politically active white women wanted women voters to use their ballots for reform, and male party leaders wanted to make sure that loyal white women voters went to the polls. By contrast, neither white men nor white women saw the consistent promotion of female officeholding as particularly advantageous. Southern white men occasionally promoted white women for public office or party council to curry favor with white women voters, and female reformers often believed that women officeholders would be more friendly to their policy goals. Nevertheless, the leading white men of the South recognized that they did not have to provide women with equal representation to win their votes. And organized southern white women realized that they could not successfully pursue their political goals on the backs of a few women legislators.

While some white women privately lamented the lack of female representation or publicly clamored for more women in office, organizations of southern white women specifically rejected a political strategy of electing their own. Many contemporary observers used female officeholding as a marker of the effects of the Nineteenth Amendment, but organized southern white women did not see it that way. In an age of interest group politics, white female activists used their legislative successes, not their legislative representation, to measure the weight of their votes.

By this measure, of course, African American women in the South had little to show for woman suffrage. Comments that appeared in the *Crisis* expressed the unfulfilled promise of the Nineteenth Amendment for southern black women. When told that the Nineteenth Amendment had provided "*all* women in the United States with the weapon of the ballot," one woman replied, "If I wish to arm a woman whose hands are tied, which must I do first, untie her hands, or just leave the gun around somewhere?"[197] As a result of disfranchisement, the majority of southerners remained unarmed, despite the ratification of the Nineteenth Amendment. For those women who were able to cast ballots, however, the Nineteenth Amendment marked a transformation in their relationship to the state. And these new voters posed a substantial challenge to the Solid South. For the first time since the passage of the disfranchisement statutes at the turn of the century, southern political leaders were forced to acknowledge the demands of more than a million new voters. The white and black women who entered the political system for the first time after 1920 insisted that southern political leaders respond to them as constituents and court their votes. The changes in the political culture and legislative policy of southern states in the 1920s testify to politicians' efforts, as one candidate put it, "to hold the lady votes."[198]

Conclusion

hen I began this project, some skeptics warned that I would be lucky to find enough evidence of southern women's political activism to fill an article, let alone a book. Indeed, the consensus among historians suggested that the empowering effects of the Nineteenth Amendment had been attenuated and short-lived. Yet in every archive, in every southern town, and in seemingly every women's club yearbook, southern women left evidence of their persistent and remarkably successful efforts to take advantage of their new ballots. From the movable registration booth that Atlanta's white women founded in a NuGrape truck to Gertrude Weil's destruction of marked ballots in North Carolina, and Elizabeth Little's campaign to register African American voters in Birmingham to the election of an all-female government in Winslow, Arkansas, the vigorous participation of women in the region's formal politics defies the notion that southern political life remained unchanged by woman suffrage.

To be sure, southern politics in the 1920s was democratic in name only. Political elites used legal and extralegal methods to prevent most southerners from voting, and the tight control of politics by a few elites alienated many of those citizens who were able to cast ballots. Yet in that decade, southern women not only voted but joined interest groups and lobbied their legislators *as constituents*. The remarkable ability of southern white women, and occasionally even southern black women, to seize political power and policy concessions from this closed system has long been obscured by our focus on the failure of national women's organizations to obtain all of the federal legislation that they demanded. This book is an attempt to recover that colorful and influential participation of southern women in local politics, and it suggests that scholars interested in the role of enfranchised women in politics focus their attention where politically active women did — at the state and local levels.

By the 1920s, a devotion to white supremacy and disfranchisement among the region's political leaders had helped give rise to a distinctive, some might say stunted, civic culture in the South. African Americans were systematically excluded from southern political life, and the region seemed increasingly isolated from national political trends. Even as they challenged many aspects of the political status quo, southern white women embraced elements of the hierarchical social order that benefited them. And, ironically, disfranchisement may have given the white women who could vote additional leverage within the region's political system, even as those same women worked to bring new voters to the polls. The peculiarities of the region's politics do not explain southern women's political success, however. Certainly what constituted political success may have been different for southern women than for women in other parts of the country, but the cultural shift that women precipitated at the polls, the lobbying tools that they developed, and the legislative successes that they enjoyed were part of an important, unrecognized national trend.

Before the ratification of the Nineteenth Amendment, one antisuffragist warned his fellow southerners that "suffrage does not mean women merely voting."[1] By the end of the decade, his prescience had become clear. Contrary to what Democratic leaders had hoped and many scholars have assumed, woman suffrage did not simply double the strength of the existing political structure. The ratification of the Nineteenth Amendment gave southern women the power to challenge the political hegemony of white men in their region. During their first decade of participation in the region's formal politics, southern women permanently altered the social drama of politics, used the threat of their ballots to extract legislative change from the region's political leadership, and began the long, slow process of opening up the South's political system to all comers. While African American women continued their struggle to take advantage of the few opportunities that the amendment offered to them, southern white women eagerly embraced the ballot and used it effectively to pursue their own political goals.

In the years that followed, southern women built upon these early successes as they continued to go to the polls and to use their votes to demand political change. What had been unthinkable in 1919 and extraordinary in 1920 became commonplace in the years that followed as women's "invasion" into party councils, polling places, and public politics continued unabated. Progressive reforms championed by women made a dramatic difference in the lives of many southerners, and women continued to press for more legislative changes as the Depression loomed. Throughout the 1930s, white political women from the South played essential roles in organizing women voters for the Democratic Party and encouraging their support for the New Deal. African American women continued to vote where they could, and the New Deal encouraged growing black political participation. Southern black women joined black men of their region in civic clubs and voters leagues as they increasingly pressed for access to the polls and admission to the all-white Democratic primaries. In 1936, the realignment of black voters that had its roots in black women voters' first, unsatisfying encounters with the Republican Party, was complete. By 1940, organized white women voters in Tennessee and Alabama were spearheading campaigns in their states for the elimination of the poll tax and southern white women in the Southern Conference for Human Welfare were demanding federal action to end the poll tax. Although the Democratic Party enjoyed dramatic successes during the 1930s, southern political leaders recognized that women's voter mobilization efforts, as well as their increasingly direct attacks on disfranchisement, remained a serious threat to politicians' control over southern politics. Long after the ratification of the Nineteenth Amendment, white southern men exerted a great effort to maintain their position atop the social order. Their ongoing struggle to contain women's political power demonstrates the profound changes that woman suffrage wrought.

By the 1940s, reliable political polling data provided candidates and politicians with increasingly detailed information about the electorate. And from the earliest days of political polling, these statistical samples identified differences between men and women on policy issues. Year after year, a gender gap consistently emerged on issues related to peace, military aggression, defense spending, capital punishment, and social welfare.[2] Since the 1950s, pollsters have also consistently identified a gender gap in political party preference.[3] Attention in recent elections to the voting power of "soccer moms," voting in the suburbs, and, more recently, the political potency of "security moms" worried about terrorism suggests the enduring significance of gendered divisions within the electorate. Yet the absence of polling data in the 1920s does not demonstrate the absence of a gender gap in the first years following the enfranchisement of women.

Indeed, even without the benefit of scientific polling data, politicians suspected that women voted differently, and they targeted special advertisements and appeals to women voters based on that assumption. Women in the 1920s went to the polls, and organized clubwomen pioneered modern interest group lobbying methods. Throughout their efforts these organized women insisted that there were particular issues that women voters cared deeply about, and they warned politicians that women voters would make their presence felt at the polls. Politicians' campaign appeals, as well as their legislative decisions, suggest that they took these organized women at their word. Certainly a gender gap did not exist on every issue in the 1920s, nor did it make itself felt in every election. Other factors, such as class and race, played central roles in determining how newly enfranchised women cast their votes. Nevertheless, the vote provided women with a powerful political weapon that, like women today, they were able to leverage as they fought for legislative change.

In her study of the demise of the white primary, Darlene Clark Hine observed that "the vote has been the most effective, prized means by which Americans made their wills felt in politics."[4] This is what suffragists believed as they fought for the Nineteenth Amendment. It is what African American activists believed as they fought the poll tax and the white primary and demanded equal access to southern polls. Yet even as historians highlight the significance of the 1965 Voting Rights Act, they largely reject the notion that the Nineteenth Amendment transformed American politics or the political power of American women. To be sure, it did not solve the problems of gender discrimination or place women on an equal playing field in politics, just as the Voting Rights Act could not eliminate racial prejudice or compensate for the long history of disfranchisement. Nevertheless, the Nineteenth Amendment gave women a critical weapon, which they skillfully added to their already formidable persuasive arsenal as they lobbied their legislators for political change. In short, the ability of southern women, white and black, to seize political power and policy concessions from the closed system of politics in the Jim Crow South demonstrates the importance of the vote, and it suggests important lessons about how ordinary people can employ the power of this form of civic engagement to make their voices heard.

Appendix

Data for tables A.1 though A.4 are from a variety of sources. For state-level presidential election returns, I consulted the *U.S. Historical Election Returns* online database. For primary data, I consulted Heard and Strong, *Southern Primaries and Elections, 1920–1949*. Louisiana was the only state in this study to collect registration data by race and gender. Those statistics were published annually in the *Report of Secretary of State to His Excellency the Governor of Louisiana* and are represented in table A.4.

There is reason to be skeptical of all southern election data from the 1920s. Despite the Herculean efforts of Heard and Strong to collect precise county-level election returns, data from several counties in any given election remain missing. Moreover, reports of fraud were prevalent enough to question the accuracy of registration lists and ballot counts. Nevertheless, the aggregate, state-level data presented here provides an important sense of the magnitude of woman suffrage as well as the patterns of voting and nonvoting in the various states.

Table A.1. Presidential Election Returns, 1916–1920

State	1916				1920				1916–1920		
	Total Vote	Democratic Vote	Republican Vote	Total Other Votes	Total Vote	Dem. Vote	Repub. Vote	Total Other Votes	Change in Total Vote	Change in Repub. Vote	Change in Dem. Vote
Alabama	130,435	99,116	28,662	2,657	233,951	156,064	74,719	3,168	103,516	46,057	56,948
Arkansas	170,104	112,211	48,879	9,014	183,621	107,406	71,107	5,108	13,517	22,228	−4,805
Georgia	160,681	127,754	11,294	21,633	149,651	106,112	42,981	558	−11,030	31,687	−21,642
Kentucky	520,078	269,990	241,854	8,234	918,342	457,203	451,480	9,659	398,264	209,626	187,213
Louisiana	92,974	79,875	6,466	6,633	126,236	87,355	38,539	342	33,262	32,073	7,480
Mississippi	86,159	80,422	4,253	1,484	82,418	69,252	11,527	1,639	−3,741	7,274	−11,170
North Carolina	289,837	168,383	120,890	564	538,649	305,367	232,819	463	248,812	111,929	136,984
South Carolina	63,950	61,845	1,550	555	66,808	64,170	2,244	394	2,858	694	2,325
Tennessee	272,190	153,280	116,223	2,687	428,036	206,558	219,229	2,249	155,846	103,006	53,278
Texas	373,310	287,415	64,999	20,896	486,449	288,933	114,384	83,132	113,139	49,385	1,518
Virginia	152,025	101,840	48,384	1,801	231,000	141,670	87,456	1,874	78,975	39,072	39,830

Table A.2. Primary Voter Strength, First Primary with Women Voters

State	Races Compared	Primary without Women	Primary with Women	Total Change in Voters	Percent Change
Alabama[a]	Primary for senator 1920 v. 1926	132,949	215,660	82,711	62%
Georgia[b]	Primary for governor 1920 v. 1922	231,435	213,003	−18,432	−8%
Louisiana	Primary for governor 1920 v. 1924	143,553	239,529	95,976	67%
Mississippi	Primary for governor 1919 v. 1923	148,411	254,141	105,730	71%
North Carolina	Primary for governor 1920 v. 1924	128,233	234,770	106,537	83%
South Carolina	Primary for senator 1920 v. 1924	117,827	200,420	82,593	70%
Tennessee	Primary for governor 1920 v. 1922	113,972	163,061	49,089	43%

[a] Alabama voters in the 1920s cast "preferential ballots" in state primaries. That is, voters selected their first and second choice candidates in each race. For purposes of this analysis, I counted only first-choice votes.

[b] In the first primary in which Georgia women voted, the gubernatorial primary featured a rematch from 1920 with an incumbent running, which may have depressed turnout.

Table A.3. Presidential Elections Returns, 1912 – 1932

State	Total Vote 1912	Total Vote 1916	Total Vote 1920	Total Vote 1924	Total Vote 1928	Total Vote 1932
Alabama	117,959	130,435	233,951	162,355	248,981	245,128
Arkansas	125,104	170,104	183,621	138,433	197,731	216,569
Georgia	121,470	160,681	149,651	166,247	229,158	255,590
Kentucky	452,714	520,078	918,342	813,859	940,631	983,086
Louisiana	79,248	92,974	126,236	121,951	215,815	268,804
Mississippi	64,483	86,159	82,418	111,889	151,435	146,013
North Carolina	243,776	289,837	538,649	481,608	635,150	711,495
South Carolina	50,403	63,950	66,808	50,755	68,605	104,411
Tennessee	251,933	272,190	428,036	301,030	352,024	390,263
Texas	300,961	373,310	486,449	659,116	709,344	870,444
Virginia	136,975	152,025	231,000	223,603	305,364	297,939

Table A.4. Louisiana Voter Registration Data, 1920–1932

	March 20, 1920	October 2, 1920	March 22, 1924	October 4, 1924	March 17, 1928	October 6, 1928	March 19, 1932
White men	194,072	211,831	220,691	227,035	254,575	261,827	305,520
White women	0	45,451	87,929	90,101	108,482	115,136	162,154
Black men	1,292	1,632	599	791	1,653	1,734	1,445
Black women	0	1,901	99	164	307	320	114
Total voters	195,364	260,815	309,318	318,091	365,017	379,017	469,233
Women as fraction of total	0.0%	18.2%	28.5%	28.4%	29.8%	30.5%	34.6%
Black voters as fraction of total	0.7%	1.4%	0.2%	0.3%	0.5%	0.5%	0.3%

Notes

Abbreviations Used in the Notes

ADAH
 Alabama Department of Archives and History, Montgomery, Alabama
ALDECP
 [Alabama] State Democratic Executive Committee Papers, Alabama
 Department of Archives and History, Montgomery, Alabama
ALLWVC
 Alabama League of Women Voters Collection, Auburn University, Special
 Collections and Archives Department, Auburn, Alabama
BPL
 Birmingham Public Library, Special Collections Department, Birmingham,
 Alabama
DSU
 Delta State University, Archives Department, Cleveland, Mississippi
DU
 Duke University, William Perkins Library, Durham, North Carolina
ESLC
 Equal Suffrage League (of Virginia) Collection, Virginia State Library and
 Archives, Richmond, Virginia
FBCP
 Florence B. Cotnam Papers, University of Arkansas, Special Collections
 Division, Fayetteville, Arkansas
FHL
 Friends Historical Library, Swarthmore College, Swarthmore, Pennsylvania
GDAH
 Georgia Department of Archives and History, Atlanta, Georgia
GHS
 Georgia Historical Society, Savannah, Georgia
JMWP
 Josephine Mathewson Wilkins Papers, Woodruff Library Special Collections,
 Emory University, Atlanta, Georgia
KYDPP
 Kentucky Democratic Party Papers, Samuel Wilson Collection, University of
 Kentucky, M. I. King Library, Special Collections, Lexington, Kentucky
KYDWCP
 Kentucky Democratic Women's Clubs Papers, Samuel Wilson Collection,
 University of Kentucky, M. I. King Library, Special Collections, Lexington,
 Kentucky

LWVKYP

League of Women Votes of Kentucky Papers, University of Kentucky, M. I. King Library, Special Collections, Lexington, Kentucky

LC

Library of Congress, Manuscript Division, Washington, D.C.

LWV

League of Women Voters

MDAH

Mississippi Department of Archives and History, Jackson, Mississippi

MGA

Middle Georgia Archives, Washington County Regional Library, Macon, Georgia

MLWP

Maggie Lena Walker Papers, Maggie Lena Walker National Historic Site, Richmond, Virginia

NAACPBF

National Association for the Advancement of Colored People Branch Files, Library of Congress, Manuscript Division, Washington, D.C.

NAACPP

National Association for the Advancement of Colored People Papers, Library of Congress (microfilm), Manuscript Division, Washington, D.C.

NACWCP

National Association of Colored Women's Clubs Papers, Library of Congress, Manuscript Division, Washington, D.C.

NCDAH

North Carolina Division of Archives and History, Raleigh, North Carolina

NCLWVP

North Carolina League of Women Voters Papers, North Carolina Division of Archives and History, Raleigh, North Carolina

NLWVP

National League of Women Voters Papers, Library of Congress, Manuscript Division, Washington, D.C.

NLWVPM

National League of Women Voters Papers on Microfilm, Library of Congress, Manuscript Division, Washington, D.C.

PLC

Paul Lewinson Collection, Schomburg Center for Research in Black Culture, New York Public Library, New York

SCDEC

Charleston County (S.C.) Democratic Party Executive Committee

SCHS

South Carolina Historical Society, Charleston, South Carolina

SCL

South Caroliniana Library, University of South Carolina, Columbia, South Carolina

SCLWV
South Carolina League of Women Voters
SHC
Southern Historical Collection, Wilson Library, University of North Carolina, Chapel Hill, North Carolina
SSWP
Sue Shelton White Papers, Arthur and Elizabeth Schlesinger Library, Radcliffe College, Cambridge, Massachusetts
SWLC
Southern Women Legislators Collection, University of Mississippi, Archives and Special Collections, Oxford, Mississippi
TC
Tuskegee Institute News Clippings File, Tuskegee Institute, Division of Behavioral Science Research, Carver Research Foundation, Tuskegee, Alabama
TSLA
Tennessee State Library and Archives, Nashville, Tennessee
TU
Manuscripts Department, Howard-Tilton Memorial Library, Tulane University, New Orleans, Louisiana
UGA
Hargrett Rare Book and Manuscript Library, Special Collections, University of Georgia, Athens, Georgia
UKY
Special Collections and Archives, Margaret I. King Library, University of Kentucky, Lexington, Kentucky
UVA
Alderman Library, Special Collections, University of Virginia, Charlottesville, Virginia
VCU
Special Collections and Archives Department, James Branch Cabell Library, Virginia Commonwealth University, Richmond, Virginia
VHS
Virginia Historical Society, Richmond, Virginia
VSLA
Virginia State Library and Archives, Richmond, Virginia

Introduction

1. Lyndon Baines Johnson to Martin Luther King Jr., 15 January 1965, phone conversation, from Miller Center of Public Affairs, WhiteHouseTapes.org.

2. For this study of "the South," I have chosen to include all the states of the former Confederacy, except Florida. Florida, with its large Hispanic community and limited connections to the network of southern women suffragists, seemed to challenge my attempts to write a coherent analysis of women's postsuffrage activity in the region. The most important works on the woman suffrage campaign in the

South, Elna Green's *Southern Strategies* and Marjorie Spruill Wheeler's *New Women of the New South*, do not substantially include Florida. Moreover, neither Michael Perman's recent work on disfranchisement, *Struggle for Mastery*, nor Edward Ayers's seminal work on the New South, *Promise of the New South*, make substantial reference to Florida. Although V. O. Key included a chapter on Florida in his classic *Southern Politics in State and Nation*, even he concluded that "it is scarcely a part of the South" (83). While Kentucky was not a Confederate state, I have included it here alongside the states of the former Confederacy because Kentucky played an important role in the woman suffrage movement in the South, and its status as a southern state that ratified the Nineteenth Amendment provides useful contrasts between ratification and nonratification states in the region. Both major studies of woman suffrage in the region devote considerable attention to Kentucky women.

3. Grantham, *Life and Death of the Solid South*, chap. 4.

4. Ibid., 78.

5. In her 1970 classic, *The Southern Lady*, Anne Firor Scott found that "the removal of legal and customary barriers to female participation in public affairs did not lead large numbers of women to assume civic or political responsibility" (211). William Chafe (*American Woman*, 46) concurred that "it was unrealistic to expect that extending the vote to women would transform the nation's political and social institutions." Since then, scholars have refined their conclusions and reconceptualized the role of women in American politics. Many have emphasized the continuities in women's pre- and postsuffrage reform activities. Yet this focus on continuity in women's political activities before and after 1920 assumes that women's political behavior was essentially unchanged by enfranchisement. Theda Skocpol (*Protecting Soldiers and Mothers*) has gone so far as to argue that women's particular style of nonpartisan politics made them more powerful *before* they were enfranchised than after. A few recent studies have specifically rejected the argument that enfranchisement itself was a failure in this period but nevertheless concede that women's legislative power declined dramatically by the end of the decade. See, for example, Andersen, *After Suffrage*; Freeman, *A Room at a Time*; and Harvey, *Votes Without Leverage*.

6. Quotation from Cott, "Across the Great Divide." For recent works on women's partisan political activity and the role of gender in the shaping of politics in the presuffrage era, see Rebecca Edwards, *Angels in the Machinery*; and Varon, *We Mean to Be Counted*.

7. For examples of works that examine the role of women and/or gender ideology in southern politics, see Dailey, *Before Jim Crow*; Laura F. Edwards, *Gendered Strife and Confusion*; Gilmore, *Gender and Jim Crow*; MacLean, *Behind the Mask of Chivalry*; and Varon, *We Mean to Be Counted*. On the woman suffrage movement in the South, see Green, *Southern Strategies*; Lebsock, "Woman Suffrage and White Supremacy"; and Wheeler, *New Women of the New South*.

8. See, for example, Chafe, "Women's History and Political History"; Clemens, *People's Lobby*; Cott, *Grounding of Modern Feminism*; Harvey, *Votes Without Leverage*; McGerr, "Political Style and Women's Power"; Muncy, *Creating a Female Dominion*; and Scott, *Natural Allies*.

9. For example, see Dailey, *Before Jim Crow*; Gilmore, *Gender and Jim Crow*;

Judson, "Building the New South City"; Kelley, *Race Rebels*; McArthur, *Creating the New Woman*; Sims, *Power of Femininity*; John Douglas Smith, *Managing White Supremacy*; Thomas, *New Woman in Alabama*; Turner, *Women, Culture, and Community*; and Wilkerson-Freeman, "Women and the Transformation of American Politics."

10. Seminal works in the political history of the New South give little attention to woman suffrage, apparently assuming that the enfranchisement of women made little difference in a political system dominated by segregation and single-party rule. (See, for example, Key, *Southern Politics in State and Nation*, and George B. Tindall, *Emergence of the New South*). Instead, scholars have focused on recurrent agricultural crises, labor unrest, a rising tide of African American activism, and the Great Migration, as well as social changes symbolized by flappers and an increasingly independent youth culture, as the major challenges to the social order of the South in the 1920s. (See, for example, Grossman, *Land of Hope*; Hale, *Making Whiteness*; Hall, "Disorderly Women"; Hall et al., *Like a Family*; Kelley, *Race Rebels*; and Tindall, *Emergence of the New South*). A few recent works, however, have begun to challenge this standard interpretation of the effects of woman suffrage in the South, notably Gilmore, *Gender and Jim Crow*; Gilmore, "False Friends and Avowed Enemies"; and Wilkerson-Freeman, "Women and the Transformation of American Politics."

11. Green, *Southern Strategies*, 176.

12. Baker, "Domestication of Politics"; Clemens, *People's Lobby*.

13. Skocpol, *Protecting Soldiers and Mothers*, 10.

14. Muncy, *Creating a Female Dominion*, xvi.

15. Skocpol, *Protecting Soldiers and Mothers*, 372.

16. For particularly detailed accounts of women's lobbying strategies in the pre-suffrage era, see Clemens, *People's Lobby*; Skocpol, *Protecting Soldiers and Mothers*; and Horstmann, "Political Apprenticeship."

17. Skocpol, *Protecting Soldiers and Mothers*, 361.

18. Muncy, *Creating a Female Dominion*.

19. Wheeler, *New Women of the New South*, 96.

20. Elna Green, Suzanne Lebsock, and Marjorie Wheeler have all studied the woman suffrage movement in the South, including the significance of states' rights issues, white supremacy, and white women's status in the development of a viable prosuffrage base. In broader studies of southern women's activism, Judith N. McArthur, Anne Firor Scott, Anastatia Sims, Mary Martha Thomas, and Elizabeth Hayes Turner have examined the suffrage movement in southern states and considered the importance of white supremacy in the southern suffrage debates. While all of these historians acknowledge the benefits that white women obtained from white supremacy, not all agree about the relative importance of white suffragists' racism. Green, Lebsock, McArthur, Scott, Sims, and Turner deemphasize the racism of white suffragists, and often highlight the differences of opinion between white men and women of the same class on issues of race. By contrast, Thomas and Wheeler emphasize the racism of white suffragists and highlight the centrality of white supremacy to both suffragist and antisuffragist ideology. Green, *Southern Strategies*; Lebsock, "Woman Suffrage and White Supremacy"; and Wheeler, *New Women of*

the New South; McArthur, *Creating the New Woman*; Scott, *Southern Lady*; Sims, *Power of Femininity*; Thomas, *New Woman in Alabama*; Turner, *Women, Culture, and Community*.

21. Elisabeth Israels Perry, "Men Are from the Gilded Age," 37.

22. Ibid.

23. Bryant Simon's examination of the political power of white South Carolina millhands provides a notable exception to this trend. His study demonstrates both the power and the limitations of electoral mobilization. See Simon, *Fabric of Defeat*. Glenda Elizabeth Gilmore's work provides welcome models for blending these two streams of historical study, demonstrating both the political potency of extrapolitical protest and the very real power of the ballot. See Gilmore, *Gender and Jim Crow*; Gilmore, "False Friends and Avowed Enemies." Although she does not find New Orleans women responding immediately to the ratification of the Nineteenth Amendment, Pamela Tyler's work highlights the value of electoral mobilization to organized white women when coupled with the political strategies developed in the presuffrage era. See Tyler, *Silk Stockings*.

24. For some of the earliest articulations of this "declension" argument, see Chafe, *American Woman*; Lemons, *Woman Citizen*; and Lichtman, *Prejudice and the Old Politics*. Like the scholars who would follow, Lemons argued for the persistence of social feminism in the 1920s but concluded that the last half of the decade was a period of declining female activism and effectiveness. Even the latest revisions by political scientists, which take seriously the *potential* power of the ballot, do not take substantial issue with the declension argument. See, for example, Andersen, *After Suffrage*; Freeman, *A Room at a Time*; and Harvey, *Votes Without Leverage*.

25. For information on the use of the vote by African American women outside the South, see Hendricks, "African American Women"; Higginbotham, "Clubwomen and Electoral Politics"; and Materson, "Respectable Partisans."

26. Helen S. Riley to Mrs. Cowper, 18 January 1927, Box 62, Folder Correspondence January–March 1927, Weil Papers, NCDAH.

Chapter One

1. Broadside: "What Will You Be?," Folder 113, Cameron Papers, SHC.

2. For an important essay on changes in the social drama of politics, see Rebecca Edwards, "Gender, Class, and the Transformation of Electoral Campaigns."

3. Green, *Southern Strategies*, 78–91. See also Wheeler, *New Women of the New South*.

4. Broadside: "Woman Suffrage is Here Opposed Because," Folder 113, Cameron Papers, SHC.

5. Broadside: "Opposing Woman Suffrage," Folder 113, Cameron Papers, SHC.

6. Broadside: "Household Hints," Folder 113, Cameron Papers, SHC.

7. Broadside: "America When Femininized [*sic*]," Reel 1, Box 1, Folder 4, Pearson Papers, TSLA.

8. Broadside: "What Will You Be?," Folder 113, Cameron Papers, SHC.

9. For works on challenges to the social order in the South in the 1920s, see Fass, *Damned and the Beautiful*; Grossman, *Land of Hope*; Hale, *Making Whiteness*; Hall,

"Disorderly Women"; Hall et al., *Like a Family*; Kelley, *Race Rebels*; John Douglas Smith, *Managing White Supremacy*; and Tindall, *Emergence of the New South*.

10. MacLean, *Behind the Mask of Chivalry*.

11. Quotation from Sims, *Power of Femininity*, 188. In her 1970 classic, Anne Firor Scott (*Southern Lady*, 211) found that "the removal of legal and customary barriers to female participation in public affairs did not lead large numbers of women to assume civic or political responsibility." Elna Green (*Southern Strategies*) and Marjorie Spruill Wheeler (*New Women of the New South*) make similar arguments in their conclusions.

12. While the majority of southern women enjoyed no voting rights until the ratification of the Nineteenth Amendment, there were some exceptions. For example, Arkansas granted women primary suffrage in 1917, a right that Texas women were granted in 1918; Atlanta women were granted local primary suffrage in 1919; Kentucky women were granted presidential suffrage in 1920; property-owning, taxpaying women of Louisiana obtained the right to vote on issues of taxation during the state constitutional convention of 1898; and in 1919 the women of Tennessee were granted the right to vote in municipal and presidential elections.

13. Wheeler, *New Women of the New South*, 181.

14. *Richmond Times Dispatch*, 24 January 1923, Scrapbook, Box 207, Clark Papers, VCU.

15. The data utilized to create the figure were made available by the Inter-University Consortium for Political and Social Research. The data set "Electoral Data for Counties in the United States: Presidential and Congressional Races, 1840–1972" was originally collected by professors Jerome M. Clubb, William H. Flanigan, and Nancy H. Zingale.

16. Statement of Registered Voters of Louisiana, 20 March 1920 and 2 October 1920, *Report of Secretary of State*.

17. The data referenced in this paragraph were made available through the University of Virginia Geospatial and Statistical Data Center, *U.S. Historical Election Returns*.

Political scientists J. Kevin Corder and Christina Wolbrecht ("Political Context and the Turnout of New Women Voters") are currently exploring ways of identifying more precisely how many women voted and how they cast their ballots. Using sophisticated statistical modeling, these scholars have begun work on data from many northern states. The lack of reliable local-level data for southern states has hampered their work in this region, however. In five northern states, Corder and Wolbrecht conclude, "the responsiveness of women's turnout overall was remarkably similar to that of men, and quickly became more so over time" (46). According to this study, women's turnout lagged men's by approximately 20 percent and was responsive to the same contextual factors that increased or depressed men's turnout; rural women voted in numbers comparable to their urban sisters.

18. *Richmond Times Dispatch*, 3 November 1920.

19. Ibid.

20. SCLWV Scrapbook, 1:69, SCL. For other examples, see SCLWV Scrapbook, 1:65, 67–70, 76, SCL; *Charlotte Observer*, 3 November 1920; and Bowron Scrapbook, 24–25, BPL.

21. *Charlotte Observer*, 3 November 1920.

22. Clipping in *Chattanooga News*, 10 June 1919, Reel 2, Frame 184, 284–85, Milton Papers, TSLA.

23. Undated clipping: "Ladylike Election," SCLWV Scrapbook, 1:68, SCL.

24. Undated clipping: "Sun Still Shines," SCLWV Scrapbook, 1:69, SCL.

25. Undated clipping: "Comment," SCLWV Scrapbook, 1:71–72, SCL.

26. Undated clipping: "Women at Booths Attract Attention," SCLWV Scrapbook, 1:69, SCL.

27. *Butler (Ga.) Herald*, 21 September 1922, Box 4, Folder 30c, Napier Papers, MGA.

28. According to Pamela Tyler (*Silk Stockings*, 132), this fight continued for decades in New Orleans, "where swaggering policemen boldly flaunted their allegiance to one faction, where mayhem was not uncommon, where the simple act of placing a paper ballot into a wooden box could be accompanied by taunts, leers, threats, or even fisticuffs." While Tyler does not find the immediate change in atmosphere at New Orleans polling places that seems evident elsewhere in the South after the ratification of the Nineteenth Amendment, her analysis similarly suggests that it was women's presence that ultimately tamed the "decidedly masculine atmosphere still prevalent at the polls in the 1940s." For information on women cleaning up the polling places, see Chapters 3 and 4.

29. Undated essay: "The recent and disgraceful episode," Box 18, Series 11, Folder 28, Atlanta LWV Papers, GDAH.

30. Eloise G. Franks to Mary Cowper, 8 October 1924, Box 9, Folder Correspondence September[–October] 1924, Cowper Papers, DU; Wake County LWV Minutes, 17 November 1924, Folder Minutes 1921–34, Wake County Chapter Records, NCLWVP, NCDAH.

31. Meeting Minutes, 12 May 1924, Collection 28, Box 621, Folder 1, SCDEC Papers, SCHS.

32. Ethel Deal, "W. A. Boyter," 4 September 1939, North Carolina Writers Project, *American Life Histories*.

33. S. Rene Harris to Mrs. Samuel Wilson, 21 August 1920, Box 1912–20, Folder January–August 1920, KYDPP.

34. *Fortnightly Bulletin*, 7 October 1922, Box 1910–24, Folder 1922, KYDWCP.

35. *Butler (Ga.) Herald*, 21 September 1922, Box 4, Folder 30c, Napier Papers, MGA.

36. John Garland Pollard to Mary Munford, 1 December 1920, Section 11, Munford Family Papers, VHS.

37. Undated clipping: "Macon Elects 'Alderwoman,'" SCLWV Scrapbook, 2:1, SCL.

38. Undated clipping: "Over 900 Women Registered Here During Yesterday," Bowron Scrapbook, BPL.

39. *The Pilgrim*, January 1926, 7.

40. "To the Voters of Jackson County," *Newport Independent*, 29 October 1920, Reel 11, Frame 871, TC.

41. See, for example, District Chairman to Dr. J. D. Buchanan, 25 April 1922; Dis-

trict Chairman to Mr. F. A. Jackson, 25 April 1922; District Chairman to Mr. R. W. Ervin, 17 April 1922, Box 1, Correspondence Jan. – May 1922, Combs Papers, UVA; C. Henry Harman to Dear Sir and Friend, April 1924, Box 2, File L. P. Summers #2, Slemp Papers, UVA.

42. Handbill advertising Lebanon, Virginia, political meeting, 2 September 1924, Box 2, File L. P. Summers, Slemp Papers, UVA.

43. Undated cartoon: "The Right Man on the Job!," Box 65, Folder 1928 Clippings, Montague Papers, VSLA.

44. Undated clipping: "960 Women Register," SCLWV Scrapbook, 1:65, SCL.

45. Clipping, *Chattanooga News*, 10 June 1919, Reel 2, Frame 184, 284 – 85, Milton Papers, TSLA.

46. Undated clipping: "23,000 Women Qualify for Participation in the General Election," Bowron Scrapbook, BPL.

47. *Richmond News Leader*, 18 September 1920, quoted in Lebsock, "Woman Suffrage and White Supremacy," 84.

48. M[ary] W[hite] O[vington] to Dr. A. M. Rivers, 8 October 1920, Box G-147, Folder Greensboro, NC, 1914 – 22, Group I, Series G, NAACPBF.

49. Gilmore, *Gender and Jim Crow*, xxi.

50. Statement of Registered Voters of Louisiana, 2 October 1920, *Report of Secretary of State*.

51. Florence Catrill to Mary Shelby Wilson, 7 October 1920, Box September – December 1920, Folder October 1 – 10, 1920, KYDPP.

52. "Thousands of Colored Voters Swooped Down on Polling Places," *Houston Informer*, 6 November 1920, Reel 11, Frame 894, TC.

53. Mrs. N. G. Evans to Mrs. Salley, 6 October [1920], Correspondence Box 2, Folder 35, Salley Papers, SCL.

54. "Negro Women Alarm Southern Politicians," *Savannah Tribune*, 16 October 1920, Reel 12, Frame 185, TC.

55. "Registration Office Gets Assistance; Women Swamp Place; Race Segregation," *Richmond News Leader*, 17 September 1920, Reel 12, Frame 155, TC.

56. Ibid.

57. Lewinson, *Race, Class and Party*, 134; see also Qre Quotes, Index Tab VIII Specific State Politics and Negro Suffrage, Louisiana, Box 1, PLC.

58. "Ballot Boxes Filled Early," 2 November 1920, Reel 12, Frame 8, TC.

59. "A Negro Woman 'Told Her to Her Teeth,'" Box 309, Folder National League of Republican Colored Women Miscellaneous, Burroughs Papers, LC.

60. "Negro Women to Help Registration," *Nashville Banner*, 10 October 1920, Reel 12, Frame 152, TC; "Colored Women Voters to Meet at School House," *Charlotte Observer*, 15 October 1920, Reel 12, Frame 181, TC; Chas. A. J. McPherson to Dear Sirs, 18 November 1920, Reel 1, Group 1, "Voting, November 10 – 30, 1920," Part 4: Voting, NAACPP; Response from Mrs. F. D. Robinson to Inaugural Questionnaire, Box 309, Folder National League Republican Colored Women 1929 Inaugural Questionnaire, Burroughs Papers, LC.

61. Interview with Christia V. Adair by Dorothy R. Robinson, 25 April 1977, Houston, Texas, in Hill, ed., *Black Women Oral History Project*, 60.

62. "The First Colored Women Voters Club of Ettrick," DeCosta Papers, Special Collections, Johnston Memorial Library, Virginia State University, Petersburg, Virginia.

63. Undated clipping: "23,000 Women Qualify for Participation in the General Election," Bowron Scrapbook, BPL.

64. *Richmond Evening Dispatch*, 5 August 1921, Scrapbook, Box 208, Clark Papers, VCU.

65. "Negro Women in South Hasten to Register as Voters," *New York World*, 3 October 1920, Reel 12, Frame 190, TC.

66. Ibid.

67. Annie G. Wright to Miss Jane Judge, 16 August 1920, Box 174, Folder 2909, Jane Judge Papers, Hartridge Collection, GHS. For an example of poll tax nonpayment by husbands, see Minutes of League of Women Voters, 3 November 1927, Box 26, Folder 8, Hill Papers, UGA.

68. Untitled essay, undated, Box 2, Folder 4, Hutson Papers, Manuscripts Collection #14, TU.

69. *Arkansas Gazette*, 12 March 1919; *Arkansas Gazette*, 15 January 1919.

70. Jackson, "Petticoat Politics," 16–17.

71. Daisy Thompson, "Women and the Changing Times," 16 February 1940, Georgia Writers Project, *American Life Histories*.

72. Undated clipping: "The Woman Voter," SCLWV Scrapbook, 1:87, SCL.

73. See, for examples, "For Canvassing File," Typed Results for Capitol View District, Box 10, Series 5, Folder 12, Atlanta LWV Papers, GDAH; undated draft essay: "Stop! Listen! Do You Know?," I&O 2205, Folder 1915–20, SCLWV Papers, SCL; *The National Notes*, December 1924, Reel 23, Frame 921, Part 1, NACWCP, LC; Report of Organization Work in Waycross, Georgia, 13–14 November 1923, Reel 4, Frames 315–16, Part 3, Series A, National Office Subject Files, NLWVPM; undated handwritten notes, "Merriam and Gosnell Not Voting — 6000," Box 27, Folder University of Virginia Extension Series Pamphlets, Pidgeon Family Papers, FHL.

74. Undated draft essay: "Stop! Listen! Do You Know?"

75. Clipping: "Women and Politics," 18 December 1921, SCLWV Scrapbook, 1:85–86, SCL.

76. Leola[?] T. Bradley, "Reminiscence," 10 October 1939, Georgia Writers Project, *American Life Histories*.

77. Scott, *Southern Lady*, 209.

78. Undated draft essay: "Stop! Listen! Do You Know?"

79. Report of Organization Work in Waycross, Georgia, 13–14 November 1923, Reel 4, Frames 315–16, NLWVPM.

80. Mrs. George McArthur to Viola Ross Napier, undated, Box 2, Folder 8h, Napier Papers, MGA.

81. Interview with Margaret Burnett by Vickie Morton, 20 February 1977, 7, University of Alabama in Birmingham, Oral History Research Project, Mervyn H. Sterne Library, University of Alabama, Birmingham, Alabama.

82. Ibid., 4.

83. Ibid., 3–4.

84. Ibid., 5.

85. Ibid.

86. Green, *Southern Strategies*, 83.

87. Annah Robinson Watson, "Attitudes of Southern Women on the Suffrage Question," *Arena* 63 (February 1895): 365, quoted in Green, *Southern Strategies*, 84.

88. McCurry, *Masters of Small Worlds*.

89. Mrs. Clay Conrad to Mary Shelby Wilson, 9 October 1920, Box September–December 1920, Folder October 1–10, 1920, KYDPP.

90. Ibid.

91. "Not an Old Maid," *Putnam County Herald*, 1 October 1923, quoted in Keith, *Country People in the New South*, 184. In chapter 10, Keith provides a thorough analysis of the debates over woman's proper role that appeared in the *Putnam County Herald* in 1923.

92. Quoted in Keith, *Country People in the New South*, 194.

93. Ibid., 192.

94. Quoted in ibid., 187–88.

95. Ibid., 186–87.

96. Quoted in ibid., 192.

97. *Southwest American*, 8 April 1925.

98. Ibid.

99. Broadside: "Woman Suffrage Is Here Opposed Because," Folder 113, Cameron Papers, SHC.

100. "Our Women Should Pay Their Taxes and Register," *Atlanta Independent*, 3 November 1921, Reel 14, Frame 250, TC.

101. Ibid.

102. "The Registration of Women," *Savannah Tribune*, 2 October 1920, Reel 12, Frame 155, TC.

103. Ibid.

104. *The Crisis*, November 1920.

105. Attachments to Letter, Addie W. Hunton to Miss Ovington, 25 October 1920, Reel 1, Group 1, File "Voting, October 21–31, 1920," NAACPP.

106. Ibid.

107. "Thanks to Women," *Savannah Tribune*, 13 November 1920, Reel 12, Frame 179, TC.

108. Lewinson, *Race, Class and Party*, 203–13. Although the survey responses have not survived, Lewinson's notes based on those surveys are part of the Paul Lewinson Collection at the Schomburg Library. On the question of reasons for nonvoting, the notes revealed no reasons that had not been included in Lewinson's appendix, Box 1, PLC.

109. "Negro Women at the Polls," *Savannah Tribune*, 1920, Reel 12, Frame 174, TC.

110. "Our Women Should Pay Their Taxes and Register," *Atlanta Independent*, 3 November 1921, Reel 14, Frame 250, TC.

111. Response to Colored Women in Politics Questionnaire from Lottie McDonald, Box 308, Folder National League Republican Colored Women in Politics Questionnaire, Burroughs Papers, LC.

112. Ibid.

113. Butler Nance to James Weldon Johnson, 17 September 1920, Reel 1, Group 1, Folder Voting, November 1 – 9, 1920 [letter misfiled], NAACPP.

114. Letter from Butler M. Nance, 12 September 1920, Box G-196, Folder Columbia, SC 1915 – 23, NAACPBF.

115. "The Women Voters' Club," *Birmingham Reporter*, 1921, Reel 14, Frame 244, TC.

116. Chas. A. J. MacPherson to Dear Sirs, 18 November 1920, Reel 1, Group 1, Folder Voting, November 1 – 9, 1920, NAACPP.

117. Mrs. Black to Mr. Bagnall, 12 May 1928, Box G-13, Folder Pine Bluff, Arkansas 1924 – 28, NAACPBF.

118. Assistant Secretary to Mrs. William Mann, 3 November 1920, Reel 1, Group 1, Folder Voting, November 1 – 9, 1920, NAACPP.

119. *Charlotte Observer*, 4 October 1920, quoted in Gilmore, *Gender and Jim Crow*, 212.

120. *The Crisis*, March 1921.

121. Dr. A. M. Rivers to James Weldon Johnson, 6 October 1920, Box G-147, Folder Greensboro, NC, 1914 – 22, NAACPBF.

122. "Dr. Dudley Explains His 'Famous' Letter," *New York Age*, 30 October 1920, Reel 12, Frame 166 – 67, TC.

123. Chairman of the Board to President James B. Dudley, 4 November 1920, Reel 1, Group 1, Folder Voting, November 1 – 9, 1920, NAACPP.

124. Minutes of League of Women Voters, 3 November 1927, Box 26, Folder 8, Hill Papers, UGA.

125. *The Crisis*, March 1921.

126. "Suffrage Has Stirred Negro People of B'ham," *Birmingham Reporter*, 9 September 1920, Reel 12, Frame 174, TC.

127. Mrs. William Mann to Mr. Walter White, 30 October 1920, Reel 1, Group 1, Folder Voting, November 1 – 9, 1920, NAACPP; Mrs. J. J. Black to Mr. Bagnall, 12 May 1928, Box G-13, Folder Pine Bluff, Arkansas 1924 – 28, NAACPBF; "Strenuous Labor in Interest of Bond Issue," 28 May 1921, *Savannah Journal*, Reel 14, Frame 249, TC.

128. James B. Dudley to Mary White Ovington, 28 October 1920, Reel 1, Group 1, Folder Voting, November 1 – 9, 1920, NAACPP.

129. "Strenuous Labor in Interest of Bond Issue," 28 May 1921, *Savannah Journal*, Reel 14, Frame 249, TC.

130. "The Negro Vote in the South," *St. Louis Argus*, 7 January 1921, Reel 14, Frame 233, TC.

131. Notecard "Not Allowed to Vote," Index Tab VIII: Specific State Politics and Negro Suffrage, North Carolina, Box 1, PLC.

132. "Mailing Lists of Qualified Voters by County," Box 29, Folders 6 and 7, ALDECP.

133. "Editorial," *Savannah Journal*, 28 May 1921, Reel 14, Frame 250, TC.

134. Undated clipping: "Goldsboro Woman Destroys Marked Ballots in Wayne" and *Roanoke-Chowan Times* (Rich Square, N.C.), 8 June 1922, Box 61, Folder NCLWV Correspondence 1921 – 22, Weil Papers, NCDAH.

135. Sallie S. Cotten to Gertrude Weil, 5 June 1922; LBA to Gertrude Weil, 6 June

1922; John M. Stivers to Gertrude Weil, 7 June 1922; J. A. Livingstone to Gertrude Weil, 20 June 1922; Cornelia P. Jerman to Gertrude Weil, 21 June 1922, Box 61, Folder NCLWV Correspondence 1921–22, Weil Papers, NCDAH.

136. LBA to Gertrude, 6 June 1922, Box 61, Folder NCLWV Correspondence 1921–22, Weil Papers, NCDAH.

137. "Negro Women in South Hasten to Register as Voters," *New York World*, 3 October 1920, Reel 12, Frame 190, TC.

138. Lewinson, *Race, Class and Party*, 134.

139. Charles Russell, "Is Woman Suffrage a Failure?" *Century Magazine* 35 (March 1924): 724–30, quoted in Andersen, *After Suffrage*, 5.

140. Mollie Dowd to Miss McReynolds, 26 July 1928, Box 15, Folder 20, ALLWVC (reproduced from NLWVP).

141. "New Voter News from the Washington Office — NLWV — October 1926," Box 82, Folder New Voters Committee 1926–28, Clark Papers, VCU.

142. Undated clipping: "Aiken Women Register," SCLWV Scrapbook 1:61, SLC.

143. Meeting Minutes, 21 April 1924, Collection 28, Box 621, Folder 1, SCDEC Papers, SCHS.

144. "Negro Women in South Hasten to Register as Voters," *New York World*, 3 October 1920, Reel 12, Frame 190, TC.

145. Meeting Minutes, 13 January 1922, Box 11, Folder 30, ALDECP.

146. Meeting Minutes, 28 April 1922, Box 14, Folder 13, ALDECP.

147. "Raleigh Women Take Hand in Precinct Meetings," *Raleigh News and Observer*, 28 March 1920, Scrapbook Volume 2, Riddick Papers, SHC.

148. Ibid.

149. Clipping: "Five Women Go to State Democratic Convention With County Delegation," 3 April 1920, Scrapbook Volume 2, Riddick Papers, SHC.

150. *The Bulletin*, May 1926, SCL.

151. Undated essay, "Women Must Still Fight for Their Rights," I&O 2205/2152, Folder 13, SCLWV Papers, SCL.

152. Broadside: "Men! Are You Politically a 'Subject Sex'?" Reel 1, Folder 4, Pearson Papers, TSLA.

153. Broadside: "What Will You Be?," Folder 113, Cameron Papers, SHC.

154. Broadside: "Men! Are You Politically a 'Subject Sex'?" Reel 1, Folder 4, Pearson Papers, TSLA.

155. Broadside: "Woman Suffrage Is Here Opposed," Folder 113, Cameron Papers, SHC.

156. *Southwest American*, 8 April 1925; *New York Times*, 9 January 1927.

157. Clipping: "Changes in Wake of Woman Legislator," Scrapbook Package I, Part I, Flanery Papers, UKY.

158. Viola Ross Napier to Miss Edith E. Moriarty, 5 May 1923, Box 2, Folder 8a, Napier Papers, MGA.

159. Untitled list, "A Personal Letter to the names here listed might be helpful," Box 52, File Personal Papers — Campaign for the Legislature, Lewis Papers, NCDAH.

160. Walter Sillers, Jr., to Hon. M. S. Conner, 18 August 1922, Box 24, Folder 12a, Sillers Jr. Collection, DSU.

161. *The Henry Bulletin* (Martinsville, Va.), 30 September 1927, 21 October 1927. Thank you to Brent Tarter who did the research on Sallie Cook Booker and provided me with his notes.

162. *The Woman Voter*, 10 August 1922.

163. Undated clipping: "Mrs. Harrold Denies Charges," Box 3, Folder 32, Harrold Family Papers, MGA.

164. Undated clipping: "Mrs. Harrold Denies Charges," and undated clipping: "1,000 Women Hear Mrs. Harrold Discuss Issues in Present Race," Box 3, Folder 32, Harrold Family Papers, MGA.

165. Wilkerson-Freeman, "Women and the Transformation of American Politics," 343.

166. John to Mrs. Marie B. Owen, 8 April 1922, Box 15, Folder 19, ALLWVC.

167. *The Woman Voter*, 17 August 1922.

168. Ibid.

169. Undated clipping: "Mrs. Harrold," Box 3, Folder 32, Harrold Family Papers, MGA.

170. D. A. Spivey to John Eldred Swearingen, 8 September 1922, Box III, Folder 83, Swearingen Papers, SCL.

171. Undated clipping: "Mrs. Napier's Candidacy," Box 4, Folder 30c, Napier Papers, MGA.

172. Ibid.

173. Undated clipping: "1,000 Women Hear Mrs. Harrold Discuss Issues in Present Race," Box 3, Folder 32, Harrold Family Papers, MGA.

174. Undated clipping: "Mrs. Harrold Denies Charges" and undated clipping: "1,000 Women Hear Mrs. Harrold Discuss Issues in Present Race," Box 3, Folder 32, Harrold Family Papers, MGA.

175. *The Henry Bulletin* (Martinsville, Va.), 7 October 1927. Thank you to Brent Tarter who did the research on Sallie Cook Booker and provided me with his notes.

176. Viola Ross Napier to Hon. Sam Rutherford, 13 September 1924, Box 2, Folder 8c, Napier Papers, MGA.

177. Clipping: "Let All Be Women," Viola Ross Napier Folder, SWLC.

178. Clipping: "The Women in Politics," enclosure, John to Mrs. Marie B. Owen, 8 April 1922, Box 15, Folder 19, ALLWVC.

179. Undated clipping: "Mrs. Flanery, Politician, Likes Housework," Scrapbook Package I, Part I, Flanery Papers, UKY.

180. Undated obituary, "Woman Senator of 1929 – 1934 Dies," Folder 1, Ellis Reference Files, SCL.

181. Undated clipping: "Woman Senator Talks Politics," Folder 5, Ellis Reference Files, SCL.

182. *New York Times*, 6 December 1925, quoted in Paulissen and McQueary, *Miriam*, 117.

183. Frances Fisher Dubuc, "A Southern Woman as Governor?" *Success*, July 1924, 57.

184. McArthur and Smith, *Minnie Fisher Cunningham*, 137.

185. Undated clipping: "Woman Senator Talks Politics," Folder 5, Ellis Reference Files, SCL.

186. See, for example, Marie Bankhead Owen to Pattie Ruffner Jacobs, 26 July 1922, box unnumbered, papers unprocessed, Folder "Democratic Party," Owen Papers, ADAH; Lamar, *When All Is Said and Done*, 213–14; and Thomas, *New Woman in Alabama*, 208.

187. Marie Bankhead Owen to Mr. C. A. Beasley, 6 December 1923, Democratic Party Folder, Owen Papers, ADAH.

188. Untitled speech written by Ivy G. Hill, undated, papers unprocessed, Smith Family Papers, DSU.

189. Broadside: "To the Voters of Bolivar County," Smith Family Papers, DSU.

190. Lamar, *When All Is Said and Done*, 214.

191. Sims, "'Powers that Pray,'" 220–21.

192. For discussions of the role of gender in white supremacist ideology, see Gilmore, *Gender and Jim Crow*; Green, *Southern Strategies*; Hale, *Making Whiteness*; Hall, *Revolt Against Chivalry*; MacLean, *Behind the Mask of Chivalry*; Wheeler, *New Women of the New South*; and Williamson, *Rage for Order*.

193. *Birmingham Age-Herald*, 10 April 19[20], Bowron Scrapbook, BPL.

Chapter Two

1. Clipping: "Demand of the Women," 25 March 1930, Box 13, Series 10, Folder 3, Atlanta LWV Papers, GDAH.

2. "Registration Week—1924," Report by Mrs. Frances Neal, Box 11, Series 6, Folder 1, Atlanta LWV Papers, GDAH.

3. Information on specific voting requirements was taken from Lewinson, *Race, Class and Party*, appendix; "A Handy Digest of Election Laws," Reel 23, Frame 285–372, Part 3, Series A, National Office Subject Files, NLWVPM; and "The ABC of Voting," Reel 4, Frames 25, 29–40, NLWVPM. Keyssar, *Right to Vote*, and Perman, *Struggle for Mastery*, provide important insights into the implications of different disfranchisement methods.

4. Information on specific poll tax requirements was taken from Lewinson, *Race, Class and Party*, appendix; "A Handy Digest of Election Laws," Reel 23, Frame 285–372, NLWVPM; and "The ABC of Voting," Reel 4, Frames 25, 29–40, NLWVPM.

5. Stoney, "Suffrage in the South," 5.

6. Ogden, *Poll Tax in the South*, 34–35, 52–53.

7. Key, *Southern Politics in State and Nation*, 592.

8. Although it is nearly impossible to separate the disfranchising effects of the poll tax from other methods used in the South in this period, the experience of Louisiana suggests that many hundreds of thousands of southerners were disfranchised by the poll tax alone. In Louisiana, voter registration soared by 240,000 in the immediate aftermath of the repeal of the poll tax. Frederic Ogden (*Poll Tax in the South*, 125–26) has estimated that "at least 100,000" voters became enfranchised in Louisiana as a direct consequence of the tax removal in 1934.

9. Information on specific literacy and understanding requirements was taken from Lewinson, *Race, Class and Party*, appendix, and Key, *Southern Politics in State and Nation*, chap. 26.

10. Lewinson, *Race, Class, and Party*, 230 and 226.

11. Ibid., 242.

12. Key, *Southern Politics in State and Nation*, 555.

13. Grantham, *Life and Death of the Solid South*, 65, 78.

14. Quoted in Green, *Southern Strategies*, 87.

15. Broadside: "Shall History Repeat Itself?" Box 1, Folder 4, Reel 1, Pearson Papers, TSLA.

16. Green, *Southern Strategies*, 36.

17. L. J. H. Mewborn to Miss Gertrude [Weil], 26 August 1920, Box 19, Folder 5, Weil Papers, NCDAH.

18. *The Crisis*, November 1920; Pickens, "Woman Voter Hits the Color Line," 373.

19. Pickens, "Woman Voter Hits the Color Line," 372.

20. Ibid., 373.

21. Ibid.

22. Ibid.

23. Ibid.

24. Ibid.

25. Ibid.

26. Ibid.

27. Ibid.

28. L. W. Taylor to Eulalie Salley, 20 September 1920, Correspondence Box 2, Folder 34, Salley Papers, SCL.

29. "Many Citizens Hear Mrs. South Discuss Issues," *Frankfort (Ky.) State Journal*, 2 October 1920, Reel 12, Frame 162, TC.

30. "Savannah Women Run Gauntlet of South to Vote at Election," *Cleveland Advocate*, 13 November 1920, ‹http://dbs.ohiohistory.org/africanam/page .cfm?ID=9957›; "Atlanta Blocks Vote of Colored Women; Oust White Women," *Cleveland Advocate*, 13 November 1920 ‹http://dbs.ohiohistory.org/africanam/page. cfm?ID=9953› (accessed 5 April 2005).

31. "The Women — God Bless Them," *Houston Informer*, 6 November 1920, Reel 12, Frame 172, TC.

32. Diary Entries 12 September 1920, 13 September 1920, 17 September 1920, Maggie Lena Walker Diary, MLWP.

33. Unknown representative of Fairfax County Branch of NAACP to National, 20 September 1920 [first page missing and end of letter not signed]; J. B. Tinner et al. to Members of the Fairfax County Branch NAACP, 11 November 1920; and E. B. Henderson to Miss Lealtad, 1 December 1920, Box G-207, Folder Falls Church, Virginia (1915 – 20), Group I, Series G, NAACPBF.

34. Chas. A. J. McPherson to Dear Sirs, 18 November 1920, Reel 1, Group 1, "Voting, November 10 – 30, 1920," Part 4: Voting, NAACPP.

35. "Outstanding Features of the Mississippi State Work," *The National Notes*, July 1924, Reel 23, Frame 912, NACWCP.

36. "Negro Women to Help Registration," 10 October 1920, *Nashville Banner*, Reel

12, Frame 152; "To Instruct Colored Women in the Vote," *Nashville Banner*, 27 October 1920, Reel 12, Frame 164, TC.

37. Program of the Third Annual Meeting of the Savannah Federation of Negro Women's Clubs, 29 July 1921, Box 3, Folder 12, Heyward-Howkins Collection, GHS.

38. "Negro Women Seek Permission to Vote," *Savannah Morning News*, 3 November 1920, Williams Clippings File, GHS; "Mass Meeting of Negro Women Held at Second Baptist Church Friday Night," *Savannah Journal*, 16 October 1920, Reel 12, Frame 184, TC; "Suffrage Meeting," *Savannah Tribune*, 27 March 1920, TC.

39. Program of the Third Annual Meeting of the Savannah Federation of Negro Women's Clubs, 29 July 1921, Box 3, Folder 12, Heyward-Howkins Collection, GHS; "Negro Women Seek Permission to Vote," *Savannah Morning News*, 3 November 1920, Williams Clippings File, GHS.

40. Clipping, *Savannah Morning News*, 5 October 1920, Williams Clippings File, GHS.

41. Program of the Third Annual Meeting of the Savannah Federation of Negro Women's Clubs, 29 July 1921, Box 3, Folder 12, Heyward-Howkins Collection, GHS.

42. Gilmore, *Gender and Jim Crow*, 219.

43. "Thousands of Colored Voters Swooped Down on Polling Places," *Houston Informer*, 6 November 1920, Reel 11, Frame 894, TC.

44. See, for examples, Pickens, "Woman Voter Hits the Color Line," 373; Gilmore, *Gender and Jim Crow*, 219; R. McCants Andrews to William T. Andrews, 27 April 1928, Reel 1, Group 1, Folder Voting 1928, NAACPP; Addie W. Huntington to Miss Ovington [and attachments], 25 October 1920, Reel 1, Group 1, Folder Voting, October 21–31, 1920, NAACPP; S. S. Humbert to The National Association A.C.P., 9 November 1920, Reel 1, Group 1, Folder Voting, November 1–9, 1920, NAACPP; and Mrs. Hubert Seligman to Dear Sirs, 8 November 1920, Reel 1, Group 1, Folder Voting, November 1–9, 1920, NAACPP.

45. *Cleveland Advocate*, 18 September 1920 ‹http://dbs.ohiohistory.org/africanam/nwspaper/index.cfm› (accessed 14 October 2002).

46. Response from Mrs. F. D. Robinson to Inaugural Questionnaire, Box 309, Folder National League Republican Colored Women 1929 Inaugural Questionnaire, Burroughs Papers, LC.

47. Undated clipping: "By National Negro Press Association," Reel 11, Frame 961, TC.

48. Quoted in *The Crisis*, October 1920.

49. Quoted in ibid., November 1920.

50. R. R. Williams to Mr. Chambliss, 30 October 1920, Reel 1, Group 1, Folder Voting, October 21–31, 1920, NAACPP.

51. *Cleveland Advocate*, 13 November 1920 ‹http://dbs.ohiohistory.org/africanam/nwspaper/index.cfm› (accessed 14 October 2002).

52. Pickens, "Woman Voter Hits the Color Line," 373; D. B. Brooks to Miss Lealtad, 20 September 1920, Box G-196, Folder Columbia, SC, 1915–93, NAACPBF.

53. D. B. Brooks to Miss Lealtad, 20 September 1920, Box G-196, Folder Columbia, SC, 1915–23, NAACPBF.

54. Clipping: "South Denies Rights That Russia Grants," undated, Reel 12, Frame 173, TC.

55. Mrs. L. F. Beuckenstein to Minnie Fisher Cunningham, 17–18 July 1918, Mc-Callum Family Papers, I, Austin History Center, Austin, Texas, quoted in Winegarten, *Black Texas Women*, 189.

56. "Mr. Ritter Falls Down on Test," *Norfolk Journal and Guide*, 6 November 1920, Reel 12, Frame 143, TC.

57. A. A. Graham to James Weldon Johnson, 26 October 1920, Reel 1, Group 1, Folder Voting, October 21–31, 1920, NAACPP.

58. Chas. A. J. McPherson to Dear Sir, 9 November 1920, Reel 1, Group 1, Folder Voting, November 1–9, 1920, NAACPP.

59. Clipping in *New York World*, 20 January 1926, Box G-1, Folder Birmingham, Alabama 1920–26, NAACPBF.

60. W. G. Young to National Republican Legal Department, 9 November 1920, Reel 1, Group 1, Folder Voting, November 1–9, 1920, NAACPP.

61. Dr. A. M. Rivers to James Weldon Johnson, 6 October 1920, Box G-147, Folder Greensboro, NC 1914–22, NAACPBF.

62. "Negro Women Registering," *Lexington Dispatch*, 28 September 1920, Reel 12, Frame 180, TC.

63. *The Crisis*, April 1921.

64. Ibid.

65. Undated, Untitled Report, Reel 2, File: Woman Suffrage April 4–May 17, 1921, NAACPP.

66. Ibid.

67. "Aftermath of Women's Convention," *Wilmington Advocate*, 26 February 1921, Reel 14, Frame 266, TC.

68. *The Crisis*, April 1921; "Negro Women Seek Franchise Probe," *Constitution*, 13 February 1921, Reel 14, Frame 266, TC.

69. "Republicans Waking Up," *New York Age*, Reel 14, Frame 217, TC.

70. *The Crisis*, the NAACP Branch Records, and Part 4 of the NAACP Papers on microfilm all provide examples of these reports from southern communities in response to the NAACP request for information.

71. "National Association Appears," *Bee*, 29 January 1921, Reel 14, Frame 230, TC.

72. "Congress Is Urged to Reduce Strength of South in House," *Atlanta Constitution*, 20 December 1920, Reel 12, Frame 130, TC; "Accuse Southern Congressmen of Cowardly Tactics," *Bee*, 29 January 1921, Reel 14, Frame 220, TC.

73. "Claims Tenn. Law More Liberal Than Mass.," *Guardian*, 5 February 1921, Reel 12, Frame 122, TC.

74. "Congress Is Urged to Reduce Strength of South in House," *Atlanta Constitution*, 20 December 1920, Reel 12, Frame 130; "Accuse Southern Congressmen of Cowardly Tactics," *Washington Bee*, 29 January 1921, Reel 14, Frame 230, TC.

75. "The South and Negro Suffrage," *Asheville (N.C.) Citizen*, 23 May 1921, Reel 14, Frame 234, TC.

76. "Reduction of Southern Representation a Failure," *New York Dispatch*, 31 December 1920, Reel 12, Frame 120, TC.

77. "Congress, Republican or Democratic, Refuses to Tackle Disfranchisement," *Savannah Tribune*, 21 May 1921, Reel 14, Frame 235, TC.

78. "Virginia League of Women Voters," Box 113, Folder Handbills, Clark Papers, VCU.

79. See, for examples, "Program of the Alabama League of Women Voters Citizenship School," 1–2 October 1924, Box 15, Folder 19, ALLWVC; Program for Citizenship School, Box 1, Folder 3, Keystone Composition Book, FBCP; First Vice-President of the National League of Women Voters Organization Department to Dear State Presidents, 25 October 1921, Box 56, Folder National League of Women Voters Correspondence June–December 1928 [letter is misfiled], Weil Papers, NCDAH; Program of the Annual Conference of the Tennessee League of Women Voters, Citizenship School, 15 March 1929, Reel 1, Frame 36, Milton Papers, TSLA; and "School of Citizenship," *University of Virginia Record Extension Series*, vol. 5, no. 6, February 1920, Box 6, Folder 363, ESLC.

80. See, for examples, "Lectures on Citizenship: Subjects Offered," Box 6, Folder 363, ESLC; Report on Plans for Citizenship, 24 March 1920, Legal Folder, Correspondence 15 March 1919–27 July 1920, Salley Papers, SCL; and Jessie S. Clayton to Salley, 20 April 1920, Correspondence Box 1, Folder 19, Salley Papers, SCL.

81. Myra Howard to Mary Elizabeth Pidgeon, 2 March 1923, Box 27, Folder University of Virginia Correspondence 1923, Pidgeon Family Papers, FHL.

82. For examples of ballot-marking classes, see "Program of the Alabama League of Women Voters Citizenship School," 20–22 September 1920, Box 60, Folder National League of Women Voters State Publications, Weil Papers, NCDAH; *The Pilgrim*, March 1926; SCLWV Scrapbook, 2:19, SCL; President's Address and Annual Report to the Tennessee League of Women Voters, 14–15 March 1929, p. 4, Reel 1, Frame 46, Milton Papers, TSLA; "Order of the Day for Meeting of League May 29 at 3pm at YWCA," Box 5, Folder 323, ESLC; Memo "County Fairs," Box 107, Folder Virginia State Fair Association, Clark Papers, VCU; *The News Bulletin*, May 1927; and "Report From Virginia," Legal Folder, Correspondence 15 March 1919–27 July 1920, Salley Papers, SCL.

83. For information on election procedures in southern states, see Lewinson, *Race, Class and Party*; Kousser, *Shaping of Southern Politics*; and Perman, *Struggle for Mastery*.

84. "Wants Women to Lead — Men to Follow," undated letter to editor of *Ledger-Dispatch* written by Earnest Woman, Box 1, Scrapbook II, Fearing Papers, DU.

85. Local League Committee Activities, Box 205, Folder Texas League of Women Voters — Miscellaneous, Series III, NLWVP.

86. Ibid.

87. For examples of compilations of election laws, see handbill "Election Day is November 4, 1924," Box 5, Folder 1, Alabama Association Records, ADAH; "A Syllabus on Studies in Citizenship," University of Arkansas Bulletin, March 1920, Box 3, Folder 1, FBCP; "Studies in Citizenship for Georgia Women," Box 28, Series 14, Folder 10, Atlanta LWV Papers, GDAH; "A Handbook for League Members 1930," Box 10, Folder 8-5-04, Atlanta LWV Papers, GDAH; *The Woman Voter*, 7 December 1923, 14 December 1923; "Studies in Citizenship for North Carolina Women," Folder 1200, Series 5, Tillett Papers, SHC; "Handbook of Election Law for the Virginia

Voter," University of Virginia Record Extension Series, March 1925, Box 6, Folder 364, ESLC; and "The ABC of Voting," Published by the National League of Women Voters, 1924, Reel 4, Frames 25–40, NLWVPM.

88. Clipping: "Women May Vote in Next Primary," hand dated c. March 1920, Scrapbook of Woman Suffrage Clippings; Attorney General Sam'l M. Wolfe to Mrs. Julian Salley, 23 March 1920, Correspondence Box 1, Folder 16, Salley Papers, SCL.

89. Undated clipping: "End of Convict Leasing Is Demand of Women," Bowron Scrapbook, 20, BPL.

90. "The Voters Calendar," Box 205, Folder Texas League of Women Voters — Miscellaneous, Series III, NLWVP.

91. For examples of women contacting the leagues for information about registration and voting, see Mrs. C. A. Bost to National League of Women Voters, 9 August 1924, Box 9, Folder Correspondence August 1924, Cowper Papers, DU; Winifred Kirkland to Secretary, League of Women Voters, 1 September 1924, Box 9, Folder Correspondence September 1924, Cowper Papers, DU; Miss Wilhelmina Salley to Eulalie Salley, 10 September 1920, Correspondence Box 2, Folder 33, Salley Papers, SCL; Elizabeth Door to Eulalie Salley, 28 February 1921, Correspondence Box 3, Folder 51, Salley Papers, SCL; and Rosabella Cooper to Richmond League of Women Voters, 28 January 1924, Box 65, Folder Richmond League of Women Voters Correspondence 1921–29, Clark Papers, VCU.

92. *The Woman Voter*, 3 August 1922.

93. "Get Out the Vote: Why, When, How," National League of Women Voters, August 1924, Reel 5, Frames 894–95, NLWVPM.

94. Report of Organization Work in Lawrenceville, Winder, and Buford, Georgia, 1–2 November 1923, Reel 4, Frame 300, NLWVPM.

95. Report to Organization Department from Huldah Moorhead, 29 September–1 October [1927], Box 62, Folder Correspondence August–September 1927, Weil Papers, NCDAH.

96. Mrs. Allan Dudley Jones to Roberta Wellford, 16 June [1921], Box 1, Folder League of Women Voters May–July 1921, Wellford Papers, UVA.

97. Jennie Bates Hagood to Eulalie Salley, 3 October 1921, Correspondence Box 4, Folder 68, Salley Papers, SCL.

98. Report of the Work of the Tennessee League of Women Voters, 1921, Correspondence Box 4, Folder 62, Salley Papers, SCL; Frances Taylor to Roberta Wellford, 12 July 1921, Box 1, Folder League of Women Voters May–July 1921, Wellford Papers, UVA.

99. Watkins Report on Texas, 1921, Box 2, Folder Texas League of Women Voters, Series II, NLWVP.

100. Registration — Woman's Club, Richmond League of Women Voters, 30 November 1920, Box 5, Folder 307, ESLC; Undated Remarks, Series Four, Folder 1022, Tillett Papers, SHC.

101. Greetings to DAR Convention, Raleigh, 27 March 1928, Box 61, Folder North Carolina League of Women Voters General Records 1922–33, Weil Papers, NCDAH.

102. Handbill "Atlanta League of Women Voters," [1924], Box 28, Series 14, Folder 3, Atlanta LWV Papers, GDAH. "Every Citizen an Intelligent Voter" was the Atlanta LWV slogan, but the determination to create an informed electorate was shared by all leagues. The leaders of the League of Women Voters during the 1920s were most

often former suffragists, and I have relied on Elna Green's analysis of the membership of suffrage and antisuffrage organizations in my generalizations about the demographics of league leaders. See Green, *Southern Strategies*, 56–77.

103. Miss Ruth Shuler to Eulalie Salley, 22 November 1920, Correspondence Box 2, Folder 37, Salley Papers, SCL; Mrs. Warren Miller to Extension Division, University of Virginia, 7 October 1922, Box 27, Folder University of Virginia Correspondence 1921–22, Pidgeon Family Papers, FHL.

104. 1921–22 Program of Study, Box 1, Folder 5, Wednesday Morning Study Club Papers, Atlanta Historical Society, Atlanta, Georgia.

105. Anne B. Graham to Mrs. Cowper, 22 March [1927], Box 62, Folder Correspondence January–March 1927, Weil Papers, NCDAH.

106. Undated notes, "Organize Women," Box 1, Folder 3, Prudential Insurance Company Notebook, FBCP.

107. Report of Miss Eleanor Laird to National League of Women Voters Organization Department, 22 December 1922 [with accompanying notes and attachments], Reel 4, Frames 214–48, NLWVPM.

108. Meeting Minutes, 16 March 1923, Folder Minutes 1921–34, Wake County Chapter Records, NCLWVP.

109. Archie Beverley to Roberta Wellford, Box 2, Folder January–March 1922 League of Women Voters; Margaret Pickett Stokes to Roberta Wellford, 28 July 1921, Box 1, Folder May–July 1921 League of Women Voters, Wellford Papers, UVA.

110. Minutes of the League of Women Voters, 14 March 1922, Box 25, Folder 8; Minutes of the League of Women Voters, 5 January 1927, Box 26, Folder 7; Minutes of the League of Women Voters, 3 November 1927, Box 26, Folder 8, Hill Papers, UGA.

111. Loka Rigby to Eulalie Salley, 15 September 1920, Correspondence Box 2, Folder 33, Salley Papers, SCL.

112. Lonny Landrum to Mrs. W. L. Dunovant, 16 July 1926, I&O 2205/2152, Folder 11, SCLWV Papers, SCL; Emily Newell Blair to Mrs. Gellhorn, 24 February 1921, Correspondence Box 3, Folder 51, Salley Papers, SCL.

113. *The Bulletin*, July 1926, SCL; undated clipping: "In Union Is Strength," SCLWV Scrapbook, 2:71, SCL.

114. Report on the Alabama State League, by Elizabeth Laird, 4 January 1923–8 January 1923, Reel 4, Frame 233–34, NLWVPM.

115. Bertha Munsell to Salley, 25 March 1921, Correspondence Box 2, Folder 44, Salley Papers, SCL.

116. Miller, "Lobbyist for the People," 68.

117. For examples of county fair work, see Mrs. Jack Lovett to Miss Gladys Harrison, 14 October 1927, Box 15, Folder 20, ALLWVC, reproduced from NLWVPM; Report of Organization Work in Valdosta, Georgia, 9–11 November 1923, Reel 4, Frames 307–8, NLWVPM; *Monthly News*, October 1924; Meeting Minutes, 15 September 1924, Folder Minutes 1921–34, Wake County Chapter Records, NCLWVP; Meeting Minutes, 17 November 1924, Folder Minutes 1921–34, Wake County Chapter Records, NCLWVP; and memo titled "County Fairs," Box 107, Folder Virginia State Fair Association, Clark Papers, VCU.

118. "Slogans for Blackboard Use at County Fairs," Box 81, Folder Get Out the Vote Campaign, Clark Papers, VCU.

119. "Six Reasons Why Farmers' Wives Should Vote," Box 113, Folder Handbills, Clark Papers, VCU.

120. Agnes Henry to Miss Weil, 3 February 1928, Box 63, Folder Correspondence January – March 1928, Weil Papers, NCDAH.

121. Undated essay, "Why a League of Women Voters?," Folder 13, SCLWV Papers, SCL.

122. Quotation is from Report on Registration Week 1926, Box 11, Series 6, Folder 3, Atlanta LWV Papers, GDAH. See also Sixth Ward Report, 12 January 1925, Box 4, Series 1, Folder 45; and Summary Report of Get Out the Vote Campaign for 1928, Box 11, Series 6, Folder 4, Atlanta LWV Papers, GDAH.

123. News Bulletin, Alabama League of Women Voters, 26 February 1923, Birmingham LWV Papers, BPL.

124. Gidlow, *Big Vote*, 130.

125. Ibid., 131.

126. *Labor Advocate*, 18 October 1924, quoted in ibid., 131.

127. News Bulletin, Alabama League of Women Voters, 26 February 1923, Birmingham LWV, BPL. Liette Gidlow has argued forcefully that the white clubwomen active in the city's voter mobilization campaigns "placed an explicit emphasis on getting out a certain segment of the potential electorate . . . while excluding 'problem voters.'" In particular, she argues that their efforts to mobilize "qualified voters" were specifically intended to reinforce class and racial hierarchies in ways that aligned with disfranchisement. While I agree that labor leaders and African Americans had goals that were different from "League ladies," the work of organized white women was more subversive than Gidlow acknowledges. In seeking out labor leaders, and, in particular, by encouraging union members to *qualify* to vote, league leaders did more than pay lip service to mobilizing industrial workers. These politically sophisticated women recognized that they would not be able to control how these workers voted, and league leaders nevertheless provided the Trades Council with information and encouragement to help laborers qualify as voters. See Gidlow, *Big Vote*, quotes pp. 132, 125 – 33.

128. Report of Eleanor Laird to National League of Women Voters, 14 January – 21 January 1923, Reel 4, Frames 239 – 42, NLWVPM.

129. Thomas, *New Woman in Alabama*, 144.

130. Clipping: "Enforcement of Race Purity is Important Issue Before Women Voters' League in Convention," 10 February 1921, Scrapbook, p. 46, Box 3, Folder 32, Harrold Family Papers, MGA.

131. Liette Gidlow, in her study of voter mobilization campaigns in the 1920s, argues that GOTV campaigns staged by the League of Women Voters and other good government organizations in the 1920s "succeeded spectacularly in their efforts to contain the radical potential of universal suffrage." Rather than working genuinely to expand the electorate, Gidlow argues, reformers instead worked to limit rhetorically and culturally an electorate that had become "nearly universal." While it is certainly true that many of these reformers believed that some people were more fit to vote than others, I think that Gidlow underestimates the radical potential of these GOTV campaigns, particularly in the South. Even she admitted that during the campaign in Birmingham, "local actors transformed the GOTV campaigns ini-

tiated by national organizations into campaigns that served their own purposes." Black women and labor leaders worked alongside businessmen and white women's organizations in Birmingham and elsewhere to increase voter turnout. Moreover, her description of suffrage as "nearly universal" in the United States in this period has little meaning given the thoroughgoing disfranchisement of the Jim Crow South. In the South, at least, efforts to mobilize voters and disseminate information about how to register successfully was clearly subversive of the closed political system that southern Democrats had created with disfranchisement. The dearth of information about how to register and the lack of opportunity to register were significant methods of disfranchisement. Once the registrars began to sit for voter enrollment and once the qualifications were publicly explained, even reformers intent on "exclusion" could not control who took advantage of the GOTV campaigns to qualify to vote. See Gidlow, *Big Vote*, 194, 133.

132. Interview with Adéle Clark by Winston Broadfoot, 28 February 1964, 20, transcribed by Jean Houston, Southern Oral History Project, SHC.

133. See, for examples, Publicity Director to Mr. James C. Latimer, 20 July 1921, Box 83, Folder Press Department, Clark Papers, VCU; Bulletin of the Charlottesville and Albemarle League of Women Voters, 22 April 1924, Box 2, Folder League of Women Voters 1924–26, Wellford Papers, UVA; Report, 19 September, Box 2, Folder League of Women Voters April–September 1922, Wellford Papers, UVA; Get Out the Vote Campaign File, Box 81, Clark Papers, VCU; and Press Department Folder, Box 83, Clark Papers, VCU.

134. Report "To Qualify for Voting in Virginia," 4, Box 104, Folder Norfolk Women's Registration Committee, Clark Papers, VCU.

135. Meeting Minutes, 24 May 1924, Box 5, Folder 323, ESLC.

136. *Texas Federation News*, February 1928, attachment to Ida K. Lane to Julia M. Hicks, 16 April 1928, Box 132, Folder Texas, Series II, NLWVP.

137. Only voters in cities were subject to any registration requirements in Kentucky, and even there registration continued through the first week in October in advance of a November election. See Lewinson, *Race, Class and Party*, 228–29.

138. Plans for "Kentucky Citizenship Days," 18–29 September [1923], Box 10, Folder Political Parties 1923–24, LWVKYP.

139. Anna H. Settle to the Ministers of Jefferson County, 13 September 1923, Box 10, Folder Pre-Election Activities 1923–24, LWVKYP.

140. AHS to Mrs. May D. Pope, 5 November 1923, Box 10, Folder Pre-Election Activities 1923–24, LWVKYP; AHS to Mrs. B. L. Hutchinson, 26 September 1923, Box 10, Folder Correspondence 1920–25, LWVKYP.

141. Plans for "Kentucky Citizenship Days," 18–29 September [1923], Box 10, Folder Political Parties 1923–24, LWVKYP.

142. Kentucky League of Women Voters GOTV, Box 165, Folder Kentucky League of Women Voters — Get Out the Vote, Series III, NLWVP.

143. "Registration Week — 1924," Report by Mrs. Frances Neal, Box 11, Series 6, Folder 1, Atlanta LWV Papers, GDAH.

144. Mrs. R. L. Turman to Mr. Walter Taylor, 7 May 1926, Box 11, Series 6, Folder 3, Atlanta LWV Papers, GDAH.

145. For examples of league voter mobilization efforts, see typed copy of news

article, "Round Table is a Success," *Fairhope Courier*, 17 October 1924, Box 1, Folder 1, ALLWVC; "Get Out the Vote, To the Fraternal Organizations of Alabama," Box 15, Folder 19, ALLWVC; Report on Get Out the Vote Campaign, 29 November 1924, SPR 380, Folder 4, State Campaign Committee for the Abolishment of the Convict Contract System Papers, ADAH; Get Out the Vote Committee Report, Box 1, Series 1, Folder 10, Atlanta LWV Papers, GDAH; Yearbook and Convention Proceedings, 1922, p. 141, Box 57, Folder National League of Women Voters Convention Proceedings 1921–22, Weil Papers, NCDAH; Myrtle Miller to Miss Gertrude, 7 May 1928, Box 63, Folder Correspondence April–June 1928, Weil Papers, NCDAH; *Monthly News*, October 1924; Get Out the Vote Campaign File, Box 81, Clark Papers, VCU; and Press Department Folder, Box 83, Clark Papers, VCU.

146. Mildred H. Morris to Dear League Member, undated, Box 165, Folder Kentucky League of Women Voters — Local Leagues, Series III, NLWVP.

147. Undated clipping in scrapbook: "Tennessee Women and the Duties of Citizenship," Reel 2, Frame 93, Milton Papers, TSLA.

148. Ibid.

149. Quoted in McArthur and Smith, *Minnie Fisher Cunningham*, 103.

150. Bertha T. Munsell to Mrs. Dunovant, 26 September 1920, I&O 2205/2152, Folder 10, SCLWV Papers, SCL.

151. Program of the Eighth Annual Conference of the Tennessee League of Women Voters, Box 60, Folder National League of Women Voters State Publications, Weil Papers, NCDAH.

152. "Feminine Voters President Resigns," *Montgomery Advertiser*, 7 May 1926, Box 15, Folder 20, ALLWVC.

153. *The News Bulletin*, May 1927.

154. For examples of league support for permanent registration, see Responses from Georgia, Summary of Answers to Questions 1 and 2 of Efficiency in Government Questionnaire, March 1925, Reel 5, Frames 160–73, NLWVPM; *The Georgia Voter*, October 1928; *Monthly News*, December 1928; President's Address and Annual Report to the Tennessee League of Women Voters, 14–15 March 1929, p. 4, Reel 1, Frame 46, Milton Papers, TSLA; and "Summary of Facts Concerning the Executive Council Meeting," 16–17 July 1923, Box 2, Folder League of Women Voters 1923, Wellford Papers, UVA. Although the leagues were primarily interested in making sure voters got registered and remained registered, there were a few occasions in which leagues supported reregistration or purging of the enrollment books in order to curtail voter fraud.

155. Sarah B. Killam to Nora Houston, 14 March 1923, Box 90, Folder Legislative Committee — 1923, Clark Papers, VCU.

156. Patti S. Jenkins to Nora Houston, 14 March 1923, Box 90, Folder Legislative Committee — 1923, Clark Papers, VCU.

157. Ibid.

158. Perman, *Struggle for Mastery*, 21.

159. Ibid., 300.

160. Michael Perman describes in persuasive terms the ways in which Australian ballot laws served as a "transition on the road to disfranchisement" by serving as an "impartial" test of literacy. In the absence of poll taxes, residency requirements,

literacy tests, and white primaries, the secret ballot dramatically limited the electorate, and demonstrated to southern leaders a way to do so without resort to fraud. By the time women were enfranchised, however, the electorate was already so tightly controlled, it is hard to imagine ways in which the secret ballot could have further constricted it. Moreover, just as Perman points to the "eager endorsements" of Democratic leaders as testimony to the disfranchising effects of the secret ballot, the vigorous opposition of party leaders in North Carolina to the Australian ballot suggests the extent to which they relied on fraud and corruption to maintain their hold on power. See Perman, *Struggle for Mastery*, 21.

161. Key, *Southern Politics in State and Nation*, 457.

162. Pettus to Mr. C. S. Goodwin, 14 June 1930, Box 24, Folder 3, ALDECP.

163. Lewinson, *Race, Class and Party*, 119.

164. Jane Judge, "What Savannah Has Done with 1923," *The New Citizen*, May 1923, and draft version, Box 174, Folder 2909, Hartridge Collection, GHS.

165. "A Woman Looks at North Carolina," Spring 1927, Box 44, Speeches, Lewis Papers, NCDAH.

166. Ibid.

167. *Monthly News*, 28 February 1927.

168. See especially Podolefsky, "Illusion of Suffrage"; and Wilkerson-Freeman, "Second Battle for Woman Suffrage."

169. U.S. Census Bureau, *Statistical Abstract of the United States*.

170. Podolefsky, "Illusion of Suffrage," 198.

171. Ibid.

172. Quoted in Wilkerson-Freeman, "Second Battle for Woman Suffrage," 347.

173. For discussion of white and black men's response to women voting and its relationship to poll tax payment, see Chapter 1.

174. Mrs. Brenton K. Fisk to Miss Belle Sherwin, 20 September 1924, Series II, Box 46, Folder Get Out the Vote: Alabama; and Report on the Get Out the Vote Campaign, 29 November 1924, Series II, Box 47, Folder Get Out the Vote Registration Figures, Series II, NLWVP.

175. Mrs. Brenton K. Fisk to Miss Belle Sherwin, 20 September 1924, Box 46, Folder Get Out the Vote: Alabama, Series II, NLWVP.

176. Jennings Perry, *Democracy Begins at Home*, 211–12.

177. Despite all of these efforts to ameliorate the effects of the poll tax, white women in South Carolina and Tennessee petitioned that women not be exempted from the tax, as they objected to different political treatment of men and women. See, for examples, *The Bulletin*, April 1927, and undated clipping: "Women Endorse Legislative Call," Reel 2, Frame 308, Milton Papers, TSLA.

178. Summary of Answers to Questions 1 and 2 of Efficiency in Government Questionnaire, March 1925, Reel 5, Frames 160–73, NLWVPM.

179. Minutes of League of Women Voters, 3 November 1927, Box 26, Folder 8, Hill Papers, UGA.

180. Typed copy of news article, "Round Table Is a Success," *Fairhope Courier*, 17 October 1924, Box 1, Folder 1, ALLWVC.

181. Annie Carrick Gravois to Miss Adéle Clark, 16 March 1925, Box 18, Folder Third Region, Series II, NLWVP; undated notes, "Organize Women," Box 1, Folder

3, Prudential Insurance Company Notebook, FBCP; Miller, "Lobbyist for the People," 43; Yearbook and Convention Proceedings, 1922, p. 141, Box 57, Folder National League of Women Voters Convention Proceedings 1921–22, Weil Papers, NCDAH; President's Address and Annual Report to the Tennessee League of Women Voters, 14–15 March 1929, Reel 1, Frame 48, Milton Papers, TSLA; Get Out the Vote Campaign File, Box 81, Clark Papers, VCU; Scott, "After Suffrage," 312. Scott contends that politically active southern women opposed the poll tax in the 1920s but encouraged their followers to pay it in order to retain their ability to vote. I have not found evidence of any active opposition to the poll tax, however. Women in Kentucky and North and South Carolina were exempt from payment of the poll tax.

182. Hine, *Black Victory*, ix.

183. See Appendix for full tables of election statistics.

184. Jackson, "Petticoat Politics," 17.

185. Heard and Strong, *Southern Primaries and Elections*, 106–9. See Appendix A.2.

Chapter Three

1. Quoted in Green, *Southern Strategies*, 85, 96.

2. See, for example, Baker, "Domestication of Politics," 627–32; Rebecca Edwards, *Angels in the Machinery*; and Varon, *We Mean to Be Counted*.

3. Ida Thompson to Mrs. Lee, 28 July 1921, Box 68, Clark Papers, VCU.

4. Clipping: "Buncombe Gives Women Right Hand," *Raleigh News and Observer*, 4 April 1920, Scrapbook Volume 2, Riddick Papers, SHC.

5. Cartoon: "In the Spring the Young Man's Fancy," Reel 2, Frame 311, Milton Papers, TSLA.

6. Broadside: "The Other Side of Vardaman," Broadside File 1919–23, MDAH.

7. Handbill: "Lamar Jeffers Candidate for Congress," Box 11, Folder 16, ALDECP.

8. "Patriots Register, Catholic Women Are in Hordes," *The Searchlight*, 14 January 1922.

9. Program, Convention of Tennessee Woman Suffrage Association and Congress League of Women Voters, May 18–19, 1920, Box 3, File 1, FBCP.

10. *The Woman Voter*, 31 August 1922.

11. See, for example, *The Pilgrim*, August 1926. See also "Report of The Pilgrim's Status by Mrs. S. D. Halley, Editor," undated, Box 10, Folder 8-05-01, Georgia LWV Papers, GDAH.

12. Arthur Lucas to Mrs. Lamar R. Lipscomb, 24 July 1922, Box 114, Folder 4, Seydell Papers, Woodruff Library Special Collections, Emory University, Atlanta, Georgia.

13. Congressman Butler B. Hare to Mrs. Dunovant, 15 January 1927, I&o 2205 / 2152, Folder 12, SCLWV Papers, SCL.

14. Undated and untitled letter, Box 1, Folder 40, ESLC.

15. Mrs. Mary Inge Hoskins to AC Patterson, 13 September 1922, Box 13, Folder 3, ALDECP.

16. Report of Organization Work in LaGrange, Georgia, 26 November 1923, Reel 4, Frames 317–18, Part 3, Series A, National Office Subject Files, NLWVPM.

17. J. E. West to Clark, 9 March 1921; Harry St. George Tucker to Friend, 23 July 1921; Clark to C. Bascom Slemp, 11 July 1921, President/Executive Secretary Correspondence File, Box 68, Clark Papers, VCU. For further examples, see Candidate Replies File, Box 91, Clark Papers, VCU.

18. E. Lee Trinkle to Clark, 4 January 1921, President/Executive Secretary Correspondence File, Box 67, Clark Papers, VCU.

19. C. R. Warren to Mrs. F. C. Beverley, 6 July 1921, Candidate Replies File, Box 91, Clark Papers, VCU.

20. "Tom Heflin Boldly Faces Suffragists," *Montgomery Advertiser*, undated, Reel 12, Frame 145, TC.

21. Lamar Jeffers to Miss Burnice Summers, 18 March 1921, Box 11, Folder 16, ALDECP.

22. Broadside: "The Other Side of Vardaman," Broadside File 1919–23, MDAH.

23. *Arkansas Gazette*, 1 August 1920.

24. Pattie R. Jacobs to Salley, 6 May 1921, Correspondence Box 3, Folder 61, Salley Papers, SCL.

25. Undated clipping: "He Got His," SCLWV Scrapbook, 2:15, SCL.

26. Proceedings of the Sixth Annual Convention of the National League of Women Voters, 1925, pp. 80–82, Box 57, Folder National League of Women Voters Convention Proceedings 1924–27, Weil Papers, NCDAH.

27. Year Book of the National League of Women Voters and Proceedings of the Third Annual Convention and Pan-American Conference of Women, 1922, pp. 159–60, Box 57, Folder National League of Women Voters Convention Proceedings 1921–22, Weil Papers, NCDAH; J. H. Webb to Hon. T. J. Bedole [*sic*] et al., 2 March 1922, Box 13, Folder 1, ALDECP.

28. Treadway, "Sarah Lee Fain," 131.

29. Undated handwritten list of candidates, Series 1, Box 1, Folder 9, Arkansas State Republican Party Papers, Special Collections Division, University of Arkansas Libraries, Fayetteville.

30. Jones and Winegarten, *Capitol Women*, 32.

31. *Fortnightly Bulletin*, Democratic Women's Clubs, 7 October 1922, Box 1910–24, Folder 1922, KYDWCP.

32. *Danville Bee*, 17 October 1925. Thanks again to Brent Tarter for his help with the information on Sallie Booker.

33. Typed summary of Lillian Exum Clement Stafford, Folder North Carolina Legislature, SWLC.

34. Undated clipping: "Booming Mrs. Flanery," Scrapbook Package I, Part I, Flanery Papers, UKY.

35. Oldfield stepped down at the conclusion of her husband's unexpired term. In accordance with her husband's dying wish, and with the support of both Republicans and Democrats in the state, Wingo served out her husband's unexpired term and one additional term before stepping down.

36. Paulissen and McQueary, *Miriam*, 128.

37. Undated clipping: "Survey to Show Part of Women in Public Life," Reel 13, Frame 392, SSWP.

38. McNeel to Nesbitt, 12 January 1922, Box 13, Folder 2, ALDECP.

39. John G. Dawson to Mary O. Cowper, 3 June 1924, Box 9, Folder Correspondence June 1924, Cowper Papers, DU.

40. Ibid.

41. W. D. Nesbitt to Mrs. John McNeel, 16 January 1922, Box 13, Folder 2, ALDECP.

42. J. H. Webb to Jon. T. J. Bedole et al., 2 March 1922, Box 13, Folder 1, ALDECP.

43. *Richmond Times Dispatch*, 1 October 1920.

44. Report of the Work of the Tennessee League of Women Voters, 1921, Correspondence Box 4, Folder 62, Salley Papers, SCL.

45. Josephus Daniels to Mary Hinton Fearing, 18 June 1928, Box 1, Scrapbook 2, Fearing Papers, DU.

46. Clipping, *Atlanta Journal*, 5 September 1937, "Former Fulton Legislator Married to Engineer in Quiet Ceremony," Box 98-64-5-1 to 98-64-6-24, Folder Kempton, SWLC.

47. Undated clipping: "Threatening Legislators," Box 4, Folder 30c, Napier Papers, MGA.

48. Wilkerson-Freeman, "Women and the Transformation of American Politics," 405.

49. Ibid.

50. Hawks and Ellis, "Heirs of the Southern Progressive Tradition," 83.

51. Brinkley, *Voices of Protest*, 47.

52. *Arkansas Gazette*, 10 May 1932.

53. *New York Times*, 20 November 1931.

54. Creel, "Woman Who Holds Her Tongue," 55.

55. Eulalie Salley to Mrs. Dunovant, 13 March 1920, I&O 2205/2152, Folder 9, SCLWV Papers, SCL.

56. *Hanover (Va.) Herald*, 20 July 1927, Box 33, Henry Taylor Wickham Scrapbook, vol. 5, Wickham Family Papers, VHS.

57. Mrs. Sarah B. Killam to Nora Houston, 8 July 1923, Legislative Committee File (1922), Box 90, Clark Papers, VCU.

58. "Urge Election of Men of Unquestioned Character," *Raleigh News and Observer*, 22 May 1926, Folder Minutes, 1921–24, Wake County Chapter Records, NCLWVP.

59. "Candidates Meek as Women Voters Opine What's What," *Charlotte Observer*, 23 April 1926, Series 4, Folder 1022, Tillett Papers, SHC.

60. *The Woman Voter*, 10 August 1922.

61. Interview with Adéle Clark by Winston Broadfoot, 28 February 1964, 25, transcribed by Jean Houston, Southern Oral History Project, SHC.

62. Undated clipping: "Those Tempting Plums," SCLWV Scrapbook, 1:63, SCL.

63. *The Sunday Journal*, 22 August 1920, Scrapbook, Box 208, Clark Papers, VCU.

64. Undated clipping: "Women's Vote May Decide It," Reel 2, Frame 278, Milton Papers, TSLA.

65. Walter E. Duncan to Governor James M. Cox, 7 August 1920, Correspondence Box 2, Folder 30, Salley Papers, SCL.

66. *Richmond News Leader*, 24 May 1922, Scrapbook, Box 208, Clark Papers, VCU.

67. *Richmond Times Dispatch*, 14 August 1921, Scrapbook, Box 208, Clark Papers, VCU.

68. Undated clipping: "Hundreds of Women Vote in Macon Primary Election," Scrapbook, p. 72, Folder 32, Box 3, Harrold Family Papers, MGA; *Richmond Times Dispatch*, 24 April 1922, Scrapbook, Box 208, Clark Papers, VCU.

69. Mrs. Dique Eldred to Mrs. Wilson, undated, Box September – December 1920, Folder October 1 – 10, 1920, KYDPP.

70. Clipping: "Comment," Fall 1920, SCLWV Scrapbook, 1:72, SCL.

71. Clipping: "Comment," 7 November 1920, SCLWV Scrapbook, 1:69, SCL.

72. Undated clipping: "Women Prove Their Mettle," Reel 2, Frame 275, Milton Papers, TSLA.

73. Undated clipping: "Women Vote Convictions," Reel 2, Frame 311, Milton Papers, TSLA.

74. S. T. Clover to Miss Marianne E. Meade, 30 August 1920, Folder Samuel Travers Clover, Section 12, Valentine Papers, VHS.

75. Clipping: "Three Suffragists Say Women Will Not Vote as Husbands Do," 26 March 1920, Scrapbook of Woman Suffrage Clippings, Salley Papers, SCL.

76. See, for examples, Gilmore, *Gender and Jim Crow*; Green, *Southern Strategies*; Hale, *Making Whiteness*; Hall, *Revolt Against Chivalry*; Lebsock, "Woman Suffrage and White Supremacy"; MacLean, *Behind the Mask of Chivalry*; Wheeler, *New Women of the New South*; and Williamson, *Rage for Order*.

77. Undated and untitled list of quotes, Folder North Carolina League of Women Voters General Records 1922 – 33, Weil Papers, NCDAH.

78. Undated clipping: "The Woman Voter," SCLWV Scrapbook, 1:87, SCL.

79. Clipping: "Name Mrs. Bowron Chairman League of Women Voters," *Birmingham Age-Herald*, 10 April 1920, Bowron Scrapbook, BPL.

80. Lebsock, "Woman Suffrage and White Supremacy," 85.

81. "Simply Doing Their Duty," Box 1912 – 20, Folder January – August 1920, KYDPP.

82. "Notice to the Democrats of Lunenburg County," Box 51, Folder Virginia State Central Democratic Committee, Clark Papers, VCU.

83. Clipping: "Patriotic Obligation," Fall 1920, SCLWV Scrapbook, 1:73, SCL.

84. *Bristol Herald Courier*, 10 October 1920, Box 116, Folder Newspaper Clippings, Clark Papers, VCU.

85. Untitled clipping, *McKinney (Texas) Examiner*, 28 October 1920, Reel 12, Frame 184, TC.

86. "Negress Pays Poll Tax," *McKinney (Texas) Examiner*, 28 October 1920, Reel 12, Frame 185, TC.

87. "Hysteria of South Increases as Women of Race Get Ballot," *Cleveland Advocate*, 16 October 1920, Reel 12, Frame 175, TC.

88. "More Negro Women Register Than White," *Savannah Journal*, 23 October 1920, Reel 12, Frame 191, TC; "Outnumber White Women in Ward 3," *Newport News Press*, Reel 12, Frame 181, TC.

89. "Necessity of Registration by Georgia Women Is Urged," *The Atlantan*, 28 October 1920, Reel 12, Frame 176, TC.

90. "Whites Must Vote in Negro Homes," *Glasgow Times*, 13 October 1920, Reel 11, Frame 878, TC.

91. *Atlanta Constitution*, 6 November 1921, Reel 14, Frame 252, TC.

92. "Teaching Colored Women," *Chattanooga Times*, 16 October 1920, Reel 12, Frame 174, TC.

93. For an examination of the relationship of women to the Democratic Party after the ratification of the Nineteenth Amendment, see Brodkin, "For the Good of the Party," chaps. 1 and 2.

94. "Raleigh Women Take Hand in Precinct Meetings," *Raleigh News and Observer*, 28 March 1920, Scrapbook Volume 2, Riddick Papers, SHC.

95. Meeting Minutes, 13 January 1922, Box 11, Folder 30, ALDECP.

96. *Richmond Times Dispatch*, 1 October 1920.

97. Mrs. Wilson to Mr. Klair, [March 1921], Box 1910 – 24, Folder 1921, KYDWCP.

98. See file of letters, Mary Shelby Wilson to multiple recipients, 25 August 1920, Box 1912 – 20, Folder January – August 1920, KYDPP.

99. J. H. Murray to Mrs. Samuel Wilson, 23 August 1920, Box 1912 – 20, Folder January – August 1920, KYDPP.

100. Ibid.

101. Ibid.

102. Brodkin, "For the Good of the Party," 95.

103. For more information on these fights, see Chapter 6.

104. See ALDECP.

105. Mary Shelby Wilson to Charles A. Hardin, undated, Box 1910 – 24, Folder 1921, KYDWCP.

106. *The Woman Voter*, 31 August 1922.

107. Ida M. Thompson to Carrie Chapman Catt, 16 September 1920, Box 1, Folder 38, ESLC.

108. Chas. A. Hammer to the Women of Virginia, 10 July 1920, Box 1, Folder 38, ESLC.

109. Charles R. Crisp to Emily B. Woodward, 28 April 1922, Box 1, Folder 6, Emily B. Woodward Collection, Hargrett Rare Book and Manuscript Library, Special Collections, UGA.

110. Broadside: "Republican Campaign Opens at Berryville," Box 4, Series 1, Subseries 4, Folder 7, Arkansas State Republican Party Papers, Special Collections Division, University of Arkansas Libraries, Fayetteville.

111. "An Address to the People of Alabama," Judge L. H. Reynolds, Chairman Republican State Campaign Committee, Official Records: Correspondence Alabama League of Women Voters, Jacobs Papers, BPL.

112. Ibid.

113. Wilkerson-Freeman, "Women and the Transformation of American Politics," 340 – 43.

114. Ibid., 344 – 46.

115. *Greensboro Daily News*, 12 September 1920, quoted in ibid., 343.

116. Wilkerson-Freeman, "Women and the Transformation of American Politics," 345.

117. Ibid., 345–54.

118. Quoted in ibid., 344.

119. Gilmore, "False Friends and Avowed Enemies," 222.

120. "Negro Women in South Hasten to Register as Voters," *New York World*, 3 October 1920, Reel 12, Frame 190, TC.

121. "Would Frighten White Women Voters with a 'Black Menace,'" *Norfolk Journal and Guide*, 25 September 1920, Reel 12, Frame 161, TC.

122. "Ballot Boxes Filled Early," 2 November 1920, Reel 12, Frame 8, TC.

123. "Republicans Hope to Carry Virginia," *New York Post*, 8 September 1921, Reel 14, Frame 162, TC.

124. Ibid.

125. "Still Shaking Skeleton of Negro Issue," *Norfolk Journal and Guide*, 29 October 1921, Reel 14, Frame 68, TC.

126. *Norfolk Ledger-Dispatch*, quoted in "Slurring a Race for Political Party Gain," *Norfolk Journal and Guide*, 2 April 1921, Reel 14, Frame 2, TC.

127. Press Release from Democratic Campaign Headquarters, 16 September 1921, quoted in John Douglas Smith, *Managing White Supremacy*, 65.

128. Ibid.

129. Ibid.

130. "Republicans Hope to Carry Virginia," *New York Post*, 8 September 1921, Reel 14, Frame 162, TC.

131. "Republicans Are to Let Negro Stay Outside," *Sun* (Durham, N.C.), 22 October 1920, Reel 12, Frame 173, TC.

132. "Democrats Hit by Negro Issue," *Charlotte Observer*, 29 October 1920, Reel 12, Frame 167, TC.

133. For an important analysis of this letter see Gilmore, *Gender and Jim Crow*, 214–15.

134. "Republicans Are to Let Negro Stay Outside," *Sun* (Durham, N.C.), 22 October 1920, Reel 12, Frame 173, TC.

135. Ibid.

136. "Democrats Hit By Negro Issue," *Charlotte Observer*, 29 October 1920, Reel 12, Frame 167, TC.

137. "Light Thrown on Activity of Negroes," *Times* (Concord, N.C.), 18 October 1920, Reel 12, Frame 157, TC.

138. Hathorn, "Republican Party in Arkansas," 22–27.

139. "G.O.P.'s Drive in the South," *New York Times*, 19 June 1921, Reel 14, Frame 21, TC.

140. Quoted in Jackson, "Petticoat Politics," 38.

141. Ibid.

142. "Georgia Republicans Are Organizing the Women with Colored Barred," *St. Louis Argus*, 29 February 1922, Reel 16, Frame 413, TC.

143. "The Republican Party in Georgia," 14 July 1923, Reel 19, Frame 56, TC.

144. "Many Citizens Hear Mrs. South Discuss Issues," *Frankfort State Journal*, 2 October 1920, Reel 12, Frame 162, TC.

145. Mrs. Clay Conrad to Mary Shelby Wilson, 9 October 1920, 1 October 1920,

Box September–December 1920, Folder October 1–10, 1920, KYDPP; Nellie L. Blackburn to Mary Shelby Wilson, 4 November 1920, 1 October 1920, Box September–December 1920, Folder November–December 1920, KYDPP.

146. Georgia Dunn to Mrs. Samuel Wilson, 1 October 1920, Box September–December 1920, Folder October 1–10, 1920, KYDPP. See also Florence Catrill to Mary Shelby Wilson, 7 October 1920, 1 October 1920, Box September–December 1920, Folder October 1–10, 1920, KYDPP.

147. "Many Citizens Hear Mrs. South Discuss Issues," *Frankfort State Journal*, 2 October 1920, Reel 12, Frame 162, TC.

148. "Race Issue Already Strong in Kentucky," *Baltimore Evening Sun*, 7 September 1920, Reel 12, Frame 180, TC.

149. "Democrats Look to Women to Give Kentucky Victory," *New York World*, 19 October 1920, Reel 12, Frame 164, TC; "Judge Bingham Takes High Stand in Politics," *Louisville News*, 20 November 1920, Reel 12, Frame 55, TC.

150. Lewinson, *Race, Class and Party*, 185. For information on the independent Republican protests of Louisville's black Republicans, see Reel 14, Frames 196–205, TC.

151. Election data used in this paragraph and in table 2 come from *Historical Statistics of the United States*, 1078, and the University of Virginia Geospatial and Statistical Data Center's online database *U.S. Historical Election Returns*. The county-level data utilized to create the figure were made available by the Inter-University Consortium for Political and Social Research. The data set "Electoral Data for Counties in the United States: Presidential and Congressional Races, 1840–1972" was originally collected by professors Jerome M. Clubb, William H. Flanigan, and Nancy H. Zingale.

152. Sims, "'Powers that Pray,'" 220–21.

153. Sherman, *Republican Party and Black America*, 143.

154. Webb, *Two-Party Politics in the One Party South*, 5; "G.O.P.'s Drive in the South," *New York Times*, 19 June 1921, Reel 14, Frame 21, TC.

155. "G.O.P.'s Drive in the South," *New York Times*, 19 June 1921, Reel 14, Frame 21, TC.

156. Ibid.

157. Ibid.

158. Mary Henderson, "The Woman Voter of North Carolina: Where She Votes and Where She Does Not" (Raleigh: North Carolina Democratic Executive Committee, 1924), Pamphlet Collection, DU.

159. Ibid., Foreword (emphasis in original).

160. Ibid.

161. *Richmond Times Dispatch*, 10 April 1923, Scrapbook, Box 208, Clark Papers, VCU.

162. SCLWV Scrapbook, 1:87, SCL.

163. Thompson, "After Suffrage," 37–38.

164. Report of the North Carolina League of Women Voters, undated, Box 61, Folder North Carolina League of Women Voters General Records 1922–23, Weil Papers, NCDAH.

165. President to Mrs. James Leech, 29 September 1924, Box 10, Folder State Pre-Election Activities 1923–24, LWVKYP.

166. Clipping: "Democrats Are None Too Sure of Tennessee," *New York Sun*, Reel 21, Frame 322, TC.

167. Minutes of Campaign Committee Meeting, 22 September 1922, Box 14, Folder 19, ALDECP, 17.

168. Ibid., 5–6.

169. Ibid., 8.

170. The data utilized to create figure 3 were made available by the Inter-University Consortium for Political and Social Research. The data set "Electoral Data for Counties in the United States: Presidential and Congressional Races, 1840–1972" was originally collected by professors Jerome M. Clubb, William H. Flanigan, and Nancy H. Zingale. In the map, each county was coded into one of four competitiveness categories based on the outcome of the 1920 presidential election. The competitiveness rankings were divided as follows: Democratic Majority (Republican won fewer than 40 percent of the votes); Borderline Competitive (Republican won 40–44.99 percent of the votes); Republican Competitive (Republican won 45–49.99 percent of the votes) and Republican Majority (Republican won 50 percent or more votes). A county was considered to have increased in competitiveness if it changed category in the direction of being more competitive between 1916 and 1920 (e.g., a Borderline Competitive County in 1916 became Republican Competitive in 1920, or a Democratic Majority County in 1916 became Borderline Competitive in 1920).

171. Mapp to Miss E. A. Elmer, Box 2, Folder 204, Mapp Papers, Swem Library, College of William and Mary, Williamsburg, Virginia.

172. "The Reluctant Voter," *Monthly News, Membership*, November 1923, Scrapbook Volume 2, Riddick Papers, SHC.

173. The data used in this analysis is drawn from Heard and Strong, *Southern Primaries and Elections*. In particular, this analysis includes gubernatorial races in Alabama, Arkansas, Georgia, Louisiana, Mississippi, North Carolina, South Carolina, Tennessee, Texas, and Virginia for the period 1919–30. Primary elections in Arkansas, Tennessee, and Texas, in which the incumbent Democratic governor sought renomination, were not included in the totals. V. O. Key provides a similar analysis of southern primary elections for the period 1920–40 in his famous *Southern Politics in State and Nation*. His conclusions for the longer period are similar to my own. See Key, *Southern Politics in State and Nation*, esp. 15–18. See Appendix for full information.

174. The University of Virginia Geospatial and Statistical Data Center, *Virginia Elections*.

175. The data used in this analysis is drawn from Heard and Strong, *Southern Primaries and Elections*. Because of variations in the timing of southern primary elections, Heard and Strong provide data for pre- and postenfranchisement comparisons in the following states only: Alabama, Georgia, Louisiana, Mississippi, North Carolina, and Tennessee. See Appendix for additional data.

176. Prince, "*Woman Voter* and Mississippi Elections."

177. *The Woman Voter*, 24 August 1922.

178. "Yearbook and Convention Proceedings, 1922," 142–43, Box 57, Folder National League of Women Voters Convention Proceedings 1921–22, Weil Papers, NCDAH.

179. Ibid.

180. Report of the Work of the Tennessee League of Women Voters, 1921, Correspondence Box 4, Folder 62, Salley Papers, SCL.

181. Judson, "Building the New South City," 210.

182. Clark, "17,000,000 Women to Vote for President This Fall," 32.

183. Quoted in McArthur and Smith, *Minnie Fisher Cunningham*, 94.

184. Quoted in ibid., 93.

185. Heard and Strong, *Southern Primaries and Elections*, 134.

186. McArthur and Smith provide an important and thorough analysis of this race in *Minnie Fisher Cunningham*, 92–94.

187. *The Woman Voter*, 31 August 1922.

188. Tipton, "'It Is My Duty,'" 110–13.

189. Undated clipping: "Mrs. Somerville Cleans Up County," Scrapbook Volume 8, Reel 3, Somerville-Howorth Papers, Arthur and Elizabeth Schlesinger Library, Radcliffe College, Cambridge, Massachusetts; interview with Lucy Somerville Howorth by Mary Meredith, 15 February 1974, DSU; Mrs. Totty Meredith, "Nellie Nugent Somerville," Presentation to Washington County Historical Society, 19 November 1978, Vertical Files: Mississippi—Bolivar County—Cleveland—Citizens —Somerville Family, Bolivar County Public Library, Cleveland, Mississippi, 69.

190. Mrs. John McNeel to W. D. Nesbitt, 12 January 1922, Box 13, Folder 2, ALDECP.

Chapter Four

1. Sam B. Cook to Oscar Underwood, 13 January 1915, Box 36, Oscar Underwood Papers, ADAH, quoted in Green, *Southern Strategies*, 36.

2. For information on the ideology of southern suffragists, see Wheeler, *New Women of the New South*, and Green, *Southern Strategies*.

3. Goodstein, "Rare Alliance," 231–35.

4. Ibid., 220.

5. Ibid., 229.

6. Kenny to Catt, 5 January 1920, quoted in ibid., 236–37.

7. *Nashville Tennessean*, 19 May 1920, quoted in Goodstein, "Rare Alliance," 239.

8. See, for example, Frederickson, "'Each One Is Dependent on the Other'"; Gilmore, *Gender and Jim Crow*; and Judson, "Building the New South City."

9. Lewinson, *Race, Class and Party*, 149.

10. Goodstein, "Rare Alliance," 237.

11. See, for example, Baker, "Domestication of Politics"; Clemens, *People's Lobby*; Harvey, *Votes Without Leverage*; McGerr, "Political Style and Women's Power"; and Skocpol, *Protecting Soldiers and Mothers*. Recent historians have begun to challenge the notion that nineteenth-century women were nonpartisan, highlighting women's involvement in partisan activities and partisan identities even before they were enfranchised. See, for example, Rebecca Edwards, *Angels in the Machinery*; Freeman,

A Room at a Time; and Varon, *We Mean to Be Counted*. Nevertheless, political expediency demanded for the most part that women activists before 1920 *appear* to be nonpartisan, and as Kimberly Anne Brodkin ("For the Good of the Party," 30) has noted, "even after they secured the vote, women continued to be imagined as disinterested (rather than self-interested) participants, as nonpartisan citizens concerned about good government and issue education."

12. Gustafson, "Partisan Women," 11.

13. Ibid.

14. See, for example, Clemens, *People's Lobby*, and Harvey, *Votes Without Leverage*.

15. Gustafson, "Partisan Women."

16. *The Crisis*, May 1922.

17. Gilmore, "False Friends and Avowed Enemies," 224.

18. Materson, "Respectable Partisans," 116.

19. "Mr. Elmnm and Ella Elmnm," Box 10, Folder 28, Illinois Writers Project, quoted in Materson, "Respectable Partisans," 86.

20. Ibid.

21. "Campaign Experiences — Tennessee," *The National Notes*, December 1924, Reel 23, Frame 921, Part 1, NACWCP.

22. "Annual National Meeting of Colored Women," *Wilmington* (Delaware) *Advocate*, 12 March 1921, Reel 14, Frame 264, TC.

23. Roster of Women in Politics, Box 309, Folder National League of Republican Colored Women — Membership Lists, Burroughs Papers, LC.

24. Memo, Mr. H. M. Kingsley, Director of Negro Work — Home Mission Society, 9 November 1920, Reel 1, Folder Voting November 1 – 9, 1920, NAACPP.

25. First quotation: "The Women Voters' Club," *Birmingham Reporter*, undated, Reel 14, Frame 244, TC; second and third quotations: "The Colored Women's Voters' League," *Birmingham Reporter*, 14 April 1921, Reel 14, Frame 244, TC.

26. "Women Voters Hear Speakers," *Norfolk Journal and Guide*, 20 October 1928, Reel 32, Frame 669, TC.

27. Program of the Third Annual Meeting of the Savannah Federation of Negro Women's Clubs, 29 July 1921, Box 3, Folder 12, Heyward-Howkins Collection, GHS.

28. Ibid.

29. 1922 Convention Minutes, Reel 1, Frames 653 – 54, NACWCP.

30. 1920 Convention Minutes, Reel 1, Frames 608 – 9; and 1924 Convention Minutes, Reel 1, Frame 709, NACWCP.

31. "Colored Doctor Speaks for Roberts," *Nashville Banner*, 27 August 1920, Reel 12, Frame 171, TC.

32. *The Crisis*, October 1920.

33. 1922 Convention Minutes, Reel 1, Frames 653 – 54, NACWCP.

34. Report of the National Chairman on Legislation, p. 77, 1926 NACW Convention Minutes, Reel 1, Frames 790 – 92, NACWCP.

35. "To The Negro Women of Georgia," *Savannah Journal*, 4 September 1920, Reel 12, Frame 188, TC.

36. *The Crisis*, September 1920.

37. Ibid., October 1920.

38. *The National Notes*, November 1925, Reel 24, Frames 33 and 37, NACWCP.

39. *The Crisis*, February 1923.

40. "Ballot Boxes Filled Early," 2 November 1920, Reel 12, Frame 8, TC.

41. Interview with Christia V. Adair by Dorothy R. Robinson, 25 April 1977, Houston, Texas, in Hill, ed., *Black Women Oral History Project*, 60–61.

42. Maggie Lena Walker Diary, October–November 1921, MLWP.

43. "The Campaign," *Richmond Planet*, 12 November 1921, Reel 14, Frames 154–15, TC; Maggie Lena Walker Diary, 7 November 1921, MLWP.

44. "Negroes Win Their Point in Virginia," *St. Louis Argus*, 17 November 1922, Reel 16, Frame 390, TC.

45. Ibid.

46. "Lily Whites Lose," *Richmond Planet*, 11 November 1922, Reel 16, Frame 381, TC.

47. "Black and Tan Nominees Accept Nominations," *Houston Informer*, 11 September 1920, Reel 11, Frame 896, TC.

48. "The Women — God Bless Them," *Houston Informer*, 6 November 1920, Reel 12, Frame 172, TC.

49. "Women, Some Others, and the Election," 6 November 1920, Reel 12, Frame 173, TC.

50. Quotation in ibid.; see also "The Women — God Bless Them," *Houston Informer*, 6 November 1920, Reel 12, Frame 172, TC.

51. "The Women — God Bless Them," *Houston Informer*, 6 November 1920, Reel 12, Frame 172, TC.

52. Ibid.

53. "Women at the Polls," *Savannah Tribune*, 14 April 1921, Reel 14, Frame 247, TC.

54. "Women Stop Working Under Scales," *Louisville News*, 1 July 1922, Reel 16, Frame 415, TC.

55. Ibid.

56. Undated Meeting Minutes, Box 309, Folder National League of Republican Colored Women, Burroughs Papers, LC.

57. Ibid.

58. "Colored Republican Women Hold Executive Session," *Washington Times*, 6 September 1924, Reel 21, Frame 391, TC.

59. Clipping: "No Such People," August 1920, SCLWV Scrapbook, 1:58, SCL.

60. Undated clipping: "Party Lines Will Not Bind Women, Says Mrs. Milton," Reel 2, Frame 313, Milton Papers, TSLA.

61. Clipping: "Would Frighten White Women Voters with a 'Black Menace,'" *Norfolk Journal and Guide*, 25 September 1920, Reel 12, Frame 161, TC.

62. Mrs. W. P. Nesbitt to Governor Thos. E. Kirby, 24 June 1919, Box 15, Folder 19, ALLWVC.

63. EAD to Salley, 5 June 1920, Correspondence Box 2, Folder 26, Salley Papers, SCL.

64. Mrs. Clay Conrad to Mary Shelby Wilson, 9 October 1920, Box September– December 1920, Folder October 1–10, 1920, KYDPP.

65. W. D. Cardwell to Mr. Roy Smith et al., 20 September 1920, Box 1, Folder 38, ESLC [response on back].

66. Lula Parks to Mrs. Settle, 9 August 1923, Box 10, Folder Efficiency in Government 1923–25, LWVKYP.

67. Undated clipping: "Clubwomen Urged to Vote," Reel 1, Frame 524, Milton Papers, TSLA.

68. Undated clipping: "Call to Polls Made to Women," Scrapbook, vol. 12, Cotten Papers, SHC.

69. Gustafson, "Partisan Women," 20.

70. *Rappahannock Record*, 3 August 1921, Scrapbook, Box 207, Clark Papers, VCU.

71. "What Women May Accomplish," *Lessons for the Study of Citizenship*, published by the National League of Women Voters, Reel 1, Frame 692, Milton Papers, TSLA.

72. Undated clipping: "Comment," SCLWV Scrapbook, 2:67–68, SCL.

73. Clipping: "Advice to Women Voters," 21 May 1922, SCLWV Scrapbook, 2:9, SCL.

74. Undated essay, "Citizenship," Box 5, Folder 323, ESLC.

75. Program of the Eighth Annual Conference of the Tennessee League of Women Voters, Box 60, Folder National League of Women Voters State Publications, Weil Papers, NCDAH.

76. Typed copy of news article, "Round Table Is a Success," *Fairhope Courier*, 17 October 1924, Box 1, Folder 1, ALLWVC.

77. Clipping: "League of Women Voters Holds Interesting Meet," Record of Meetings of League of Women Voters of Mecklenburg County, North Carolina 1924–25, Series Four, Folder 1022, Tillett Papers, SHC.

78. Clippings, 18 September [1924], Record of Meetings of League of Women Voters of Mecklenburg County, North Carolina 1924–25, Series Four, Folder 1022, Tillett Papers, SHC.

79. Clipping: "League of Women Voters Holds Interesting Meet," Record of Meetings of League of Women Voters of Mecklenburg County, North Carolina 1924–25, Series Four, Folder 1022, Tillett Papers, SHC.

80. Mrs. Neil R. Wallace to Miss Rocca, 21 October 1924, Box 20, Folder Alabama League of Women Voters, Series II, NLWVP.

81. Ibid.

82. First Vice President to Mr. Nate Lord, 10 November 1928, Box 11, Folder Louisville — November 1926–April 1929, LWVKYP.

83. Agenda, Louisiville League of Women Voters Pre-Election Meeting, 26 October 1928, Box 11, Folder Louisville — November 1926–April 1929, LWVKYP.

84. Undated clipping: "Ask Women to Vote for Right Men for Office," Scrapbook, vol. 12, Cotten Papers, SHC.

85. McGerr, *Decline of Popular Politics*; Rebecca Edwards, "Gender, Class, and the Transformation of Electoral Campaigns." See also Kleppner, *Who Voted?*, and Kornbluh, *Why America Stopped Voting*.

86. Kleppner, *Who Voted?*, 62–63.

87. Report of Liba Pashokova and Gertrude Watkins, 5–10 June 1922, Reel 1, Frame 740, Milton Papers, TSLA.

88. Jackson, "Petticoat Politics," 45.

89. Report on Get Out the Vote Campaign, 29 November 1924, SPR 380, Folder 4, State Campaign Committee for the Abolishment of the Convict Contract System Papers, ADAH.

90. Clipping: "Account of Get Out Vote Luncheon Held October 8, 1924," 9 October 1924, Series Four, Folder 1022, Tillett Papers, SHC.

91. President to Mr. Lawrence Mackey, 16 March 1929, Box 11, Folder Louisville — November 1926 – April 1929, LWVKYP.

92. See, for example, Press Release, 8 April 1928, Box 11, Folder Louisville — November 1926 – April 1929, LWVKYP.

93. See, for example, President to Mr. John C. Doolan, 30 July 1923; and President to Mr. J. H. Scales, undated, Box 10, Folder Political Parties 1923–24, LWVKYP.

94. Anna Settle to Miss Louise Dorsey, 13 June 1923, Box 10, Folder Political Parties 1923–24, LWVKYP.

95. President to Mrs. James Leech, 29 September 1924, Box 10, Folder State Pre-Election Activities 1923–24, LWVKYP.

96. Mary Bronaugh to Mrs. Marie Stuart Edwards, [April 1921], Box 1, Folder Kentucky League of Women Voters, Series II, NLWVP.

97. Mrs. F. C. Beverley to Mary Elizabeth Pidgeon, 18 June 1923, Box 27, Folder University of Virginia Correspondence, Pidgeon Family Papers, FHL.

98. W. M. Brown to Mrs. Charles G. Doak, 19 September 1924, Folder Miscellaneous, Wake County Chapter Records, NCLWVP.

99. *The Woman Voter*, 7 September 1922.

100. Technically, nonpartisanship prevented all leagues from endorsing candidates, but throughout the South local and state leagues engaged in election-season activities that tested the limits of their nonpartisanship. Moreover, on rare occasions some leagues even went so far as to issue endorsements, as the Mississippi league did on behalf of Belle Kearney.

101. *The Woman Voter*, 7 September 1922.

102. Undated clipping: "What Do You Know About Your Government," SCLWV Scrapbook, 2:7, SCL.

103. Clement Eaton, "Breaking a Path," 197–98. See also Goodman, *Ellen Glasgow*, 155.

104. McArthur and Smith, *Minnie Fisher Cunningham*, 119.

105. Quoted in ibid.

106. Alice Paul to Sue Shelton White, 7 August 1924, Reel 13, Frame 73; Paul to White, 8 August 1924, Reel 13, Frame 73; White to Paul, 8 August 1924, Reel 13, Frame 74; White to Mrs. Howard, 8 August 1924, Reel 13, Frame 75; White to Mrs. Mary Giles Howard, 8 August 1924, Reel 13, Frame 76, SSWP.

107. For important works on women's partisan identities in the presuffrage era, see Rebecca Edwards, *Angels in the Machinery*, and Varon, *We Mean to Be Counted*.

108. See, for example, Marie Bankhead Owen to Mr. C. A. Beasley, 6 December 1923, Democratic Party Folder, box unnumbered, papers unprocessed, Owen Papers, ADAH.

109. For examples, see Mrs. John McNeel to W. D. Nesbitt, 12 January 1922, Box 13, Folder 2, ALDECP; undated clipping: "Survey to Show Part of Women in Public Life," Reel 13, Frame 392, SSWP; and Thompson, "After Suffrage," 37–38.

110. Louisiana League of Women Voters' Platform, undated, Box 166, Folder Louisiana, Series III, NLWVP; Jessie Daniel Ames to Miss Julia M. Hinaman, 1 March 1921, Box 5, Folder Legislative Reports, Series II, NLWVP; "Legislation Won in the Equal Rights Campaign 1921–1929," Collection 24, Box 4, Folder 6, Pollitzer Papers, SCHS; "Legal Status of Women: Laws Passed from January 1920 to June 1930 with League Support," Reel 3, Frames 646–69, Part 3, Series A, National Office Subject Files, NLWVPM.

111. *Monthly News*, June 1924.

112. New Orleans was one of the few places where the partisanship of league members resulted in the league becoming overtly aligned with a single party and faction within state politics. The league lost its national charter as a consequence, but the episode stands as an exception to the rule in other states where political women worked hard to safeguard the nonpartisanship of the organization. See Tyler, *Silk Stockings*, esp. 79–82.

113. Mattie T. Pou to Mrs. Thos. O'Berry, 13 November 1930, Series 5, Folder 1097, Tillett Papers, SHC.

114. Undated clipping: "Mrs. Somerville Cleans Up County," Scrapbook, vol. 8, Reel 3, Somerville-Howorth Papers, Arthur and Elizabeth Schlesinger Library, Radcliffe College, Cambridge, Massachusetts.

115. Ibid.

116. SCLWV Scrapbook, 2:15, SCL.

117. *The Woman Voter*, 31 August 1922.

118. Goebel, *Government by the People*, 71.

119. Kousser, *Shaping of Southern Politics*, 73. For additional information on the direct primary in the South, see also Perman, *Struggle for Mastery*, chap. 14.

120. *The Woman Voter*, 31 August 1922.

121. Ibid.

122. Clipping: "Demand of the Women," *Atlanta Constitution*, 25 March 1930, Box 13, Series 10, Folder 3, Atlanta LWV Papers, GDAH.

123. Mary Elizabeth Pidgeon to Eleanor Coleman Johnston, 11 November 1924, Box 27, Folder University of Virginia Correspondence 1926–27 and undated, Pidgeon Family Papers, FHL.

124. *Monthly News*, January 1926; Adéle Clark to Harry Flood Byrd, 6 June 1923, Box 29, Folder Political and Civic Activities — Virginia League Legislative Program, Pidgeon Family Papers, FHL.

125. League of Women Voters Quarterly Meeting Minutes, 15 May 1923, Box 4, Series 1, Folder 43, Atlanta LWV Papers, GDAH.

126. Adéle Clark to Mrs. L. L. Hendren, 1 October 1924, Box 21, Folder Georgia League of Women Voters, Series II, NLWVP.

127. "Slogans for Blackboard Use at County Fairs," Box 81, Folder Get Out the Vote Campaign, Clark Papers, VCU.

128. Untitled list of slogans, Box 81, Folder Get Out the Vote Campaign, Clark Papers, VCU.

129. "A Woman Looks at North Carolina," Spring 1927, Speeches, Box 44, Lewis Papers, NCDAH.

130. Ibid.

131. *The Woman Voter*, 17 August 1922.

132. Mary Elizabeth Pidgeon to Nora Houston and Adéle Clark, 2 January 1921, Box 90, Folder Legislative Committee (1920–21), Clark Papers, VCU.

133. Eloise G. Franks to Mary Cowper, 8 October 1924, Box 9, Folder Correspondence September[–October] 1924, Cowper Papers, DU.

134. Undated clipping: "Goldsboro Woman Destroys Marked Ballots in Wayne," and *Roanoke-Chowan Times* (Rich Square, N.C.), 8 June 1922, Box 61, Folder North Carolina League of Women Voters Correspondence 1921–22, Weil Papers, NCDAH.

135. Miller, "Lobbyist for the People," 49–50.

136. *The Crisis*, August 1925.

137. *Atlanta Constitution*, 13 December 1922; Lewinson, *Race, Class and Party*, 148.

138. *Atlanta Constitution*, 13 December 1922.

139. Ibid., 14 December 1922.

140. Ibid., 13 December 1922, 14 December 1922.

141. *The Crisis*, August 1925.

142. *Atlanta Constitution*, 10 January 1923.

143. Roster of Women in Politics, Box 309, Folder National League of Republican Colored Women — Membership Lists, Burroughs Papers, LC.

144. Lewinson, *Race, Class and Party*, 149.

145. Ibid., 148; *The Crisis*, August 1925.

146. Goodstein, "Rare Alliance," 242–43.

147. Ibid., 243.

148. Mrs. H. R. Butler to NAACP, 24 September 1920; Assistant Director of Branches, NAACP to Mrs. H. R. Butler, 28 September 1920, Reel 2, Group 1, Subject File — Suffrage Woman — March 15–November 11, 1920, NAACPP.

149. Quarterly Meeting Minutes, 4 April 1921, Box 4, Series 1, Folder 41, Atlanta LWV Papers, GDAH; Report of the Second Quarterly Meeting of the League, 14 April 1921, Box 10, Series 4, Folder 5, Atlanta LWV Papers, GDAH.

150. Note to folder, Marion Napier Smith, 21 August 1993, Box 6, Folder 40, Napier Papers, MGA.

151. Joan Marie Johnson, "'This Wonderful Dream Nation!,'" 430.

152. *The National Notes*, May 1928, Reel 24, Frame 323–24, Part 1, NACWCP.

153. AHS to Miss Marguerite Owens, 1 October 1923; AHS to Miss Edith Rockwood, 25 September 1923; AHS to Mrs. Paul Rittenhouse, 17 December 1923, Box 10, Folder African Americans 1923–24, LWVKYP.

154. Gidlow, *Big Vote*, 130.

155. Wilkerson-Freeman, "Women and the Transformation of American Politics," 391.

156. Maggie Lena Walker Diary, 20 November 1920, MLWP; interview with Adéle Clark by Winston Broadfoot, 28 February 1964, transcribed by Jean Houston, Southern Oral History Project, SHC.

157. Clark interview with Broadfoot, 21.

158. "Negro Women in the South Hasten to Register as Voters," *New York World*, 3 October 1920, Reel 12, Frame 190, TC.

159. Addie W. Huntington to Miss Ovington [and attachments], 25 October 1920, Reel 1, Group 1, File Voting October 21–31, 1920, NAACPP.

160. Bessie McD. Bricken to Mrs. Minnie Fisher Cunningham, 5 October 1922, Box 15, Folder 19, ALLWVC.

Chapter 5

1. "Responses of Hon. Chas. I. Dawson and Hon. Wm. J. Fields Candidates for Governor," 16 October 1923, Box 10, Folder Questionnaires, LWVKYP; Julia R. Gunn to Mrs. Solon Jacobs, 29 February 1924, Box 14, Folder Legislative Reports, Series II, NLWVP.

2. *The Woman Voter*, 9 February 1923.

3. Virginia League of Women Voters First Bulletin, November 1920, Box 5, Folder 301, ESLC.

4. Undated draft essay: "Stop! Listen! Do You Know?" I&O 2205, Folder 1915–20, SCLWV Papers, SCL.

5. *The Pilgrim*, July 1926; undated clipping: "Women Urged by President to Use Ballot," Scrapbook, vol. 12, Cotten Papers, SHC.

6. Undated clipping: "Clubwomen Urged to Vote," Reel 1, Frame 524, Milton Papers, TSLA.

7. Although the "blame" for the failure of women's policy demands has shifted over time, nearly all scholars agree that by the end of the 1920s, the inability of newly enfranchised women voters to extract additional policy concessions based on their position as voters was clear. For examples, see Chafe, *American Woman*; Cott, *Grounding of Modern Feminism*; Lemons, *Woman Citizen*; Lichtman, *Prejudice and the Old Politics*; McGerr, "Political Style and Women's Power"; Scott, *Southern Lady*; and Skocpol, *Protecting Soldiers and Mothers*. A few recent studies have highlighted the importance of women's participation in formal, electoral politics, but like earlier studies, these more recent works have found that enfranchised women were unable to sustain sufficient electoral threat to secure additional policy outcomes by the end of the 1920s. See, for example, Andersen, *After Suffrage*; Freeman, *A Room at a Time*; and Harvey, *Votes Without Leverage*.

8. See, for example, Clemens, *People's Lobby*; Harvey, *Votes Without Leverage*; and Skocpol, *Protecting Soldiers and Mothers*.

9. Clemens, *People's Lobby*, 232.

10. See, for example, Chafe, "Women's History and Political History"; Cott, *Grounding of Modern Feminism*; McGerr, "Political Style and Women's Power"; Muncy, *Creating a Female Dominion*; and Scott, *Natural Allies*.

11. Horstmann, "Political Apprenticeship." In recent years a number of studies have examined the ideology, political activities, and accomplishments of white women's reform organizations in the South during the late nineteenth and early twentieth centuries. See, for example, Enstam, *Women and the Creation of Urban Life*; Hewitt, *Southern Discomfort*; McArthur, *Creating the New Woman*; Sims,

Power of Femininity; Thomas, *New Woman in Alabama*; Turner, *Women, Culture, and Community*, and Joan Marie Johnson, *Southern Ladies*. A number of dissertations have also examined similar themes: Hudson, "Maintaining White Supremacy"; Judson, "Building the New South City"; Roydhouse, "'Universal Sisterhood of Women'"; and Wilkerson-Freeman, "Women and the Transformation of American Politics."

12. "Dear Presidents, Legislative Chairmen, and Individual Members," 1 March 1924, Legislative Committee File (1924–25), Box 90, Clark Papers, VCU.

13. Skocpol, *Protecting Soldiers and Mothers*, 362.

14. Ibid., 367.

15. Thomas, *New Woman in Alabama*, 100.

16. Suggested Helps for Committees Furthering Legislation, Box 4, Folder 41, Pidgeon Papers, FHL.

17. Horstmann, "Political Apprenticeship," 400.

18. *Georgia Bulletin* 10, no. 8 (August 1915), quoted in Horstmann, "Political Apprenticeship," 401 (emphasis added).

19. Josephine E. Houston to Senator Carter Glass, 23 January 1921, Legislative Committee File (1920–21), Box 90, Clark Papers, VCU (emphasis added).

20. Adéle Clark to Senator Claude Swanson, 23 January 1921, Legislative Committee File (1920–21), Box 90, Clark Papers, VCU (emphasis added).

21. League of Women Voters Quarterly Meeting Minutes, 21 June 1921, Box 4, Series 1, Folder 41, Atlanta LWV Papers, GDAH (emphasis added).

22. Gertrude Weil to Hon. Hallett S. Ward, 9 December 1921, Box 61, Folder North Carolina League of Women Voters Correspondence 1921–22, Weil Papers, NCDAH; Eulalie Salley to Hon. Richard Wade, 27 January 1921, Correspondence Box 3, Folder 45, Salley Papers, SCL.

23. Horstmann, "Political Apprenticeship," 402.

24. Undated clipping: "Why Should Women Vote," SCLWV Scrapbook, 2:45, SCL.

25. Horstmann, "Political Apprenticeship," 421.

26. Mrs. E. L. Hutchinson to Fellow-Voter, 19 January 1924, Box 14, Folder Legislative Reports, Series II, NLWVP.

27. Jackson, "Petticoat Politics," 229–30.

28. Unsigned to Mrs. James R. Hagan, 6 August 1921, Correspondence Box 4, Folder 65, Salley Papers, SCL.

29. Ibid.

30. Minnie Fisher Cunningham to Eulalie Salley, 2 September 1921, Correspondence Box 4, Folder 67, Salley Papers, SCL.

31. "Suggested Program of Work of Small Town or Village Leagues," undated, published by the National League of Women Voters, Folder National League of Women Voters Reports 1922–30, Weil Papers, NCDAH.

32. Horstmann, "Political Apprenticeship," 427.

33. Mecklenburg County League of Women Voters to Dear Madam, undated, Series 4, Folder 1022, Tillett Papers, SHC.

34. Bertha Munsell to Dear Chairmen, 7 December 1920, Correspondence Box 2, Folder 40, Salley Papers, SCL.

35. Sims, *Power of Femininity*, 170.

36. Undated Talk on Federal Government, Box 31, Folder 12, Raoul Family Papers, Woodruff Library Special Collections, Emory University, Atlanta, Georgia.

37. Viola Ross Napier to Mrs. John Dozier Pou, 1 November 1921, Box 1, Folder 6d, Napier Papers, MGA.

38. Form letter from North Carolina League of Women Voters, 14 December 1920, Box 61, Folder North Carolina League of Women Voters Correspondence 1920, Weil Papers, NCDAH.

39. Mrs. H. B. Chamberlin to Dear Madam, 16 June 1923, Box 2, Folder 8a, Napier Papers, MGA.

40. Miss Parna B. Hill to Hon. William J. Harris, 17 December 1928, Box 27, Folder 5, Hill Papers, UGA.

41. Minutes, 7 February 1923, Council of Women's Clubs Papers, BPL.

42. Form letter by Mrs. A. P. Brantley, undated, Box 11, Folder 3, Wilkins Papers, Woodruff Library Special Collections, Emory University, Atlanta, Georgia.

43. Undated clipping: "Call to Polls Made to Women," Scrapbook, vol. 12, Cotten Papers, SHC.

44. *Knoxville News*, 8 June 1922, Reel 1, Frame 541, Milton Papers, TSLA.

45. AHS to Richard P. Ernst, 2 February 1924, Box 10, Folder Political Parties 1923–24, LWVKYP.

46. Jessie Leigh Hutchinson to Fellow-Worker, 23 May 1924, Box 10, Folder Correspondence 1920–25, LWVKYP.

47. Examples taken from the membership of the Virginia Women's Council of Legislative Chairmen of State Organizations. See Box 6, Folder 376, ESLC.

48. "The Legislative Council of Alabama Women," Report Spring 1924, Box 15, Folder 19, ALLWVC (reproduced from NLWVP).

49. *Monthly News*, March 1924.

50. Legislative Program of the Legislative Council of Alabama Women, April 1923, Box 15, Folder 19, ALLWVC.

51. For purposes of this study, I have chosen to focus primarily on white women's demands for gender equality, labor reform, and social welfare reforms because these were the issues that southern politicians most often identified as "women's issues." When southern white women worked for government reforms such as the short ballot, city manager form of government, or governmental efficiency, they often worked with men's organizations, which makes it harder to isolate the response of politicians to women's new status as voters.

52. Horstmann, "Political Apprenticeship," esp. 460–66. While many state studies of women's Progressive Era reform efforts demonstrate the frequency with which white clubwomen formed coalitions in support of some specific causes, these coalitions were sporadic and ad hoc. The innovation of the Legislative Councils rests in part in their ability to set a single agenda and to represent it as the priority of all clubwomen. Moreover, these councils were permanent organizations for legislative coordination, not temporary coalitions in pursuit of a single cause.

53. Quotation from Clemens, *People's Lobby*, 230. For examples of women's partisan activity before 1920, see Rebecca Edwards, *Angels in the Machinery*, and Varon, *We Mean to Be Counted*.

54. Mary Johnston to Edith Clark Cowles, 9 October 1920, Voter Registration Correspondence and Lists File, Box 124, Clark Papers, VCU.

55. *Richmond News Leader*, 27 May 1921, Scrapbook with clippings labeled "History of Virginia League of Women Voters," Box 207, Clark Papers, VCU. For a discussion of the league's nonpartisanship and early fears that the league might constitute a third party or woman's bloc, see Young, *In the Public Interest*, 47.

56. *Lessons for the Study of Citizenship* by Marie B. Ames, published by the National League of Women Voters, Reel 1, Frame 692, Milton Papers, TSLA.

57. "Women Voters, Duty Calls You," 10 September 1922, SCLWV Scrapbook, 2:13, SCL; "Facts for Women Voters," 11 March 1922, SCLWV Scrapbook 2:7, SCL.

58. *The Woman Voter*, 31 August 1922.

59. Much recent scholarship has focused on the continuities in women's reform activities before and after they won the right to vote. Emphasis on the continuities in women's pre- and postsuffrage reform activity, however, suggests that the nonpartisanship of women's organizations in the 1920s was simply a holdover from presuffrage days. Indeed, Clemens argues that "having mobilized around identities and organizational forms defined in opposition to party politics, women activists found it difficult to mobilize as a bloc within the electoral system" once the vote was won. Anna Harvey equates organized women's nonpartisanship with a failure to pursue an electoral strategy. Theda Skocpol has gone so far as to argue that women's particular style of nonpartisan politics made them more powerful *before* they were enfranchised than after. Yet, as both Clemens and Harvey acknowledge, nonpartisan or "extrapartisan" organizing could enhance the power of groups of voters pursuing legislative change. Interest groups composed of new women voters, like all interest groups, are more powerful when their loyalty is in question. Nonpartisanship, then, is not evidence of the tendency of newly enfranchised women to avoid electoral politics. Rather, it was a strategic choice made by women to make them more effective as lobbyists. Quote, Clemens, *People's Lobby*, 232. See also Cott, *Grounding of Modern Feminism*; Harvey, *Votes Without Leverage*; and Skocpol, *Protecting Soldiers and Mothers*.

60. Legislative Chairman to Dear Sir, 18 August 1921, Legislative Committee File (1920–21), Box 90, Clark Papers, VCU.

61. Nora Houston to Presidents, Legislative Chairmen and Individual Members, 17 June 1924, Legislative Committee File (1924–25), Box 90, Clark Papers, VCU.

62. Undated essay, "Citizenship," Box 5, Folder 323, ESLC.

63. See, for example, Hansen, *Gaining Access*, and Harvey, *Votes Without Leverage*. Although many political scientists root the power of interest groups in the voters that the groups represent, this is a point of substantial disagreement among scholars.

64. *Birmingham Age-Herald*, 3 September 1922, quoted in Miller, "Lobbyist for the People," 45.

65. *Hanover (Va.) Herald*, 20 July 1927, Box 33, Henry Taylor Wickham Scrapbook, vol. 5, Wickham Family Papers, VHS; *Richmond News Leader*, 19 February 1923, Box 207, Clark Papers, VCU.

66. *The Pilgrim*, July 1926; undated clipping: "Put It in Writing," Scrapbook, vol. 12, Cotten Papers, SHC.

67. Undated clipping: "Put It in Writing," Scrapbook, vol. 12, Cotten Papers, SHC.

68. Ibid.

69. *An Aid for Voters: Election of November 1921*, Box 165, Folder Kentucky League of Women Voters — Get Out the Vote, Series III, NLWVP.

70. Hand-dated clipping: "Register and Join!," 5 March 1922, SCLWV Scrapbook, 2:6, SCL.

71. Thomas B. Bailee to Virginia League of Women Voters, 23 September 1923, Legislative Measures and Programs File, Box 92, Clark Papers, VCU.

72. Mary Elizabeth Pidgeon to State Legislative Chairmen, 15 June 1925, Virginia Women's Council of Legislative Chairmen of State Organizations File, Box 92, Clark Papers, VCU.

73. Ibid.

74. Bert. to Eulalie, 24 July 1920, Correspondence Box 2, Folder 29, Salley Papers, SCL.

75. Horstmann, "Political Apprenticeship," 434. Horstmann discusses the timing of unenfranchised women's lobbying activities, and she concludes that many clubwomen withheld their pressure from legislators "until their legislative success seemed imminent." According to Horstmann, UDC members often waited for men to request their assistance before entering the political fray. None of the activity she describes took place during election cycles, although white clubwomen recognized that the election of new men to office could sometimes make legislative bodies more receptive to women's demands.

76. Jane Judge, "What Savannah Has Done with the 1923," *The New Citizen*, May 1923, Reprint, Box 174, Folder 2909, Hartridge Papers, GHS.

77. As many scholars have demonstrated, newly enfranchised women did not vote as a bloc. In fact, most observers at the time probably recognized that such a voting bloc was neither possible nor seriously considered by suffragists. Talk of a women's voting bloc — or the failure of women to create one — was rather, as one scholar recently termed it, "a political myth" (Freeman, *A Room at a Time*, 2). Attacks against it served to defend politics as usual, condemning women who sought to organize women outside of the parties, and repeated references to women's failure to create one helped politicians justify their resistance to women's policy demands. Nevertheless, a monolithic woman's voting bloc is not the same thing as an interest group. Women's interest groups did exist, and they comprised important blocs of voters who could use their ballots to help determine the outcome of an election. For information on the "failure" to create a women's voting bloc, see Lichtman, *Prejudice and the Old Politics*. For two important studies that demonstrate that the women's voting bloc was a political construct rather than a realistic possibility, see Cott, *Grounding of Modern Feminism*, and Freeman, *A Room at a Time*.

78. For examples of candidate responses, see *The Pilgrim*; *The Georgia Voter*; *FACTS*; *An Aid for Voters: Election of November 1921*, Box 165, Folder Kentucky League of Women Voters — Get Out the Vote, Series III, NLWVP; *Kentucky League Bulletin*; *The Woman Voter*; *Monthly News*; and Candidate's Replies File, Box 91, Clark Papers, VCU.

79. Candidate's Replies File, Box 91, Clark Papers, VCU.

80. Ibid.

81. Quotation from J. S. Barron to Nora Houston, 11 July 1923, Candidate's Replies File, Box 91, Clark Papers, VCU.

82. "Citizens! By Voting You Can," Handbills Folder, Box 113, Clark Papers, VCU.

83. Reprinted in *The Pilgrim*, August 1926.

84. "Notable Meeting of Women Voters," 16 February 1923, SCLWV Scrapbook, 2:21, SCL.

85. *Monthly News*, February 1928.

86. Sims, *Power of Femininity*, 185.

87. Minutes, 23 October 1922, Council of Women's Clubs Papers, BPL.

88. Many scholars writing about the 1920s continue to draw sharp distinctions between the activities of women reformers and those of women "in politics." According to these accounts, activist women could choose to continue their voluntarist reform efforts *or* to engage in partisan politics. For example, scholars as diverse as William Chafe and Anna L. Harvey have distinguished between electoral and nonelectoral reform strategies pursued by women. Felice Gordon characterized activist women in the 1920s as either "moral prodders" or "equal righters." Even a more recent account by Jo Freeman draws distinctions between "feminists," "reformers," and "party women." While scholars generally admit that many women participated in both kinds of activities, such distinctions — in particular the common dichotomies between electoral and nonelectoral activities — fail to acknowledge the very political nature of lobbying. Organized women reformers in the 1920s engaged in sophisticated lobbying campaigns that were based on electoral strategies. These activities were not separate from the partisan political fray but rather used the electoral threat that organized women posed to command the attention of political parties and elected officials. See Chafe, "Women's History and Political History"; Harvey, *Votes Without Leverage*; Felice Gordon, *After Winning*; and Jo Freeman, *A Room at a Time*.

89. *The Woman Voter of Virginia*, October 1926, Membership Bulletin File, Box 115, Clark Papers, VCU.

90. Undated Convention Program, Box 15, Folder 20, ALLWVC.

91. Clipping: "Comment," hand-dated 5 February 1922, SCLWV Scrapbook, 2:4, SCL.

92. President to Mrs. G. A. Barret, 14 April 1928, Box 11, Folder Louisville — November 1926 – April 1929, LWVKYP.

93. Marie Holmes to Mrs. Cowper, Box 62, Folder Correspondence January – March 1927, Weil Papers, NCDAH.

94. Clemens, *People's Lobby*, 217.

95. *Monthly News*, 14 March 1927.

96. Unsigned to Miss Weil, 19 November 1927, Box 62, Folder Correspondence October – November 1927, Weil Papers, NCDAH.

97. *The Pilgrim*, April 1926.

98. A Summary of the Atlanta League of Women Voters from 1920 – 29, Box 12, Series 9, Folder 1, Atlanta LWV Papers, GDAH.

99. Mrs. C. A. Bost to Cowper, 13 October 1924, Box 9, Folder Correspondence September[– October] 1924, Cowper Papers, DU.

100. In a particularly blatant example of such protests, an article in the bulletin of the Georgia League of Women Voters disingenuously stated that "influencing the individual voter is quite beyond our province," while just a few sentences later the author lambasted the policy regarding salaries for county officials and detailed the records of each candidate on that particular issue. See *The Pilgrim*, February 1926.

101. Mrs. J. W. Dodd and Elizabeth Tompkins to Members of the General Assembly, Virginia Women's Council File, Box 92, Clark Papers, VCU.

102. Nora Houston to the Presidents of Local Leagues of Women Voters, 21 February 1922, Legislative Committee File (1922), Box 90, Clark Papers, VCU.

103. Mrs. Brenton K. Fisk to Hon. George Huddleston, 30 August 1921, Correspondence Box 4, Folder 67, Salley Papers, SCL.

104. Mrs. Brenton K. Fisk to Mrs. G. E. Kirkland et al., 19 July 1923, Folder 2, State Campaign Committee for the Abolishment of the Convict Lease System Papers (SPR #380), ADAH.

105. Ibid.

106. Gertrude Weil to Hallett S. Ward, 9 December 1921, Box 61, Folder North Carolina League of Women Voters Correspondence 1921–22, Weil Papers, NCDAH.

107. Hansen, *Gaining Access*, 29.

108. Edith Clark Cowles to Mrs. Woods Jordan, 29 November 1920, Box 1, Folder 39, ESLC.

109. Clipping: "Register and Vote," 27 February 1926, *Birmingham Reporter*, Reel 26, Frame 508, TC.

110. Charlotte Hawkins Brown to James B. Dudley, 3 May 1920, Reel 2, Frame 845, Brown Papers. For additional information on the ideology of African American suffragists, see Terborg-Penn, *African American Women in the Struggle for the Vote*, esp. 76.

111. *The National Notes*, November 1925, Reel 24, Frame 33, Part 1, NACWCP.

112. *The National Notes*, September 1927, Reel 24, Frame 214, NACWCP.

113. *Atlanta Independent*, 3 February 1921, quoted in Judson, "Building the New South City," 226.

114. Report of the National Chairman on Legislation, Convention Minutes 1926, Reel 1, Frames 792–93, NACWCP.

115. Ibid.

116. Ibid.

117. *The Kentucky Club Woman* (Louisville, Ky.), 31 May 1921, Box 2, Folder 14, Fouse Family Papers, UKY.

118. *The Crisis*, August 1925.

119. J. Douglas Smith discusses the paternalistic race relations of the Jim Crow South in general and the alternating friendship and derision shown by white politicians to black southerners in *Managing White Supremacy*, esp. 65–66.

120. Joan Marie Johnson, *Southern Ladies*, 169.

121. *The National Notes*, March 1926, Reel 24, Frame 65, NACWCP.

122. For information on Virginia's racial integrity legislation in the 1920s, see Sherman, "'The Last Stand,'" and Smith, *Managing White Supremacy*, esp. 76–106.

123. *The National Notes*, March 1926, Reel 24, Frame 65, NACWCP.

124. *Monthly News*, October 1930.

125. McKendrick Barr to Salley, 6 January 1921, Correspondence Box 2, Folder 43a, Salley Papers, SCL.

126. Johnson, *Southern Ladies*, 185.

127. Wesley, *History of the National Association of Colored Women's Clubs*, 328.

128. Ibid., 312.

129. Charlotte Hawkins Brown to Mrs. R. J. Reynolds-Johnson, 25 October 1921, Reel 3, Frame 212, Brown Papers, Arthur and Elizabeth Schlesinger Library, Radcliffe College, Cambridge, Massachusetts.

130. Wesley, *History of the National Association of Colored Women's Clubs*, 312.

131. Program of the Legislative Council of North Carolina Women, 1925, Box 53, Folder Legislative Reports, Series II, NLWVP.

132. *Monthly News*, 23 January 1925.

133. President and Executive Secretary to Judge W. H. Young, 21 March 1927, Box 62, Folder Correspondence January–March 1927, Weil Papers, NCDAH.

134. Speech at Madison Square Garden, 1943, Brown Papers, Arthur and Elizabeth Schlesinger Library, Radcliffe College, Cambridge, Massachusetts, quoted in Roydhouse, "'Universal Sisterhood of Women,'" 236.

135. Undated essay: "In 1925 the Georgia Federation of Business and Professional Women's Clubs," Box 4, Folder 17, Napier Papers, MGA.

136. Cox, *Women State and Territorial Legislators*.

137. *St. Louis Post Dispatch*, 17 December 1926.

138. Kate Neal Workman to Eulalie Salley, undated, Correspondence Box 2, Folder 30, Salley Papers, SCL.

139. Mrs. Frank Haskins to Viola Ross Napier, 30 May 1922, Box 1, Folder 7a, Napier Papers, MGA.

140. Hawks and Ellis, "Heirs of the Southern Progressive Tradition," 83–84.

141. For specific information on legislators' club memberships, see SWLC.

142. Tipton, "'It Is My Duty,'" 128–29.

143. Undated clipping: "Mrs. Napier's Bills," Box 4, Folder 30c, Napier Papers, MGA.

144. Mrs. Robert K. Rambo to Viola Ross Napier, 18 August 1925, Box 2, Folder 8d, Napier Papers, MGA.

145. *The Bulletin*, July 1926.

146. Mrs. W. B. Puett to Mrs. Mary O. Cowper, 4 February 1927, Box 62, Folder Correspondence January–March 1927, Weil Papers, NCDAH.

147. Mrs. W. B. Puett to Mrs. Mary O. Cowper, 4 February 1927, Box 62, Folder Correspondence January–March 1927, Weil Papers, NCDAH.

148. Eulalie Salley to Mrs. Dunovant, 3 March 1921, I&O 2205/2152, Folder 11, SCLWV Papers, SCL.

149. Mary Cowper to Belle Sherwin, 27 January 1927, Box 123, Series II, NLWVP, quoted in Roydhouse, "'Universal Sisterhood of Women,'" 241.

150. "A Decade of League Work," Tenth Annual Convention Drama File, Box 86, Clark Papers, VCU; A Summary of the Atlanta League of Women Voters from 1920 thru 1929, Box 12, Series 9, Folder 1, Atlanta LWV Papers.

151. *Monthly News*, February 1928 [emphasis added].

152. Undated clipping: "Conclusions from Elections," SCLWV Scrapbook, 2:63.

153. Cox, *Women State and Territorial Legislators.*

154. Sarah S. Matthews to Nora Houston, 3 January 1926, Box 13, Folder Political, Subfolder Suffrage and Virginia LOWV 1916–38, Houston Family Papers, VHS.

155. Response penciled on back of letter, Georgia May Jobson to Mrs. Townsend, 23 February 1921, Box 1, Folder 41, ESLC.

156. Nellie Nugent Somerville to Mrs. Thompson, 6 March [year not noted], Box 1, Folder 6, Lily Wilkinson Thompson Papers (#1265), MDAH.

157. Undated clipping: "Efficiency Rather Than Sex," Scrapbook, vol. 12, Cotten Papers, SHC.

158. Undated clipping: "Boom Mrs. Hook for State Legislature," Scrapbook, vol. 11, Folder 11, Cotten Papers, SHC.

159. Report of the Work of the Tennessee League of Women Voters, 1921, Correspondence Box 4, Folder 62, Salley Papers, SCL.

160. Mary E. Jagoe to Miss Caspar Whitney, 25 May 1926, Box 97, Folder Get Out the Vote — State Reports, Series II, NLWVP.

161. McArthur and Smith, *Minnie Fisher Cunningham*, 118–19; Paulissen and Mc-Queary, *Miriam*, esp. 94–116.

Chapter 6

1. James C. Derieux to Mrs. F. S. Munsell, 24 March 1920, Correspondence Box 1, Folder 16, Salley Papers, SCL.

2. Interview with Adéle Clark by Winston Bradfoot, 28 February 1964, transcribed by Jean Houston, Southern Oral History Project, SHC, 15.

3. Emily McDougald, Georgia League of Women Voters, to Eulalie Salley, 17 July 1921, Correspondence Box 4, Folder 64, Salley Papers, SCL.

4. Undated clipping: [1922] "A Revelation of Power," Scrapbook, vol. 11, Folder 11, Cotten Papers, SHC.

5. *The Woman Voter,* 14 September 1922.

6. E. A. Dunnovant to Salley, 1 March 1921, Correspondence Box 3, Folder 52, Salley Papers, SCL.

7. Ibid.

8. "Addresses Delivered Yesterday by Equal Suffrage Leaders," *Raleigh News and Observer,* 3 February 1915, quoted in Sims, *Power of Femininity,* 169.

9. "Report of the Legislative Chairman of the VA League of Women Voters [1922]," Legislative Reports and Summaries File, Box 91, Clark Papers, VCU.

10. T. W. Harrison to Nora Houston, 11 October 1924, Legislative Committee File (1924–25), Box 90, Clark Papers, VCU.

11. Hamilton McWhorter Jr. to Viola Ross Napier, 2 September 1925, Box 2, Folder 8d, Napier Papers, MGA.

12. Speech by Congressman J. T. Deal, December 1921, Child Welfare Committee — Bulletins, Correspondence, Miscellaneous (1921–25) File, Box 79, Clark Papers, VCU.

13. Ibid.

14. *The Woman Voter,* 3 August 1922.

15. MacLean, *Behind the Mask of Chivalry,* 88.

16. Perhaps because the legislative councils in each state were coalitions of many organizations, freestanding collections of council papers are rare. Consequently, most of the information on the councils presented here comes from the reports compiled by the state Leagues of Women Voters. The national League of Women Voters regularly inquired about the existence of such councils, and in their own legislative reports, state leagues generally indicated which legislative activities had been undertaken in coordination with other women's groups.

17. "Laws Passed from January 1920 to June 1930 with League Support," Reel 3, Frames 646–69, Part 3, Series A, National Office Subject Files, NLWVPM; *Knoxville News*, 8 June 1922, Reel 1, Frame 541, Milton Papers, TSLA.

18. *Promotion of the Welfare and Hygiene*, 46.

19. Ibid., 1928, 33–34.

20. Hanger and Eno, *History of the Arkansas Federation of Women's Clubs*, 87.

21. Georgia Legislation Enacted Since 1920, Reel 17, Frames 484–85, NLWVPM; Report of Ida Blount Cheatham to the Atlanta League of Women Voters, 1921, Box 1, Series 1, Folder 3, Atlanta LWV Papers, GDAH; League of Women Voters Third Regional Bulletin, 29 June 1922, Box 2, Folder 7d, Napier Papers, MGA.

22. Harper, ed., *History of Woman Suffrage*, 6:142.

23. Legislative Program [1922] From the Report of the Legislative Chairman, Mrs. Frank McIntire, Box 5, Series 4, Folder 1, Atlanta LWV Papers, GDAH; Reports from Thirty Five States of Legislation Endorsed and Supported by State Leagues Since Formation of National League in 1920, Reel 6, Frames 900–926, NLWVPM; *Promotion of the Welfare and Hygiene*, 1929, 2; Georgia Legislation Enacted Since 1920, Reel 17, Frames 484–85, NLWVPM.

24. Legislative Program [1922] From the Report of the Legislative Chairman, Mrs. Frank McIntire, Box 5, Series 4, Folder 1, Atlanta LWV Papers, GDAH; Reports from Thirty Five States of Legislation Endorsed and Supported by State Leagues Since Formation of National League in 1920, Reel 6, Frames 900–926, NLWVPM; *Promotion of the Welfare and Hygiene*, 1929, 2; Georgia Legislation Enacted Since 1920, Reel 17, Frames 484–85, NLWVPM.

25. "Laws Passed from January 1920 to June 1930 with League Support," Reel 3, Frames 646–69, NLWVPM.

26. Ibid.

27. *Promotion of the Welfare and Hygiene*, 1929, 2; *Biennial Report of the State Treasurer of the Commonwealth of Kentucky*, 1923 and 1924.

28. "Louisiana Laws Discriminating Against Women," National Woman's Party, Collection 24, Box 41, Folder 6, Pollitzer Papers, SCHS, 11.

29. Ibid., 11–14; "Louisiana National Woman's Party Plans Active Season," 5 February 1922, *Times-Picayune*, Box 38, Collection 24, Pollitzer Papers, SCHS.

30. "Louisiana Laws Discriminating Against Women," National Woman's Party, Collection 24, Box 41, Folder 6, Pollitzer Papers, SCHS, 11–14; "Louisiana National Woman's Party Plans Active Season," 5 February 1922, *Times-Picayune*, Box 38, Collection 24, Pollitzer Papers, SCHS.

31. *New York Times*, 26 August 1923.

32. *Promotion of the Welfare and Hygiene*, 1929, 2; Swain, "Organized Women in Mississippi," 99.

33. *The Woman Voter*, 3 August 1922.

34. Form Letter from North Carolina LWV, 14 December 1920, Box 61, Folder North Carolina League of Women Voters Correspondence 1920, Weil Papers, NCDAH; "The North Carolina League of Women Voters," undated report, Box 61, Folder North Carolina League of Women Voters General Records 1922–23, Weil Papers, NCDAH; Memo by Lillian M. Thompson, 19 March 1921, Correspondence Box 3, Folder 56, Salley Papers, SCL; *Promotion of the Welfare and Hygiene*, 1929, 2; "Legal Status of Women: Laws Passed from January 1920 to June 1930 with League Support," Reel 3, Frames 646–69, NLWVPM; Skocpol, *Protecting Soldiers and Mothers*, 457; U.S. Department of Labor, Children's Bureau, *A Tabular Summary of State Laws Relating to Public Aid to Children in Their Own Homes in Effect January 1 1925 and the Text of the Laws of Certain States* (Washington, D.C.: Government Printing Office, 1925), 16–17, Box 10, Folder 18, JMWP.

35. "The North Carolina League of Women Voters," undated report, Box 61, Folder North Carolina League of Women Voters General Records 1922–23, Weil Papers, NCDAH; *Promotion of the Welfare and Hygiene*, 1929, 2.

36. "The North Carolina League of Women Voters," undated report, Box 61, Folder North Carolina League of Women Voters General Records 1922–23, Weil Papers, NCDAH.

37. Memo by Lillian M. Thompson, 19 March 1921, Correspondence Box 3, Folder 56, Salley Papers, SCL; Sims, "'Sword of the Spirit,'" 410.

38. Skocpol, *Protecting Soldiers and Mothers*, 457; *Promotion of the Welfare and Hygiene*, 1929, 2.

39. Memo by Lillian M. Thompson, 19 March 1921, Correspondence Box 3, Folder 56, Salley Papers, SCL.

40. Bertha Munsell to Mrs. Dnonavant [*sic*], 7 March 1921, I&O 2205 / 2152, Folder 11, SCLWV Papers, SCL.

41. "Legal Status of Women: Laws Passed from January 1920 to June 1930 with League Support," Reel 3, Frames 646–69, NLWVPM; Reports from Thirty Five States of Legislation Endorsed and Supported by State Leagues Since Formation of National League in 1920, Reel 6, Frames 900–926, NLWVPM; "Year book and Convention Proceedings, 1922," Box 57, Folder National League of Women Voters Convention Proceedings 1921–22, Weil Papers, NCDAH.

42. "Legal Status of Women: Laws Passed from January 1920 to June 1930 with League Support," Reel 3, Frames 646–69, NLWV Papers (on microfilm), LC; *Promotion of the Welfare and Hygiene*, 1929, 2.

43. Proceedings of the Fifth Annual Convention of the National League of Women Voters, 1924, pp. 34–38, Box 57, Folder National League of Women Voters Convention Proceedings 1924–27, Weil Papers, NCDAH.

44. Ibid.

45. Report of the Work of the Tennessee League of Women Voters, 1921, Correspondence Box 4, Folder 62, Salley Papers, SCL.

46. Ibid.; U.S. Department of Labor, Children's Bureau, *Tabular Summary*, 20–21.

47. Report of the Work of the Tennessee League of Women Voters, 1921, Correspondence Box 4, Folder 62, Salley Papers, SCL.

48. "Legislation Won in the Equal Rights Campaign 1921–1929," Collection 24,

Box 4, Folder 6, Pollitzer Papers, SCHS; *Promotion of the Welfare and Hygiene*, 1929, 2; "Legal Status of Women: Laws Passed from January 1920 to June 1930 with League Support," Reel 3, Frames 646–69, NLWVPM.

49. Senate Document No. 6, Communication from the Governor Transmitting the Report of the Children's Code Commission, *Journal of the Senate of the Commonwealth of Virginia*, 1922.

50. The league documents consistently cite that eighteen of the children's code commission recommendations passed into law that year, but all of their lists of those bills include the passage of Virginia's Sheppard-Towner legislation, which was not one of the original twenty-six proposals. See *Journal of the Senate of the Commonwealth of Virginia*, 1922; *Journal of the House of Delegates of the Commonwealth of Virginia*, 1922; and Child Welfare Bulletin submitted by Elizabeth Sims Brownlow [1921], n.d.; "Personnel of the Virginia Children's Code Commission"; and Child Welfare Committee Report signed by Mrs. Louis Brownlow [1922], n.d.; all in Child Welfare Committee File (1921–25), Box 79, Clark Papers, VCU; and answers to questionnaire sent out by National Congressional Secretary, Legislative Committee Reports and Summaries File, Box 91, Clark Papers, VCU.

51. *Journal of the Senate of the Commonwealth of Virginia*, 1922; *Journal of the House of Delegates of the Commonwealth of Virginia*, 1922.

52. *Richmond Times Dispatch*, 3 November 1921, Scrapbook, Box 208, Clark Papers, VCU.

53. Response to Colored Women in Politics Questionnaire from Lottie McDonald, Box 308, Folder National League Republican Colored Women, Colored Women in Politics Questionnaire, Burroughs Papers, LC.

54. Clark, "17,000,000 Women to Vote for President This Fall," 32.

55. The story of this remarkable election is told in Goodstein, "Rare Alliance." For additional information on this election, see Chapter 4.

56. Judson, "Building the New South City," 216.

57. Sarah Mercer Judson provides an excellent analysis of these two bond elections in ibid., 215–33.

58. Wilson Lovett to Mr. John L. Patterson, 19 June 1920, Reel 2, Frame 57, Part 4: Voting, NAACPP.

59. Ibid., Frame 58.

60. Ibid., Frame 60, 65–66; "To the Colored People of Louisville: Why We Intend to Vote No on the Million Dollar Bond Issue," *Evening Post*, 29 October 1920, Reel 2, Frame 71, Part 4: Voting, NAACPP.

61. Lovett to W. E. B. DuBois, 23 July 1920, Reel 2, Frame 63, Part 4: Voting, NAACPP.

62. Ibid.

63. "University of Louisville to the Colored People of Louisville," *Louisville Herald*, 27 October 1920, Reel 2, Frame 68, Part 4: Voting, NAACPP.

64. "To the Colored People of Louisville: Why We Intend to Vote No on the Million Dollar Bond Issue," *Evening Post*, 29 October 1920, Reel 2, Frame 71, Part IV, NAACPP.

65. Lovett to Walter White, 18 November 1920, Reel 2, Frame 79, Part 4: Voting, NAACPP.

66. Lewinson, *Race, Class and Party*, 151.

67. Ibid., 105.

68. Clipping: "Negro Vote Issue in Raleigh Election," 4 May 1927, Reel 29, Frame 367; clipping: "Negroes Using the Vote Effectively," 14 May 1927, Reel 29, Frame 348, TC.

69. Clipping: "Negro Vote Issue in Raleigh Election," 4 May 1927, Reel 29, Frame 367, TC.

70. Ibid.

71. Clipping: "One Lesson of Election," 12 May 1927, Reel 29, Frame 209; clipping: "A Political Firebrand," 6 May 1927, Reel 29, Frame 367, TC.

72. Clipping: "One Lesson of Election," 12 May 1927, Reel 29, Frame 209, TC.

73. Ibid.

74. Lewinson, *Race, Class and Party*, 146–48.

75. Ibid., 150–52.

76. Jessie Daniel Ames to Miss Julia M. Hinaman, 1 March 1921, Box 5, Folder Legislative Reports, Series II, NLWVP.

77. Ibid.

78. Ibid.

79. Ibid.

80. Legislative Program of the Legislative Council of Alabama Women, April 1923, Box 15, Folder 19, ALLWVC (reproduced from NLWVP).

81. Ibid.

82. Ibid.

83. Ibid.

84. Ibid.

85. Ibid.

86. Legislative Council Report, Spring 1924, Box 15, Folder 19, ALLWVC.

87. Ibid.

88. "Laws Passed from January 1920 to June 1930 with League Support," Reel 3, Frames 646–69, NLWVPM; *Knoxville News*, 8 June 1922, Reel 1, Frame 541, Milton Papers, TSLA.

89. For an important study of early age-of-consent campaigns, see Odem, *Delinquent Daughters*, esp. chap 1.

90. Quoted in Sims, "'Sword of the Spirit,'" 410.

91. Bertha Munsell to Mrs. Dunnovant, undated, I&O 2205/2152, Folder 11, SCLWV Papers, SCL.

92. "The Legislative Council of Alabama Women," Report Spring 1924, Box 15, Folder 19, ALLWVC.

93. E. A. Dunnovant to Salley, 1 March 1921, Correspondence Box 3, Folder 52, Salley Papers, SCL.

94. *Promotion of the Welfare and Hygiene*, 1928, 33–34.

95. *Biennial Report of the State Treasurer of the Commonwealth of Kentucky*, 1923. (Amount includes federal matching funds.)

96. *Promotion of the Welfare and Hygiene*, 1929, 2. (These figures include federal matching funds.)

97. *Report of the Treasurer of Virginia*, 1923.

98. Quarterly Meeting Minutes, 21 June 1921, Box 4, Series 1, Folder 41, Atlanta LWV Papers, GDAH; Report of Ida Blount Cheatham to the Atlanta League of Women Voters, 1921, Box 1, Series 1, Folder 3, Atlanta LWV Papers, GDAH; League of Women Voters Third Regional Bulletin, 29 June 1922, Box 2, Folder 7d, Napier Papers, MGA.

99. *Annual Report of the Treasurer of the State of Georgia*, 1924, 1926; E. B. Chamberlain to Mrs. Jacobs, 31 January 1923, Box 14, Folder Legislative Reports, Series II, NLWVP; State Council of Social Agencies Newsletter, 15 September 1923, Box 14, Folder Legislative Reports, Series II, NLWVP.

100. "The Woman Voter," *Montgomery Journal*, 18 September 1923 and 24 September 1923, quoted in Miller, "Lobbyist for the People," 42.

101. In addition to obvious general pressures on state budgets in times of fiscal crisis, southern states also devoted considerable resources to Confederate pension programs. Six decades after the end of the war, these entitlement programs absorbed a substantial portion of southern state resources. In Virginia, for example, state lawmakers spent between $750,000 and $1.1 million annually to support Confederate pensioners. According to historian Kathleen Gorman, "The percentage of state expenditures spent on pensions never dipped below 10 percent" in Georgia before 1921. As late as 1933, pensions absorbed 5 percent of Georgia's budget, and at no time during the 1920s did the state spend less than $1 million a year on its Confederate pensioners. See Gorman, "Confederate Pensions," 27; *Report of the Treasurer of Virginia*, 1919 – 33; and *Annual Report of the Treasurer of the State of Georgia*, 1920 – 33.

102. Most white female political leaders in the 1920s were former suffragists (or antisuffragists), and I have relied on Elna Green's analysis of the membership of suffrage and antisuffrage organizations in my generalizations about the class background of these women. See Green, *Southern Strategies*, 56 – 77.

103. Ibid., 52.

104. Jessie Daniel Ames to Miss Julia M. Hinaman, 1 March 1921, Box 5, Folder Legislative Reports, Series II, NLWVP; Jackson, "Petticoat Politics," 214 – 33.

105. Quoted in Scott, "After Suffrage," 306.

106. Memo by Lillian M. Thompson, 19 March 1921, Correspondence Box 3, Folder 56, Salley Papers, SCL.

107. *The Woman Voter*, 24 August 1922.

108. Ibid.

109. *The Bulletin*, October 1926.

110. Memo by Lillian M. Thompson, 19 March 1921, Correspondence Box 3, Folder 56, Salley Papers, SCL.

111. Ibid.; Report of the Work of the Tennessee League of Women Voters, 1921, Correspondence Box 4, Folder 62, Salley Papers, SCL.

112. Memo by Lillian M. Thompson, 19 March 1921, Correspondence Box 3, Folder 56, Salley Papers, SCL.

113. Louisiana League of Women Voters' Platform, undated, Box 166, Folder Louisiana, Series III, NLWVP.

114. Recent scholarship has examined women's involvement in partisan activities and the response of the parties after women's enfranchisement. See, for example,

Brodkin, "For the Good of the Party"; Freeman, *A Room at a Time*; and Gustafson, *Women and the Republican Party*.

115. Quoted in Jackson, "Petticoat Politics," 237.

116. For examples, see Legislative Program of the Legislative Council of Alabama Women, April 1923, Box 15, Folder 19, ALLWVC; and Legislative Council of Women's State Organizations of Georgia, "Legislative Calendar for 1927," Box 103, Folder Legislative Questionnaires, Series II, NLWVP. See Chapter 5 for additional information on the battles in North and South Carolina.

117. *The News Bulletin*, February 1928.

118. Undated handwritten note "For Mrs. Dieckerson," Box 36, Folder Virginia Women's Council of Legislative Chairmen of State Organizations, Clark Papers, VCU.

119. Quoted in Gilmore, *Gender and Jim Crow*, 211.

120. For examples of women's important role in southern interracial work, see Frederickson, "'Each One Is Dependent on the Other'"; Gilmore, *Gender and Jim Crow*; Judson, "Building the New South City"; and John Douglas Smith, *Managing White Supremacy*, esp. 48–49.

121. Townsend to Mrs. Minnie Fisher Cunningham, 15 July 1922, Box 1, Folder 45, ESLC.

122. Sadie S. Matthews, "Our First Political Campaign," reprinted in *The Woman Citizen*, 2 April 1921.

123. "Talk at the Jewish Synagogue," Spring of 1927, Box 44, Folder Speeches, Lewis Papers, NCDAH.

Chapter 7

1. Clipping: "Looking Them Over," hand-dated 28 June 1930, SCLWV Scrapbook, 2:34, SCL.

2. Clipping: "A Political Rally," *Herald Progress*, 3 August 1923, Box 33, Henry Taylor Wickham Scrapbook, vol. 5, Wickham Family Papers, VHS.

3. Lichtman, *Prejudice and the Old Politics*, 165.

4. Ibid.

5. For some of the earliest articulations of this "declension" argument, see Chafe, *American Woman*, and Lemons, *Woman Citizen*. Like the scholars who would follow, Lemons argued for the persistence of social feminism in the 1920s but concluded that the last half of the decade was a period of declining female activism and effectiveness. Several recent studies have specifically rejected the argument that enfranchisement itself was a failure in this period but nevertheless concede that women's legislative power had declined dramatically by the end of the decade. See, for example, Andersen, *After Suffrage*, and Freeman, *A Room at a Time*. In the most recent treatment of the relationship between woman suffrage and women's lobbying, Anna Harvey (*Votes Without Leverage*) concedes that women's political power was enhanced by enfranchisement as women pursued their legislative demands as constituents rather than as supplicants. Nevertheless, she, too, argues that women's power waned as political party elites co-opted the voting power of women without

giving them policy concessions in exchange, and women's organizations were unable to match the institutional power of parties in mobilizing women's votes.

6. Broadside: "Men! Are You Politically a Subject Sex?" Reel 1, Folder 4, Pearson Papers, TSLA; Lichtman, *Prejudice and the Old Politics*, 165.

7. The data utilized to create figure 4 and referenced in this paragraph were made available through the *U.S. Historical Election Returns* online database. See also table A.3 in Appendix.

8. See Appendix for full statistics. The only exceptions were Tennessee and Alabama. In Tennessee, the number of voters increased substantially in the presidential election of 1920, but after the imposition of the poll tax on women in 1921, the number of voters declined by 120,000. Consequently, the rate of growth in voters across the decade is uneven. Alabama had one of the highest rates of new voters in 1920. While the population of the state grew 12 percent from 1920 to 1930, voting basically stabilized at approximately 90 percent of the 1916 figure. In short, the number of voters did not grow substantially after 1920, but it stabilized quickly at a high rate relative to other southern states. Moreover, the poll tax was applied to Alabama women after 1920, but the number of voters at the polls did not decline substantially, as they did in Tennessee. See *Historical Census Browser.*

9. Statement of Registered Voters of Louisiana, in *Report of Secretary of State*. See table A.4 in Appendix.

10. The election data referenced in this paragraph were made available through the *U.S. Historical Election Returns* online database.

11. Minutes of the Board of Directors Meeting, Texas League of Women Voters, 9 January 1929, Box 205, Folder Texas League of Women Voters — Minutes, pp. 2, 4–5, Series II, NLWVP.

12. Ida Blacke Smedley to Miss Sherwin, 22 September 1928, Box 15, Folder 20, ALLWVC (reproduced from NLWVP).

13. See, for example, "Programme for Saturday May 22nd, 1926," Box 11, Series 6, Folder 3; "Organizations Co-Operating in Get Out The Vote Campaign in 1927," Box 11, Series 6, Folder 4; and Director to Mr. S. V. McArthur, General Outdoor Advertising Company, 3 September 1930, Box 11, Series 6, Folder 4, all in Atlanta LWV Papers, GDAH.

14. Gidlow, *Big Vote*, 78.

15. *The News Bulletin*, October 1927.

16. *Monthly News*, November 1926.

17. Alice Lloyd to Mrs. Wilson, 16 October 1924, Box 1924–25, Folder 1924, KYDPP.

18. *Augusta Chronicle*, 4 May 1930.

19. *The Bulletin*, July 1926.

20. Ibid.

21. *Studies in Citizenship for Georgia Women*, p. 6, Box 28, Series 14, Folder 10, Atlanta LWV Papers, GDAH.

22. "The Legislative Council of Alabama Women," Participating Organizations, Box 15, Folder 19, ALLWVC; Legislative Calendar for 1929, Georgia Legislative Council of Women's State Organizations, Box 11, File 16, JMWP; Report of Legislation, KY LWV, 1930, Box 232, Folder Legislative Department State Reports, Series

II, NLWVP; Program of the Legislative Council of North Carolina Women 1929, Box 10, Folder Printed Materials 1930–33, Cowper Papers, DU; Report of Legislation, Texas LWV, 25 March 1927, Box 103, Folder Legislative Questionnaires, Series II, NLWVP; Elizabeth Tompkins to Legislative Chairmen of State Organizations, 6 January 1928, Box 92, Folder Virginia Women's Council Bulletins 1923–44, Clark Papers, VCU.

23. In Texas, the legislative council disbanded late in the decade as a consequence of what some women's clubs viewed as excessive focus on prohibition. Even there, however, the struggles among various women's organizations about the proper priorities for the council seem to have taken place largely beyond the view of the public and even politicians. By contrast, historians J. Stanley Lemons (*Woman Citizen*, esp. chaps. 7 and 8) and Nancy Cott (*Grounding of Modern Feminism*, esp. chap. 8) have found that public divisions among women's clubs at the national level and accusations that some women's organizations were part of a "spider web" of communist activity crippled Progressive reform efforts in the late 1920s. In the records of southern legislative councils, however, evidence of these national battles was scant. White southern clubwomen at the state and local level seemed largely unaffected by these national fights, perhaps as a consequence of overlapping club memberships.

24. Legislative Calendar for 1929, Folder 16, Box 11, JMWP; Report to the Virginia State League of Women Voters, 1928, Box 84, Folder Committee Reports, Clark Papers, VCU.

25. Quoted in Andersen, *After Suffrage*, 1 n. 1.

26. "Notes of the Third Regional Conference of Democratic Women," Box 11, Folder League of Women Voters: *Monthly News* January 1924, Cowper Papers, DU.

27. Meeting Minutes, 21 April 1924, Collection 28, Box 621, Folder 1, SCDEC Papers, SCHS; Meeting Minutes, 13 January 1922, Box 11, Folder 30, ALDECP.

28. *The Democratic Woman's Journal* (Louisville: Democratic Woman's Club of Kentucky), Box 1924–45, KYDWCP.

29. Miss Maude McClure Kelly to Pettus, 13 August 1930, Box 24, Folder 11, ALDECP.

30. Beckham for Governor Campaign Committee to Miss Mary Elliott Flanery, 25 July 1927, Box 1, Folder Correspondence 1924–29, Flanery Papers, UKY.

31. McArthur and Smith, *Minnie Fisher Cunningham*, 143.

32. Finance Committee Chairman to Miss Florence Harrison, 14 December 1926, Box 37, Folder Louisville November 1926–April 1929, LWVKYP.

33. Ibid.

34. Ibid.

35. G. Walter Mapp to Mr. and Mrs. E. Hugh Smith, 24 July 1925, Box 1, Folder 48, ESLC.

36. T. W. Costen, Sr., to Mary Hinton Fearing, 6 February 1930, Box 1, Folder Correspondence 1928–30, Fearing Papers, DU.

37. *Richmond Times Dispatch*, 10–11 March 1926; *Richmond News Leader*, 13 March 1926; *Richmond Times Dispatch*, 20 March 1926, in scrapbook with clippings labeled "History of Virginia League of Women Voters," Box 207, Clark Papers, VCU.

38. *Richmond News Leader*, 13 June 1927, in scrapbook with clippings labeled "History of Virginia League of Women Voters," Box 207, Clark Papers, VCU.

39. Quoted in Miller, "Lobbyist for the People," 71.

40. Helen S. Riley to Mrs. Cowper, 18 January 1927, Box 62, Folder Correspondence January–March 1927, Weil Papers, NCDAH.

41. *Hanover (Va.) Herald*, 20 July 1927, Box 33, Henry Taylor Wickham Scrapbook, vol. 5, Wickham Family Papers, VHS.

42. *The Pilgrim*, April 1926, 2.

43. Heard and Strong, *Southern Primaries and Elections*.

44. See Chapter 6 for further discussion of initial efforts to eliminate the primary.

45. North Carolina Report of State Legislation 1925, Box 54, Folder Legislative Reports, Series II, NLWVP; Tennessee Report of State Legislation 1929, Box 232, Folder Legislative Department State Reports, Series II, NLWVP.

46. Questionnaire, Virginia, 29 March 1924, Box 14, Folder Legislative Reports, Series II, NLWVP.

47. Jessie Daniel Ames to Mrs. Jacobs, 1 January 1924, Box 14, Folder Legislative Reports, Series II, NLWVP; Jackson, "Petticoat Politics," 465.

48. Jackson, "Petticoat Politics," 465.

49. Quoted in Adéle Clark to Nora Houston, 20 August 1925, Box 1, Folder Correspondence with Nora Houston, Clark Papers, VHS.

50. Ibid.

51. Ibid.

52. Clipping: "Race Played Big Part in Hot Springs Election," Reel 29, Frame 186, TC.

53. Ibid.

54. Ibid.

55. Clipping: "Negroes Using the Vote Effectively," Reel 29, Frame 348, TC; clipping: "Race Played Big Part in Hot Springs Election," Reel 29, Frame 186, TC.

56. Clipping: "Race Played Big Part in Hot Springs Election," Reel 29, Frame 186, TC.

57. Clipping: "Negroes Using the Vote Effectively," Reel 29, Frame 348, TC.

58. *New York Sun*, 20 October 1924, Reel 21, Frame 322, TC.

59. Mrs. Elliott Brand to Mrs. Solomon Van Meter, 3 October 1924, Box 1924–45, Folder 1924, KYDWCP.

60. MSW to Mrs. Brown, 2 December 1924, Box 1924–25, Folder 1924, KYDWCP.

61. Report from the State of Mississippi, File Election Figures, Box 157, Campaign and Transition Files, Herbert Hoover Presidential Library, West Branch, Iowa.

62. I. T. Quinn to Pettus, 30 August 1930, Box 25, Folder 11, ALDECP.

63. Miss Maude McClure Kelly to Pettus, 13 August 1930, Box 24, Folder 11, ALDECP.

64. Montague to John A. Dutton, 13 January 1929, Box 22, Folder DEF, Montague Papers, VSLA.

65. The data utilized in this paragraph were made available by the Inter-University Consortium for Political and Social Research. The data for the "Electoral Data for Counties in the United States: Presidential and Congressional Races, 1840–

1972" were originally collected by professors Jerome M. Clubb, William H. Flanigan, and Nancy H. Zingale. Neither the collector of the original data nor the consortium bear any responsibility for the analyses or interpretations presented here.

66. Speech by Congressman J. T. Deal, December 1921, Child Welfare Committee — Bulletins, Correspondence, Miscellaneous (1921–25) File, Box 79, Clark Papers, VCU.

67. Minutes, Norfolk League of Women Voters, 28 September, Box 5, Folder 323, ESLC.

68. Charles R. Crisp to Emily Woodward, 11 July 1928, Box 1, Folder 13, Emily B. Woodward Collection, Hargrett Rare Book and Manuscript Library, Special Collections, UGA.

69. Tom to Governor, 29 September 1928, Box 21, Correspondence 1927–28 (M), Montague Papers, VSLA.

70. Marie Bankhead Owen to Pat Harrison, 17 September 1928, papers unprocessed, box unnumbered, Folder "Democratic Party," Owen Papers, ADAH.

71. *New York Times*, 14 October 1928.

72. Marie Bankhead Owen to Pat Harrison, 17 September 1928, papers unprocessed, box unnumbered, Folder "Democratic Party," Owen Papers, ADAH.

73. Neil Craig to Miss Gertrude Weil, 4 October 1928, and Weil to Craig, 3 October 1928, Box 63, Folder Correspondence July–October 1928, Weil Papers, NCDAH.

74. Millard E. Tydings to Mrs. Lamar Rutherford, undated, Box 114, Folder 4, Seydell Papers, Woodruff Library Special Collections, Emory University, Atlanta, Georgia.

75. O. M. Mull to Mary Hinton Fearing, 28 July 1928, and undated clipping: "Mrs. James G. Fearing Ignored Mull's Call," Box 1, Scrapbook 2, Fearing Papers, DU.

76. Annual Address of Mrs. Nellie N. Somerville to the WCTU of Mississippi, 11 October 1928, Reel 6, Folder 60, Somerville-Howorth Papers, Arthur and Elizabeth Schlesinger Library, Radcliffe College, Cambridge, Massachusetts.

77. Clipping: "An Open Letter to Mrs. Nellie Somerville," hand-dated 23 October 1928, MDAH Subject File: Nellie Nugent Somerville; and Statement of Mrs. Nellie N. Somerville in Support of Herbert Hoover, Reel 5, Folder 48, Somerville-Howorth Papers, Arthur and Elizabeth Schlesinger Library, Radcliffe College, Cambridge, Massachusetts.

78. Jackson, "Petticoat Politics," 580.

79. For an important analysis of the 1928 Hoover campaign and the way campaign workers targeted interest groups for specialized campaign messages, see Balogh, "'Mirrors of Desires.'"

80. Final Report, Hoover-Curtis Organization Bureau, Box 30, Casefile 83 (3), MacChesney Papers, Herbert Hoover Presidential Library, West Branch, Iowa.

81. Jennings C. Wise to A. H. Lloyd, 12 October 1928; Wise to Duncan Curry, 12 October 1928; Wise to Clarence E. Smithers, 10 October 1928; Wise to Gentlemen at Republican District Committee Headquarters, 14 September 1928, 1928 Letterbook, pp. 356, 362, 344–45, 194–95, Wise Papers, VHS.

82. *The Georgia Voter*, September 1928.

83. Quoted in Jackson, "Petticoat Politics," 584.

84. Report of Women's Activities: Arkansas, Final Report of the Hoover-Curtis Organization Bureau, Box 30, Casefile 83 (3), MacChesney Papers, Herbert Hoover Presidential Library, West Branch, Iowa.

85. Press Release: "League of Women Voters at Rosedale, Nov. 1," *Fairhope Courier*, 25 October 1928, Box 1, Folder 1, ALLWVC.

86. Quoted in Jackson, "Petticoat Politics," 586.

87. *Mississippi Woman's Magazine*, October 1928, p. 12, Box 2, Fortnightly Club Scrapbook, McLemore Papers, MDAH.

88. Mollie Dowd to Miss Sherwin, 21 July 1928, Box 15, Folder 20, ALLWVC.

89. Sue Shelton White to Molly Dewson, 23 November 1928, Reel 12, Frames 481–82, SSWP.

90. Adeline C. Bernard to NBL, 13 November 1928, Box 1, File Correspondence 1928, Lewis Papers, NCDAH.

91. "Talk at the Jewish Synagogue," Spring of 1927, Box 44, Folder Speeches, Lewis Papers, NCDAH.

92. *New York Times*, 19 July 1929.

93. Scott, "After Suffrage"; Davidson, *Child Labor Legislation*, 272–78; List of legislation supported by state Leagues, hand-dated, 1927, Reel 6, Frames 939–53, Part 3, Series A, National Office Subject Files, NLWVPM; Skocpol, *Protecting Soldiers and Mothers*, 457; Thompson, "After Suffrage," 62, 97; Index to Acts of the Assembly of the Commonwealth of Virginia, 1912–59; and "A Decade of League Work," Tenth Annual Convention Drama File, Box 86, Clark Papers, VCU.

94. Report of Legislation of Kentucky, April 1930, Folder Legislative Department State Reports, Box 232, Series II, NLWVP.

95. Jessie Daniel Ames to Miss Julia M. Hinaman, 1 March 1921, Box 5, Folder Legislative Reports, Series II, NLWVP. See Chapter 6 for further information on Texas's women's early legislative battles after their enfranchisement.

96. Questionnaire, 1 March 1923, Folder Legislative Reports, Box 14, Series II, NLWVP.

97. Jessie Daniel Ames to Mrs. Jacobs, 1 January 1924, Folder Legislative Reports, Box 14, Series II, NLWVP.

98. Quoted in Jackson, "Petticoat Politics," 94.

99. Jackson, "Petticoat Politics," 521; Actions on Bills Sponsored by the Texas League of Women Voters, 26 August 1929, Folder Legislative Departments — State Reports, Box 232, Series II, NLWVP; Report of State Legislation for the State of Texas, 19 March 1929, Folder Legislative Departments — State Reports, Box 232, Series II, NLWVP; Lucko, "'Next Big Job,'" 83.

100. Jackson, "Petticoat Politics," 601.

101. Quoted in ibid., 436.

102. Quotation from Ruth Burke to Miss Gertrude, 8 May 1928, Box 63, Folder Correspondence April–June 1928, Weil Papers, NCDAH. For information on the legislative accomplishments of organized white women discussed in this paragraph, see *Monthly News*, April 1929.

103. Thomas, *New Woman in Alabama*, esp. 92–117.

104. *Annual Report of the Treasurer of the State of Alabama*, 1920.

105. Ibid., 1921 and 1922.

106. Ibid., 1924, 1925, and 1926.

107. Ibid., 1928.

108. Ibid., 1930.

109. Legislative Activities in 1924, Virginia Women's Council Legislative Chairmen of State Organizations, Box 4, Folder 41, Pidgeon Papers, FHL.

110. *Report of the Treasurer of Virginia*, 1919–24.

111. Legislative Activities in 1924, Virginia Women's Council Legislative Chairmen of State Organizations, Box 4, Folder 41, Pidgeon Papers, FHL; Measures of Legislation Advocated by the Virginia League of Women Voters Session of the General Assembly of 1926, Box 54, Folder Legislative Reports, Series II, NLWVP; Report of Legislation, Virginia LWV, 1 April 1928, Box 103, Folder Legislative Reports, Series II, NLWVP; Report of Legislation, Virginia LWV, 1 April 1930, Box 232, Folder Legislative Department State Reports, Series II, NLWVP.

112. *Report of the Treasurer of Virginia*, 1925–28.

113. Ibid., 1929, 1930.

114. Ibid., 1931.

115. Skocpol, *Protecting Soldiers and Mothers*, 424–80.

116. Ibid., 462.

117. U.S. Department of Labor, Children's Bureau, *A Tabular Summary of State Laws Relating to Public Aid to Children in Their Own Homes in Effect January 1 1925 and the Text of the Laws of Certain States* (Washington, D.C.: Government Printing Office, 1925), Box 10, Folder 18, JMWP.

118. For two important works on mothers' pensions, see Linda Gordon, *Pitied but Not Entitled*, esp. chap. 3; and Skocpol, *Protecting Soldiers and Mothers*, esp. chap. 8.

119. Skocpol, *Protecting Soldiers and Mothers*, 479.

120. Ibid.

121. *Biennial Report of the Treasurer of North Carolina*, 1924, 1925.

122. Ibid., 1928, 1929, 1931, 1932.

123. Report of Legislation of the Kentucky League of Women Voters, April 1928, Folder Legislative Reports, Box 103, Series II, NLWVP.

124. Report of Legislation of the Mississippi League of Women Voters, April 1928, Folder Legislative Reports, Box 103, Series II, NLWVP; Report of Legislation of the Mississippi League of Women Voters, April 1930, Folder Legislative Department State Reports, Box 232, Series II, NLWVP.

125. *Report of the Treasurer of Virginia*, 1933.

126. *Promotion of the Welfare and Hygiene*, 1929, 2.

127. Chepaitis, "First Federal Social Welfare Measure," 354–55.

128. Ibid.; *Monthly News*, September 1929; *Acts of the General Assembly of the Commonwealth of Virginia*, 1928–34; "The Maternity and Infancy Measures in the 71st Congress 1929–1930," Reel 34, Frame 129, NLWVPM. Each of these states' appropriations equaled or nearly equaled the combination of federal and state appropriations before the federal withdrawal. Texas's funds were "not quite equal."

129. "Reports from 38 State Health Officers Showing Effect of Withdrawal of Sheppard-Towner Funds on Maternity and Infancy Hygiene Work in the States," Reel 26, Frame 762, NLWVPM.

130. "The Maternity and Infancy Measures in the 71st Congress 1929–1930," Reel 34, Frame 129, NLWVPM.

131. "Reports from 38 State Health Officers Showing Effect of Withdrawal of Sheppard-Towner Funds on Maternity and Infancy Hygiene Work in the States," Reel 26, Frame 767, NLWVPM.

132. Ibid., Frames 762, 765, 767; "The Maternity and Infancy Measures in the 71st Congress 1929–1930," Reel 34, Frame 129, NLWVPM.

133. "Reports from 38 State Health Officers Showing Effect of Withdrawal of Sheppard-Towner Funds on Maternity and Infancy Hygiene Work in the States," Reel 26, Frame 762, NLWVPM.

134. Ibid., Frames 760–61.

135. Lemons, *Woman Citizen*, 176.

136. "Reports from 38 State Health Officers Showing Effect of Withdrawal of Sheppard-Towner Funds on Maternity and Infancy Hygiene Work in the States," Reel 26, Frame 765, NLWVPM.

137. Theda Skocpol agrees that "national leaders of the organized women's coalition in American politics chose not to go to a full test of their political strength against the forces that wanted to kill Sheppard-Towner" and that the deal they struck with Congress to extend the program in 1927 prevented any grassroots mobilization in support of the bill. She takes issue with Chepaitis and others who argue that Children's Bureau leaders were "forced to capitulate" once it became clear that women would not vote as a bloc. Instead, she argues that women *and* men *underestimated* "women's political prowess" by the end of the decade. Robin Muncy similarly suggests that a grassroots battle was never joined; instead, she argues, much of Sheppard-Towner's defeat was due to the determination of the "female child welfare dominion" to retain bureaucratic control over the program. By 1929, she writes, "the issue was now pretty much dead. Although the female child welfare dominion could not find the votes in Congress to renew the Sheppard-Towner Act, it retained enough power to keep such work out of the Public Health Service. The women's monopoly thus shrank, but no outsider took over a piece of it." See Skocpol, *Protecting Soldiers and Mothers*, 512–24 (quotation on 520); Chepaitis, "First Federal Social Welfare Measure," 276; and Muncy, *Creating a Female Dominion*, 148. For another example of scholars who view Sheppard-Towner's defeat as evidence of the absence of an effective women's voting bloc, see Lemons, *Woman Citizen*, 174.

138. Confidential Memorandum to Miss Clark from Department of Legislation, 14 November 1924, Box 54, Folder Legislative Department—Summary of Legislation, Series II, NLWVP.

139. Report of the Department of Legislation on the Status of Ratification in the States to the National Board, 14 April 1925, Box 54, Folder Legislation—State League Material, Series II, NLWVP.

140. Report of Legislation of the Georgia League of Women Voters, for the year beginning April 1924, Folder Legislative Reports, Box 53, Series II, NLWVP; Report of Legislation of the North Carolina League of Women Voters, for the year beginning April 1924, Folder Legislative Reports, Box 53, Series II, NLWVP; Lemons, *Woman Citizen*, 220.

141. See, for example, Harvey, *Votes Without Leverage*, 6 – 7; and Lemons, *Woman Citizen*, 225.

142. Lemons, *Woman Citizen*, 225.

143. See, for example, Report of Legislation, North Carolina LWV, 25 March 1927, Box 103, Folder Legislative Questionnaires, Series II, NLWVP; Report of Legislation, Georgia LWV, 20 March 1926, Box 54, Folder Legislative Reports, Series II, NLWVP; Scott, *Southern Lady*, 188 – 89; and Davidson, *Child Labor Legislation*, 277. Shelley Sallee agrees that state legislators responded to Alabama women's demands for reform, but she characterizes this as a "victory by forfeit" as manufacturing opposition in the state declined. See Sallee, *Whiteness of Child Labor Reform*, esp. chap. 7 (quotation on 145).

144. See, for example, Kerber, *No Constitutional Right to Be Ladies*, 128 – 51; and Ritter, "Jury Service and Women's Citizenship."

145. Women in Kentucky were given the privileges of jury service automatically upon enfranchisement; women became eligible jurors as a consequence of being voters. Women in Arkansas and Louisiana secured that right from their legislators in 1920 and 1921, respectively, as those states elaborated the rights of women as officeholders and in other duties following the ratification of the Nineteenth Amendment. In the South as elsewhere, women who did not receive jury service automatically (or immediately) upon enfranchisement faced an uphill battle to secure that right. See "The Case for Women Jurors," Collection 24, Box 41, Folder 6, Pollitzer Papers, SCHS; Swain, "Organized Women in Mississippi," 102; Shankman, "Jury of Her Peers," 113; Lemons, *Woman Citizen*, 69; and Kerber, *No Constitutional Right to be Ladies*, 136 – 51.

146. Harper, ed., *History of Woman Suffrage*, 6:587, quoted in Ritter, "Gender and Citizenship," 372.

147. *The Woman Voter*, 29 February 1924.

148. *Monthly News*, November 1924.

149. Untitled essay, undated, Box 2, Folder 4, Hutson Papers, Manuscripts Collection #14, TU.

150. At different points, Leagues of Women Voters in Tennessee, Texas, and Virginia each put jury service for women on their legislative agendas. In no case, however, did the state league make jury service its highest priority, and the state legislative councils never took it up. See Jessie Daniel Ames to Miss Julia Hinaman, 1 March 1921, Box 5, Folder Legislative Reports, Series II, NLWVP; Report of Legislation, Virginia LWV, 1926, Box 54, Folder Legislative Reports, Series II, NLWVP; and Thompson, "After Suffrage," 151.

151. Mrs. Walter Clark to Miss Hicks, 8 April 1928, Box 103, Folder Legislative Reports, Series II, NLWVP.

152. Ibid.

153. Ritter, "Jury Service and Women's Citizenship," 14 (in online version); Lemons, *Woman Citizen*, 73.

154. Clipping: "Cong. Upshaw Succeeds in Closing White Hospitals to Negroes," Reel 26, Frame 360, TC.

155. Ibid.

156. Ethel Hutson to Ida Harper, 21 April 1921, Box 1, Folder 9, Hutson Papers, TU.

157. Larson, *Sex, Race, and Science*, 131–39.

158. *Monthly News*, October 1926.

159. Record of Legislation Supported and Opposed by State Leagues, 1924–25, Reel 6, Frame 747 and 775, NLWVPM; Record of Legislation Supported and Opposed by State Leagues, 1925–26, Reel 6, Frame 841, NLWVPM.

160. *Monthly News*, 12 March 1925.

161. Eulalie Salley to Mrs. Dunovant, 3 March 921, I&O 2205/2152, Folder 11, SCLWV Papers, SCL.

162. Mrs. W. B. Puett to Mrs. Mary O. Cowper, 4 February 1927, Box 62, Folder Correspondence January–March 1927, Weil Papers, NCDAH.

163. "A Survey of the Legal Status of Women in the Forty-eight States," published by the National League of Women Voters, 1930, Box 10, Folder Printed Materials 1920–33, n.d., Cowper Papers, DU.

164. The only year in which Kentucky women saw dramatic reversal of their pattern of legislative success was 1926, but in 1928 and in 1930 they resumed their pattern of regular successes, and even in 1926 all of their demands for appropriations were granted. See Reports of Legislation of the State of Kentucky, Folder Legislative Reports, Boxes 14, 53, 54, 103, and 232, Series II, NLWVP.

165. Lucy J. Ozmer to Miss Alice W. Owens, 10 June 1931, Folder Legislative Reports and Questionnaires, Box 231, Series II, NLWVP.

166. Ibid.

167. Ibid.

168. The county unit system in Georgia allotted primary votes by county, with almost no regard to population. Each county was classified as rural, urban, or town. Urban counties received six votes in statewide primaries, town counties received four votes, and rural counties received two unit votes each. As a consequence, urban voters had difficulty sustaining electoral pressure in statewide primary races because their votes counted for little compared to the votes of rural Georgians. Candidates often focused their campaigning in rural areas because they could secure the same number of county unit votes in the primary by appealing to far fewer actual voters.

169. It is surprising that the numbers of new voters in these two ratification states were proportionately so small. Tennessee's experience of first permitting women to vote without a poll tax penalty and then imposing the poll tax demonstrates the enormous disfranchising effect that the poll tax had on women in the state. Nevertheless, Arkansas's election qualifications looked much like those of Texas, and Tennessee's were more liberal than Virginia's. Yet Texas and Virginia showed greater rates of increase in voters after women voted than did Tennessee. Per capita income figures can account for some of the difference, as Arkansas had one of the lowest per capita incomes in the region, but they do not explain it sufficiently. Arkansas and Tennessee had larger numbers of men at the polls for presidential elections in the presuffrage era than did states like Virginia and Georgia, but the rates of increase in Virginia and Georgia substantially outstripped the rate of increase in Arkansas and Tennessee during the 1920s. Indeed, as soon as women began vot-

ing, the number of voters at the polls for presidential elections in both Georgia and Virginia exceeded those in Arkansas, despite Georgia's cumulative poll tax.

170. In Tennessee and Arkansas, more voters participated in presidential elections than in primaries. In Mississippi and South Carolina, more voters participated in primaries than in general elections. Yet the percentage increase in Mississippi and South Carolina primary voters after woman suffrage was more substantial than the percentage increase in Arkansas presidential voters or Tennessee voters in either general or primary elections. Moreover, the raw number of new voters in Mississippi and South Carolina primaries outstripped the number of new voters at Arkansas presidential polls or at Tennessee primaries. (Data for Arkansas primaries before woman suffrage is not readily available). See Appendix.

171. Because they were unable to effectively mobilize electoral pressure, women in Arkansas and Tennessee, for example, benefited in no obvious ways from the political circumstances that led state lawmakers to enfranchise them. For information on ratification states versus nonratification states in the South, see Green, *Southern Strategies*, esp. 179–83; and Elizabeth A. Taylor's studies of suffrage in the southern states.

172. Quoted in McArthur and Smith, *Minnie Fisher Cunningham*, 67.

173. Cott, "Across the Great Divide," 367.

174. Untitled essay, undated, Box 2, Folder 4, Hutson Papers, TU.

175. Public Welfare Progress, 1 February 1922, Box 14, Folder Legislative Reports, Series II, NLWVP.

176. "Reports from 38 State Health Officers Showing Effect of Withdrawal of Sheppard-Towner Funds on Maternity and Infancy Hygiene Work in the States," Reel 26, Frame 767, NLWVPM.

177. Child Welfare Committee Report signed by Mrs. Louis Brownlow [1922], n.d., Box 79, Folder Child Welfare Committee Reports, Box 79, Clark Papers, VCU.

178. Clipping: "Looking Them Over," hand-dated 28 June 1930, SCLWV Scrapbook, 2, SCL.

179. "Accuse Southern Congressmen of Cowardly Tactics," *Washington Bee*, 29 January 1921, Reel 14, Frame 230, TC.

180. Historians disagree about the fate of black women voters in the 1920s. Rosalyn Terborg-Penn (*African-American Women*, chap. 7) contends that southern black women "lost the vote within less than a decade" (156). Disfranchisement and disillusionment, she contends, resulted in waning voter participation by black women, despite their early efforts to take advantage of the Nineteenth Amendment. By contrast, Glenda Gilmore (*Gender and Jim Crow*, 224) argues that black women "registered in ever-increasing numbers throughout the 1920s." Because voting registration records were kept by race and gender only in Louisiana, it is difficult to accurately determine the number of black women voters in the region. Those Louisiana records and my own research suggest that the number of black women who were able to cast ballots did decline by the end of the decade. Nevertheless, I agree with Glenda Gilmore that black women were persistent in their political activism throughout the decade, and their voter mobilization drives laid important foundations for black electoral mobilization during the New Deal.

181. Statement of Registered Voters of Louisiana, *Report of Secretary of State*. See table A.4 in Appendix.

182. Lewinson, *Race, Class and Party*, 126.

183. "Republican Colored Women Hold Three Day Session Behind Closed Doors," 12 – 14 May [1928], Box 309, Folder National League of Republican Colored Women — Miscellaneous, Burroughs Papers, LC.

184. Summary of Report by Miss Nannie H. Burroughs, Washington, D.C., [1928], Box 309, Folder National League of Republican Colored Women, Miscellaneous, Burroughs Papers, LC.

185. "Republican Colored Women Hold Three Day Session Behind Closed Doors," 12 – 14 May [1928], Box 309, Folder National League of Republican Colored Women — Miscellaneous, Burroughs Papers, LC.

186. *The National Notes*, September 1927, Reel 24, Frame 217, Part 1, NACWCP.

187. Ibid.

188. "G.O.P. Is Warned by Negro Woman," *New York World*, 29 November 1929, Reel 35, Frame 2, TC.

189. Gilmore has examined the issue of African American women's "realignment" in the 1920s through a close analysis of "men's" politics in North Carolina. In "False Friends and Avowed Enemies," she argues that the roots of realignment can be traced to the effects of the Nineteenth Amendment in the South, as the Republican Party in the region courted white women voters by driving black voters from the party.

190. Clipping: "Negroes Turn Election in Arlington, Va.," 11 November 1927, Reel 29, Frame 439, TC.

191. Diary entry, 3 November 1925, Maggie Lena Walker Diary, MLWP.

192. List of Registrars and Judges for Primary and Election, 1928, Box 52, File Personal Papers — Campaign for the Legislature, Lewis Papers, NCDAH.

193. List of Precinct Committees, Box 52, File Personal Papers — Campaign for the Legislature, Lewis Papers, NCDAH.

194. Letter to the Democratic Voters of Wake County, undated, Box 52, File Personal Papers — Campaign for the Legislature, Lewis Papers, NCDAH.

195. Ibid.

196. R. H. Lewis Jr. to Nell Battle Lewis, 18 January 1928, Box 10, File Personal Correspondence 1926 – 45, Lewis Papers, NCDAH.

197. *The Crisis*, April 1926 (emphasis added).

198. D. A. Spivey to John Eldred Swearingen, 8 September 1922, Box III, Folder 83, Swearingen Papers, SCL.

Conclusion

1. Broadside: "Opposing Woman Suffrage," Folder 113, Cameron Papers, SHC.

2. Elshtain, "Woman Suffrage and the Gender Gap," 138 – 39.

3. Kenski, "Gender Factor in a Changing Electorate."

4. Hine, *Black Victory*, 3.

Bibliography

Manuscript Collections and Interviews

Athens, Georgia
    University of Georgia, Hargrett Rare Book and Manuscript Library,
        Special Collections
        Marion Colley Boyd Papers
        Walter B. Hill Papers
        Mildred Lewis Rutherford Papers
        Emily B. Woodward Collection
Atlanta, Georgia
    Atlanta Historical Society
        Wednesday Morning Study Club Papers
    Emory University, Woodruff Library Special Collections
        Raoul Family Papers
        Mildred Seydell Papers
        Josephine Mathewson Wilkins Papers
    Georgia Department of Archives and History
        Atlanta League of Women Voters Papers
        Georgia League of Women Voters Papers
        Rhoda Kaufman Papers
Auburn, Alabama
    Auburn University, Special Collections and Archives Department
        Alabama League of Women Voters Collection
Birmingham, Alabama
    Birmingham Public Library, Special Collections Department
        Council of Women's Clubs Papers
        Birmingham League of Women Voters Papers
        Lillian Bowron Scrapbook
        Pattie Ruffner Jacobs Papers
    University of Alabama in Birmingham, Mervyn H. Sterne Library, Oral
        History Research Project
        Interview with Margaret Burnett by Vickie Morton
Cambridge, Massachusetts
    Arthur and Elizabeth Schlesinger Library, Radcliffe College
        Charlotte Hawkins Brown Papers (microfilm)
        Somerville-Howorth Papers (microfilm)
        Sue Shelton White Papers (microfilm)

Chapel Hill, North Carolina
    University of North Carolina at Chapel Hill, Wilson Library, Southern
        Historical Collection
        Benneham Cameron Papers
        Sallie Southall Cotten Papers
        Elsie Riddick Papers
        Southern Oral History Project Interviews
        Gladys Avery Tillett Papers
Charleston, South Carolina
    South Carolina Historical Society
        Charleston County (S.C.) Democratic Executive Committee Papers
        Anita Pollitzer Papers
Charlottesville, Virginia
    University of Virginia, Alderman Library, Special Collections
        Everett R. Combs Papers
        Mary Johnston Papers
        Oral History of Adéle Clark
        Oral History of Elizabeth Pidgeon
        Oral History of Elizabeth Otey
        Political Papers of G. Walter Mapp
        Campbell Bascom Slemp Papers
        Roberta Wellford Papers
Cleveland, Mississippi
    Bolivar County Public Library
        Oral History with Lucy Somerville Howorth
        Recollections of Nellie Nugent Somerville
        Vertical Files
    Delta State University, Archives Department
        Interview with Lucy Somerville Howorth by Mary Meredith
        Walter Sillers Sr. Collection
        Walter Sillers Jr. Collection
        Hill Cassibry Smith Family Papers
Columbia, South Carolina
    University of South Carolina, South Caroliniana Library, Manuscripts
        Department
        Mary Ellis Papers
           Reference Files
        Eulalie Chafee Salley Papers
        South Carolina League of Women Voters Papers
        South Carolina League of Women Voters Scrapbooks. Vols. 1 and 2
        John Eldred Swearingen Papers
Durham, North Carolina
    Duke University, William Perkins Library
        Mary Octavine Thompson Cowper Papers
        Mary Hinton Fearing Papers

Lucy Randolph Mason Papers
Pamphlet Collection
Fayetteville, Arkansas
   University of Arkansas Libraries, Special Collections Division
      Arkansas State Republican Party Papers
      Florence B. Cotnam Papers
      Ft. Smith Fortnightly Club Papers
      League of Women Voters of Washington County Collection
Hattiesburg, Mississippi
   University of Southern Mississippi, Mississippi Oral History Program
      Mary Elizabeth Brown Oral History
      Mary Sheldon House Oral History
      Lucy Somerville Howorth Oral History
Jackson, Mississippi
   Mississippi Department of Archives and History
      Broadside File
      Henrietta Mitchell Henry Papers
      Lucy Somerville Howorth Papers
      Belle Kearney Papers
      Richard Aubrey McLemore Papers
      Nellie Nugent Somerville Papers
      Subject Files
      Lily Wilkinson Thompson Papers
      Ellen Woodward Papers
Lexington, Kentucky
   University of Kentucky, M. I. King Library, Special Collections
      Mary Elliott Flanery Papers
      Fouse Family Papers
      League of Women Voters of Kentucky Papers
      Samuel Wilson Collection
         Democratic Party Papers
         Democratic Women's Club Papers
Macon, Georgia
   Washington County Regional Library, Middle Georgia Archives
      Harrold Family Papers
      Viola Ross Napier Papers
Montgomery, Alabama
   Alabama Department of Archives and History
      Alabama Association Records
      Alabama Child Welfare Department Papers
      Alabama Equal Suffrage Association Papers
      Alabama Woman's Anti-Ratification League Papers
      Marie Bankhead Owen Papers
      State Campaign Committee for the Abolishment of the Convict Lease
        System Papers

State Democratic Executive Committee Papers
    Oliver Day Street Papers
Nashville, Tennessee
  Tennessee State Library and Archives
    Abby Crawford Milton Papers (microfilm)
    Josephine Anderson Pearson Papers (microfilm)
New Orleans, Louisiana
  Tulane University, Howard-Tilton Memorial Library, Manuscripts
      Department
    Ida Weis Friend Papers
    Hilda Phelps Hammond Papers
    Ethel Hutson Papers
    New Orleans League of Women Voters Papers
    Martha Gilmore Robinson Papers
New York, New York
  Schomburg Center for Research in Black Culture, New York Public Library
    Paul Lewinson Collection
Oxford, Mississippi
  University of Mississippi, Archives and Special Collections
    Southern Women Legislators Collection
Petersburg, Virginia
  Virginia State University, Johnston Memorial Library, Special Collections
    E. S. DeCosta Papers
Raleigh, North Carolina
  North Carolina Division of Archives and History
    Nell Battle Lewis Papers
    North Carolina League of Women Voters Papers
    Gertrude Weil Papers
Richmond, Virginia
  Maggie Lena Walker National Historic Site
    Maggie Lena Walker Papers
  Valentine Richmond History Center, Archives Division
    Cook Collection of Photographs
  Virginia Commonwealth University, James Branch Cabell Library, Special
      Collections and Archives Department
    Adéle Clark Papers
  Virginia Historical Society
    Adéle Clark Papers
    Houston Family Papers
    David Mays Diary
    Munford Family Papers
    Lila Meade Valentine Papers
    Wickham Family Papers
    Jennings C. Wise Papers
  Virginia State Library and Archives

        Equal Suffrage League Collection
        Andrew Jackson Montague Papers
    Rock Hill, South Carolina
        Winthrop University, Archives and Special Collections
            Mary Ellis Biographical File
            Harriet P. Lynch Papers
    Savannah, Georgia
        Georgia Historical Society
            Walter Charlton Hartridge Jr. Collection
            Heyward-Howkins Collection
            Helen Dortch Longstreet Papers
            Mrs. George S. Williams Clippings Files
    Swarthmore, Pennsylvania
        Friends Historical Library, Swarthmore College
            Mary Elizabeth Pidgeon Papers
            Pidgeon Family Papers
    Tuskegee, Alabama
        Tuskegee Institute, Division of Behavioral Science Research, Carver Research
            Foundation
            Tuskegee Institute News Clippings File (microfilm)
    Washington, D.C.
        Library of Congress, Manuscript Division
            Nannie Helen Burroughs Papers
            National Association for the Advancement of Colored People Branch Files
            National Association for the Advancement of Colored People Papers
                (microfilm)
            National Association of Colored Women's Clubs (microfilm)
            National League of Women Voters Papers (microfilm)
            National League of Women Voters Papers (Series II and Series III)
            National Woman's Party Papers (Group II)
    West Branch, Iowa
        Herbert Hoover Presidential Library
            George Akerson Papers
            Campaign and Transition Files
            Lou Henry Hoover Papers
            Nathan William MacChesney Papers
            Presidential Papers — Subject Files
            Lewis L. Strauss Papers
            Jack Summerbell File — *Hoover Bulletin of Georgia*
    Williamsburg, Virginia
        College of William and Mary, Swem Library
            Anne T. Chapman Papers
            G. Walter Mapp Papers
            William M. Tuck Papers

Newspapers

Arkansas Gazette (Little Rock, Ark.)
Atlanta Constitution (Atlanta, Ga.)
Augusta Chronicle (Augusta, Ga.)
The Bulletin (South Carolina League of Women Voters, Edgefield, S.C.)
Cleveland Advocate (Cleveland, Ohio)
The Crisis
FACTS (Atlanta League of Women Voters, Atlanta, Ga.)
The Georgia Voter (Georgia League of Woman Voters, Atlanta, Ga.)
Kentucky League Bulletin (Lexington, Ky.)
Monthly News (North Carolina League of Women Voters, Durham, N.C.)
The National Notes (official organ of the National Association of Colored Women)
The News Bulletin (Richmond League of Women Voters, Richmond, Va.)
New York Times
The Pilgrim (Georgia League of Woman Voters, Decatur, Ga.)
Richmond Times Dispatch (Richmond, Va.)
The Searchlight (Atlanta, Ga.)
The Southwest American (Ft. Smith, Ark.)
The Woman Citizen (National League of Women Voters)
The Woman Voter (Mississippi League of Women Voters, Clarksdale, Miss.)

Government Documents and Official Statistics

Acts of the General Assembly of the Commonwealth of Virginia. Richmond: Division of Purchase & Printing, 1916–34.

Annual Report of the Treasurer of the State of Alabama. Montgomery: The Brown Printing Company, State Printers and Binders, 1920–35.

Annual Report of the Treasurer of the State of Georgia. Atlanta: Byrd Printing Co., 1920–35.

Biennial Report of the State Treasurer of the Commonwealth of Kentucky. Frankfort: Treasury Department, 1917–34.

Biennial Report of the State Treasurer to the Governor of the State of Louisiana. Baton Rouge: Ramires-Jones Printing Co., 1922–34.

Biennial Report of the Treasurer of North Carolina. Raleigh: Mitchell Printing Company, State Printers, 1921–35.

Historical Statistics of the United States: Colonial Times to 1970. Washington, D.C.: U.S. Department of Commerce, Bureau of the Census, 1976.

Index to Acts of the Assembly of the Commonwealth of Virginia, 1912–1959. Richmond: Commonwealth of Virginia, 1972.

Journal of the House of Delegates of the Commonwealth of Virginia. Richmond: Commonwealth of Virginia, 1910–34.

Journal of the Senate of the Commonwealth of Virginia. Richmond: Commonwealth of Virginia, 1910–34.

The Promotion of the Welfare and Hygiene of Maternity and Infancy. Washington, D.C.: Children's Bureau, 1921–29.

Report of the Secretary of State to His Excellency the Governor of Louisiana. Baton Rouge: Ramires-Jones Printing Co., 1921–34.

Report of the State Treasurer of South Carolina. Columbia: Gonzales & Bryan, State Printers, 1919–34.

Report of the Treasurer of the State of Texas. Austin: Texas Treasury Department, 1920–34.

Report of the Treasurer of Virginia. Richmond: Office of the Treasurer, 1919–34.

State of Tennessee Biennial Report of the Treasurer of State. Nashville: Office of the Treasurer, 1919–34.

Online Resources and Statistical Databases

American Life Histories: Manuscripts from the Federal Writers' Project, 1936–1940. ‹http://memory.loc.gov / ammem / wpaintro / wpahome.html›.

Electoral Data for Counties in the United States: Presidential and Congressional Races, 1840–1972. Data made available by the Inter-University Consortium for Political and Social Research. Data originally collected by Jerome M. Chubb, William H. Flanigan, and Nancy H. Zingale.

Miller Center of Public Affairs. White House Tapes.org. ‹http://www .whitehousetapes.org / pages / listen_tapes_lbj_tel.htm›.

The University of Virginia Geospatial and Statistical Data Center. *Historical Census Browser*. ‹http://fisher.lib.virginia.edu / collections / stats / histcensus / index .html›.

———. *U.S. Historical Election Returns*. ‹http://fisher.lib.virginia.edu / collections / stats / elections / us.elections / ›.

———. *Virginia Elections and State Elected Officials Database Project, 1776–2004*. ‹http://fisher.lib.virginia.edu / collections / stats / valeg / ›.

U.S. Census Bureau. *Statistical Abstract of the United States*. 2003. ‹http://www .census.gov / statab / hist / HS-35.pdf›.

Published Works

Alexander, Adele Logan. "Adella Hunt Logan and the Tuskegee Woman's Club: Building a Foundation for Suffrage." In *Stepping Out of the Shadows: Alabama Women, 1819–1990*, edited by Mary Martha Thomas, 96–113. Tuscaloosa: University of Alabama Press, 1995.

Alexander, Charles C. "Defeat, Decline, Disintegration: The Ku Klux Klan in Arkansas, 1924 and After." *Arkansas Historical Quarterly* 22 (Winter 1963): 311–31.

Alpern, Sara, and Dale Baum. "Female Ballots: The Impact of the Nineteenth Amendment." *Journal of Interdisciplinary History* 16 (Summer 1985): 43–67.

Andersen, Kristi. *After Suffrage: Women in Partisan and Electoral Politics Before the New Deal*. Chicago: University of Chicago Press, 1996.

———. "Women and Citizenship in the 1920s." In *Women, Politics and Change*, edited by Louise A. Tilly and Patricia Gurin, 177–98. New York: Russell Sage Foundation, 1990.

Anderson, Kathryn. "Steps to Political Equality: Woman Suffrage and Electoral

Politics in the Lives of Emily Newell Blair, Anne Henrietta Martin, and Jeannette Rankin." *Frontiers* 18 (1997): 101 – 21.

Ayers, Edward L. *The Promise of the New South: Life after Reconstruction*. New York: Oxford University Press, 1992.

Baker, Paula. "The Domestication of Politics: Women and American Political Society, 1780 – 1920." *American Historical Review* 89 (June 1984): 620 – 47.

Balogh, Brian. " 'Mirrors of Desires': Interest Groups, Elections and the Targeted Style in Twentieth-Century America." In *The Democratic Experiment: New Directions in American Political History*, edited by Meg Jacobs, William Novak, and Julian Zelizer, 222 – 49. Princeton: Princeton University Press, 2003.

Becker, Susan. "International Feminism Between the Wars: The National Woman's Party Versus the League of Women Voters." In *Decades of Discontent: The Women's Movement, 1920 – 1940*, edited by Lois Scharf and Joan M. Jenson, 223 – 42. Westport, Conn.: Greenwood Press, 1983.

Bland, Sidney R. " 'Mad Women of the Cause': The National Woman's Party in the South." *Furman Studies* 26 (December 1980): 82 – 91.

Breckenridge, Sophonisba P. *Women in the Twentieth Century: A Study of Their Political, Social, and Economic Activities*. New York: McGraw-Hill Book Company, 1933.

Brinkley, Alan. *Voices of Protest: Huey Long, Father Coughlin, and the Great Depression*. New York: Knopf, 1982.

Bryan, Mary L. *Proud Heritage: A History of the League of Women Voters of South Carolina, 1920 – 1976*. Columbia: League of Women Voters of South Carolina, 1978.

Bucy, Carole Stanford. " 'The Thrill of History Making': Suffrage Memories of Abby Crawford Milton." *Tennessee Historical Quarterly* 55 (Fall 1996): 224 – 39.

Bull, Emily L. *Eulalie*. Aiken, S.C.: Kalima Press, 1973.

Burner, David. *The Politics of Provincialism: The Democratic Party in Transition, 1918 – 1932*. New York: W. W. Norton, 1967.

Carlton, David L. *Mill and Town in South Carolina, 1880 – 1920*. Baton Rouge: Louisiana State University Press, 1982.

Chafe, William H. *The American Woman: Her Changing Social, Economic, and Political Roles, 1920 – 1970*. New York: Oxford University Press, 1972.

——. *The Paradox of Change: American Women in the Twentieth Century*. New York: Oxford University Press, 1991.

——. "Women's History and Political History: Some Thoughts on Progressivism and the New Deal." In *Visible Women: New Essays on American Activism*, edited by Nancy A. Hewitt and Suzanne Lebsock, 101 – 18. Urbana: University of Illinois Press, 1993.

Clark, Ida Clyde. "17,000,000 Women to Vote for President This Fall." *Pictorial Review*, March 1920, 6 – 7, 30, 32.

Clemens, Elisabeth S. "Organizational Repertoires and Institutional Changes: Women's Groups and the Transformation of U.S. Politics 1890 – 1920." *American Journal of Sociology* 98 (January 1993): 755 – 98.

——. *The People's Lobby: Organizational Innovation and the Rise of Interest*

Group Politics in the United States, 1890–1925. Chicago: University of Chicago Press, 1997.

Corder, J. Kevin, and Christina Wolbrecht. "Political Context and the Turnout of New Women Voters after Suffrage." *Journal of Politics* 68 (February 2006): 34–49.

Corrales, Barbara Smith. "Parlors, Politics, and Privilege: Clubwomen and the Failure of Woman Suffrage in Lafayette, Louisiana, 1897–1922." *Louisiana History* 38 (Fall 1997): 453–71.

Cott, Nancy. "Across the Great Divide: Women in Politics before and after 1920." In *Women, Politics and Change,* edited by Louise A. Tilly and Patricia Gurin, 153–76. New York: Russell Sage Foundation, 1990.

———. "Feminist Politics in the 1920s: The National Woman's Party." *Journal of American History* 71 (June 1984): 43–68.

———. *The Grounding of Modern Feminism.* New Haven: Yale University Press, 1987.

———. "What's in a Name?: The Limits of 'Social Feminism'; or, Expanding the Vocabulary of Women's History." *Journal of American History* 76 (December 1989): 809–29.

Cox, Elizabeth M. *Women State and Territorial Legislators, 1895–1995.* Jefferson, N.C.: McFarland and Company, 1996.

Creel, George. "The Woman Who Holds Her Tongue." *Colliers,* 18 September 1937, 22, 55.

Dabney, Wendell P. *Maggie L. Walker and the I.O. Order of Saint Luke: The Woman and Her Work.* Cincinnati: Dabney Publishing Co., 1927.

Dailey, Jane. *Before Jim Crow: The Politics of Race in Postemancipation Virginia.* Chapel Hill: University of North Carolina Press, 2000.

Davidson, Elizabeth H. *Child Labor Legislation in the Southern Textile States.* Chapel Hill: University of North Carolina Press, 1939.

Dinkin, Robert J. *Before Equal Suffrage: Women in Partisan Politics from Colonial Times to 1920.* Westport, Conn.: Greenwood Press, 1995.

Dubay, Robert W. "Political Pioneers: Georgia's Gubernatorial Lady Campaigners." *Atlanta Historical Society Journal* (Spring 1982): 33–44.

Dubuc, Frances Fisher. "A Southern Woman as Governor?" *Success,* July 1924, 56–58, 109.

Eaton, Clement. "Breaking a Path for the Liberation of Women in the South." *Georgia Review* 28 (Summer 1974): 187–99.

Edwards, Laura F. *Gendered Strife and Confusion: The Political Culture of Reconstruction.* Urbana: University of Illinois Press, 1997.

Edwards, Rebecca. *Angels in the Machinery: Gender in American Party Politics from the Civil War to the Progressive Era.* New York: Oxford University Press, 1997.

———. "Gender, Class, and the Transformation of Electoral Campaigns in the Gilded Age." In *We Have Come to Stay: American Women and Political Parties, 1880–1960,* edited by Melanie Gustafson, Kristie Miller, and Elisabeth I. Perry, 13–22. Albuquerque: University of New Mexico Press, 1999.

Ellis, M. Carolyn, and Joanne V. Hawks. "Ladies in the Gentlemen's Club: South Carolina Women Legislators, 1928–1984." *Proceedings of the South Carolina Historical Association* (1986), 17–32.

Elshtain, Jean Bethke. "Woman Suffrage and the Gender Gap." In *Votes for Women! The Woman Suffrage Movement in Tennessee, the South and the Nation*, edited by Marjorie Spruill Wheeler, 129–43. Knoxville: University of Tennessee Press, 1995.

Enstam, Elizabeth York. *Women and the Creation of Urban Life: Dallas, Texas, 1843–1920.* College Station: Texas A&M University Press, 1998.

Evins, Janie Synatzske. "Arkansas Women: Their Contribution to Society, Politics, and Business, 1865–1900." *Arkansas Historical Quarterly* 44 (Summer 1985): 118–33.

Fass, Paula. *The Damned and the Beautiful: American Youth in the 1920s.* New York: Oxford University Press, 1979.

Frederickson, Mary E. " 'Each One Is Dependent on the Other': Southern Churchwomen, Racial Reform, and the Process of Transformation, 1880–1940." In *Visible Women: New Essays on American Activism*, edited by Nancy A. Hewitt and Suzanne Lebsock, 296–324. Urbana: University of Illinois Press, 1993.

———. "Shaping a New Society." In *Women in New Worlds: Historical Perspectives on the Wesleyan Tradition*, edited by Hilah F. Thomas and Rosemary Skinner Keller, 345–61. Nashville, Tenn.: Parthenon Press, 1981.

Freedman, Estelle B. "The New Woman: Changing Views of Women in the 1920s." *Journal of American History* 61 (1974): 372–93.

———. "Separatism as Strategy: Female Institution Building and American Feminism, 1870–1930." *Feminist Studies* 5 (Fall 1979): 512–29.

Freeman, Jo. *A Room at a Time: How Women Entered Party Politics.* Lanham, Md.: Rowman and Littlefield, 2000.

Fry, Joseph A., and Brent Tarter. "The Redemption of the Fighting Ninth: The 1922 Congressional Election in the Ninth District of Virginia and the Origins of the Byrd Organization." *South Atlantic Quarterly* 77 (Summer 1978): 352–70.

Gaddy, Carol T. "Women of Arkansas." *Historical Report of the Secretary of State, Arkansas.* Vol. 3. Little Rock, Ark., 1978.

Gidlow, Liette. *The Big Vote: Gender, Consumer Culture, and the Politics of Exclusion, 1890s–1920s.* Baltimore: Johns Hopkins University Press, 2004.

Gidlund, Lenora. "Georgia Feminists Before and after the Franchise." *The Proceedings and Papers of the Georgia Association of Historians* (1983), 28–35.

———. "Southern Suffrage and Beyond: Eleonore Raoul and the Atlanta League of Women Voters, 1920–1935." *Atlanta History* 40 (3–4): 30–43.

Gilmore, Glenda Elizabeth. "False Friends and Avowed Enemies: Southern African Americans and Party Allegiances in the 1920s." In *Jumpin' Jim Crow: Southern Politics from Civil War to Civil Rights*, edited by Jane Dailey, Glenda Elizabeth Gilmore, and Bryant Simon, 219–38. Princeton: Princeton University Press, 2000.

———. *Gender and Jim Crow: Women and the Politics of White Supremacy in North Carolina, 1896–1920.* Chapel Hill: University of North Carolina Press, 1996.

Goebel, Thomas. *A Government by the People: Direct Democracy in America, 1890 – 1940*. Chapel Hill: University of North Carolina Press, 2002.

Goodman, Susan. *Ellen Glasgow: A Biography*. Baltimore: Johns Hopkins University Press, 1998.

Goodstein, Anita Shafer. "A Rare Alliance: African American and White Women in the Tennessee Elections of 1919 and 1920." *Journal of Southern History* 64 (May 1998): 219 – 46.

Gordon, Felice. *After Winning: The Legacy of the New Jersey Suffragists, 1920 – 1947*. New Brunswick: Rutgers University Press, 1986.

Gordon, Linda. *Pitied but Not Entitled: Single Mothers and the History of Welfare*. Cambridge, Mass.: Harvard University Press, 1994.

Gorman, Kathleen. "Confederate Pensions as Southern Social Welfare." In *Before the New Deal: Social Welfare in the South, 1830 – 1930*, edited by Elna C. Green, 24 – 39. Athens: University of Georgia Press, 1999.

Graham, Sara Hunter. *Woman Suffrage and the New Democracy*. New Haven: Yale University Press, 1996.

———. "Woman Suffrage in Virginia: The Equal Suffrage League and Pressure-Group Politics, 1909 – 1920." *Virginia Magazine of History and Biography* 101 (April 1993): 227 – 50.

Grantham, Dewey. *The Life and Death of the Solid South: A Political History*. Lexington: University Press of Kentucky, 1988.

Green, Elna C. *Southern Strategies: Southern Women and the Woman Suffrage Question*. Chapel Hill: University of North Carolina Press, 1997.

Grossman, James R. *Land of Hope: Chicago, Black Southerners and the Great Migration*. Chicago: University of Chicago Press, 1989.

Gruberg, Martin. *Women in American Politics: An Assessment and Sourcebook*. Oshkosh, Wisc.: Academia Press, 1968.

Gustafson, Melanie. "Partisan Women in the Progressive Era: The Struggle for Inclusion in American Political Parties." *Journal of Women's History* 9 (Summer 1997): 8 – 23.

———. *Women and the Republican Party, 1854 – 1924*. Urbana: University of Illinois Press, 2001.

Hale, Grace Elizabeth. *Making Whiteness: The Culture of Segregation in the South, 1890 – 1940*. New York: Pantheon Books, 1998.

Hall, Jacquelyn Dowd. "Disorderly Women: Gender and Labor Militancy in the Appalachian South." *Journal of American History* 73 (September 1986): 354 – 82.

———. *Revolt Against Chivalry: Jessie Daniel Ames and the Women's Campaign Against Lynching*. Rev. ed. New York: Columbia University Press, 1993.

Hall, Jacquelyn Dowd, James Leloudis, Robert Korstad, Mary Murphy, Lu Ann Jones, and Christopher B. Daly. *Like a Family: The Making of a Southern Cotton Mill World*. Chapel Hill: University of North Carolina Press, 1987.

Hanger, Mrs. Frederick, and Clara B. Eno. *History of the Arkansas Federation of Women's Clubs, 1897 – 1934*. Lewisville: Arkansas Federation of Women's Clubs, 1935.

Hansen, John Mark. *Gaining Access: Congress and the Farm Lobby, 1919 – 1981*. Chicago: University of Chicago Press, 1991.

Harper, Ida Husted, ed. *History of Woman Suffrage, 1900–1920.* Vols. 5 and 6. New York: Arno and the New York Times, 1969.

Harvey, Anna L. *Votes Without Leverage: Women in American Electoral Politics, 1920–1970.* New York: Cambridge University Press, 1998.

Hawks, Joanne Varner. "Like Mother, Like Daughter: Nellie Nugent Somerville and Lucy Somerville Howorth." *Journal of Mississippi History* 45 (February–November 1983): 116–28.

Hawks, Joanne Varner, and Mary Carolyn Ellis. "Heirs of the Southern Progressive Tradition: Women in Southern Legislatures in the 1920s." In *Southern Women*, edited by Carolina Matheny Dillman, 81–92. New York: Hemisphere Publishing Corporation, 1988.

Hawks, Joanne Varner, Mary Carolyn Ellis, and J. Byron Morris. "Women in the Mississippi Legislature (1924–1981)." *Journal of Mississippi History* 43 (November 1981): 266–93.

Heard, Alexander, and Donald S. Strong. *Southern Primaries and Elections, 1920–1949.* Freeport, N.Y.: Books for Libraries Press, 1970.

Hendricks, Wanda A. "African American Women as Political Constituents in Chicago, 1913–1915." In *We Have Come to Stay: American Women and Political Parties, 1880–1960*, edited by Melanie Gustafson, Kristie Miller, and Elisabeth Israels Perry, 55–64. Albuquerque: University of New Mexico Press, 1999.

Hewitt, Nancy A. *Southern Discomfort: Women's Activism in Tampa, Florida, 1880s–1920s.* Urbana: University of Illinois Press, 2001.

Higginbotham, Evelyn Brooks. "Clubwomen and Electoral Politics in the 1920s." In *African American Women and the Vote, 1837–1965*, edited by Ann D. Gordon and Bettye Collier-Thomas, 134–55. Amherst: University of Massachusetts Press, 1997.

———. *Righteous Discontent: The Women's Movement in the Black Baptist Church, 1880–1920.* Cambridge, Mass.: Harvard University Press, 1993.

Hill, Ruth Edmonds, ed. *The Black Women Oral History Project.* Vol. 1. Westport, Conn.: Meckler Publishing, 1991.

Hine, Darlene Clark. *Black Victory: The Rise and Fall of the White Primary in Texas.* Millwood, N.Y.: KTO Press, 1979.

Hine, Darlene Clark, and Christie Anne Farnham. "Black Women's Culture of Resistance and the Right to Vote." In *Women of the American South*, edited by Christie Anne Farnham, 204–19. New York: New York University Press, 1997.

Humphreys, Hubert. "Rev. Lula Wardlow: Louisiana's First Elected Woman Mayor." *North Louisiana Historical Association Journal* 18 (1987): 3–10.

Jacoway, Elizabeth, ed. *Behold, Our Works Were Good: A Handbook of Arkansas Women's History.* Little Rock: Arkansas Women's History Institute and August House Publishers, 1988.

Jemison, Marie Stokes. "Ladies Become Voters: Pattie Ruffner Jacobs and Women's Suffrage in Alabama." *Southern Exposure* 7 (Spring 1979): 48–59.

Johnson, Dorothy E. "Organized Women as Lobbyists in the 1920's." *Capitol Studies* 1 (Spring 1972): 41–58.

Johnson, Joan Marie. *Southern Ladies, New Women: Race, Region, and Club-*

women in South Carolina, 1890 – 1930. Gainesville: University Press of Florida, 2004.

Jones, Nancy Baker, and Ruthe Winegarten. *Capitol Women: Texas Female Legislators, 1923 – 1999*. Austin: University of Texas Press, 2000.

Keith, Jeanette. *Country People in the New South: Tennessee's Upper Cumberland.* Chapel Hill: University of North Carolina Press, 1995.

Kelley, Robin D. G. *Race Rebels: Culture, Politics and the Black Working Class.* New York: The Free Press, 1994.

Kemp, Kathryn W. "Jean and Kate Gordon: New Orleans Social Reformers, 1898 – 1933." *Louisiana History* 24, no. 4 (1983): 389 – 401.

Kenski, Henry C. "The Gender Factor in a Changing Electorate." In *The Politics of the Gender Gap: The Social Construction of Political Influence*, edited by Carol M. Mueller, 38 – 60. Newbury Park, Calif.: Sage Publications, 1988.

Kerber, Linda K. *No Constitutional Right to Be Ladies: Women and the Obligations of Citizenship.* New York: Hill and Wang, 1998.

Key, V. O., Jr. *Southern Politics in State and Nation.* New York: Knopf, 1949; Knoxville: University of Tennessee Press, 1984.

Kincheloe, Joe L., Jr. "Transcending Role Restrictions: Women at Camp Meetings and Political Rallies." *Tennessee Historical Quarterly* 40, no. 2 (1981): 158 – 69.

Kleppner, Paul. "Were Women to Blame? Female Suffrage and Voter Turnout." *Journal of Interdisciplinary History* 12 (Spring 1982): 621 – 43.

———. *Who Voted? The Dynamics of Electoral Turnout, 1870 – 1980.* New York: Praeger Publishers, 1982.

Keyssar, Alexander. *The Right to Vote: The Contested History of Democracy in the United States.* New York: Basic Books, 2000.

Kornbluh, Mark Lawrence. *Why America Stopped Voting: The Decline of Participatory Democracy and the Emergence of Modern American Politics.* New York: New York University Press, 2000.

Kousser, J. Morgan. *The Shaping of Southern Politics: Suffrage Restriction and the Establishment of the One-Party South, 1880 – 1910.* New Haven: Yale University Press, 1974.

Lamar, Dolly Blount. *When All Is Said and Done.* Athens: University of Georgia Press, 1952.

Larson, Edward J. *Sex, Race, and Science: Eugenics in the Deep South.* Baltimore: Johns Hopkins University Press, 1995.

Lawson, Steven F. *Black Ballots: Voting Rights in the South, 1944 – 1969.* New York: Columbia University Press, 1976.

———. *In Pursuit of Power: Southern Blacks and Electoral Politics, 1965 – 1982.* New York: Columbia University Press, 1985.

Lebsock, Suzanne. "Woman Suffrage and White Supremacy: A Virginia Case Study." In *Visible Women: New Essays on American Activism*, edited by Nancy A. Hewitt and Suzanne Lebsock, 62 – 100. Urbana: University of Illinois Press, 1993.

———. "Women and American Politics, 1880 – 1920." In *Women, Politics and Change*, edited by Louise A. Tilly and Patricia Gurin, 35 – 62. New York: Russell Sage Foundation, 1990.

Lemons, J. Stanley. "The Sheppard-Towner Act: Progressivism in the 1920s." *Journal of American History* 55 (March 1969): 776–86.

———. *The Woman Citizen: Social Feminism in the 1920s*. Urbana: University of Illinois Press, 1973; Charlottesville: University Press of Virginia, 1990.

Lewinson, Paul. *Race, Class and Party: A History of Negro Suffrage and White Politics in the South*. New York: Oxford University Press, 1932.

Lichtman, Alan. *Prejudice and the Old Politics: The Presidential Election of 1928*. Chapel Hill: University of North Carolina Press, 1979.

Lindig, Carmen. *The Path from the Parlor: Louisiana Women, 1879–1920*. Lafayette: University of Southwestern Louisiana, 1986.

Link, William A. *The Paradox of Southern Progressivism, 1880–1930*. Chapel Hill: University of North Carolina Press, 1992.

Lisenby, William Foy. "Brough, Baptists, and Bombast: The Election of 1928." *Arkansas Historical Quarterly* 32 (Summer 1973): 120–31.

Lucko, Paul M. "The 'Next Big Job': Women Prison Reformers in Texas, 1918–1930." In *Women and Texas History*, edited by Fane Downs and Nancy Baker Jones, 72–87. Austin: Texas State Historical Association, 1993.

MacLean, Nancy. *Behind the Mask of Chivalry: The Making of the Second Ku Klux Klan*. New York: Oxford University Press, 1994.

Marshall, Susan E. "The Gender Gap in Voting Behavior: Evidence from a Referendum on Woman Suffrage." *Research in Political Sociology* 8 (1998): 189–207.

Matthews, Glenna. *The Rise of Public Woman: Woman's Power and Woman's Place in the United States, 1630–1970*. New York: Oxford University Press, 1992.

Mayo, Edith P. "Be a Party Girl: Campaign Appeals to Women." In *Hail to the Candidate: Presidential Campaigns from Banners to Broadcasts*, edited by Keith Melder, 149–60. Washington, D.C.: Smithsonian Institution Press, 1992.

McArthur, Judith N. *Creating the New Woman: The Rise of Southern Women's Progressive Culture in Texas, 1893–1918*. Urbana: University of Illinois Press, 1998.

McArthur, Judith N., and Harold L. Smith. *Minnie Fisher Cunningham: A Suffragist's Life in Politics*. New York: Oxford University Press, 2003.

McCurry, Stephanie. *Masters of Small Worlds: Yeoman Households, Gender Relations, and the Political Culture of the Antebellum South Carolina Low Country*. New York: Oxford University Press, 1995.

McGerr, Michael. *The Decline of Popular Politics: The American North, 1865–1928*. New York: Oxford University Press, 1986.

———. "Political Style and Women's Power, 1830–1930." *Journal of American History* 77 (December 1990): 864–85.

Meckel, Richard A. *"Save the Babies": American Public Health Reform and the Prevention of Infant Mortality, 1850–1929*. Baltimore: Johns Hopkins University Press, 1990.

Moneyhon, Carl H. *Arkansas and the New South, 1874–1929*. Fayetteville: University of Arkansas Press, 1997.

Monoson, S. Sara. "The Lady and the Tiger: Women's Electoral Activism in New York City before Suffrage." *Journal of Women's History* 2 (Fall 1990): 100–135.

Muncy, Robin. *Creating a Female Dominion in American Reform, 1890–1935*. New York: Oxford University Press, 1991.

Nasstrom, Kathryn L. "More Was Expected of Us: The North Carolina League of Women Voters and the Feminist Movement in the 1920s." *North Carolina Historical Review* 68 (July 1991): 307–19.

Neverdon-Morton, Cynthia. *Afro-American Women of the South and the Advancement of the Race, 1895–1925*. Knoxville: University of Tennessee Press, 1989.

Nichols, Carole. *Votes and More for Women: Suffrage and after in Connecticut*. New York: Haworth Press, 1983.

O'Dell, Samuel. "Blacks, the Democratic Party, and the Presidential Election of 1928: A Mild Rejoinder." *Phylon* 48 (Spring 1987): 1–11.

Odem, Mary E. *Delinquent Daughters: Protecting and Policing Adolescent Female Sexuality in the United States, 1885–1920*. Chapel Hill: University of North Carolina Press, 1995.

Ogden, Frederic D. *The Poll Tax in the South*. University: University of Alabama Press, 1958.

Olson, Mancur. *The Logic of Collective Action: Public Goods and the Theory of Groups*. Cambridge, Mass.: Harvard University Press, 1965.

Parker, Frank R. *Black Votes Count: Political Empowerment in Mississippi after 1965*. Chapel Hill: University of North Carolina Press, 1990.

Paulissen, May Nelson, and Carl McQueary. *Miriam: The Southern Belle Who Became the First Woman Governor of Texas*. Austin, Tex.: Eakin Press, 1995.

Perman, Michael. *Struggle for Mastery: Disfranchisement in the South, 1888–1908*. Chapel Hill: University of North Carolina Press, 2001.

Perry, Elizabeth Israels. "Men Are from the Gilded Age, Women Are from the Progressive Era." *Journal of the Gilded Age and Progressive Era* 1 (January 2002): 25–48.

———. "Women's Political Choices after Suffrage: The Women's City Club of New York, 1915–1990." *New York History* 71 (October 1990): 417–34.

Perry, Jennings. *Democracy Begins at Home: The Tennessee Fight on the Poll Tax*. Philadelphia: J. B. Lippincott Co., 1944.

Pickens, William. "The Woman Voter Hits the Color Line." *The Nation*, 6 October 1920, 372–73.

Podolefsky, Ronnie L. "The Illusion of Suffrage: Female Voting Rights and the Women's Poll Tax Repeal Movement after the Nineteenth Amendment." *Columbia Journal of Gender and Law* 7 (1998): 185–224.

Prince, Vinton M., Jr. "Will Women Turn the Tide? Mississippi Women and the 1922 United States Senate Race." *Journal of Mississippi History* 42 (August 1980): 212–20.

———. "The *Woman Voter* and Mississippi Elections in the Early Twenties." *Journal of Mississippi History* 49 (May 1987): 105–14.

———. "Women, Politics and the Press: The Mississippi *Woman Voter*." *Southern Studies* 19 (Winter 1980): 365–72.

Puryear, Elmer L. *Democratic Party Dissension in North Carolina, 1928–1936*. Chapel Hill: University of North Carolina Press, 1962.

Reagan, Hugh D. "Race as a Factor in the Presidential Election of 1928 in Alabama." *Alabama Review* (January 1966): 5–19.

Reichard, Gary W. "The Aberration of 1920: An Analysis of Harding's Victory in Tennessee." *Journal of Southern History* 36 (February 1970): 33–49.

Reynolds, George M. *Machine Politics in New Orleans, 1897–1926*. New York: Columbia University Press, 1936.

Ritter, Gretchen. "Gender and Citizenship after the Nineteenth Amendment." *Polity* 32 (Spring 2000): 345–75.

———. "Jury Service and Women's Citizenship before and after the Nineteenth Amendment." *Law and History Review* 20 (Fall 2002): 479–516.

Ross, Francis Mitchell. "The New Woman as Club Woman and Social Activist in Turn-of-the-Century Arkansas." *Arkansas Historical Quarterly* 50, no. 4 (1991): 317–51.

Rouse, Jacqueline Anne. *Lugenia Burns Hope: Black Southern Reformer*. Athens: University of Georgia Press, 1989.

Roydhouse, Marion W. "Bridging Chasms: Community and the Southern YWCA." In *Visible Women: New Essays on American Activism*, edited by Nancy A. Hewitt and Suzanne Lebsock, 270–95. Urbana: University of Illinois Press, 1993.

Ryan, Mary. *Women in Public: Between Banners and Ballots, 1825–1880*. Baltimore: Johns Hopkins University Press, 1990.

Sallee, Shelley. *The Whiteness of Child Labor Reform in the New South*. Athens: University of Georgia Press, 2004.

Schweiger, Beth Barton. "Putting Politics Aside: Virginia Democrats and Voter Apathy in the Era of Disfranchisement." In *The Edge of the South: Life in Nineteenth-Century Virginia*, edited by Edward L. Ayers and John C. Willis, 194–218. Charlottesville: University of Virginia Press, 1991.

Scott, Anne Firor. "After Suffrage: Southern Women in the Twenties." *Journal of Southern History* 30 (August 1964): 298–318.

———. "Most Invisible of All: Black Women's Voluntary Associations." *Journal of Southern History* 56 (February 1990): 3–22.

———. *Natural Allies: Women's Associations in American History*. Urbana: University of Illinois Press, 1991.

———. *The Southern Lady: From Pedestal to Politics, 1830–1930*. Chicago: University of Chicago Press, 1970; Charlottesville: University Press of Virginia, 1995.

Shankman, Arnold. "A Jury of Her Peers: The South Carolina Woman and Her Campaign for Jury Service." *South Carolina Historical Magazine* (April 1980): 102–21.

Shawhan, Dorothy S., and Martha H. Swain. *Lucy Somerville Howorth: New Deal Lawyer, Politician, and Feminist from the South*. Baton Rouge: Louisiana State University Press, 2006.

Sherman, Richard B. "'The Last Stand': The Fight for Racial Integrity in Virginia in the 1920s." *Journal of Southern History* 54 (February 1988): 69–92.

———. *The Republican Party and Black America from McKinley to Hoover, 1896–1933*. Charlottesville: University of Virginia Press, 1973.

Simon, Bryant. *A Fabric of Defeat: The Politics of South Carolina Millhands, 1910–1948*. Chapel Hill: University of North Carolina Press, 1998.

Sims, Anastatia. *The Power of Femininity in the New South: Women's Organiza-*

tions and Politics in North Carolina, 1880–1930. Columbia: University of South Carolina Press, 1997.

———. "'Powers that Pray' and 'Powers that Prey': Tennessee and the Fight for Woman Suffrage." *Tennessee Historical Quarterly* 50 (Winter 1991): 203–25.

———. "'The Sword of the Spirit': The WCTU and Moral Reform in North Carolina, 1883–1933." *North Carolina Historical Review* 64 (October 1987): 394–415.

Skocpol, Theda. *Protecting Soldiers and Mothers: The Political Origins of Social Policy in the United States.* Cambridge, Mass.: Belknap Press, 1992.

Smith, Constance E. *Voting and Election Laws.* New York: Oceana Publications, 1960.

Smith, John Douglas. *Managing White Supremacy: Race, Politics, and Citizenship in Jim Crow Virginia.* Chapel Hill: University of North Carolina Press, 2002.

Stephenson, William. *Sallie Southall Cotten: A Woman's Life in North Carolina.* Greenville, N.C.: Pamlico Press, 1987.

Stoney, George C. "Suffrage in the South, Part I: The Poll Tax." *Survey Graphic* 29 (January 1940): 5.

Swain, Martha H. "Ellen S. Woodward: The Gentlewoman as Federal Administrator." *Furman Studies* 26 (December 1980): 92–103.

———. "Organized Women in Mississippi: The Clash over Legal Disabilities in the 1920s." *Southern Studies* 22 (1984): 91–102.

———. "The Public Role of Southern Women." In *Sex, Race and the Role of Women in the South*, edited by Joanne V. Hawks and Sheila Skemp, 37–58. Jackson: University Press of Mississippi, 1983.

Sweeny, James R. "Rum, Romanism, and Virginia Democrats: The Party Leaders and the Campaign of 1928." *Virginia Magazine of History and Biography* 90 (October 1982): 403–31.

Swenson, Mary E. "To Uplift a State and Nation: The Formative Years of the Alabama League of Women Voters, 1920–1921." *Alabama Historical Quarterly* (Summer 1975): 115–35.

Taylor, A. Elizabeth. "The Last Phase of the Woman Suffrage Movement in Georgia." *Georgia Historical Quarterly* 43 (March 1959): 11–28.

———. "South Carolina and the Enfranchisement of Women: The Early Years." *South Carolina Historical Magazine* 77 (April 1976): 115–26.

———. "South Carolina and the Enfranchisement of Women: The Later Years." *South Carolina Historical Magazine* 80 (October 1979): 298–310.

———. "The Woman Suffrage Movement in Arkansas." *Arkansas Historical Quarterly* 15 (Spring 1956): 17–52.

———. "The Woman Suffrage Movement in Mississippi, 1890–1920." *Journal of Mississippi History* 30 (February 1968): 1–34.

———. "The Woman Suffrage Movement in North Carolina." *North Carolina Historical Review* 38 (January 1961): 45–62; 38 (April 1961): 173–89.

Terborg-Penn, Rosalyn. *African American Women in the Struggle for the Vote, 1850–1920.* Bloomington: Indiana University Press, 1998.

———. "Discontented Black Feminists: Prelude and Postscript to the Passage of the Nineteenth Amendment." In *Decades of Discontent: The Woman's Move-*

ment, 1920–1940, edited by Lois Scharf and Joan Jensen, 261–78. Westport, Conn.: Greenwood Press, 1983.

Thomas, Mary Martha. "The 'New Woman' in Alabama, 1890–1920." *Alabama Review* 46 (July 1990): 163–80.

———. *The New Woman in Alabama: Social Reforms and Suffrage, 1890–1920*. Tuscaloosa: University of Alabama Press, 1992.

Thurner, Manuela. "'Better Citizens Without the Ballot': American Antisuffrage Women and Their Rationale during the Progressive Era." *Journal of Women's History* 5 (Spring 1993): 33–60.

Tindall, George B. *The Emergence of the New South, 1913–1945*. Baton Rouge: Louisiana State University Press, 1967.

Treadway, Sandra Goia. "Sarah Lee Fain: Norfolk's First Woman Legislator." *Virginia Cavalcade* 30 (Winter 1981): 125–33.

Turner, Elizabeth Hayes. *Women, Culture, and Community: Religion and Reform in Galveston, 1880–1920*. New York: Oxford University Press, 1997.

Tyler, Pamela. *Silk Stockings and Ballot Boxes: Women and Politics in New Orleans, 1920–1963*. Athens: University of Georgia Press, 1996.

Varon, Elizabeth. "Tippecanoe and the Ladies, Too: White Women and Party Politics in Antebellum Virginia." *Journal of American History* 82 (September 1995): 494–521.

———. *We Mean to Be Counted: White Women and Politics in Antebellum Virginia*. Chapel Hill: University of North Carolina Press, 1998.

Watson, Richard L., Jr. "The Defeat of Judge Parker: A Study in Pressure Groups and Politics." *Mississippi Valley Historical Review* 50 (September 1963): 213–34.

———. "A Political Leader Bolts—F. M. Simmons in the Presidential Election of 1928." *North Carolina Historical Review* 37 (October 1960): 516–43.

Webb, Samuel L. "From Independents to Populists to Progressive Republicans: The Case of Chilton County, Alabama, 1880–1920." *Journal of Southern History* 59 (November 1993): 707–36.

———. *Two-Party Politics in the One-Party South: Alabama's Hill Country, 1874–1920*. Tuscaloosa: University of Alabama Press, 1997.

Wesley, Charles Harris. *The History of the National Association of Colored Women's Clubs: A Legacy of Service*. Washington, D.C.: National Association of Colored Women's Clubs, 1984.

Wheeler, Marjorie Spruill. *New Women of the New South: The Leaders of the Woman Suffrage Movement in the Southern States*. New York: Oxford University Press, 1993.

White, Deborah Gray. *Too Heavy a Load: Black Women in Defense of Themselves, 1894–1994*. New York: W. W. Norton, 1999.

Whitney, Susan E. *The League of Women Voters: Seventy-five Years Rich: A Perspective on the Woman's Suffrage Movement and the League of Women Voters in Georgia*. Atlanta: League of Women Voters of Georgia, 1995.

Wilkerson-Freeman, Sarah. "From Clubs to Parties: North Carolina Women in the Advancement of the New Deal." *North Carolina Historical Review* 68 (July 1991): 320–39.

———. "The Second Battle for Woman Suffrage: Alabama White Women, the Poll

Tax, and V. O. Key's Master Narrative of Southern Politics." *Journal of Southern History* 68 (May 2002): 333–74.

Williamson, Joel. *A Rage for Order: Black-White Relations in the American South Since Emancipation*. New York: Oxford University Press, 1986.

Winegarten, Ruthe. *Black Texas Women: A Sourcebook*. Austin: University of Texas Press, 1996.

Winn, Robert G. *The Story of Winslow's Maud Duncan*. Fayetteville, Ark.: Washington County Historical Society, 1992.

Young, Louise M. *In the Public Interest: The League of Women Voters, 1920–1970*. New York: Greenwood Press, 1989.

Dissertations and Unpublished Works

Brodkin, Kimberly Anne. "For the Good of the Party: Gender, Partisanship, and American Political Culture from Suffrage to the 1960's." Ph.D. diss., Rutgers, The State University of New Jersey, 2001.

Chepaitis, Joseph Benedict. "The First Federal Social Welfare Measure: The Sheppard-Towner Maternity and Infancy Act, 1918–1932." Ph.D. diss., Georgetown University, 1968.

Deskins, S. C. "The Presidential Election of 1928 in North Carolina." Ph.D. diss., University of North Carolina at Chapel Hill, 1944.

Elliott, Jane Whiteside. "Lucy Somerville Howorth: Legislative Career, 1932–1935." M.A. thesis, Delta State University, 1975.

Hathorn, Billy Burton. "The Republican Party in Arkansas, 1920–1982." Ph.D. diss., Texas A&M University, 1983.

Horstmann, Stacey Michelle. "Political Apprenticeship of Southern Women: The Political History of White Women's Organizations in Georgia, 1880–1920." Ph.D. diss., Emory University, 2000.

Hudson, Janet Goodrum. "Maintaining White Supremacy: Race, Class, and Reform in South Carolina, 1917–1924." Ph.D. diss., University of South Carolina, 1996.

Jackson, Emma Louise Moyer. "Petticoat Politics: Political Activism Among Texas Women in the 1920s." Ph.D. diss., University of Texas at Austin, 1980.

Johnson, Joan Marie. " 'This Wonderful Dream Nation!': Black and White South Carolina Women and the Creation of the New South." Ph.D. diss., University of California at Los Angeles, 1997.

Judson, Sarah Mercer. "Building the New South City: African American and White Clubwomen in Atlanta, 1895–1930." Ph.D. diss., New York University, 1997.

Kennedy-Haflett, Cynthia. " 'To Raise Oneself to a Higher Plane': The Political Activism of Adéle Clark, 1909–1930." M.A. thesis, University of Richmond, 1989.

Materson, Lisa Gail. "Respectable Partisans: African American Women in Electoral Politics, 1877–1936." Ph.D. diss., University of California at Los Angeles, 2000.

Meredith, Mary Louise. "The Mississippi Woman's Rights Movement, 1889–1923: The Leadership Role of Nellie Nugent Somerville and Greenville in Suffrage Reform." M.A. thesis, Delta State University, 1974.

Miller, Mary Elizabeth Swenson. "Lobbyist for the People: The League of Women Voters of Alabama, 1920 – 1975." M.A. thesis, Auburn University, 1978.

Roydhouse, Marion Winifred. "The 'Universal Sisterhood of Women': Women and Labor Reform in North Carolina, 1900 – 1932." Ph.D. diss., Duke University, 1980.

Shawhan, Dorothy Sample. "Women Behind the Woman Voter." Paper presented at the "Journals, Journalists and the Reading Public" Conference, Jackson, Mississippi, April 1986.

Thompson, Ruth Anne. "After Suffrage: Women, Law and Policy in Tennessee, 1920 – 1980." Ph.D. diss., Vanderbilt University, 1994.

Tipton, Nancy Carol. "'It Is My Duty': The Public Career of Belle Kearney." M.A. thesis, University of Mississippi, 1975.

Wilkerson-Freeman, Sarah. "Women and the Transformation of American Politics: North Carolina, 1898 – 1940." Ph.D. diss., University of North Carolina at Chapel Hill, 1995.

Index

tion in, 104; primaries in, 128, 243 (n. 12); registration barriers in, 45, 46, 65; registration drives in, 62–63, 65–66

Orange (Texas), 53

Organizations, black: lobbying by, 154–55; national vs. local, 154–55; non-partisanship of, 112–17. *See also specific organizations*

Organizations, white: conflicting priorities in, 194, 293 (n. 23); cooperation among, for reform, 143, 279 (n. 52); in courtship of voters, 196; on female officeholders, 162–63, 226; lobbying by, 143–46; nonpartisanship of, 119–26, 143–46, 193, 219, 280 (n. 59). *See also specific organizations*

Owen, Marie Bankhead, 43, 125, 202

Owsley, Alvin, 195

Parent Teacher Association (PTA), 65, 135, 193

Parker, John, 94

Parnell, Governor, 82

Partisan identities: of black women, 112; gender gap in, 229; presuffrage, 110, 270 (n. 11); of white women, 110, 125. *See also* Nonpartisanship; Party loyalty

Party leaders, 75–106; as antisuffragists, 75–76; courtship of voters by, 75–81, 194–97; female candidates nominated by, 79–80; and female party officeholders, 80–81; on loyalty of women, 85–86; reaction to 1920 elections among, 97–105

Party loyalty: among black women, 111–17; to Democratic Party, 7–8, 85–91; to Republican Party, 91–96; of white women, 85–96

Party organizations: incorporation of women into, 38–39, 80–81, 89–90, 125–26, 184; resistance to women in, 27, 39

Perman, Michael, 68, 240 (n. 2), 260 (n. 160)

Phoebus (Virginia), 32, 132–33

Pierce, J. Frankie, 109

Pine Bluff (Arkansas), 33

Pittsylvania (Virginia), 124

Political participation: effect of suffrage on, 3, 240 (n. 5); before vs. after suffrage, 3. *See also* Voter turnout

Polling data, 229

Polling places: cleaning up of, 20–21, 37; gender segregation at, 26; location of, 20–21; presuffrage election day rituals at, 13–14, 19–21; racial segregation challenged at, 25

Polls, feminization of: black women in, 22–26, 27; and language, 21–22; and rituals, 20–21

Poll taxes: abolition of, support for, 70, 71; as barrier to registration, 45, 46, 69–70, 251 (n. 8); black men on women's, 32, 33; cumulative, 45, 46, 70; education on, 64; fund-raising for, 70–71; in 1920 elections, 72–73; and turnout, 218; vs. wages, 69–70; white men refusing to pay women's, 27, 34, 70; white women's response to, 64, 69–71, 262 (n. 181)

Poll watchers, female, 37, 129

Power: and control of households, 28–32, 35; electoral mobilization and, 6–7; limits on women's, 9, 183–84; before vs. after suffrage, 3–4; women's attacks on men's, 36–43, 178–80

Presidential election(s): early suffrage in, 243 (n. 12); of 1924, 70; of 1928, 8, 201–5, 222–23; trends in turnout for, 190, *191*, 192, *232*, *234*

Presidential election of 1920: black women voters in, 115; competitiveness of, 73; poll taxes and, 70; Republican competitiveness after, 101, *102*, 269 (n. 171); Republican turnout in, 97–99, *98*, *99*; turnout in, 16, *18*, *19*, *232*; white supremacy in, 35

Pressure, electoral, 215–17, 219–20

Primary elections: direct, 127–28; early suffrage in, 73, 243 (n. 12); lobbying before, 148; and women's political authority, 183, 198. *See also* Democratic primaries; White primaries

Prohibition, 2, 4, 202

Salley, Eulalie, 58

Savannah (Georgia): ballots in, 68; black women registering in, 50, 51; interracial alliances in, 130–31; lobbying in, 148–49; machine politics in, 130–31; men's response to suffrage in, 32, 35; 1923 elections in, 148–49; nonpartisanship in, 116

Savannah Federation of Negro Women's Clubs, 51

Savannah League of Women Voters, 148–49

Scott, Anne Firor, 240 (n. 5), 241 (n. 20), 243 (n. 11), 262 (n. 181)

Seabrook, Paul, 130

Segregation, gender, at polls, 26

Segregation, racial: challenged by integrated polling places, 25; in schools, 174–75

Sheppard-Towner Infancy and Maternity Protection Act of 1921: funding for, 180, 182, 210–12; lobbying for, 5, 8, 152–53, 159, 210, 298 (n. 137); state legislator response to, 167–72, 178, 180, 182, 210–12

Silverstreet (South Carolina), 159

Simmons, Furnifold McLendl, 196

Simon, Bryant, 242 (n. 23)

Sims, Anastatia, 241 (n. 20)

Skocpol, Theda, 138, 208, 240 (n. 5), 280 (n. 59), 298 (n. 137)

Slemp, C. Bascom, 77, 99, 116

Smith, Alfred E., 201–4, 223

Smith, J. Douglas, 283 (n. 119)

Somerville, Nellie Nugent, 126, 161, 203

South: black women in, vs. North, 11; states included in definition of, 239 (n. 2)

South Carolina: ballots in, 57–58, 68; black women voters in, 22–24, 48–49; courtship of voters in, 77, 78–79, 83–84, 86, 87–88; disfranchisement in, 48–49, 66–67; female candidates in, 41, 42–43; female officeholders in, 159, 160–61; inter-

racial alliances in, 131; language in, 22; legislator responsiveness in, 166, 171–72, 179, 180, 215; literacy tests in, 48–49; lobbying in, 136, 141, 145, 147, 148, 150, 151, 157, 159–61, 193–94; men's response to suffrage in, 28, 33; 1920 elections in, 19, 20, 73–74, 100; nonpartisanship in, 118, 120, 124; party organization in, 38, 39; poll taxes in, 261 (n. 177); primaries in, 21, 183, 218, 301 (n. 170); registration barriers in, 46, 48–49; registration efforts in, 38, 48–49, 59; rejection of amendment by, 16; rural women in, 61–62; in ten years after suffrage, 193–94, 218; voter education in, 58

South Carolina League of Women Voters, 62, 120, 145

Southeastern Federation of Colored Women's Clubs, 223

Spruce Pine (North Carolina), 62

Stephens, Hubert D., 76, 105

Stewart, M. M., 130

Stokes, Ora Brown, 50, 117, 222

Strong, Donald S., 231, 269 (n. 174), 269 (n. 176)

Supreme Court, U.S., 223

Swanson, Senator, 139

Sylacauga (Alabama), 63

Taylor, Rebecca Stiles, 113, 114

Tennessee: antisuffragist women in, political activities of, 44; ballots in, 68; black women voters in, 24; courtship of voters in, 81; early suffrage in, 108, 243 (n. 12); electoral reform in, 67; female officeholders in, 81, 82, 162; gender relations in rural, 30–31; interracial alliances in, 131; legislator responsiveness in, 172, 175, 205–6, 211; 1920 elections in, 19–20, 72, 73, 97, 100; in 1920 presidential election, 70, 73, 97; nonpartisanship in, 112, 118, 121, 123, 125; party organization in, 81, 89, 184; polling places in, location of, 21; poll taxes in, 70 – 72, 218, 261 (n. 177), 300 (n. 169); presidential turnout in, 190, *191*, 292 (n. 8); primaries in, 104, 183, 198; ratification by, 16; registration barriers in, 46; registration drives in, 50 – 51, 66; in ten years after suffrage, 205 – 6, 211, 218

Tennessee League of Women Voters, 77, 81, 118, 162, 172

Terborg-Penn, Rosalyn, 301 (n. 180)

Terrell (Texas), 60

Texas: black candidates in, 116; black leverage in, 176; black women voters in, 24, 26, 50; courtship of voters in, 79, 80, 88, 95; female candidates in, 79; legislator responsiveness in, 177, 182, 206, 216 – 17; lobbying in, 140; men's response to suffrage in, 28; 1920 elections in, 73; in 1928 presidential election, 203, 204; nonpartisanship in, 123, 125; party organization in, 89, 184; poll taxes in, 46, 64, 73; presidential turnout in, 190, *191*; primaries in, 104 – 5, 198; primary suffrage in, 243 (n. 12); ratification by, 16; registration barriers in, 53; Republican lily-whitism in, 94 – 95, 116; rural women in, 60; in ten years after suffrage, 192, 198, 206, 216 – 17; voter education in, 58

Texas League of Women Voters, 104, 198

Texas Women's Democratic Association, 198

Thomas, Mary Martha, 241 (n. 20)

Thomason, Robert, 104 – 5

Thursday Afternoon Book Club, 60

Tinkham, George Holden, 55, 56

Trades Council, 63

Turner, Elizabeth Hayes, 241 (n. 20)

Turnout. *See* Voter turnout

Tyler, Pamela, 242 (n. 23), 244 (n. 28)

Understanding clauses, 47, 69

Underwood, Senator, 43

Union workers, 63, 258 (n. 127)

United Daughters of the Confederacy (UDC), 66, 88, 150, 281 (n. 75)

Upshaw, W. D., 214

Vardaman, James K., 78, 105

Violence, 24, 35, 49, 109

Virginia: black leverage in, 176, 224; black nonpartisanship in, 113, 115 – 17; black women voters in, 24 – 26, 27; courtship of voters in, 77 – 79, 81, 83, 86 – 88, 91 – 93, 196; electoral reform in, 67; female candidates in, 42, 79; female officeholders in, 81, 160, 161; interracial alliances in, 131, 132 – 33; language in, 22; legislator responsiveness in, 166 – 68, 172 – 73, 180 – 81, 206, 208 – 10, 216 – 17; lobbying in, 136, 139, 145 – 49, 153, 156, 185; men's response to suffrage in, 26, 32; 1920 elections in, 17 – 19, 100; in 1928 presidential election, 8, 203 – 4; party organization in, 81, 89, 90; poll taxes in, 70; presidential turnout in, 190, *191*; primaries in, 128 – 29, 198 – 99; questionnaires in, 147 – 49, 201; registration barriers in, 46, 47, 52 – 54; rejection of amendment by, 16; Republican lily-whitism in, 92 – 93, 114, 115 – 16; rural women in, 61; segregation challenged at polls of, 25; in ten years after suffrage, 196, 198 – 200, 206, 208 – 10, 216 – 17; voter education in, 57, 59, 64; white nonpartisanship in, 119, 124 – 25, 145, 146. *See also* Richmond

Virginia League of Women Voters: legislator responsiveness to, 167 – 68, 172 – 73; lobbying by, 145, 153; and primaries, 128 – 29

Virginia Women's Council, 148, 185

Voter education. *See* Education, voter

Voter mobilization: by black women, 47 – 56; and competition, 73 – 74; Democratic vs. Republican views of, 7–8; disfranchisement challenged by, 47, 192; feminization of, 37–38; in lobbying strategies, 149–51; power of, 6–7; for primaries, 126–27; of rural women, 10, 30, 60–62; throughout 1920s, 192; by white women, 56–67

Voter registration. *See* Registration, voter

Voter turnout: before 1920s, 13, *19*; during 1920s, 2, 31, 190, *191*, 192; for Democratic primaries, 197–98, *233*; in 1916 elections, 72, *232*; in 1920 elections, 16–17, *18*, *19*, 72–74, 97–99, *232*; nonpartisanship influencing, 122–23; poll taxes and, 218; for presidential elections, trends in, 190, *191*, 192, *232*, *234*

Voting Rights Act (1965), 230

Wake County (North Carolina), 21, 61, 124, 224–25

Walker, Maggie Lena, 50, 115, 132, 224

Warren, C. R., 78

Watson, Tom, 80

Waycross (Georgia), 28

Wayne County (North Carolina), 36

Weil, Gertrude: on black institutions, 158; and election fraud, 36, 129, 130; and mobilization, 60; in 1928 presidential election, 202; and roll-call records, 152–53

Wheeler, Marjorie Spruill, 240 (n. 2), 241 (n. 20)

White, Sue Shelton, 80, 125

White men: in campaigns against female candidates, 41; erosion of power of, 36–43, 178–80; on female officeholding, 40; feminization of polls threatening, 24; households controlled by, 28–32; language of, 22; public authority of, attacks on, 36–43; response to suffrage by, 26–32, 34; threats to social order and, 14–15

White primaries: black leverage in states without, 175–76; competition in, 127–29; Supreme Court on, 223; white women on, 71

White supremacy: black voters threatening, 25; and courtship of voters, 86–88, *87*; effect on women vs. men, 24, 35; feminization of polls and, 24; within suffrage movement, 5; white primaries and, 128; white women's views of, 186, 214

White women: antisuffragist, political activities of, 43–44; attacks on white men's authority by, 36–43; black men at polls with, 25; disfranchisement challenged by, 56–72, 74, 192; legislator responsiveness to, 165–73, 177–87, 205–12; lobbying for black women's reform priorities, 156–58, 184–86; lobbying strategies of, 135–53; and machine politics, 108–10, 130–33; nonpartisanship of, 110–11, 117–30, 143–46; as registrars, 37. *See also* Interracial alliances

Whitfield, Henry, 103

Widow appointments, 80, 82

Wilkerson-Freeman, Sarah, 132

Williams, Mrs. George, 114, 130, 154

Winder (Georgia), 59

Wingo, Effigene, 80, 263 (n. 35)

Winslow (Arkansas), 31, 40, 160

Wolbrecht, Christina, 243 (n. 17)

Woman's Christian Temperance Union (WCTU), 140, 150, 203, 204

Woman suffrage movement: naïveté in, 5–6; views on importance of, 1

Women's Joint Congressional Committee, 219, 220

Working-class women, 62–63, 258 (n. 127)

Worley, Anne, 82

YWCA, 60